A NEW HISTORY OF SCOTLAND

by

William Croft Dickinson, D.Lit., LL.D.

Fraser Professor of Scottish History and Palaeography in the University of Edinburgh

and

George S. Pryde, M.A., Ph.D.

Professor of Scottish History and Literature in the University of Glasgow

Vol. 2

A New History of Scotland

1 SCOTLAND FROM THE EARLIEST TIMES TO 1603
William Croft Dickinson, D. Lit., LL.D.

2 SCOTLAND FROM 1603 TO THE PRESENT DAY
George S. Pryde, M.A., Ph.D.

Scotland

from 1603 to the present day

George S. Pryde

Thomas Nelson and Sons Ltd
London Edinburgh Paris Melbourne Johannesburg
Toronto and New York

THOMAS NELSON AND SONS LTD
Parkside Works Edinburgh 9
36 Park Street London W1
117 Latrobe Street Melbourne C1
302-304 Barclays Bank Buildings
Commissioner and Kruis Streets
Johannesburg

THOMAS NELSON AND SONS (CANADA) LTD
91-93 Wellington Street West Toronto 1

THOMAS NELSON AND SONS
18 East 41st Street New York 17, N.Y.

SOCIÉTÉ FRANÇAISE D'ÉDITIONS NELSON
97 rue Monge Paris 5

First published February 1962
Reprinted May 1962

Printed in Great Britain by
ROBERT CUNNINGHAM AND SONS LTD, ALVA

Contents

Tables

Foreword

THIS book was planned and written as the second part of a two-volume survey of Scottish history, Professor W. Croft Dickinson, of the University of Edinburgh, having taken the story down to the Union of the Crowns in 1603. The genesis and aim of our collaborative effort have been explained by him in the Foreword to Volume I, and it remains for me to make brief mention of one or two points which have special reference to the scope and content of the present volume.

Hume Brown's *History of Scotland* virtually stopped at 1843, dealing with post-Disruption matters only in an admittedly sketchy postscript. Many 'general' histories devote even less space to modern times, while other recent commentaries are in one way or another unsatisfactory. Now, in our view, the choice of 1746, 1843, or any other date well 'beyond the memory of man', as the *terminus ad quem* of a new 'History of Scotland' is quite indefensible. In the twentieth century, Scotland remains a nation, with a character, heritage and culture distinctive enough to endow its history at all stages, modern as well as ancient, with value and interest. My volume is accordingly as nearly 'up-to-date' as it is possible for me to make it.

Moreover, an attempt has been made to interpret the past in a way that is in keeping with historical attitudes today. Each generation has its own outlook on the record of times gone by – perhaps no better than, but certainly different from, that of any preceding epoch – and one marked tendency nowadays is to attach as much importance to constitutional, social, economic and 'cultural' studies as to the more traditional aspects of 'history' – political and diplomatic, military and ecclesiastical. This newer approach (of particular relevance to recent times) is, I hope, apparent in the chapters that follow: the intention has been to accord, within each period, something like equality of treatment to each branch of the story – the political narrative, constitutional change, agriculture and industry, social progress, religious developments, education, the arts and letters. None of these has been – consciously, at all events – relegated to an inferior or subsidiary status.

If a historical writer is presumptuous enough, after his kind, to detect flaws in the works of his forerunners, he must expect others to find his own account 'in one way or another unsatisfactory': he dare not hope, uniquely, to have avoided mistakes, whether of assertion or of omission. Striving from afar to approach the unattainable ideal – perfect accuracy, judicial impartiality and warm human sympathy – he can, along the route, endeavour to eliminate the grosser errors and the more glaring misconceptions. In this spirit we trust that our two volumes will be found not wholly unworthy of their great theme.

GEORGE S. PRYDE

The University,
Glasgow.
January, 1960.

George Pryde, as he was affectionately known to his friends and colleagues, died suddenly on 6 May 1961. His early death was a grievous loss to Scottish historical scholarship.

Although he had corrected all the page-proofs, and had filled in the cross-references, he was unhappily denied the satisfaction of seeing his own volume of our *History* in its final form.

It was always a pleasure and a satisfaction to work with him in our joint effort. His book is its own tribute to his labours.

W. Croft Dickinson

CHAPTER I

Crown and Covenants

JAMES VI's accession to the throne of England in March 1603 was no accident. The link between the royal houses of Scotland and England, forged exactly a hundred years earlier, had been the outcome of dynastic policy; and King James, especially after his mother's death in 1587, had made it his aim to commend himself, as a suitable successor, to Queen Elizabeth and to the advisers likely to take control on her demise. And, from 1603 onward, the Union of the Crowns under the house of Stuart[1] was the dominant fact in Scottish history. It is therefore important to remember what that union meant, and also what it did not mean.

The man who was by right of birth king of Scotland became by right of birth king of England. And, apart from a successful rebellion, or the breakaway of one of the kingdoms, or perhaps a disputed succession leading to different solutions in each country, his descendants would likewise be kings of both Scotland and England. This was all that was implied by the 'regal union' of 1603; it did not unite the two countries. Sharing the same monarch, each country still had its own parliament and privy council, its own laws and law-courts, its own national church, its own ways of levying taxes and regulating trade; and, to the extent to which it was free from royal control, each country could pursue its own foreign policy.

That was the legal position; yet something more needs to be said. For one thing, James VI, though he intended to revisit the land of his fathers from time to time,[2] in fact lived in London instead of Edinburgh; only once (in 1617) during the twenty-two remaining years of his life did he come back to Scotland. Now, Scotland had had 'absentee monarchs' before. William the Lion, David II, James I and Queen Mary had spent long periods abroad, but in each case it had been warfare, with capture or threat of capture, which had forced them to

[1] The accepted convention about the spelling of the name of the royal dynasty is here followed. The change, under French influences, from the older and native form 'Stewart' (derived from the office of Steward of Scotland) to the later 'Stuart' (which has little beyond mere usage to commend it) is taken as belonging to the reign of James VI and I.

[2] Cf. *supra*, VOL. I, p. 370.

reside in other countries. Thus their sojourns in England or France had been temporary: each of them eventually came home to rule in Scotland. James VI and I, however, now chose to live in England permanently, and his relations with his native land were bound to be different from those of his forebears.

Placed in this new situation, the king, it is clear, had several real assets, which, properly used, might enable him to be a highly successful 'absentee monarch'. His very absence could be turned to advantage; no longer would he have to endure the personal insults, the rough treatment, even the fear of assassination, that previous kings had had to face. Believing, as did Claudius in *Hamlet*, that 'divinity doth hedge a king', James thought that respect for that 'divinity' might be accorded to him more readily as a distant, mysterious and glamorous personage, than as the familiar figure of the royal occupant of Holyroodhouse, almost rubbing shoulders with the turbulent populace of Edinburgh. No longer must he thole captivity under the Ruthvens, or meet the wild threats of a madcap Earl of Bothwell, or be plucked by the sleeve by Andrew Melville and told he was 'God's sillie vassal'. His 'king-craft' might get wider scope through 'remote control'. Not only was he immune in the south from personal danger: he also had command of the great resources of the English monarchy – its wealth, patronage and prestige, its experienced advisers and its loyal subjects. Could these be brought into service to enable James to govern Scotland wisely and competently? The answer would depend largely on his own character and conduct.

So much for the effect of the Union on the crown; but for the people too the position had changed, and we must look below the surface for the deeper meaning of this historic event. The two nations, tied to each other even loosely, might be expected to be better friends after 1603 than they had been before. At the very lowest, they could hardly make war on each other, for it was the king (assisted, it is true, by Parliament) who declared war, and it would be absurd for a king to declare war against himself. And, in point of fact, though relations have at times been strained between the two peoples, they have never since resorted to war.[1] Again, the presence of the king in London would inevitably draw to his side, and far from their native land,

[1] Scotsmen and Englishmen have on occasion been opposed to each other in battles, such as Dunbar (1650), Worcester (1651), Sheriffmuir (1715), Prestonpans (1745), Falkirk and Culloden (1746), but these were episodes in civil wars, not in armed conflicts between the two nations.

Scottish nobles, courtiers and high officials, who would thereby learn English ways, perhaps admire English people, possibly even acquire English speech. There would be much more coming and going between the nations than had ever been the case. The way was open for a fruitful exchange of ideas at many levels – in the relations of church and state, in methods of government, in legal practice, in education, in trade and social life, in language and literature. In such an exchange, Scotland had much to offer – for example, the noble ideal, expressed in the First Book of Discipline, that every parish should have a schoolmaster to teach the rudiments to all boys, whatever their birth or means. She had also much to gain from contacts with her wealthy and powerful neighbour – for example, the knowledge and experience gained by English traders in overseas markets.

On the other hand, there was some menace to the freedom and security of the smaller and poorer country: she might be 'dragged at the heels of England', obliged to take part in enterprises, domestic or foreign, of interest to England but of none to herself, governed by a monarch who would regard himself first and foremost as king of England and only in a secondary capacity as king of Scotland. It would be ironical if Scotland, giving a king to 'the auld enemy', should find herself at the end of the day, after all her struggles to defend her hard-won independence, a mere province of England. There was thus danger as well as opportunity, for those who lived north of the Tweed, in the Union of the Crowns.

Soon after his arrival in England, James showed that he had strong views on the new relations between his two peoples. He induced both his Parliaments to appoint commissioners to consider the question of a complete union between the two countries. The negotiations which followed (1604-7) broke down over the refusal of the English to grant the Scots equal trading rights, but something was achieved in spite of the major failure. The old laws which treated the king's subjects on each side of the Tweed as 'enemy aliens' were repealed; instead, a Scottish statute (1607) and an English judicial decision (1608) secured rights of citizenship, in Scotland and England, for English and Scots who were born after the Union. The earliest Union 'jack' or flag was adopted at this time, and a joint Anglo-Scottish commission, appointed in 1605 with a small body of mounted police at its command, enforced order in 'the Middle Shires', as the king now called the hitherto lawless Borders. James used the prerogative of the crown to change the royal title in accordance with his own hopes and ideals: as we read to this day in the 'epistle dedicatory' prefixed to the 'Authorised Version' of the Bible of 1611, he was styled 'the most high and mighty Prince James, by the grace of God, King of Great Britain, France and Ireland'.

The same mixture of success and failure attended James's efforts to improve the internal administration of the northern kingdom. A learned and pedantic man, he declared that, where his ancestors had failed to govern by the sword, he now governed by the pen; and there was some truth in the boastful saying. His chosen instrument was the Privy Council, which, sitting in Edinburgh, received and carried out the orders sent down from London by James himself or his Scottish Secretary; the king could depend on his councillors, for it was only such nobles, bishops and lairds as stood well with him who became his trusted advisers. Moreover, Parliament (meeting once every few years) merely assembled in order to hand over its powers to the Lords of the Articles (a small business committee of thirty to forty members); and, by manoeuvring the method of election,[1] James was soon able to ensure that most of the committee members were 'king's men' and that the lords and prelates on the committee were generally privy councillors. Finally, many of the judges of the Court of Session were likewise privy councillors. Thus James's policies came to be embodied in the statutes passed by Parliament, as well as in the edicts of the Council, and, from London, he could control the legislature, the executive and the judiciary alike. Only occasionally did the three Estates show resistance to the royal wishes: the good opinion of the king, and the rewards and favours he could give, mattered too much for lords, lairds or burgesses to oppose his desires.

The field of local government proved to be harder ground. An admirer of the system which he inherited in England from his Tudor predecessors, he thought particularly well of the justices of the peace, who had been entrusted with the duty of maintaining law and order in the English localities: drawn mostly from the squires and the county

[1] The normal usage was that eight members of each estate served on the 'Articles' – bishops, nobles, barons of the shire, and burgesses. A system of 'cross-election' seems to have been practised in the sixteenth century, whereby the clergy chose the appropriate number of nobles for the committee, the nobles chose the clergy, and the burgesses elected their own representatives. There is uncertainty as to what was done in the early part of James VI's reign, but from 1612, at all events, 'cross-election' was revived with this difference, that the bishops and nobles (either all of them together, or their delegates on the committee) chose the representatives of both barons and burgesses. The royal influence over this devious procedure was sufficient to ensure that a majority of the privy council found places on the committee, either by election or *ex officio* as a 'great officer of state'.

gentry, the English J.P.s were indeed the pillars of rural society and political life. As early as 1587 James had tried to introduce similar officials in Scotland[1]; he tried again to copy the English system in 1609, when J.P.s were appointed in each shire by the Privy Council. This was a praiseworthy attempt to provide sound local administration, and it was not all James's fault that, somehow, the scheme did not work out well. Perhaps the Scottish J.P.s, now and later, paid too much heed to the whims of kings and courtiers, not enough to the needs of their own people; perhaps they had too little sympathy with the religious faith of the greater part of the nation; perhaps they were too closely bound, by family ties, to the nobility, too deeply involved in those baronial feuds which it was originally intended they should prevent. On one side, there was antipathy from the holders of heritable jurisdictions (private or feudal law-courts): Scotland was too conservative for such a radical 'reform'. On the other side, the new J.P.s were regarded by ordinary folk as the tools of an absentee king and an unpopular Privy Council, and were therefore generally disliked and suspected; this meant that they never matched their English brethren as the crown's loyal and reliable 'men-of-all-work'.

In the same year (1609), under the Statutes and Band of Icolmkill (Iona), the king tried to persuade the unruly clan chiefs in the Western Isles to adopt the Protestant faith, to answer for the peaceable conduct of their tenants and followers, and to give their sons the benefits of schooling in the Lowlands. The attempt to bring law and order through religion and education was not without some success; but the Islesmen, for the most part, retained their Roman Catholic faith, cherished the military habits of their ancestors, and clung to the Gaelic tongue. In Orkney and Shetland the abolition of Norse law and customs (1611), the annexation of the islands (1612), and the forfeiture and execution of the last, turbulent Stewart Earl (1615),[2] made the power of the crown in those remote parts less shadowy and eventually brought them under the law of the realm of Scotland administered by royal officials. In 1616, in a further effort to introduce Lowland refinement into the Highlands, as well as to improve education in general, the Privy Council decreed that a school be provided in every parish; among other things, it was hoped that a knowledge of reading

[1] See *supra*, VOL. I, p. 375.

[2] Though a rebel against royal authority, this nobleman was actually a first cousin of the king: he was the notorious Earl Patrick, the oppressor and the almost independent ruler of Orkney and Shetland, whose father, Robert Stewart (1533-92), a natural son of James V, had been created earl in 1581.

and writing in English would result in the disappearance of 'the Irish language', which was denounced as one of the principal causes of Highland barbarity and incivility. But internal strife, lack of means and lack of will defeated the plan; and many years were to pass before the General Assembly's constantly reiterated desire for a school in every parish was to be achieved throughout Scotland.

Overseas, James encouraged the 'plantation' of Ulster, which, begun in 1610, attracted many Scottish settlers and ultimately gave that province the staunchly Presbyterian character which it retains to this day. Great expectations were also aroused by the project of settling Scottish emigrants in Acadia, a maritime region of what is now the dominion of Canada. Many took shares in the ambitious scheme (1621), but the French were already on the spot and were able to make good their claim to the land. Hence the only lasting results of the enterprise were the name bestowed on the proposed colony (Nova Scotia) and the institution of the Nova Scotia baronets, the oldest order of its kind in Britain.

In his dealings with the Church, too, James accomplished much, though he met one major set-back. Long before he succeeded to the English throne he had made up his mind in favour of episcopacy and against presbyterianism, and already, by 1600, he had induced the Kirk to countenance his 'parliamentary bishops'.[1] After 1603 he strove with tenacity and cunning to bring the Church of Scotland more nearly into line with that of England. In his view, the royal dignity in the state and some of the royal authority were bound up with episcopal order in the church: he put the matter tersely in the words, 'No bishop, no king'. As early as 1597, on the basis of a clause of the Golden Act of 1592, he had asserted his right to name the time and place of the meetings of the General Assembly[2] and by 1606 he had reduced that body to a mood of sullen obedience; in that year his most formidable critic, Andrew Melville, was exiled for his resistance to the royal will. The Privy Council next secured that 'constant moderators' (acceptable to the Kirk as 'fighters against popery') should be named over synods as well as presbyteries and that, in the former case, bishops might be appointed to the post (1607). Meanwhile a statute of 1606 had authorised the return to the bishops of the revenues annexed to the crown by the Act of 1587, and another, in 1609, restored their ancient

[1] See *supra*, VOL. I, pp. 359-61.

[2] Cf. VOL. I, p. 359: his choice of towns like Dundee and Montrose made it difficult (particularly in winter) for the south-western extremists to attend.

judicial rights. In 1610 Courts of High Commission were set up at St Andrews and Glasgow, and a subservient General Assembly fully endorsed the ecclesiastical status of the bishops, who, in the same year, received consecration from their English brethren. An Act of Parliament of 1612 ratified 'the Jacobean episcopacy'.

Later events, however, taught James that there were limits to the innovations that might safely be made. The lower church courts – presbytery and kirk session – were unchanged, and, until 1618, there was no interference with the form of worship: bishops had simply been superimposed on a presbyterian system. But in that year James endangered all his work by striving, in the Five Articles of Perth, for a 'decent and comelie order' of church service. Four of the articles concerned observance of the Christian festivals such as Christmas and Easter, private baptism, episcopal confirmation at the age of eight, and private communion; but, though there was objection to some of these, it was the fifth article, enjoining the kneeling posture at communion, that aroused extreme hostility as smacking of 'papistry'. There was an immediate outcry, and James was wise enough not to insist too strongly on his 'reforms'. When he died, in 1625, Scotland was tolerably peaceful and content under the new order in church and state.

Where James had been moderate and cautious, his son Charles I (1625-49) was headstrong and foolish. Although born in Dunfermline (1600), he had been brought up in England as a devout and fanatical Anglican, so that his ideas were bound to clash with those of his Scottish subjects. He began his reign well enough with a thorough and much-needed overhaul of the tangled subject of church finance. Through a complicated series of negotiations, statutes and legal actions (1625-33), he was enabled to make adequate provision, from the lands of the old Church and from the 'teinds' (tithes),[1] for the augmentation of the stipends of the reformed clergy.[2] It was a statesmanlike measure and

[1] One-tenth of the produce of the soil and of all natural increase (grain, livestock, wool, eggs, cheese and so forth) was to be set aside for the upkeep of the church in each parish; in time this settled down as a fixed charge (teind) on each landholding – that is, on each heritor. The levy might be commuted for a money payment.

[2] Earlier legislation had affirmed the principle that teinds were liable *inter alia* to sustain the ministers' stipends, but the basic statute was Charles's Act of 1633, amplifying one of 1617 and followed by a series of similar measures down to 1693. Parliament thus periodically appointed a 'Commission for the Plantation of Kirks and the Valuation of Teinds', whose main duty was to provide for the union or suppression of depopulated parishes, or the division of congested parishes. By an Act of 1707, however, disjunctions, new erections and annexations of parishes were entrusted to the Court of Session, which became, for these purposes, the 'Teind Court' or 'Court of Teinds'. The 'reforms' of 1633 included the fixing of a legal minimum

it stood the test of time, for some of its features survived into the twentieth century. But Charles's brusque manner and critical frame of mind estranged his natural supporters, the nobles, who had made heavy inroads into the wealth of the old Church and felt themselves menaced by a close scrutiny of their titles. As early as 1633, therefore, the king had seriously weakened the position of the crown.

In June 1633 Charles paid the first of two visits to his northern kingdom. Although he was received with expressions of delight and was crowned at Holyrood with pomp and ceremony, he noted with distaste the simplicity and lack of ritual in the church services; already under the influence of William Laud (soon to become Archbishop of Canterbury), he resolved to make changes. As a first reform he added a fourteenth bishopric (Edinburgh, with St Giles as its cathedral church), and thus made Edinburgh a 'city' and gave it formal recognition as the 'capital' (1633). At the same time, the building of Parliament House and of the Tron church cost the city dear and enormously increased its debt.

Back in London, the king was sufficiently ill-advised to revive the least prudent and least successful of his father's policies – that of imposing uniformity of worship and doctrine on Scotland and England. A new book of canons (1635) and a revised prayer-book (1637) were produced solely on the king's order and without the sanction of either Parliament or General Assembly, though it is true that the Scottish bishops had been consulted and that some attempt was made to meet Scottish wishes. These measures aroused the utmost resentment of all Presbyterians, and a riot in St Giles on 23 July 1637 (traditionally associated with Jenny Geddes) was the signal for a widespread revolt against the 'novations' in church affairs. Nobles, lairds, burgesses and ministers joined to subscribe the National Covenant, in which they both professed loyalty to the crown and denounced the recent changes: 'the true worship of God and the king's authority, being so straitly joined, as that they had the same friends and common enemies, and did stand and fall together' (February 1638). In December 1638 a General Assembly at Glasgow, continuing to sit in defiance of the king's commissioner, deposed the bishops and abolished episcopacy.

The Covenanters raised an army which, during the Bishops' Wars (1639-41), occupied the northern counties of England (though it saw very little fighting). The invasion was made with the approval of

stipend for ministers: it was to be 8 chalders of victual or 800 merks (equal to £44 8s. 11d. sterling).

Charles's English opponents, who regarded the Scots as friends. By 1641 the king, at odds with both his peoples, had given way on all the grievances of his Scottish subjects; he visited Edinburgh a second time and tried to win support by conferring peerage titles and promoting his critics. In this he failed, for the outbreak of war between the English royalists and parliamentarians, in August 1642, inclined the Scots Presbyterians to intervene on the side of Parliament for their own purposes and in a quarrel which was no concern of theirs. Repeating, in reverse, Charles's own blunder, they resolved to impose Presbyterianism on England and Ireland as well as Scotland, and to this end persuaded the English Parliament to accept, not the civil league which it would have preferred, but the Solemn League and Covenant, designed to secure ecclesiastical uniformity in all three countries (September 1643).

The Scots helped the Puritans to defeat the Cavaliers at Marston Moor (July 1644), but at home the Marquis of Montrose, disgusted by the anti-royalist actions of his former colleagues, put himself at the head of a mixed force of Highlanders and Irish soldiers of fortune, and resolved to strike a blow for his king. At Tippermuir, near Perth, he defeated a Covenanting force much larger than his own (1 September 1644) and twelve days later he routed the burghers of Aberdeen and sacked their town. The rapidity of his marches and the sudden violence of his attacks dismayed his opponents, as much as the barbarity of his motley army alarmed and angered them. December found him at Inveraray, in the heart of the country of his enemy, the Marquis of Argyll, whose forces he routed, with mighty slaughter, at Inverlochy (2 February 1645). Two generals of the Covenanting levies were in turn overwhelmed by his bold tactics – Hurry at Auldearn, near Inverness (9 May), and Baillie at Alford, on Donside (2 July). The cause for which Montrose bravely fought was, however, already lost, for Charles's English supporters had been decisively defeated at Naseby in the previous month. Crossing the Forth, Montrose enjoyed one more victory – his greatest – at Kilsyth, where he again crushed Baillie and the Covenanters (15 August). Though the whole of the south of Scotland now seemed at his feet, retribution was on the way: Sir David Leslie, coming up from England with seasoned and disciplined troops, out-generalled and routed Montrose at Philiphaugh (13 September), and 'the wonderful year' ended miserably with the Covenanters' vengeful slaughter of their prisoners.

The defeat of Montrose ended any possibility of a royalist triumph in the field. In May 1646 the king surrendered to his Scottish adversaries, and this event led to long disputes over his fate. By now, however, real power in England had passed to Oliver Cromwell and his army, who were 'Independents' in religion. It was Cromwell who suppressed, at Preston (August 1648), a Scottish invasion, led by the Duke of Hamilton, in favour of the captive king, and it was Cromwell who ultimately decided, in January 1649, that Charles I, that 'man of blood', should pay with his life for his sins against the people.

During the period 1638-49 the General Assembly, inspired by covenanting ideals, played a large part in the affairs of both church and state; and the Scottish Parliament, in close sympathy with these ideals, also did more to shape policy than it had ever done before. No longer content simply to approve decisions taken by the king or a committee of king's men, it made its authority felt in politics, war and diplomacy. In June 1640 it carried through what amounted to a constitutional revolution. Ignoring the king's proclamation proroguing its meeting, it elected its own president, abolished the clerical estate, did away with the Lords of the Articles, and agreed to appoint, by free election, only such committees as it thought necessary. Above all, it passed a Triennial Act to ensure that no longer interval than three years would elapse between sessions of parliament.[1] (In accordance with the terms of the statute, the Estates were in fact convened in 1644 and again in 1648.) In August 1641 Parliament went further by claiming, and persuading the king to acknowledge, that officers of state, privy councillors and judges of the Court of Session should be chosen only with its advice; it thus became supreme over the executive and judicial, as well as the legislative, branches of government. And, from 1643 until 1651, a committee of estates sat continuously, at times when Parliament itself was not in session: this was a safeguard against even a temporary silencing of its voice. In a real and unaccustomed sense, the Scottish Parliament was a power in the land during 'the Time of the Troubles'.

These advances and experiments in parliamentary government

[1] This measure anticipated and suggested the famous English Triennial Act, passed by the Long Parliament, in similar terms and with the same aim, in February 1641. These statutes must not be confused with the wholly different English Triennial Act of 1694 or the British Septennial Act of 1716, which limited the life of any one parliament to a maximum of three and seven years respectively. (The Parliament Act, 1911, reduced the permissible period to five years.) Thus, while the Acts of 1640 and 1641 were directed against royal tyranny (rule without parliament), the later statutes were intended to prevent parliamentary oppression (continuance in power without appeal to the people by way of elections).

have an obvious and close connection with the central struggle that was then being waged for power within the state: they are part and parcel of the political history of the period. The same comment applies to certain other constitutional developments of the years 1603-49 which have already been noticed – for example, to James's manipulation of the process of choosing the Lords of the Articles, in order to ensure royal control of Parliament, to his institution of justices of the peace in an endeavour to strengthen the local machinery for maintaining law and order, and also in some measure to Charles's reorganisation of church teinds, of the 'plantation of kirks' and of clerical stipends. If such major reforms can be said to have been carried through in the full glare of publicity and to have attracted the attention both of contemporary chroniclers and of later historians, the reigns of James VI and I and of Charles I are noteworthy, in a different and quieter way, for the constitutional progress that was achieved in the field of local administration. Scarcely, if at all, affected by the main currents of national political life, a series of changes occurred, so to speak, on a minor key, and these, though often passed over in silence by the annalist of the wars of the Covenant, deserve a place here, for they left an imprint that was to endure for centuries.

The first of these local developments concerns the extension and completion of the system of shires. Hitherto the whole of the northern mainland and most of the western isles,[1] forming one-third of the country's area, had been contained within the single sheriffdom of Inverness, and certain earlier attempts to carve up this vast domain into more manageable divisions had proved impermanent or quite abortive. Now, in 1631, Sutherland became a separate shire, with Dornoch as its county-town and with the earl (who owned the whole region) as its hereditary sheriff. Next, in 1641, Ross and Caithness[2] were erected as two other sheriffdoms, though the former was not fully defined until 1661, when Lewis was declared to fall within its bounds (as it does to this day). And meanwhile the ancient but lapsed sheriffdom of Cromarty was re-created. Since the medieval sheriffdom of Tarbert was annexed to Argyll in 1633, there emerged a total of thirty-three 'counties' – thirty-two shires and the stewartry of Kirkcudbright. This 'tidying-up' process no doubt owed something to the fact that,

[1] Orkney, including the lordship of Shetland, had been recognised as a distinct sheriffdom since the reign of James V.

[2] An Act of Parliament of 1504, professing to make these erections, had not taken effect.

since 1587, the shires had been recognised as one of the estates of the realm, with their own voice in all parliaments, and, indeed, both in administration and in justice we can sense, in the records of the seventeenth century, a strengthening of the powers and authority of the shire and the sheriff-court.[1]

Something was likewise done to improve the status of the parish. With its minister, elders and deacons, its heritors and kirk session, the parish had a ready-made organisation that was adaptable as a local agency of civil, as well as ecclesiastical, government. Already before 1603, Parliament had affirmed and reaffirmed the principle that each parish, through its kirk session, was responsible for the sustenance of its own native poor, 'stenting' the parishioners, if need be, for the money required; and the legislation of 1575, 1579 and later years remained for over two and a half centuries the basis of the Scottish poor law. Enactments of the time on other parochial concerns were proofs of good intentions rather than effective measures of state polity, so that it remained for the legislature in the seventeenth century to make the parish active and effective in education and registration. Acts of the Privy Council in 1616 and of Parliament in 1633, 1640 and 1646 (the terms of which are discussed in a later chapter[2]) gave statutory force to the reformed Kirk's ideal of a school, with a salaried schoolmaster, in each parish. In 1616, too, the Privy Council instructed the minister or reader in every parish to keep 'ane famous book and register' with the names and dates of all marriages, baptisms and deaths occurring within the parish. Thereafter there was much laxity in the practice of registration: some ministers were careless, others conscientious, and the parish registers consequently vary greatly in their value as records, but at least one can say that the statutory duty, having been laid down, was partially observed. By virtue of all its new functions, the parish tended to take the place that had belonged to the medieval barony as the handiest unit of rural administration.

During this period the royal burghs received a few accessions to their number, not so much by way of new creations[3] as by the promotion to royal tenure of burghs which, having hitherto held from an ecclesiastical or baronial superior, were legally styled burghs of barony

[1] For example, even the inhabitants of royal burghs, if accused of graver offences than breaches of the peace or minor assaults, were liable to prosecution in the sheriff-court rather than (as formerly) in the burgh-court.

[2] See *infra*, pp. 35-6.

[3] Only New Galloway, Scotland's smallest burgh, was erected *de novo* during the period (in 1630).

or of regality. Much the most important of these were the episcopal burghs of Glasgow and St Andrews, which had long been associated with the royal burghs in Parliament and in the burghs' own convention, and which stood, respectively, fifth and sixth on the burghs' 'stent-roll' or tax-roll[1]; they became, in the formal sense, royal burghs in 1611 and 1620. Among the other promotions at this time were those of Queensferry (1636), Brechin (1641) and Kirkcaldy (1644), also formerly belonging to the Church, and the baronial burghs of Stranraer (1617) and Inveraray (1648). Of the new creations of burghs of barony,[2] perhaps the most interesting, because of its rivalry to Glasgow, was that of Greenock in 1635; but several others had each some local consequence – Thurso (1633), Coupar Angus (1607), Tranent (1619), Portpatrick (1620), Langholm (1621) and Moffat (1648).

It was the royal burghs that formed the burgess estate and could therefore impress their views on king and parliament, and they used their strategic position to get an Act passed in 1633, which confirmed all their privileges in the most ample manner. In particular, only the merchant burgesses were authorised to trade with France, Flanders and other foreign parts, or to sell wine, wax, silk, spices and similar imports; and it was expressly declared that these rights 'are onlie proper and competent to the frie borrowes royall that have vote in parliament . . . and to no others'.[3] The high-water mark of burghal monopoly had been reached.

In these several ways, at an epoch marked by bitter disputation and armed conflict over the major affairs of church and state, time and thought were given to the problem of rendering the shire, the parish and the burgh stronger and better instruments of local administration.

[1] Above them in the roll stood Edinburgh, Dundee, Aberdeen and Perth (in that order); but Glasgow was sharing fourth place with Perth by 1635, and was a clear fourth by 1649. The next revision of the roll, in 1670, was to put Glasgow in second place, above both Dundee and Aberdeen.

[2] The burgesses of such burghs were restricted to petty local and retail trade and to the usual burgh crafts; for some further remarks about them see *infra*, pp. 32-4.

[3] An ancient and customary exception to this rule allowed the nobles, barons and other landed men to bring in merchandise from overseas 'to their awin particular use and behuif', so long as they did not attempt to sell these again for profit.

CHAPTER II

Restoration and Revolution

THE EXECUTION of Charles I emphasised a point which had been obscured by the struggle against royal absolutism – that it was in all good faith that the Scots Presbyterians had declared in their covenants for both Crown and Kirk. Now, with their Church duly 'reformed' and with the king beheaded by the English sectarians, they saw where their duty lay. They proclaimed the late king's son as Charles II in defiance of Cromwell and his army, brought the new monarch over from Holland, and induced him to accept the two Covenants. With pathetic but misplaced trust in the word of a king, they felt that Charles II was bound to their cause for all time. At the battle of Dunbar, however (3 September 1650), Cromwell crushed the Covenanters, and, exactly a year later, he totally defeated another Scottish force, largely royalist in sentiment and led by the king himself, at the battle of Worcester. Meanwhile, in August 1651, the Committee of Estates had been captured at Alyth; her last defences gone, her authority humbled, her king fled, Scotland lay helpless at the feet of the man who was soon to be Lord Protector.

For seven years (1651-58) Oliver Cromwell tried, in Scotland as elsewhere, to disguise, under constitutional forms, the fact that his rule rested on the power of the sword. He decided to treat Scotland, not as a conquered country, but as a state conjoined with England and Ireland to form one 'Commonwealth'. In February 1652 the monarchy was formally abolished, and delegates were summoned to Dalkeith from shires and burghs, and invited to accept a 'tender of union'. Most of them did so, and Scotland was thereafter represented in the various united parliaments, with which the Protector sought to bolster his rule.

Within the enforced Cromwellian union, Scotland's share of parliamentary representation was neither large nor distinguished. In June 1653 a carefully selected body of 140 God-fearing Puritans ('Barebone's Parliament') included just five Scots. In April 1654, under the Ordinance of Union, Scotland got 30 members out of a total of 460 for the British Isles. Twenty of these were shire members (the smaller shires being grouped for the purpose in twos and threes[1]), and ten came from the burghs – two from Edinburgh (including Canongate) and the other eight from 'districts of burghs', or combinations of several neighbouring towns.[2] It cannot be denied that Cromwell was a dictator, that his 'parliaments' were something of a sham, that English army officers sat for many of the Scottish constituencies, or that the scheme did not work well at the time; nevertheless, it is still of interest, in that Cromwell's device served as a model for later use. Revived in 1707, the pairing of shires and the 'districting' of burghs for the election of a single M.P. have ever since been features of Scottish political life.

Cromwell's measures for managing the internal affairs of the country were more successful than were his parliamentary arrangements. The baron courts (in which feudal rights of justice were still exercised) were suspended; in April 1654, however, they were re-erected, though they were allowed to try only cases involving sums up to 40s. sterling. Justices of the peace were given the same powers as in England, and, in general, the people enjoyed the boon of fair and

[1] The groups of shires were:
Orkney (with Shetland) and Caithness;
Sutherland, Ross and Cromarty;
Elgin and Nairn;
Kincardine and Forfar;
Fife and Kinross;
Clackmannan, Stirling and Linlithgow;
Dumbarton, Argyll and Bute;
Ayr and Renfrew;
Peebles and Selkirk;
Wigtown and Kirkcudbright.
The remaining ten shires were each to return one member.

[2] The eight districts (with the head burgh, in which the election was to take place, named first in each case) were:
Inverness, Dornoch, Tain, Dingwall, Nairn, Elgin and Forres;
Aberdeen, Banff and Cullen;
Dundee, Forfar, Arbroath, Montrose and Brechin;
Stirling, Perth, Culross, Linlithgow and Queensferry;
Cupar, St Andrews, Crail, Anstruther Easter, Anstruther Wester, Pittenweem, Kilrenny, Dysart, Kirkcaldy, Kinghorn, Burntisland, Dunfermline and Inverkeithing;
Glasgow, Lanark, Rutherglen, Dumbarton, Renfrew, Ayr, Irvine and Rothesay;
Dumfries, Sanquhar, Lochmaben, Annan, Kirkcudbright, New Galloway, Wigtown and Whithorn;
Lauder, Haddington, Dunbar, North Berwick, Peebles, Selkirk and Jedburgh.
Of the burghs previously represented in the Scottish Parliament, Inverurie and Kintore, in Aberdeenshire, were disfranchised.

even-handed justice. Though the General Assembly was forbidden to meet after 1653 – which one perfervid minister declared to be no bad thing – the lower courts of the Church were not interfered with; but the Lord Protector forbade any persecution of such Protestant sects as Independents, Baptists or Quakers. This 'vast toleration' was distasteful to the Scots, who had no doubt that Presbyterianism was of divine origin. They thought ill, too, of the heavy taxation which was required to maintain the great military establishment, based on five large forts (Leith, Ayr, Perth, Inverlochy and Inverness) and over twenty lesser garrison towns or castles, and which threatened, in the end, to reduce their country to bankruptcy.

Life and property were safe under Cromwell, trade was 'free' and unhampered between the two countries, and there was little popular reaction against the régime. The Earl of Glencairn and General Middleton led risings in favour of Charles II (1653-54), but they gave the government little trouble and were easily suppressed. The Scottish people, chastened by turmoil and defeat, heard of the death of the Lord Protector (3 September 1658) without making a move on their own behalf. Nor did they stir while Oliver's unwarlike son, Richard, quietly took over and as quietly resigned the chief place in the government (May 1659). The 'rump' of the Long Parliament (which had first met in 1640) was twice recalled and twice dissolved before a free Parliament was convened. In the end, it was General Monck and his 'army of Scotland' who, by crossing the Tweed in January 1660, determined the course of events; but that army was, of course, composed mostly of English veterans of Cromwell's campaigns. Following Monck's lead, the English Parliament declared for the exiled king, who was proclaimed as Charles II on 8 May 1660 and entered London at the end of that month. Though welcomed in Scotland, the Restoration was planned and carried through in England.

The Scottish nation, indeed, having lived in turn under government by the godly and rule by the soldiers, was ready for a return to old-fashioned monarchy. Exhausted by civil warfare and impoverished by high taxation, it now needed a peaceful 'middle way' that would bring freedom from strife; and, if the restored king and his advisers could produce a 'moderate' settlement, there was a good chance that the nation would give it goodwill and support. Could Charles II rise to the occasion and prove himself a statesman? Could he produce sensible solutions for the difficult and still outstanding problems – the relations between England and Scotland, the bond between church and state, the choice between episcopacy and presbyterianism? The short and quick answer came in 1661 with the passing by the Scottish Parliament of the Act Rescissory, which, at one stroke, annulled the legislation 'of all pretendit parliaments since the yeer 1633'.

For the state, this far-reaching statute meant the end alike of the abortive 'covenanted union' of 1643 and of the imposed military union of 1651-60. Scotland and England were again separate kingdoms, loosely linked through a common monarch, who, so far as Scotland was concerned, was to be another 'absentee monarch'. (Not till 1822 was a reigning sovereign even to visit Scotland.) Control would rest with the king and his secretary in London, who would send orders to an amenable privy council in Edinburgh, which in turn would see to it that the parliament passed the desired laws.

The ideal of a closer union between the two countries was not entirely lost sight of during the reign of Charles II (1660-85). One result of the Restoration, as the Scottish merchants soon found, was the disappearance of free trade: England's Navigation Act of 1660 and later legislation denied the Scots any share in the rich and growing commerce with the English 'plantations' beyond the sea. Hence there was some interest in Scotland in the proposals for a commercial treaty (1667) and for a parliamentary union (1670); and, when these projects fell through (neither side being prepared for the sacrifices involved in a true compromise), disappointment was real.

In the government of the northern kingdom, the key positions, as the events of the reign showed, were held by the secretary in London and the king's commissioner in Edinburgh; these two officials were able between them to keep a tight grip on council, parliament and nation. The Lords of the Articles, again mostly 'king's men', were in power from 1661. Attendance was well maintained at Parliament House, ranging between 142 and 196; sometimes – but not very often – there were heated debates and opposition to the royal policies. One change that was made touched the mode of electing the shire members. Besides the 'forty-shilling freeholders', other tenants of crown land got the vote in 1661, if their holdings were worth £1,000 Scots a year (or £83 6s. 8d. sterling), and in 1681 this figure was lowered to £400 Scots (£33 6s. 8d.). The vote remained with the county gentry, but that group was slightly widened.

The costs of government rose (one cause being the Dutch war which broke out in 1665) and taxation remained high. Excise duties, levied on ale, beer, spirits, salt and other goods, were now an important branch of revenue, yielding the crown £40,000 sterling a year. From 1667 the 'cess' or land-tax was fixed at a monthly figure of £6,000 sterling (£5,000 from the shires, £1,000 from the burghs), and the estates would vote 'supply' by passing an act which granted the king so many months' cess to defray his expenses. The act named, for each shire, a number of the greater landowners as the commissioners who were to value the lands and apportion the tax; and these 'commissioners of supply', since they controlled the local money, came in time to be entrusted with other duties[1] and to provide a species of local government for rural Scotland.

Two other constitutional changes belong to the reign of Charles II. Criminal justice was reformed in 1671, when the Court of Justiciary (nowadays called the 'High Court') was set up at Edinburgh: it then consisted of the Justice-General, the Justice-Clerk, and five of the judges of the Court of Session. (In the nineteenth century all the 'Lords of Session' became 'Lords Commissioners of Justiciary'.) The poor law, as settled in James VI's reign, was overhauled by statutes of 1663 and 1672, suppressing vagabondage, allowing only the lame, blind and impotent poor to beg, and permitting the heritors and kirk session in each parish, if they so wished, to levy a 'poor's rate'. The 1663 act is noteworthy, because, for the first time, it provided that half the poor's rate should be levied from the heritors (or owners) and half from the tenants (or occupiers) – a division that was observed in Scotland until 1957.

For the Church, the Act Rescissory of 1661 meant a return to episcopacy as it had stood in the latter part of James VI's reign and the early years of Charles I. For the Presbyterians, this was bad, and worse followed in 1662. The bishops were formally restored and given their place as an estate of parliament, 'as in former tymes before these troubles', while the covenants were denounced as 'rebellious and treasonable', and conventicles in private houses were forbidden.

Naturally these rapid developments came as a rude shock to the Presbyterians, who were deeply disappointed in their 'covenanted king'. Despite their chagrin, however, it seems likely that, if the king and his counsellors had been content with the changes already made, and had set themselves to secure ecclesiastical peace and good order under something like the 'Jacobean episcopacy', they would have won

[1] For example, they were conjoined in 1686 with the justices of the peace (*supra* pp. 4-5) for the supervision of roads, bridges and ferries; for their responsibilities in education (1696), see *infra*, p. 36.

over moderate opinion and achieved a lasting settlement. The General Assembly, it is true, would have been missed by many, but the retention of the presbyteries and kirk sessions would have made up for part of the loss; the ideal of church unity would have had a strong appeal for the nation at large; and only the extremists (mainly in the south-west) would have regretted the covenants. These bright hopes were to be dashed; the story of how this came about occupies much of the record of the reigns of Charles II and his successor, and provides a striking memorial to the tragic folly of self-willed rulers and to the futility, as well as the wickedness, of persecution.

The rights of lay patrons to nominate clergymen to parishes had been abolished in 1649, and Parliament, obstinately unwilling to 'let bygones be bygones', ordered all ministers who had been admitted since that date to seek presentation from the patron and collation from the bishop. This measure immediately stirred up trouble. About 270 ministers refused to comply and were ejected from their livings; in the Glasgow and Ayr synod the deprived pastors outnumbered those that remained by more than two to one. Conventicles now took the shape of large field meetings and these became the rallying-points of the south-western covenanters. An Act of 1663 imposed fines on those who absented themselves from ordinary worship, while the Privy Council forbade the 'outed' ministers to reside within twenty miles of their former parishes. A small rebellion in 1666, the Pentland rising, was easily suppressed, but it convinced some of the leading politicians that the king's policy was mistaken.

In the next phase the government, headed by the Earl (later the Duke) of Lauderdale, tried the gentler method of conciliation. By two Declarations of Indulgence, issued in 1669 and 1672, over 100 'outed' ministers, who had 'lived peaceably and orderly', were allowed to return to their own churches; and a royal proclamation of 1674 granted indemnity for past offences. The mood of leniency passed, and repression was renewed from the same year, 1674, when landlords were made answerable for their tenants' behaviour. More and more people, many of them armed, attended the conventicles. To restore order in this threatening situation, the government sent more soldiers, who, as the 'Highland Host', earned an ugly name for themselves in the south-west; and the show of force evoked force from the other side. Archbishop Sharp was murdered by some brutal fanatics in May 1679. On 1 June a party of armed covenanters had a victory at Drumclog over John Graham of Claverhouse (afterwards Viscount Dundee), but three weeks later their small army was crushed at Bothwell bridge by James, Duke of Monmouth, the king's natural son.[1]

Lauderdale was now replaced in the administration of Scotland by James, Duke of York, the king's brother and an open Roman Catholic; his right to the succession, despite the 'difference in religion', was asserted by a Scottish statute of 1681. In the same year all officials were required to take a new 'test' or oath, acknowledging the royal supremacy and renouncing the covenants. Charles's last years were long remembered in Scotland as 'the Killing Time', for there was something like open war in the south-west between Claverhouse and his dragoons, ready on occasion to shoot at sight, and the extreme covenanters (called Cameronians after one of their leading preachers, Richard Cameron), who went so far as to 'disown Charles Stuart . . . for . . . his perjury and breach of covenant'.

One curious by-product of 'the Killing Time' was the impetus which it gave to Scottish colonial endeavours. The inauspicious start of that process has already been glanced at, namely, the vain scheme for a Scottish settlement of French Acadia, or Nova Scotia, in 1621.[2] Since that event, any connexion between Scotland and the English colonies in North America had been quite casual and unplanned. Hundreds of the Scottish prisoners taken at Dunbar (1650) and Worcester (1651) were shipped by the Cromwellian forces to the American plantations. After the Restoration, paupers, vagrants and chronic law-breakers were commonly transported thither by order of the Scots Privy Council or of the town councils of the larger burghs. Yet again, many a venturesome Scot bound himself to a colonial master (in need of reliable labour) as an 'indentured servant', agreeing to work for his keep for a period of years, after which he would be free; in this way, he made sure of a voyage that would otherwise be beyond his means, and of his ultimate livelihood in Massachusetts, Virginia or the West Indies. This random traffic and settlement were encouraged by the skippers and crews carrying on what was strictly 'illegal' trade with the English colonies.[3] The defeat of thc Drumclog rebellion (1679) brought America a further supply of captive Covenanters.

Such movements were, however, spasmodic, and the numbers involved were small. After 1680, emigration became more systematic,

[1] The risings of 1666 and 1679 loom so large in Presbyterian lore and legend as to disguise the facts that they concerned only the south-western uplands and involved no more than a few thousand fighting men.

[2] See *supra*, p. 6. [3] See *infra*, p. 30.

partly to relieve the sufferers from religious persecution, partly as an outlet for commercial enterprise. The proprietors of East New Jersey, who got their title to the land in 1682, included five Scotsmen, and they persuaded many hundreds of their fellow-countrymen to move in. Letters written home by the settlers brought out more friends or kinsfolk. This part of the Atlantic seaboard consequently acquired, and for long retained, a strong Scottish and Presbyterian character. The new provincial capital, Perth Amboy, was named in honour of the Earl (later Duke) of Perth, one of the proprietors. The cherished Scottish connection had much to do with the foundation and prosperity of the 'College of New Jersey' (1746), which grew into the famous Princeton University. Far to the south, meanwhile, Stuart's Town was settled by Lord Cardross and William Dunlop (later principal of Glasgow University) with Scots Covenanters. For two years (1684-86) it acted as the southern outpost of British settlement in those parts, until it was overwhelmed by a Spanish force from Florida. These were the high-lights of the 'Covenanting' phase of Scottish emigration, which had a wide, if diffuse, impact on all the North American colonies.

On Charles II's death in February 1685 his brother succeeded quietly as James VII and II (1685-88). In the west country the Earl of Argyll, in conjunction with Monmouth in England, raised another rebellion, only to be captured and executed, while the American colonies got a further supply of Scots prisoners. Parliament, loyal and submissive as ever, made a perpetual grant to the crown of the excise, but even it refused to sanction James's proposal of toleration for the Roman Catholics. The royal influence was, however, sufficient to obtain converts to the king's faith among his Scottish subjects: the Earl of Perth, the chancellor (whom we have just seen in connection with Perth Amboy), became a Romanist, and the Duke of Gordon, another Catholic, was appointed keeper of Edinburgh castle. In 1687 James had recourse to the royal prerogative in order to achieve his purpose. In two Declarations of Indulgence, he gave complete toleration to all his subjects, including Romanists, Covenanters and Quakers. The Killing Time was over, persecution was ended, but presbyterians and episcopalians alike were thoroughly alarmed about the favour being shown to the papists. The town-dwellers were made fully aware of the drift of public affairs, for the king, acting through the privy council in the most arbitrary manner, suspended the burgh elections and simply nominated as magistrates and councillors either Roman Catholics or such as were known to lean to their faith.

Wholly alienated by the king's rashness and stupidity, Scotland was as ready for the Revolution as it had earlier been ready for the Restoration; but again it was left to the English to take positive action. The news of the arrival in the south of William of Orange (November 1688) and of James's flight to France (December) provoked some rioting against the Romanists and also the 'rabbling' of episcopal clergymen; but it was not until after 'Dutch William' had become king of England (February 1689) that the all-important meeting of the Convention of Estates (summoned by him on the invitation of the Scottish politicians who had flocked to London) began in Edinburgh (14 March).

In April 1689 the Convention resolved that James had forfeited the crown and ordered the proclamation of William and Mary as king and queen of Scotland; the late monarch's misdeeds were set out in detail in the Claim of Right. Parliamentary opposition to the change of kings was slight, and, while there was some military resistance from the Highlands and other adherents of King James (now known as 'Jacobites'), this offered little real menace to the new régime.[1] King William was thus given the chance to rule which his father-in-law had so foolishly thrown away.

The contrast between England and Scotland in respect of the chain of events leading from the Restoration to the Revolution is thus sharp. The great outpouring of loyal sentiment by the English people in 1660 soon spent itself, and within a few years Parliament was addressing itself to the task of limiting the royal prerogative and perfecting constitutional 'checks' on absolutism. By 1688 the English political leaders were ready to assert, with general approval, popular rights against the mounting claims of royal autocracy. In Scotland, on the other hand, the power of the restored monarchy remained great throughout the period, the king retained firm control of the apparatus of the state, and his actions, and those of his chosen ministers, were seldom challenged by any political opponents.

The religious settlements also showed the two countries in different lights. The position of the Church of England – strongly royalist during 'the Troubles' – was utterly secure, and Protestant dissent was relatively weak. But the renewed attempt to re-shape the Church of Scotland to an episcopal mould, and so to bring it more nearly into accord with the Anglican model, was a hazardous undertaking, despite all that might be argued in favour of a 'moderate' solution, a 'middle

[1] For details of these matters, see *infra*, pp. 45-7.

way'. Popular hostility, though tending in its extreme form to be localised, was stubborn and at times violent. And yet, in the end, when the conjunction of royal despotism and Romanist subversion faced the two countries with an equal, and an equally deadly, menace, it was the political capacity of the English, supported by the outraged dignity of their Church, and not the manifold grievances of the frustrated Presbyterians of Scotland, that brought about the dispossession of James II and VII. In some sense the Revolution may be said to have cancelled out the Restoration, but the impulse for both these processes came from England.

CHAPTER III

The Economy under the Regal Union

THE DILEMMA that had long faced the Scottish economy became acute in the course of the seventeenth century, though it is easy to overlook it amid the drama of religious conflict and civil strife. We do well to remind ourselves that, whether the power of the state lay with king, parliament or general assembly, the main business of most of the people was, as before, to produce food and drink, clothes and furnishings, necessities and luxuries. In these matters of day-to-day living, the true 'curse of Scotland' was her continued poverty, and the problem to which an answer was now sought, more eagerly than ever before, was how to overcome this disability and to advance along the road to security and prosperity.

There are many reasons why Scotland was a poor country and remained one after the union of 1603 had brought about closer contacts with England, a richer and more progressive country. Agriculture, now as heretofore, was primitive in aims and backward in methods. The theory was that each region, each estate and even, as far as possible, each farm should be self-supporting: it should grow, raise or make all that its occupants needed in order to eat, to drink, to clothe themselves and to render their homes habitable. The general concept was that of a mixed farm, yielding oats (which, as oatmeal, formed the staple foodstuff), 'bere' or coarse barley (the chief drink-crop, and also used for barley bread), a little flax (for spinning into linen yarn), and some pease and beans for variety, and possessing, too, a few head of cattle (useful in those days as draught oxen apart from the value placed on beef, milk, cheese and butter), and perhaps, in addition, a number of sheep, pigs (though not in the Highlands) and poultry.

This general concept, however, was seldom to be found in practice; pure 'subsistence farming', indeed, occurred, and could occur, only in the poorest areas. Differences of climate and soil, of knowledge and skill, impelled the farmer to be more than merely a successful 'all-rounder' – just like his neighbour or his counterpart in some other region. Nature itself told him what to grow and what to avoid, and each generation handed on its knowledge and experience to the next. Thus, the richest grain-bearing farms lay in the south-eastern plain between Edinburgh and Berwick while there was also some good arable land in East Fife and in parts of Forfarshire. Clydesdale had orchards as well as cornfields and pastures, Galloway was noted for its horses and cattle, Tweeddale and Teviotdale relied on their large sheep-farms. Then there was, of course, the 'harvest of the sea': while the fishermen of the north-east coast reaped a rich haul of salmon, the lochs and bays of the west gave up a large yield of herring.

Hence the real position was one of surpluses here, deficiencies there; and the matter was complicated by seasonal fluctuations, for a poor, late harvest could turn a surplus area into a deficiency area. Most of the time there was some trade between region and region – even between Highlands and Lowlands. We are too ready to think of contacts across the Highland line in terms of plunder, blackmail and punitive expeditions, for there were peaceful links too. The clansmen could raise more cattle, but grew less grain, than they required for their own use; and they had easy access to extensive forests. Highland drovers therefore conducted herds of black cattle to the markets of Forfarshire, Perthshire and Stirlingshire, and woodmen floated timber down the Ness and the Tay to supply the 'treeless' Lowlanders. In return the Highlanders bought the meal, malt and cloth that their infertile glens could not produce in sufficient quantities.

Though the inhabitants of each district tended to barter what they could spare for what they lacked, the doctrine of self-sufficiency still had a cramping effect on the farmer's outlook and practice: by striving to produce for his own and his family's immediate needs, as well as by clinging to the short views and traditional methods of feudal agriculture, he set narrow limits to the national output, trade and wealth. For centuries there was little change in the range of the country produce available for shipping 'furth of Scotland'. There were always plenty of hides of cattle and skins of deer, goats, rabbits, otter and badgers; there were substantial quantities of wool and woolfells (or whole sheepskins); there were salmon and herring, smoked or salted and barreled; and, in times of plenty, there might be cargoes of oats, barley and cattle. These raw materials, laboriously produced and collected, formed the basis of Scottish export trade.

Farming and fishing, backward as they were, received little help from native industry. The 'trades', as they are still called in Scotland – such as those of the baker, flesher, tailor, cordiner (or shoemaker), mason, wright, weaver and litster (or dyer) – remained in the hands of the incorporated crafts within the burghs.[1] Craftsmen worked on their own or employed a 'journeyman' as a paid servant, and some of them kept an apprentice or two; in most burghs the crafts were small bodies of men. By the strict old rules that still prevailed, only a burgess could become a master-craftsman and, before admission, he had to prove his skill by performing an 'essay' or task-piece: for example, each Glasgow skinner had to dress thirty sheepskins and make a pair of gloves. Each had to pay, as entry-fee, what was known as his 'booth-upset', entitling him to set up his booth, or shop, and to practise his craft. If he had served an apprenticeship (of five, six or seven years) and so completed his 'indenture', he paid less than one who had not done so; and easier terms were also made for sons or sons-in-law of masters.[2] Once admitted, all craftsmen must abide by the craft rules. They must charge the fixed prices for their goods, ensure that they were of the proper quality, and pay their servants the agreed rate of wages; they must not lure away another man's apprentice, or 'cry down' his wares while extolling their own. They must combine against the common enemy – the 'unfree' craftsman, who, living perhaps in a suburb or a nearby village, paid no dues and endeavoured to undersell the 'free' or burgess craftsman. Thus the work carried out by the tailors of Potterrow, outside Edinburgh, by the skinners of Gorbals, across the Clyde from Glasgow, or by the weavers of the Hilltown of Dundee, was denounced as unfair competition.

The burgh crafts were essentially conservative in aims and methods. Each tailor and bonnetmaker, each weaver and cordiner, made to order for his customers, and not, as a rule, what he thought he might sell in the open market. The apprentice learned his trade, became a master in due course, and taught the same things in turn to his own apprentice. Custom and tradition governed the weight of the loaf of bread, the width of cloth, the very taste of the ale. 'Forestalling', that is, buying

[1] There were 14 crafts in Edinburgh and 14 in Glasgow; the other chief burghs, like Aberdeen, Dundee, Perth, Stirling, Ayr and St Andrews, had 7, 8 or 9 each; but most of the burghs had a smaller number – 4, 5 or 6. In many of the lesser burghs two or more crafts were often united; thus the masons (stoneworkers) and the wrights (woodworkers) were sometimes combined as the 'squaremen', while the hammermen formed a large confederation of many sub-crafts, such as goldsmiths, silversmiths, locksmiths, blacksmiths, pewterers, lorimers, saddlers and 'sword-slippers'.

[2] It was common for an apprentice to marry the daughter of the master-craftsman with whom he had boarded and from whom he had learnt his craft. The son or son-in-law was admitted, in the old Scots phrase, 'at the near hand', whereas the stranger came in, for a higher payment, 'at the far hand'.

goods before they came to market, was forbidden, as was 'regrating', or making excessive purchases in order to 'corner' supplies. These ancient abuses, far from being hailed as smart business, were constantly condemned in much the same way as was profiteering during the first World War or the black market during the second.

The craftsmen were either skilled artisans or petty shopkeepers selling their own products. In contrast, the merchants were the wholesale traders, and to them 'merchandise' meant overseas trade. They had their own organised and exclusive society: the merchant guild, under the dean of guild, had the right and duty, in each of the larger burghs, of controlling sea-borne commerce. In some burghs a skipper had to have the dean of guild's 'ticket' before he could sail, the guild dues being first paid; in all of them the guild firmly supervised trading practices, and the merchants, paying high entry-fees, formed the upper class of the burgess body. But their monopoly of trade stretched, so to speak, backward as well as forward – into the landward areas, whence they drew the raw materials that were their 'staple wares', and over the ocean to the foreign ports where they sought their return cargoes. Thus their jealous insistence on their rights had a cramping effect on rural as well as urban enterprise.

The merchants' habits altered little from age to age. The same trade-routes were followed, the same goods were exported, and the same articles were brought home. Fish, hides and skins, wool and woolfells, coarse cloth (both linen and woollen), salt and coal, and perhaps some cattle and grain, were exported from the eastern ports, such as Leith, Kirkcaldy, Dundee, Montrose and Aberdeen, to the Baltic, the Low Countries and France; while the western burghs, Glasgow, Dumbarton, Irvine and Ayr, had a little trade with Ireland, England and France. From Norway and the Baltic the incoming cargoes comprised timber, iron, tar, pitch, flax and hemp; from Bordeaux wine was brought over each year by a fleet sailing in convoy; the other French ports, the Netherlands and England sent silks and fine woollen cloth, wheat, salt (suitable for pickling fish and preserving meat), fruits, nuts and spices, and all sorts of manufactures; butter, cattle and grain sometimes came from Ireland.

Apart from the hazards of war, piracy and storms, Scottish trade was fairly steady and substantial; what can be said against it is that it was almost entirely an exchange of exported (and cheap) raw materials for imported (and costly) manufactures and articles of fashion or luxury. Foreign trade was a constant drain on the nation's natural resources; it disposed of a hard-won surplus of the produce of land and sea in order to acquire a modicum of the comfortable and gracious things of life. The position is clearly indicated in a statement of the annual values of the various classes of goods exported by sea from Scotland during the period 1611-14. The list is as follows (in thousands of pounds Scots):

	(£'000)
Bear, Cattle, Oats and Wheat	37
Hides	65
Woolfells	143
Other Skins	31
Wool	52
Lead	20
Coal	25
Salt	40
Feathers and Butter	2
Herring	100
Salmon	47
Other Fish	6
Re-exports (Wax, Salt, Timber, Cloth, etc.)	39
Woollen Cloth, Plaiding and Hose	70
Linen Cloth	12
Linen Yarn	33
Gloves and other Leather Goods	14
Total	736

It is noticeable that the cloth, yarn, gloves and other manufactured goods were worth only £129,000; even if some small allowance be made for manufactures included among the 're-exports', their worth would still be less than one-fifth of the total. The moral to be drawn from such figures is plain. What was needed was an improvement in industrial skills, so that Scotland's own manufactures could command a good price in overseas markets and so pay for what the people lacked or desired.

As early as 1605 the problem and a proposed solution were clearly set forth by Sir Thomas Craig, an eminent Scottish lawyer: 'In future our people must pay very particular attention to the manufacture of cloth, for thence will proceed our ability to import wines, merchandise, and those things on which men set store. Otherwise we shall find it hard to raise the money to pay for our imports.' The principle here stated continued to influence Scottish economic policy throughout the seventeenth century, and both Parliament and Privy Council frequently attempted, by specific acts and decrees, to put it into practice. The export of raw wool was forbidden, the bringing in of cloth of English or overseas manufacture was prohibited, and foreign weavers and dyers were encouraged to settle in Scotland and to teach native workers their more advanced processes. It is true that the very repetition of such legislation suggests that it may not have been effective: otherwise, why re-enact the same measures? It was, indeed, hard to enforce state policy in the absence of an effective system of central and local government; moreover, it was tempting for the king to reward his courtiers, or to raise money from them, by granting special export licences.

Another method favoured by the Crown for the establishment of new industries or the improvement of old ones was the issue of 'patents of monopoly', whereby the sole right to develop some trade or process was conveyed to an individual or company for an express period – often twenty-one years. In 1619, for example, Nathaniel Udwart, of Edinburgh, got a twenty-one years' monopoly of soap-making; again, from 1620, John, Lord Erskine, was authorised to bring in English tanners for the advancement of Scottish leather-making.

Perhaps the greatest progress of the time was made in coal-mining, an enterprise which (because of the rural location of the workable seams) concerned the landowners rather than the burgesses. Early in the century Sir George Bruce of Culross was a pioneer in the winning of 'sea-coal' by driving galleries under the waters of the Firth of Forth. Between 1660 and 1677 David, Earl of Wemyss, is reputed to have spent the sum of £100,000 Scots (over £8,300 sterling) on the improvement of his collieries and the building of a new harbour at Methil.[1] This investment was a sound one, for by 1677 the port was reckoned to be worth 20,000 merks a year (or £1,111 sterling) to the Wemyss family; much of the profit came from the export of coal. By way of contrast, the greatest economic failure of the period 1603-90 was sustained over the fishing industry. In an effort to combat the ascendancy of the Dutch, with their larger and better boats, in Scotland's coastal waters, Charles I in 1630 promoted a grandiose scheme for a fishing company, and his son repeated the experiment in 1661. The royal burghs, sensing a threat to their monopoly of trade, resisted these ventures and rejoiced over their complete collapse.

[1] Methil was erected (with the promotion of the coal trade in view) as a free burgh of barony in 1662.

In the time of the Cromwellian protectorate, as we have seen,[1] Scotland enjoyed the benefit of free trade with England and with the English colonies, though, for various reasons (including high taxation and Dutch wars), her merchants were unable to take full advantage of their opportunities. One town, however, that did make great advances was Glasgow, which could now trade legally as well as conveniently with the American plantations. Robert Baillie, writing in 1656, records that Glasgow 'thryves above all the land. . . . Our people has much more trade in comparison than any other: their buildings encrease strangelie both for number and fairness: it's more than doubled in our tyme'.[2]

Equal trading conditions, however much or little they signified, disappeared with the Restoration. A new English Navigation Act of 1660 treated Scotland, so far as trade was concerned, as a foreign country, and this rebuff induced the Scottish politicians to adopt a system of full 'protection'. Their own Navigation Act (1661) imposed penalties on English and foreign traders, and two years later heavy duties were expressly enacted for English cloth, hats, stockings and gloves.[3] Further statutes of the year 1661 set up a Council of Trade to regulate and promote manufactures and commerce; encouraged, especially by the promise of freedom from custom, the erection of new 'manufactories'; prohibited the export of linen yarn (so that it might be woven at home); forbade the importation of such 'made work' as could be produced within Scotland; offered advantageous terms for the settlement of overseas artisans skilled in the making of linen cloth, worsted stockings, serges and other stuffs; and disallowed the export of skins (to induce Scottish skinners to make finished gloves as articles of commerce). In its 'cold war' with England, Scotland, it must be confessed, came off none too well, though the Clyde again provides an exception. The Glasgow merchants, defying the English Navigation Act, continued to bring in odd cargoes of tobacco, sugar, mahogany and oranges in an 'illicit' trade with the American colonies and the West Indies. In 1662 they built a riverside quay at the Broomielaw, but six years later they took a bolder step to meet the challenge of the

[1] See *supra*, p. 16.

[2] By this phrase Baillie (who was born in 1599 and died in 1662) must have meant some such period as 1615-55.

[3] These duties were deliberately 'protective', i.e. they were aimed against English products that competed with the native articles; the tobacco duty, imposed at the same time, was rather 'sumptuary', i.e. it was directed against what was thought to be a fashionable fad and a needless luxury.

harbour at Greenock[1] by setting up their own 'New Port' down the estuary of the Clyde, and this soon came to be called Port Glasgow.

Trade rivalry and new enterprise sharpened in the last two decades of the century. A sweeping Act of 1681 forbade the importation of gold or silver thread, laces and buttons, of sundry silk stuffs and embroidered work, of Dutch linen, cambric, lawn, damask and calico, of foreign stockings (silk or woollen), and of gloves, shoes and many other articles of apparel. These regulations formed part of a large design, for the statute was intended to foster the development of Scottish manufactures, and under its terms at least fifty joint-stock companies came into being. Typical of these is the woollen manufactory set up in 1693 at New Mills (East Lothian), with a guarantee that all its imported raw materials, as well as its finished cloth, and even the liquor consumed by its employees, would be free from customs and excise duties for the space of twenty-one years. Other joint-stock companies were instituted for the weaving of linen (at Edinburgh and Leith), for soap-making (at Glasgow and Leith), for sugar (at Glasgow), for silk-weaving, for sail-cloth, rope and cordage, for pottery, paper-making, gunpowder and iron-founding. Meanwhile Parliament continued its policy of strict control. It was enacted in 1686 that corpses should not be buried except in Scottish-made linen 'or cloath of hards' (a coarser fabric also woven from flax), and the export of lint and linen yarn was forbidden in 1693 and again in 1695.

The end of the story presents a mixture of triumph and catastrophe. The Bank of Scotland was established in 1695, with a paid-up capital of £10,000 sterling, 'for the carying on and manageing of a publick Bank'; and that venerable and flourishing institution is with us to this day. On the other hand, the most ambitious and the best supported of the joint-stock enterprises of the time – it also was authorised in 1695 – resulted in a gigantic disaster; but an account of the Darien scheme, since it has as much political as economic significance, is reserved for a later chapter.[2]

The Darien project had the support of the burghs, but, on the whole, they were indifferent or hostile to the various industrial and trading ventures of the seventeenth century. It was the nobles and lairds, often backed up by wealth drawn from estates formerly belonging to the Church, who took up monopolies or subscribed to a 'joint

[1] It had been erected as a burgh of barony, in favour of its superior, John Shaw of Greenock, in 1635.

[2] See *infra*, chap. v, pp. 48-9.

stock', who tried to promote the fisheries and to foster weaving, who developed coal mines and introduced English, French and Flemish artisans. The royal burghs were short-sighted enough to defend and rely on the exclusive rights and restrictions which, in past centuries, had buttressed their favoured position in industry and commerce, and which now, in changed conditions, seemed to them essential props of their wealth and security. Their privileges had been confirmed, in the amplest form, by a statute of 1633.[1] After the Restoration, however, their cherished 'liberties' were menaced from several directions besides that of the joint-stock company.

A large number of burghs of barony had been erected by royal charter between 1450 and 1660,[2] generally in favour of a local noble or laird, but these 'unfree burghs' (as they were rather scornfully styled by the royal burghs) offered little serious rivalry, so long as the burgesses of the royal burghs kept a watchful eye on them,[3] to ensure that their markets contained only local produce and not the 'staple wares' of overseas commerce, and that their craftsmen did not impinge on their own rights. In the reign of Charles II, when many more burghs of barony were created,[4] the nobles and lairds, strongly represented in Parliament, sought to widen the powers of their dependent towns. A statute passed in 1672 allowed the burghs of barony to export corn, cattle and other native produce, to import timber, iron, tar and other commodities required for tillage or for building, and to sell retail all goods whatsoever. The royal burghs counter-attacked in 1681, when they induced Parliament to declare that merchandise imported by traders in the burghs of barony might be sold only for the use of the inhabitants of the barony. By a further Act of 1690 the trade of these 'unfree' burghs was restricted to native commodities and to foreign goods purchased from freemen of the royal burghs.

The basic idea of the burgh of barony – whether it worked out in practice or not – was sensible and modest enough: its aim was to meet the needs of the country dwellers and the village folk for some

[1] See *supra*, p. 13.

[2] About 100 formal 'erections' are recorded between 1450 and 1560, and about 130 between 1560 and 1660, but probably at least 50 of these charter grants were abortive; to some extent these were the 'town planning' schemes of their day, which might or might not 'come off'.

[3] For example, within Ayrshire, the men of Ayr regarded the unfree traders of Maybole with the utmost suspicion, while the men of Irvine were equally jealous of those of Kilmarnock.

[4] About 100 'erections' were authorised in the short period between 1660 and 1707, but certainly fewer than half of these resulted in real burghs.

shopping facilities and for the services of the humbler kind of craftsmen at no unreasonable distance from their homes.[1] Now, prior to 1660, all but a few of the weekly markets and annual fairs throughout the country had been held in the burghs; indeed, the market and the fair were often thought of as being among the hall-marks of a burgh. After the Restoration, Parliament, as one of its measures for improving the national economy, especially in rural parts and remote settlements, granted the landowner the right to hold a weekly market, or an annual fair, or both,[2] without any obligation on him or on the local community to establish and maintain a burgh. All that was needed for the success of such a project was a willing landlord, some local demand, and a village street, a suitable field, open space or hill-top; there was no question of incurring the burden and the cost of local government. The non-burghal market and fair obviously met a felt want and had a wide appeal. The parliamentary records for the single year 1661, for example, show grants of this kind in respect of Stenton (East Lothian), Bowden (Roxburgh), Leslie (Fife), Old Deer (Aberdeen) and Foulden (Berwick) – none of them a burgh, but each of them a village or a tiny hamlet. Each session of Parliament thereafter brought into being a substantial number of separate markets and fairs (or of the two in conjunction), until, by the time of the Union, some 250 such grants had been made.

The encroachments of the burgh of barony, and the spread of the private market and fair, alarmed the burgesses of the royal burghs and at last led them to suggest a remedy for what lay at the root of the trouble – an over-concentration of trading facilities. The outcome was the offer of 'communication of trade', whereby, in 1693, the royal burghs promised to share foreign trading rights with the burghs of barony, market towns and other 'unfree places', if they would undertake to relieve them of ten per cent of their land tax. Many of the greater burghs of barony, including Borrowstouness, Prestonpans, Greenock, Kelso, Dalkeith, Musselburgh, Alloa, Falkirk, Kilmarnock, Peterhead and Fraserburgh, joined the scheme, but there was prolonged haggling over the price of admission. The project never worked very well: the relief to the royal burghs turned out to be not ten per cent

[1] There were only 66 royal burghs to serve the inhabitants of Scotland's 33 shires; and this meant that many homes lay 20 miles and more from the nearest royal burgh.

[2] The grant included authority to the landlord to collect the booth-rents and other dues from the market or fair; and the revenue to be gained therefrom was a strong inducement to him to favour the idea.

but two, and, until well on in the eighteenth century, many 'unfree traders' preferred, to the grandiose plan of 'communication of trade', the simpler and more profitable device of what was, in the strict legal sense, smuggling.

CHAPTER IV

Seventeenth-Century Culture

THE SEVENTEENTH CENTURY saw strenuous efforts being made to promote progress in the arts of peace, no less than in material well-being, though in both cases the efforts were hampered or frustrated by political and ecclesiastical strife. Regardless of his religious creed or political leanings, the Scotsman adhered to the belief (bequeathed by Knox and the early reformers) in the value of a learned laity as well as a dedicated ministry. The first objective of those who cared for the cause of education was the provision of a network of elementary schools, covering the country and giving every boy,[1] no matter what were his parents' means, a chance to learn to read, to write and to count.

Legislation, at least, was plentiful during the century. Its basic principles had been suggested in the First Book of Discipline and amplified in later acts of the General Assembly, which advocated attention to the Christian duty of 'planting of schools', the appointment of teachers 'able in doctrine', and regular 'visitations' by the authorities to ensure that the statutes were being obeyed, and that parents and pupils were taking advantage of their opportunities. The first clear and systematic statement on the subject came in an act of the Privy Council in 1616, which directed that a school be established in every parish where 'convenient meanes may be had', at the expense of the parishioners and by the advice of the bishop of the diocese 'in his visitatioun'. The aim was to instruct 'the youth' in godliness and knowledge, to teach them to read and write in English, and, thereby, to abolish the 'Irishe' (or Gaelic) language, which was said to be a chief cause of the continued 'barbaritie and incivilitie' of the inhabitants of the Highlands and Islands – a phrase that brings vividly before us Lowland prejudice toward Gaelic culture.[2] In 1633 Parliament ratified this act, with the important addition that the bishops, in their visitations, were empowered, with the consent of the heritors and a majority of the parishioners, to impose a 'stent' or land tax

[1] The education of girls was thought to be of much less importance, and little was done before the eighteenth century, but see *infra*, p. 38.

[2] The attitude was, of course, based on ignorance, and on fear and suspicion of the unknown, but it continued well into the eighteenth century.

on each parish for the establishment and maintenance of the school.

The triumph of the Covenanters from 1638 altered some of the details of the statutory arrangements. Schoolmasters were required in 1640 to subscribe the Confession of Faith and the National Covenant. After repeated urgings from the General Assembly, Parliament passed, in 1646, the most precise legislation to date for the founding of a school and the appointment of a schoolmaster in every parish. The heritors must provide a 'commodious' school-house and tax themselves for its maintenance and for the payment of the master's stipend, which was to be not less than 100 merks (£5 11s. 1d. sterling) or more than 200 merks (£11 2s. 2d.); that stipend was to cover the teacher's duties as session clerk, an office usually held by him. If the heritors failed to act, the presbytery (coming in place of the bishops, deposed in 1638) was to appoint 'tuell honest men within the boundis' to set up the school and impose the stent.

The Act Rescissory of 1661 had the effect of annulling the statute of 1646 and restoring that of 1633, so that the duties of 'visitation' and of enforcing the school tax devolved again upon the bishops. The legislative record of the century closed in 1696 with another Act 'for settling of schools', which repeated the terms of the 1646 statute, with three main changes. Each heritor was allowed 'relief' for half of his tax from the tenants or occupiers of his lands.[1] The teacher's salary was now to be paid in full, over and above any fees that might come to him as session clerk. Most important of all, in the event of the heritors failing to carry out their duty, the presbytery would apply to the commissioners of supply for the shire to establish the school, 'modify' the salary (within the 1646 limits) and enforce the tax. The commissioners, as large landowners responsible for assessing the national land-tax, were a powerful body in each county, and the idea of bringing them in was to give the statute 'teeth'.

How far these statutes were effective it is hard to say, for our records are too scrappy to be very helpful. Times indeed were 'out of joint' and, though the ministers and many of the laity were keen educationists, the heritors were often apathetic or stingy; it is certain that, despite all the orders from Edinburgh, many parishes had no 'settled' school. On the other hand, our scant records do suggest that some progress was made. In the better shires – for example,

[1] The principle that the owner should pay half the 'rate' and the occupier the other half had been laid down for the first time in an Act of 1663 concerning poor relief. It lasted until 1957. Cf. *supra*, p. 18.

Aberdeen, Forfar and Lanark – fully half of the parishes had schools or schoolmasters at some stage during the century, though, since a fixed 'provision' (based on a permanent 'stent') was not made in every case, there was no guarantee of continuity in these arrangements. In other shires, and especially in the remote Highlands, with their poverty, large and scattered parishes, and the language difficulty, the position was much worse.

The parish schools imparted the rudiments of reading and writing, taught simple arithmetic, and gave instruction in the elements of religion. In some of them the 'dominie' went further, taking the gifted scholar – the 'lad o' pairts' – through courses of Latin and even occasionally of Greek or French. The boys attended between the ages of seven and nine or ten, after which a few would go on to a grammar school. Quarterly fees, often a shilling but sometimes more, were paid directly to the schoolmaster and formed part of his emoluments. The scholars also brought straw for the floor, peats for the fire, and candles, or gifts of money, at Candlemas (2 February), while fighting cocks, matched against each other by the boys on Fastern's E'en,[1] became the property of the teacher as they were killed. And the dominie eked out his stipend with the fees paid to him as session clerk and also often as parish registrar of births, deaths and marriages.

Parish schools, where they existed, formed the backbone of the national system, but there were others. The song school or music school of an earlier day seems to have died out in the course of the seventeenth century. The burgh school or grammar[2] school, however, situated in each large town, constituted the second stage of formal education. The main, and often the only, subject taught was Latin, in which the boys were drilled relentlessly until they had fitted themselves, if they wished, to go on to the university. A few grammar schools also gave a grounding in Greek and some other subjects, but mastery of Latin was their primary aim. Most boys attended between the ages of nine or ten and thirteen or fourteen. School hours were very long; at Stirling, for example, in 1613, they ran from six o'clock in the morning until six in the evening, with a breakfast break between nine and ten, and an hour off for dinner at noon. Saturday was a full

[1] Fastern's E'en (Shrove Tuesday), the last day before Lent, was traditionally a time of rude licence and games. Though the Church denounced cock-fighting, masters and scholars were attached to it, and the custom lingered on in some country schools until the nineteenth century.

[2] The 'grammar' of the title was Latin grammar; such a school was sometimes called 'high school' or 'Latin school'.

day like the others. As the century wore on, however, this rigorous discipline was somewhat softened. At Elgin, in 1649, the pupils got a Saturday half-holiday. At Dundee, in the 1670s, the opening was put back to seven o'clock for the winter months. By the 1690s many schools started at seven in summer and nine in winter.

The grammar schools were managed by the town councils, who appointed teachers (though often with the minister's advice), fixed the school hours and curriculum, regulated the fees (which were rather higher than in the parish schools) and saw to the repair of the buildings. A few of the burghs were helped by grants made by the Crown from the revenues of the old Church for the express purpose of running the schools – Dundee, Irvine, Renfrew, Elgin, Dunfermline, Paisley and Musselburgh – but in the main the burgh itself had to bear the cost of the schoolmaster's stipend (again at a higher rate than in the parishes), of his 'house-mail' or rent, and of the salary of his assistant, 'the doctor'. If times were hard and fees few – for example, during seasons of war, plague or famine – the town council might come to the dominie's help with a supplementary grant.

In a few of the larger burghs certain private or 'adventure' schools operated by permission of the town council, who would license a teacher of French, of dancing, or of some of the sciences, but careful watch was kept to ensure that such schools did not compete with the grammar schools and so deprive them of fees which would otherwise have come their way; they were thus largely confined to young boys and, in some cases, young girls. Moreover, Edinburgh had, by the end of the century, several schools that took in the daughters of nobles and lairds, and, for relatively high fees,[1] gave them their board and taught them writing, singing, playing, dancing and sewing.

At the highest level of the educational system, perhaps the most remarkable thing about the universities is that all five contrived to survive this strife-torn century – the three papal foundations of the middle ages, St Andrews, Glasgow and King's College, Old Aberdeen, and the two post-medieval and secular institutions, Edinburgh and Marischal College, in New Aberdeen. Of these five, Edinburgh differed from the others in that it was not an independent university but a 'toun's college'. The town council appointed and dismissed the teachers, paid their salaries, and regulated students' fees and courses of study. In the other four, the rector was chosen by the

[1] In 1700 the laird of Kilravock paid for his daughter in Edinburgh as much as £5 sterling for a quarter's board and 10s. and upwards a quarter for each subject.

regents, masters and students to protect their liberties; he was generally, at this time, a clergyman, often a well-known city minister or else a college dignitary. In 1620 a separate rector was first appointed at Edinburgh[1] and, until 1665, he was usually a person of a similar kind. In that year, however, the town council determined that the provost would always be 'rector and governor of the colledge'; in a phrase used in 1640 he was to be 'the eye of the Council of the Toun' as well as 'the mouth of the colledge'. And yet, despite its close dependence on the city fathers, Edinburgh was recognised, in a statute of 1621, as possessing all the liberties of the other colleges, including the right to confer degrees.

Changes in policy during the century affected the universities, and each turn of the wheel of fortune was apt to bring about the deprivation of principals and regents who had been too intimate with the outgoing régime. Not only so, but university finances also experienced violent fluctuations. Between 1641 and 1660, and again after 1690, the various colleges applied for, and received, generous assistance from the episcopal revenues, released by the triumph of presbytery. The Restoration, of course, dried up these sources of income, as the reinstated bishops needed them for their own upkeep; but before 1660 prosperity had made it possible to bring near to completion the century's most pleasing and successful piece of architectural planning – that of the graceful 'Old College' in the High Street of Glasgow, with its picturesque clock-tower, gateways and high gables, its two quadrangles and its spacious gardens.

The curricular reforms introduced at the older universities by, or under the inspiration of, Andrew Melville[2] failed to take lasting root, and the century was not far advanced before all of them had reverted to the antique 'regenting' method. It is true that some new chairs were founded in each of them, especially in Latin, Mathematics, Divinity, Hebrew and Medicine, but these foundations were mostly short-lived, and the 'fixed' professorship remained largely an ideal. The regent did much more actual teaching than the professor. Each regent conducted his own class through its entire four years' course, comprising (with local variations) Greek, Logic, Moral Philosophy and Natural Philosophy; additional instruction might be given in such subjects as Astronomy, Geography and Mathematics. Formal

[1] Prior to this, one man had been 'principal and rector'. In 1620 the offices were divided, the professor of divinity (and not the principal) being named rector.
[2] See *supra*, VOL. I, p. 377.

readings were delivered from Latin texts of Aristotle's works and from Dutch commentaries upon them, and there was much dictation of notes and sheer memory-work. The students, most of whom ranged from fourteen to eighteen years of age, with some older men, attended classes from six or seven o'clock until nine, and again from ten to twelve; the afternoons were occupied with disputations and examinations, and also with permitted recreations, like archery and golf.

College discipline was strict and even harsh. Most of the students lived in bare and comfortless college chambers, though a few wealthier boys boarded with regents or in private houses with 'masters', who might give them extra-mural tuition. The morning bell rang at five o'clock, and at nine in the evening one of the regents came round to see that all lights were out and all the boys in bed.[1] At the common tables the fare was simple and homely: oatmeal, bread, broth and ale were to be seen more often than eggs, fish or meat. Gowns were worn not only in college but also on the public streets, for it was thought that this conspicuous garb made disorderly conduct less likely. Speech, even informal conversation, was allowed only in Latin.

St Andrews was the fashionable university and attracted the sons of nobles as well as of lairds and merchants: Montrose, Argyll, Lauderdale and 'Bonnie Dundee' were all students there. But the great majority of the boys at the Scottish universities took the 'Arts' or 'Philosophy' course with a view to the ministry, and their simple piety and cloistered life made a strong appeal not only to Scots Presbyterians, but also to English and Irish Nonconformists, barred from Oxford and Cambridge by religious tests. Numbers accordingly rose, especially after 1690, when Edinburgh and Glasgow each had 300 or more; though St Andrews, shorn of its lustre as the ecclesiastical capital of the country and in severe financial difficulties, began to decline.[2]

Hampered as they were by political change, religious strife and financial insecurity, the universities nevertheless bred some men of note as graduates and teachers. Prominent among them were the early members of the amazing Aberdonian family of Gregory, which, for two centuries, was to produce many famous mathematicians,

[1] This was one of the duties that fell to the regents by weekly turns; as supervisor of discipline and behaviour, the regent 'on duty' for the week was called the 'hebdomadar'.

[2] A removal of the university to Perth, as a more convenient centre, was actually being discussed in 1697-98.

astronomers, physicians and chemists.[1] James Gregory, inventor of the reflecting telescope, was educated at Aberdeen and taught mathematics at St Andrews and Edinburgh, while his nephew, David, went from Edinburgh in 1691 to become professor of astronomy at Oxford. Among the latter's contemporaries were Sir Robert Sibbald and Archibald Pitcairne, the one a geographer, the other a poet, and both outstanding physicians, in whose time were laid the foundations of Edinburgh's later distinction in medicine. A botanical garden was established (for the study of medicinal plants), the Royal College of Physicians was chartered in 1685, and the College of Surgeons, dating from 1505, likewise became 'Royal' in 1694.[2] Meanwhile Glasgow, as the centre of piety and learning in the Covenanting south-west, naturally had, among its teachers, some of the country's leading divines, like Robert Baillie and David Dickson; but it also had on its staff Principal John Cameron, the great classics scholar, and James Dalrymple, later Viscount Stair,[3] whose *Institutions of the Law of Scotland* (1681) was the first work of its kind and the model for many later legal treatises.[4]

In many ways Scottish graduates contributed to the enrichment of the mental and cultural life of the nation. Among them were the three cartographers, Timothy Pont, Robert Gordon of Straloch and James Gordon of Rothiemay, whose maps (published finally in 1654 as the Scottish section of the great Dutch atlas of Willem Blaeu) for the first time depicted in detail the various Scottish regions. Another product of our universities was Sir George Mackenzie (later earl of Cromarty), who, as dean of the faculty of advocates, founded, in 1682, the Advocates' Library, now the National Library of Scotland. Dating also to this period is the Faculty of Procurators in Glasgow, which for long had more to do with the professional training of the west-country lawyers than had the University.

If formal learning held its own through the century, the same cannot be said of imaginative literature. Alexander Montgomerie, 'the last of the makars', died about 1610, and he had no successor as

[1] It is an indication of the renown of this family that the *Dictionary of National Biography* includes lives of no fewer than nine of them, stretching in time from 1627 to 1858.

[2] The corresponding Glasgow institution, the Faculty of Physicians and Surgeons, had been founded in 1599, but was not incorporated as 'Royal' until 1910.

[3] It was his son, John (created Earl of Stair in 1703), who was 'the villain of the piece' in the Massacre of Glencoe; see *infra*, pp. 47-8.

[4] The *Institutions*, indeed, laid the foundation of modern Scots Law.

a vernacular poet. The Scots dialect was now going out of fashion as a written and even as a spoken language. The change to standard English, begun in Knox's day, was furthered by the Union of the Crowns. Moreover, the 'King James' or Authorised Version of the Bible, published in 1611, was used by all Scots Protestants and it was, of course, in pure English. Again, the Confession of Faith, the Shorter Catechism, and the metrical version of the Psalms, all drawn up by order of the Westminster Assembly of Divines (1643-47), were also in English, and these were used in the education of children as well as in the worship of adults. The common speech of a devout people like the Scots was bound to be affected by these religious 'standards'.

Little wonder, then, that there survive from the seventeenth century only a few fragments of popular poetry in Scots – 'The Life and Death of Habbie Simson, Piper of Kilbarchan', and 'Epitaph on Sanny Briggs', written by Robert Sempill about 1640, and the anonymous 'Blythesome Bridal'. The Covenanting cause inspired only a few ballads – 'Blue Bonnets over the Border', 'Loudoun Hill' and 'Bothwell Brig'. Among the Cavalier poets (all of them using the fashionable English) were Sir William Alexander, Earl of Stirling, who left several long poems, William Drummond of Hawthornden, remembered for some of the loveliest sonnets in the language, and the great Marquis of Montrose, who wrote the well-known lines:–

He either fears his fate too much
Or his deserts are small,
That does not put it to the touch,
To gain or lose it all.

The prose of the century is mostly serious and even didactic in tone. The ecclesiastical and civil history of the times provided subject-matter for the Presbyterians, David Calderwood, John Row and James Kirkton, and for the Episcopalians, Archbishop John Spottiswoode and Bishop Gilbert Burnet.[1] The best of the many diarists are Robert Baillie and John Nicoll, each of whom gives us vivid little sketches from life, enlivened by Scotticisms in word and phrase. Lighter in spirit is William Lithgow's *Rare Adventures and Painfull Peregrinations* (1614), one of the most widely read, if not the most credible, of early travel books; and another talented Scots 'character',

[1] His bishopric was that of Salisbury in England; he is best remembered for his *History of his Own Times*.

Sir Thomas Urquhart, made a translation from the French of Rabelais (1653), which is justly admired for its success in conveying the spirit of the original work.

Although their literary merits were small, it is worth noting that the earliest Scottish newspapers appeared during the second half of the seventeenth century. Some of them were very short-lived, and some of them were merely Edinburgh reprints of London papers. The first of them, the *Mercurius Scoticus*, of Leith, ran for five months in 1651. The *Mercurius Politicus* lasted for seven years (1653-60), as did the curiously named *Kingdoms Intelligencer* (1661-68). In 1680 there began the very long, though broken, career of the *Edinburgh Gazette*.

Turning now to the arts we may mark the rise of portrait painting in the works of George Jamesone, a pupil of Rubens who died in 1644, and of his contemporary, John Scougall. But it is in architecture that Scottish creative talent found its best expression at this time. The day of the cathedral, the abbey and the large and ornate church was over, but the lesser barons and lairds, many of them enriched by grants of Church lands, developed the simple, old, square tower until it became the most original and picturesque of Scotland's historic buildings. Already, the so-called L-type, with one wing added to provide flanking defence,[1] was fairly common. Now, three new types appeared, which have been called the Z-type, with two wings (square or round) at opposite corners of the main rectangle; the E-type, with two wings on the same long side; and the T-type, with a short wing or projection jutting out from the middle of one of the long sides. Though the towers retained their military features, elegance rather than defensibility was now the barons' aim. The lower storeys were left severely plain, but the higher levels were enriched with fanciful and pleasing details – turrets roofed or spired, corbels, crow-stepped gables, decorative parapets, pack-saddle roofs and great coped chimneys. Blending harmoniously with an austere countryside and well suited to the vagaries of a harsh, northern climate, such towers as Hatton, Greenknowe, Claypotts, Amisfield, Coxton, Craigievar and Scotstarvit are among our 'Scots Baronial' gems. Moreover, these essentially rural dwellings inspired much of the urban architecture of the period, particularly the graceful, tall 'lands' in the High Street and Canongate of Edinburgh, and a few individual buildings elsewhere,

[1] The door, situated in the re-entrant angle of the L, could be 'covered' by fire from two sides.

like Glasgow's Old College (demolished in 1870), Loudoun Hall in Ayr, and Argyll's Lodging in Stirling. Scots Baronial, as a distinctive national style, flourished until nearly 1700 and represents the most remarkable cultural achievement of the century.

CHAPTER V

The Union of the Parliaments

THE REVOLUTION itself was accomplished in little longer than a week, but the 'Revolution Settlement' needed more than a year of negotiation, discussion and legislation (April 1689–June 1690). The outlines of the settlement had been laid down in the Claim of Right and the Articles of Grievances, which the Convention of Estates approved in April 1689. Besides condemning the illegal actions of James VII – fostering of popery, maintenance of a standing army in peace-time, arbitrary taxation, fines and imprisonment, abuse of martial law, suspension of burgh charters,[1] the use of torture, and so forth – the Convention reached several important decisions. It resolved, first, that 'prelacy' was 'a great and insupportable grievance . . . and therefore ought to be abolished'; secondly, that Parliament should meet frequently, with freedom of speech and debate; and, thirdly, that the Lords of the Articles were a grievance to the nation, and that there should be no parliamentary committees to prepare business except such as were freely chosen by the estates. These resolutions foreshadowed the later developments in church and state.

The Convention, having been turned into a Parliament in June 1689, abolished episcopacy in the following month. Next year it re-established presbyterian government in the Church as laid down in the Golden Act of 1592. The ministers who had been ejected in and after 1662 were restored, and in 1690 individual lay patronage was adjudged 'inconvenient' and therefore discontinued, the right of nominating a pastor for the approval of the congregation being transferred to the heritors and elders. The General Assembly met in October 1690 for the first time since 1653.

This ecclesiastical settlement was a sensible and moderate one, but, as a 'middle way', it aroused discontent on both flanks. Since nothing had been said of the covenants, the Cameronians stood aloof from the new establishment and formed a separate sect.[2] At the other

[1] James's 'packed' town councils were set aside by the Convention, which ordered fresh elections by direct poll of the burgesses (April-May 1689).

[2] Reorganised in 1743 as the Reformed Presbytery, this body exists to this day, though with small numbers.

extreme, the Episcopalians, strong in the north-east and with powerful friends among the noblity and gentry, presented a harder problem. Their Jacobite leanings made it difficult for king and parliament to show leniency towards them.[1] At the end of 1688 and early in 1689 the stricter Presbyterians of the south-west drove out many of the pastors who had enjoyed favour and protection under Charles II and James VII. This 'rabbling of the curates' was followed, in the summer and autumn of 1689, by the deprivation of a large number of ministers, who refused to say public prayers for William and Mary. Eventually, by statutes of 1693 and 1695, Episcopalian clergymen were given the choice of taking an oath of allegiance to William, and promising to 'behave themselves worthily', or of losing their livings. Many of them conformed in this way, but many others stayed outside.[2]

The abolition of episcopacy removed the clerical estate from Parliament, and in May 1690, after a stubborn conflict with King William (who thought the device a useful one), it was agreed that the Lords of the Articles should no longer be appointed, but that Parliament might select whatever special committees it wished; on such committees officers of state should have no vote. These changes freed the hands of the estates from the shackles which had bound them since the Restoration.

The Revolution was not effected without some resistance and bloodshed. The Duke of Gordon held out for King James in Edinburgh castle until, in June 1689, he realised the futility of his gesture and surrendered the fortress. Claverhouse, appointed Viscount Dundee in 1688, received James's commission to raise the clans on his behalf. With a force of some 3,000 Highlanders, he met and defeated General Mackay at the battle of Killiecrankie (27 July 1689); but the victory was fatal to the Jacobite cause, for 'Bonnie Dundee' was himself killed in the hour of his triumph. Within a month the clansmen, now led by Colonel Alexander Cannon, were routed in a running fight at Dunkeld by a Covenanting force under Colonel William Cleland (19-21 August). Armed resistance continued on a small scale until the Highlanders sustained a final defeat at Cromdale (1 May

[1] Early in 1689 Bishop Rose of Edinburgh, on a special mission to London, had unsatisfactory interviews with the Bishop of London (Compton) and with William himself; Rose's inability to reassure either of them about the willingness of the Scottish bishops to support the new régime probably helped to clinch William's decision in favour of the Presbyterians.

[2] These latter formed, along with their lay adherents, the nucleus of the Episcopal Church in Scotland.

1690). The Williamite cause seemed supreme, and, as a visible symbol of its success, the government built Fort William, at Inverlochy, to keep watch over Lochaber and other disaffected districts.

The Highlands, however, were not yet completely pacified, and efforts were made in 1691 to induce the Jacobite chiefs to acknowledge William and Mary. Offers of pardon were extended to the end of the year, but those who had not submitted by 1 January 1692 were to be punished with the utmost rigour of the law. Among the king's Scottish advisers in London were some (especially Sir John Dalrymple, Master of Stair) who felt that the opportunity should not be missed of teaching the troublesome Highlanders a terrible lesson; already, in December 1691, Dalrymple was thinking of 'taking a severe course' with the MacDonalds. As it happened, it was Alexander MacDonald of Glencoe, chief of what Dalrymple called 'that damnable sect, the worst in all the Highlands', who fell into the net by appearing, at the very end of the year, at Fort William, ready to take the oath. He was passed on to Inveraray, where a further delay put back his submission until 6 January 1692. The net now closed around him and his men, for the king (who may not have known the details of the transaction) issued instructions 'to extirpate that sect of thieves'. The planned massacre was carried out on 13 February by a party of Campbells, the hereditary foes of the Glencoe men, headed by Robert Campbell of Glenlyon. They had enjoyed the hospitality of their intended victims without (strangely enough) arousing suspicion, but, in the end, the scheme was bungled, for most of the MacDonalds escaped from the glen in the early hours of the wintry morning. The chief and over thirty of his followers were, however, murdered in cold blood.

Many slaughters of Highlanders are recorded in Scottish history, and, before this time, little thought had been given in the Lowlands (and still less in England) to such episodes; but the massacre of Glencoe differed in several ways from all precedents. For one thing, the gross breach of hospitality gave the transaction an air of special and revolting treachery. Next, a higher value was being placed on human life, and people were now sickened by the kind of barbarity to which their forebears had been hardened. Moreover, there were many – fellow-clansmen, Jacobites, Episcopalians and even Covenanters – who were critical of the government and ready to take up any cause likely to give it embarrassment. William and his ministers were therefore denounced on both moral and political grounds; yet no attempt was made until 1695 to fix the blame on the perpetrators of the crime, and even then the main result of an enquiry was merely the removal of Stair from his secretarial post. What happened in the pass of Glencoe became a tragic legend and an unforgotten wrong.

A few years later another kind of disaster aroused even more resentment among Scotsmen. In an effort to secure a share of colonial trade and overseas wealth, the Scottish Parliament passed, in 1695, an Act for a Company trading to Africa and the Indies. This ambitious project had an English as well as a Scottish aspect: half the capital was to come from England, half the directors were to be English, and London support was expected because the new company was planned as a rival to the East India Company, whose monopoly was disliked by many. But the English Parliament, under pressure from the East India Company and others, forbade English participation in the scheme, so that the Scots had to find all the needed capital themselves. They were now set on establishing a Scottish colony on the isthmus of Darien, or Panama, although the territory was claimed by Spain and William was particularly anxious not to alienate Spanish opinion in view of the French claims to the Spanish succession. England moved from indifference to hostility, and instructions were sent to the English colonies in that part of the world to refuse help to the intending colonists.

Far from being discouraged, the whole Scottish nation became deeply interested in the project. A large expedition reached Darien in November 1698, only to find that provisions were short and that the 'fever coast' was fatal to white men, and to abandon the place after much suffering and heavy casualties. Before the sad news could reach Scotland, second and third expeditions were sent out. The colonists defeated a Spanish force in February 1700, but two months later agreed, in the face of continuing Spanish opposition, to give up the whole enterprise. The final note of tragic failure was struck on the return journey, when most of the homecoming adventurers perished.

From first to last the affair had been dogged by mismanagement as well as ill luck. The Scots were naturally furious with 'Dutch William' and his English advisers, whom they were inclined to blame exclusively for the miscarriage of their grand scheme. Years passed before the bitterness ceased to rankle. Another and deeper lesson was, however, to be learnt from the Darien disaster. Scottish and English commercial interests had clashed head-on, and the merchants in each country had had full support from their respective Parliaments. Since the Revolution both assemblies had claimed to be sovereign bodies, able to offer the monarch advice which he was bound to accept. What if the advice tendered to the king from the two bodies was opposite and irreconcilable? How could William follow two divergent policies at the behest of his Parliaments? The weakness of a personal union between what were now 'parliamentary states' was self-evident. North and south of the border wiser heads were giving thought to the need for a more workable device than the regal union.

Their very enmities were driving Scotland and England towards a closer union, and the material results of Darien had a similar effect. The Scots had sunk so much money in the project that they had nothing left for new undertakings that were desperately needed; more than ever, therefore, they required a share of England's trading opportunities and colonial wealth. Thus both the constitutional and the economic arguments for union were gathering strength: there was no room in the one island for two parliaments, pursuing, under one king, conflicting aims in foreign and commercial relations.

And now these arguments were given fresh urgency by the dynastic problem. As William's reign wore on (Queen Mary had died in 1694), it became apparent that he would die childless, and it also seemed likely that the same would happen to his chosen successor, Anne.[1] Several children had been born to Anne and her husband, Prince George of Denmark, but they all died young – the last of them in 1700. English statesmen, with an anxious eye on the Prince of Wales, the hope of the Jacobites and of their French friends, were concerned over the safety of the Protestant succession. In 1701 the English Parliament passed the Act of Settlement, whereby the crown was to go, after William, to Anne, and after her death (if she should leave no children) to the Electress Sophia of Hanover, the granddaughter of James VI and I, and to her heirs, being Protestants. Henceforth it was the aim of English politicians to induce Scotland to adopt the same succession, and so to close what they regarded as a 'back door' for Jacobite intrigue and French aggression.

The Scottish Parliament, however, was no longer content to serve as a rubber stamp for decisions taken in London, and it was not going to be rushed into playing the English game when it had worth-while cards of its own. For the Revolution had made it a free and un-

[1] Anne, born in 1665, was the younger daughter of James VII and the only sister of Mary, William's wife (born in 1662). It was the birth of their half-brother, James, in 1688, that precipitated the Revolution by arousing fears of a permanent Roman Catholic dynasty. That boy, known as the Prince of Wales, assumed, on his father's death in 1701, the style of 'James VIII and III', but he was more commonly referred to as 'the Old Pretender' [or 'claimant']. See table on page 50.

THE LATER STUARTS

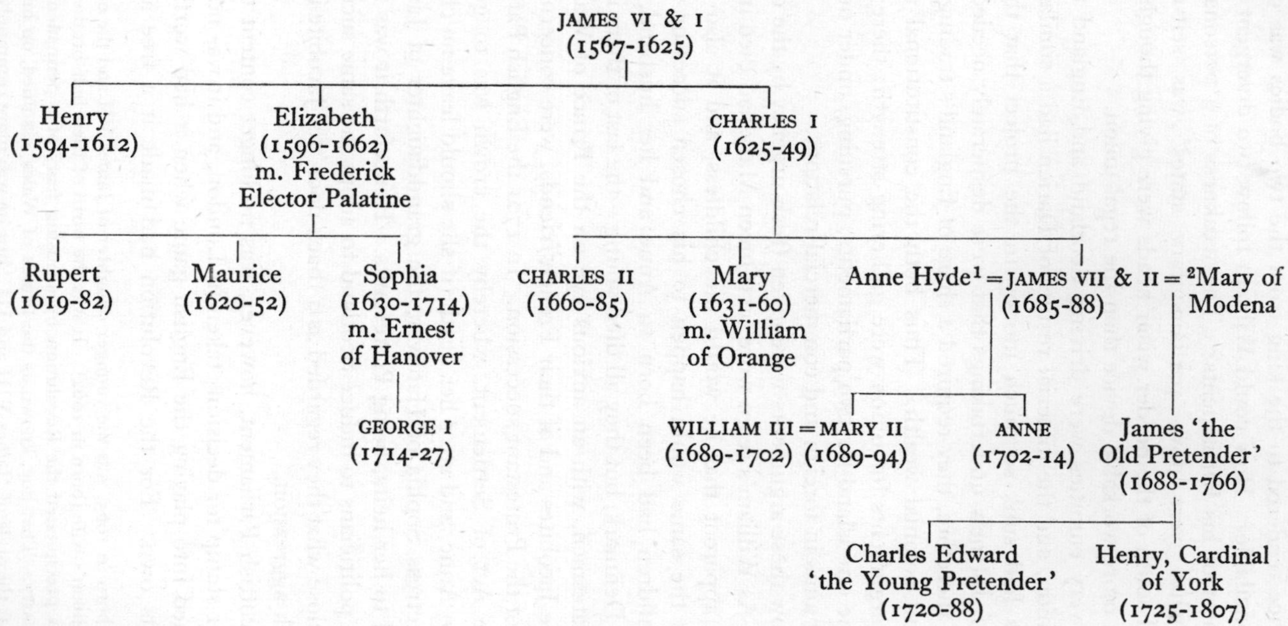

Note: Reigning kings and queens are in capitals, with their regnal years in brackets; for others the dates are those of birth and death.

trammeled assembly and, as the legislation of William's reign shows, it had exercised its new powers with vigour, good sense and responsibility. Not only did it carry through a moderate settlement in church and state. It put its own house in order by providing proper rules of debate, by having its proceedings minuted, and by deciding, in 1696, that no discussion or vote should be taken at the time of the first reading of a proposed statute. It adjusted its composition by directing the larger and wealthier shires (fifteen in number) to send three or four members instead of the two hitherto allotted to each.[1] Moreover, it found time to attend to many matters affecting the welfare of the people. It experimented with the hearth-tax and the poll-tax as alternatives to the land-tax or 'cess'. It encouraged a cloth manufactory at New Mills (East Lothian) and a soap and sugar works at Leith, and it set up the Bank of Scotland in 1695. It confirmed and extended earlier legislation in its important Education Act of 1696, it attended to the salaries of university professors and Court of Session judges, and it voted funds for the completion of the pictorial work (highly valued today) of the Dutchman, John Slezer.

Fired by patriotic sentiment, and smarting under the tragic losses of the Darien adventure, the Parliament was not disposed to settle the succession to the Scottish crown merely to assuage English anxiety. The question was still open when, in March 1702, William died, without having persuaded his two Parliaments to negotiate for a closer union. In her first year Queen Anne (1702-14) was able to appoint commissioners to treat for union, but once more, to the chagrin of the Scots, English commercial interests were opposed to Scottish participation in overseas trade without some *quid pro quo*, which the Scots would not offer; and the discussions broke down without any positive result. The new – and the last – Scottish Parliament met in 1703 in anything but a conciliatory mood. It asserted, in the Act anent Peace

[1] In detail, the following eleven counties were to send four members each:–

Berwick, Roxburgh, Haddington, Edinburgh, Lanark, Ayr, Dumfries, Fife, Perth, Forfar and Aberdeen;

four counties were to elect three representatives each:–

Stirling, Argyll, Renfrew and Kirkcudbright;

the two smallest counties, Clackmannan and Kinross, were to continue to choose only one member apiece, and the remaining sixteen shires (including Cromarty as a separate shire, but excluding Shetland, which was considered, until 1889, to form part of Orkney) were to have two members each. The total shire representation was thus ninety members. The statute of 1690 which embodied this change is memorable, for it achieved a fairer distribution of county seats than the contemporary English arrangement.

and War, its power of consenting to the making of war and peace. It showed, in the Wine Act, that it thought it right and proper to trade with France, with which England was at war. And it declared, in the Act of Security (finally passed in 1704), that it would not adopt the Hanoverian succession, except on terms securing Scotland's crown, parliament, religion, liberty and trade from English or foreign interference; this statute was, in effect, a threat to break the personal union of the crowns.

England's reply was the Alien Act, threatening to treat Scotsmen as foreigners,[1] and to ban their trade in cattle, coal and linen, unless, by Christmas day, 1705, they should accept the Hanoverian succession; but its opening clauses invited the Scots to agree to the appointment of commissioners for 'a nearer and more complete' union. These 'escape clauses' were seized upon, commissioners for both countries were named, and these men, after three months' hard work (April-July 1706), drafted a Treaty of Union. Submitted to the Scottish Parliament and discussed there at great length in the winter of 1706-7, and then passed on to Westminster, the Treaty, with only minor amendments, was approved by both assemblies and came into force on 1 May 1707.

The Treaty united the two kingdoms under the title of Great Britain, confirmed the Hanoverian succession and provided that there should be but one 'Parliament of Great Britain'. These three articles gave England what she insisted on as a minimum requirement; the remaining twenty-two articles comprised the concessions to Scotland and consequential adjustments. Trade and navigation were to be open at home and overseas to all British subjects, with one (the English) system of customs and excise applying to all, though with certain temporary exemptions in favour of Scotland – from the higher English salt-duty (for seven years) and from the very steep malt-tax (for the duration of the war). A common level was found for the different forms of land-tax: eight months' cess in Scotland (amounting to £48,000 sterling) was equated to an English levy of 4/- in the £ (yielding nearly £2,000,000).[2] To compensate Scotland for sharing the burden of England's National Debt, an 'Equivalent', nicely calculated at £398,085 10s., was promised to the northern nation – as was a

[1] Among other ill effects, this would have prevented Scotsmen from inheriting land or acting as civic officials.

[2] These rates were (as a search of the records showed) the highest imposed on each country since the Restoration.

further Equivalent (which could not be exactly reckoned beforehand) as recompense for the higher Scottish revenue resulting from the Union, since part of that would likewise go to serve the same debt. The first Equivalent was to be used to reimburse private losses sustained through the change to English coinage, and to recoup the investors in the Darien company (which was to be wound up); any surplus, and also the whole of the second Equivalent, would pay off the public debts of the Scottish crown and provide an annual sum of £2,000 for seven years for the encouragement of coarse wool manufacture and thereafter for promoting fisheries and other useful enterprises.

The law of Scotland relating to private rights was to remain unaltered 'except for evident utility of the subjects within Scotland', and all the existing law courts were to continue, 'but subject to alterations by the Parliament of Great Britain'. No appeal was allowed from any Scottish court to any ordinary law court in England; but on the delicate question of appeals to the House of Lords[1] the commissioners chose to be silent rather than to antagonise Scotland prematurely and perhaps needlessly. The baronial and higher feudal courts were safeguarded, as were the privileges of the royal burghs.

The representation of Scotland in the united Parliament was the one issue on which the commissioners clashed. The Scots, conscious of what they were sacrificing and jealous of their country's dignity, thought they should have 50 members in the House of Commons (where England had 513), but the English, used to linking the ideas of representation and taxation, and mindful of Scotland's small revenue (about one-fortieth of England's), suggested 38; the figure agreed upon was 45, with a proportional number (16) of Scottish peers to sit in the House of Lords. The Treaty also in effect created a new order of peerage, that of Great Britain, in succession to the older peerages of England and Scotland, both of which were closed in 1707.

Three further statutes, two Scottish and one English, supplemented the Treaty and formed an essential part of the Union. One of them secured the Protestant faith and the presbyterian church government of Scotland; another did the same for the Church of England and its episcopal system; and the third provided for the mode

[1] The House was accustomed to hear appeals from English law courts, and, from 1707, it would include Scottish peers as well; in English eyes, therefore, it seemed right that it should also hear Scottish appeals. Scottish Presbyterians, however, feared that the presence in the House of 22 Anglican bishops would give its judgments an Episcopalian bias.

of choosing Scotland's 16 representative peers and 45 commoners. Of the latter, 30 were allotted to the shires and 15 to the burghs. Each of the 33 shires was to return one M.P., except the six smallest, which were paired for alternate representation only. Thus, Bute would elect the M.P. for one Parliament, and Caithness was meanwhile disfranchised, but would get its turn at the next Parliament (when Bute would stand down); and so with Clackmannan and Kinross, and with Cromarty and Nairn. Of the 15 burgh members, one went to Edinburgh and the remaining 14 to the 65 other royal burghs, which were arranged, by geographical order, in 'districts' of four or five burghs, each district returning one member. Thus, in the east, Forfar, Dundee, Perth, Cupar and St Andrews between them chose one M.P., while, in the west, Glasgow, Renfrew, Rutherglen and Dumbarton chose another.[1] The 16 representative peers were to be chosen before each Parliament by all the Scottish peers, voting in person or by proxy; they still meet in the way laid down in 1707, and this is one of the few provisions of the Treaty which remain unaltered to this day. These details (worked out by the Scottish Parliament in its last session) completed the Union.

Were the arrangements fair and just? Each side, seeking union for different reasons, had to yield something of importance to the claims of the other. For Scotland the quest for commercial equality entailed the major sacrifice of her separate Parliament; true, there was no strong attachment to it as to an ancient and revered institution, and yet its record since the Revolution was full of achievement and of promise. England's need of dynastic and military security involved the sharing with her partner of her jealously guarded monopolies in

[1] In addition to the two 'districts' and nine burghs named in the text, the following twelve 'districts', with 56 burghs, were established:–

Kirkwall, Wick, Dornoch, Dingwall, Tain;
Fortrose, Inverness, Nairn, Forres;
Elgin, Banff, Cullen, Inverurie, Kintore;
Aberdeen, Inverbervie, Montrose, Brechin, Arbroath;
Crail, Kilrenny, Anstruther Easter, Anstruther Wester, Pittenweem;
Dysart, Kirkcaldy, Kinghorn, Burntisland;
Dunfermline, Inverkeithing, Culross, Stirling, Queensferry;
Linlithgow, Lanark, Peebles, Selkirk;
Haddington, Dunbar, North Berwick, Lauder, Jedburgh;
Ayr, Irvine, Rothesay, Inveraray, Campbeltown;
Dumfries, Annan, Lochmaben, Sanquhar, Kirkcudbright;
Wigtown, Whithorn, Stranraer, New Galloway.

The list may be compared with the Cromwellian arrangement of 1654 (*supra*, p. 15, n. 2), which was more flexible in that the number of burghs allotted to each 'district' in the earlier scheme varied between three and thirteen.

trade and navigation; and Scotland's bargaining position was strong enough to preserve her own church and her own laws. Turning from basic principles to practical applications, we note that England, generous in financial and economic matters, was niggardly as regards Scottish participation in the Parliament of Great Britain; and Scotland was therefore condemned to 175 years of under-representation at Westminster. In several respects the Treaty has had to be modified to meet changing needs, and it is not, in any case, the kind of agreement that would be freely made in similar circumstances today. But neither point detracts from the fact that, for its own day, the Union, grounded on common sense and reached through fair and open bargaining, was one of the most statesmanlike transactions recorded in our history.

The first fruits of the new partnership were not as sweet as might have been expected. Disagreement arose almost at once from petty misunderstandings or from differences over details that had not been sufficiently worked out beforehand. The English thought the Scottish merchants guilty of sharp practice in importing, before 1 May 1707, large quantities of American tobacco, which (in great demand on the continent) paid high duty in England but came in then almost free of custom in Scotland; once the Treaty was in force, the Scots traders could hope to reap a large and (in English eyes) unfair profit. The Scots thought ill of the English for sending the Equivalent late and paying it largely in paper money, which was seldom used north of the Tweed; nor did they approve of the new English customs officers and excisemen carrying out their duties on the Sabbath.

Worse was to come. The Scottish Privy Council was abolished in 1708; though unpopular, it was useful to the politically ambitious nobles. The very severe English penalties for treason[1] were extended to Scotland in 1709, because the Jacobite attempt of the preceding year had convinced England that the Scottish courts were too lenient to traitors. In 1710 a general election gave control of government and Parliament to the Tories, who were hostile or indifferent to the things for which the Whigs stood – the French war, the Hanoverian succession and the Treaty of Union. The change meant real trouble for Scotland, and the next four years were a testing time for the Union.

Three statutes of 1712 alarmed all Presbyterians. The Toleration

[1] Included among them was 'corruption of the blood', which punished, not only the 'attainted' person, but also his descendants. Not until 1949 was this penalty abolished, along with such other obsolete punishments as drawing and quartering, escheat, outlawry, penal servitude and hard labour.

Act permitted episcopalian worship, provided an oath of allegiance were taken; the Patronage Act restored the rights of lay patrons to nominate ministers to vacant charges; and the Yule Vacance Act forced Christmas holidays on the law courts, which to many Scots savoured of 'popery'. The Scots nobles were chagrined to learn, from 1711, that the House of Lords had no intention of seating, as members, those of their number who were created peers of Great Britain; their English colleagues took the view that the Scottish nobility was sufficiently represented by the 16 peers elected to each Parliament. Finally, the merchants were affronted by a new export duty laid on linen, a staple Scottish product, in 1711, and by the government's proposal to levy a malt-tax in open breach of the Treaty.

So loud was the outcry against this latest injustice to Scotland that the suggested tax was suspended, but not before a motion to dissolve the Union was only narrowly defeated in the House of Lords (1713). Queen Anne's reign closed amid hopes and fears that 'James VIII' would 'come into his own' and the Union would be broken, but the Tories bungled whatever chances they had, and it was to an united kingdom that George I (whose mother, Sophia, Electress of Hanover, had died earlier in the same year) succeeded without disturbance in August 1714.

CHAPTER VI

Hanoverian and Jacobite

THE REIGN of George I, the first king of the house of Hanover (1714-27), opened with the dismissal of the Tory ministers, who had been intriguing for the restoration of the exiled Stuarts, and their replacement by Whigs, who were known adherents to the principles of the Revolution, the Union and the Protestant succession. The Parliament that met in March 1715 had a large majority in favour of Hanover, and it is said that the sixteen elected Scottish peers were, to a man, those whom the government wished to see returned. The new order seemed secure; yet, before the year was out, a major insurrection of the Jacobites had taken place.

Since the defeat, in 1689-90, of the attempt by 'Bonnie Dundee' and his lieutenants to rally the clans against the Revolution, the Scots Jacobites, numerous and fervent as they were, had refrained from armed resistance. True, in the midst of Marlborough's wars, the French had sent a naval expedition, intended to coincide with a rising that would exploit Scottish discontent with the results of union (1708); but the affair miscarried through bad navigation and the watchfulness of the English seamen, so that no landing was made and no Jacobite stirred. The sole result of the episode was the passage of a new Treason Act, which, with a view to deterring future disturbers of the peace, applied to Scotland England's savagely severe code of penalties (1709).[1]

One event of 1715 that was decidedly unfavourable to the hopes of the Jacobites was the death of Louis XIV of France, the patron of the titular 'James VIII and III', the Old Pretender. The new French government, under the Regent Orléans, was disinclined to meddle in British affairs, so that little help was to be expected from that quarter. What launched the rising known to history as 'the 'Fifteen' was the personal vanity, discontent and restless ambition of one Scots noble. John, earl of Mar, had been prominent in the making of the Union, and, in 1713, had been appointed by the Tory ministry as third Secretary of State.[2] On the accession of George I, Mar was involved in the

[1] Cf. *supra*, p. 55.

[2] This office, first conferred on Queensberry in 1709, carried responsibility for Scottish affairs. Prior to 1707 the chief power in English government was held jointly by two Secretaries of State, sharing the field of home affairs and, as regards foreign

x But in any case under terms of T. of Utrecht France was forbidden to support J. cause.

disgrace of the Tories, and his vainglorious nature led him to abandon his earlier principles and to go over to the Jacobites.

On 26 August Mar held a hunting party in Braemar, which was really a screen for a political meeting with the Highland Jacobite chiefs, and on 6 September he raised the standard for King James in the same district. Proclamations were made at Aberdeen, Dundee, Perth, Inverness and elsewhere, and on 16 September, with a force of some 5,000 clansmen, Mar moved to Perth. Here for weeks he remained inactive, awaiting the arrival in Scotland of the Old Pretender and hoping for risings in England and the Lowlands. Meanwhile, his numbers increased. Whether impelled by love of war and plunder, or forced to 'come out' by the chiefs' commands and threats, Macdonalds, Camerons, Mackenzies, Macphersons, Macintoshes, Gordons, Ogilvies, Murrays, Robertsons, Drummonds and Macgregors responded in strength to Mar's appeal, and eventually he had at his back some 12,000 men, drawn mostly from the Central and West Highlands. On the other side, the Duke of Argyll and General Wightman had a much smaller body of regulars and a few companies of volunteers raised by the cities and towns. With these, they very wisely occupied Stirling (where the bridge offered the only easy crossing of the Forth) and so 'contained' the Jacobite army within the north of Scotland. The contagion of rebellion was prevented from spreading to the south.

During October the insurgents' only exploit was the bold and hazardous crossing of the estuary of the Forth, in small boats, by a party of some 1,500 under Brigadier William Mackintosh of Borlum. This intrepid soldier pushed on to Kelso and joined forces with the small bodies of Jacobites who had risen in Dumfriesshire under Lords Kenmure, Winton, Nithsdale and Carnwath, and in Northumberland under Thomas Forster and the Earl of Derwentwater. As they passed from Scotland into England, many Highlanders, disappointed in their hopes of a quick campaign and enough booty to reward their efforts, quietly took their own road home, but the rest went on by way of Penrith and Lancaster to face the government troops, under General Wills, at Preston. A fierce street battle followed, with heavy casualties on both sides, before the Jacobite survivors, numbering 1,550, surrendered (14 November).

policy, one taking the 'northern department', the other the southern: not till 1782 were separate home and foreign secretaries appointed. Between 1709 and 1746 (though with long gaps) a third Secretary of State was named: always a Scotsman, he had Scotland as his sole and special province. The last occupant of the office, Tweeddale, was dismissed in 1746.

See 'Jacobite Risings' for a different view.

By that time, the rising was virtually over. Rousing himself from his apathy, Mar moved to Auchterarder on 10 November. Argyll had only about a third of Mar's numbers, but his 4,000 men were seasoned troops, disciplined and well-led, and he did not refuse the challenge. The armies met in a confused, running fight at Sheriffmuir, in which each right wing was at first victorious. In a technical sense it may have been a drawn battle, but Argyll held the field, and that was what mattered; victory and advance were essential for Mar, whereas he was now compelled to withdraw to Perth. On the day of the battle – 13 November – Inverness was recaptured by three local lairds, Hugh Rose of Kilravock, Duncan Forbes of Culloden and Simon Fraser of Lovat. In all quarters the enterprise was doomed.

The Old Pretender, characteristically late at the supreme crisis of his life, landed at Peterhead on 22 December and proceeded to Perth, where all that remained for him was to supervise the winding-up of the scheme. Before departing, the Jacobites committed one senseless crime, which is a blot on their memory. To impede Argyll's inevitable advance – his strength was waxing as that of his opponents was waning – the insurgents, in the depth of a hard winter, burned the villages of Blackford, Auchterarder, Muthill and Crieff, exposing the pitiable inhabitants to dreadful and needless suffering. Then, on 30 January, they withdrew to Dundee and Montrose, from which latter port James and Mar escaped to France; the others dispersed soon after.

The punitive and remedial measures taken after the rebellion were not so much severe as ill-advised. The prisoners from Preston were the most unlucky victims, for many executions followed the impeachments of the great offenders and the trials of the lesser, carried out at London and Liverpool. The disarming acts were obeyed by the clansmen after their own fashion: they are said to have brought in their obsolete guns and to have retained their best. Scottish Episcopalian clergymen suffered for the cause, but what most affronted national sentiment was the removal of the prisoners taken in Scotland for trial at Carlisle.[1] Resentment was also aroused over the method of dealing with the estates forfeited to the government by such leading rebels as the Earls of Mar, Tullibardine and Seaforth and the Earl Marischal. Special commissioners were to receive the proceeds of the forfeitures,

[1] The English judges themselves seem to have had doubts as to the legality of the proceedings, for, though some Scots were formally condemned to death, and some others were transported, none were executed.

and most of the estates were purchased by the York Buildings Company, but there was widespread resistance by lawyers as well as tenants. After debts and burdens had been met from the rent-rolls, very little money found its way to the public purse.[1] The people outside the Highlands would not fight for the royal exiles, but neither would they agree in their hearts to the severe punishment of those who had done so; to this extent Jacobitism can be called popular and patriotic.

Another grandiose international plot, this time involving Swedish and Spanish aid, fell apart after the death of Charles XII of Sweden (1718) and resulted only in the landing of a few hundred Spaniards and the rising of a small number of West Highlanders, who were easily defeated by General Wightman at Glenshiel on 11 June 1719.

The year 1721 brought Sir Robert Walpole into power as prime minister, and for more than twenty years, under George I and his son, George II (1727-60), Walpole, though often opposed, denounced and thwarted, was responsible for the conduct of British affairs. For Scotland the main interest of his administration is twofold – military and financial.

The long-term measures to pacify the Highlands were intended to prevent, if possible, another insurrection, or, if that should not prove feasible, to ensure its speedy suppression. The chief government adviser was General[2] George Wade, who was sent to the Highlands in 1724. His best known memorial comprises the famous roads and bridges, built between 1726 and 1733, and linking Perth, Inverness and the Great Glen, with branches into other districts. Their object was to facilitate the rapid movement of troops and supplies, and to enable force to be brought to bear quickly on any 'trouble spot'; the work was continued and extended by Wade's successor, Colonel William Caulfeild. Another military precaution was the building, in 1726, of Fort Augustus, lying at the south-west end of Loch Ness and forming a companion stronghold to Fort William, at the southern extremity of the Great Glen.[3]

Roads and forts, useful as they might be, did not dispense with the need for men, and another aspect of the government's policy in Walpole's time was the enrolment of loyal clansmen to 'watch' or patrol the Highlands (1725). These 'independent companies', clad in

[1] For some further details of these transactions, see *infra*, p. 153.

[2] He was promoted to Field-Marshal in 1743.

[3] See *supra*, p. 47. The system of defences was completed in the years 1747-59, when Fort George was constructed on a peninsula in the Moray Firth, on the seaward side of Inverness.

tartan of sombre colours (dark green, navy and black), came to be known as 'the Black Watch'[1]; when, ultimately, they were formed into a regiment (the Forty-second), this nickname clung to them and became their title. Constituting the oldest of our Highland regiments, the Black Watch fought gallantly at Fontenoy (May 1745) and in many a later campaign; but no further use was made at this period of the superb martial qualities of the clansmen, and these remained a source of potential trouble for the future.

For the time being, however, it was the financial rather than the military policy of the state that created disquiet in Scotland. The high hopes of economic advance aroused at the Union had not yet been realised, and Scotland, to put the matter bluntly, was not paying her way as a partner in that Union. To Walpole, the great financier, this was a serious offence, and he resolved to levy from Scotland an additional revenue of £20,000 a year. A proposal for a duty of 6d. from each barrel of ale drew such an outcry that it was withdrawn in favour of the alternative of 3d. a bushel of malt (which amounted to much the same thing). The result was a riot in Glasgow (23 June 1725), in which the house of the local M.P., Daniel Campbell of Shawfield, was sacked, because he was thought to favour the hated malt-tax. Next day a party of English soldiers, under Captain Bushell, were so provoked by the Glasgow mob that they opened fire and killed a few onlookers. Bushell was tried and convicted for his action, but, to Glasgow's extreme indignation, was pardoned. Some time later the Edinburgh brewers planned a strike against the tax, but were induced to abandon their scheme. The nation finally, though sullenly, acquiesced in the malt-tax.

The episode brought about a change in the mode of administering Scotland. The Secretary of State, Roxburgh, was dismissed and his office left vacant. From now on, until near the end of his premiership, Walpole relied on the advice of the Duke of Argyll and his brother, Archibald, earl of Islay (who was to become third duke in 1743). Between them, Argyll and Islay 'managed'[2] Scotland, with the help of

[1] The name, traditionally associated with the characteristic dark tartan, may have been derived rather from the duty of putting down the 'black-mail' levied from Lowlanders.

[2] The word was used in a special sense. The 'manager' was the leading Scottish politician of the day, with enough power to control, in the interests of the government, the elections of the sixteen peers and forty-five commoners. This he did partly through family influence and personal friendship, partly through dispensing state patronage (offices, clerkships, military and naval commissions, and pensions), and

the able and patriotic lawyer, Duncan Forbes of Culloden, who was Lord Advocate from 1725 to 1737, and then Lord President (of the Court of Session) until his death in 1747.

The national addiction to smuggling and dislike of the revenue officers produced, in 1736, a more celebrated event than the Shawfield riot of 1725. Two smugglers had been caught and condemned to death for an attack on the custom-house at Pittenweem. One of them, Andrew Wilson, became a public hero by sacrificing himself to ensure the escape of his companion, a youth named Robertson, so that Wilson's execution, on 14 April, brought a noisy demonstration by a vast Edinburgh crowd. The city guard, under Captain Porteous, fired and killed or wounded some spectators. Porteous was tried, sentenced to death, but reprieved; and the parallel with Bushell's case, eleven years earlier, was too much for the mob in the capital, who, on 7 September, seized Porteous, executed 'lynch law' upon him, and quietly dispersed.[1] Inquiries having totally failed to reveal the identity of the conspirators, it was Parliament's turn to show resentment. A drastic bill of penalties was hotly debated and, thanks to English 'constitutionalist' as well as Scottish national sentiment, greatly modified by the Commons. In the end, the provost of Edinburgh was disqualified from holding any other office, and the city was fined £2,000 for the behoof of Porteous's widow.

By the 1740s Scotland was used to the rule of law; taxation was accepted as a necessary condition in a world of commerce, and the house of Hanover, if not the focus of enthusiasm or fervid loyalty, was regarded as a sound business proposition. Martial ardour was cooling, even in the Highlands. Two facts nevertheless kept Jacobite hopes alive. In the first place, Charles Edward, the elder son of the Old Pretender, had been born in 1720, and he was now a handsome and dashing young man, resolved to make one more bid for the throne of his ancestors. Secondly, France was again at war with Britain, and was as ready as ever to embarrass the government by fostering insurrection. In 1744, indeed, a large French expedition was prepared and an invasion planned, but the fleet was dispersed and the scheme defeated, partly by storms and partly by the vigilance of the British navy. The French lost heart for the Jacobite cause,

partly through simple bribery. Though the 'post' of manager was quite unofficial, his functions were clearly understood and accorded well with the lax standards of public morality which then prevailed.

[1] The Porteous riot is the central theme of Sir Walter Scott's novel, *The Heart of Midlothian*.

and 'Bonnie Prince Charlie' was thrown back on his own resources.

On 23 July 1745, after a hazardous, month-long voyage from France, the Prince landed at Eriskay, in the Outer Isles, with only seven companions – three Scots, two Englishmen and two Irishmen. The clan chiefs were slow to rise, but the adhesion (after much hesitancy) of Donald Cameron, 'the gentle Lochiel', settled the issue, and the standard was raised, in the name of 'King James VIII and III', at Glenfinnan on 19 August. Thus began, in slow tempo, the romantic but ill-advised venture of 'the Prince Regent', which seems strangely out of place in the sober annals of the mid-eighteenth century, and which was yet to last for over a year and to cover more than 1,000 miles of campaigning. On his side Charles Edward had his own youth and gallantry, Highland courage and endurance, and the help of a group of able lieutenants – especially a sound general in Lord George Murray and a competent secretary in John Murray of Broughton. Self-will, an utter attachment to the Romanist faith and lack of finance were his outstanding disabilities. Against him were arrayed the wealth and power of a prosperous state, the hostility of the loyal clans and of the Lowlanders and the English, the scattered but substantial and ultimately decisive military forces of the crown, and a number of elderly[1] and often timorous generals. The blend of assets and liabilities on each side accounts for both the quick success and the final defeat of the rising.

At the outset a military blunder played into the hands of the Jacobites. Sir John Cope, having collected the small force of regulars immediately available,[2] made the mistake of marching north from Stirling, and then, at Dalwhinnie, instead of seeking out the insurgents further west, he took the safe but pointless road to Inverness. These foolish moves opened up the entire country to the Prince, who, gathering strength as he went along, reached Perth on 4 September. After a slight show of resistance, Edinburgh surrendered on 17 September, and five days later Cope, having transported his men by sea, suffered a crushing defeat at Prestonpans. All Scotland lay at the Prince's feet.

For six weeks the Jacobites enjoyed undisputed possession of the capital, but their triumph had its limits. There was neither a French landing nor an English rising. Only a few Lowlanders came in, and

[1] The all-important exception was the king's son, William, duke of Cumberland, who was only twenty-five.

[2] Most of the troops were engaged on the Continent in the War of the Austrian Succession (1740-48).

those as individuals and not, like the Highland chieftains, as leaders with large followings. Inverness and the far north were held for the government, partly by reason of the loyalty of the Sinclairs, Mackays, Rosses, Munroes and Sutherlands, partly through the strenuous efforts of Forbes of Culloden and Lord Loudoun; although the wily old schemer, Lord Lovat, tried to 'play safe' by professing obedience and at the same time sending the Frasers out under his son (whose action he repudiated). As in the 'Fifteen, the remote Western Isles and Skye stayed out of the fight, and Argyll remained a government stronghold under General John Campbell of Mamore (who was to succeed as fourth Duke of Argyll in 1761).

When, on 31 October, the Jacobites left Edinburgh for the march into England, their forces numbered only about 6,000 – that is, half of Mar's strength in 1715. Moreover, the further the clansmen got from their glens, the more they tended to desert. The enterprise was therefore bold, not to say rash, since the Hanoverian armies, reinforced from the Continent, were growing steadily. The Prince took the western route, avoiding Wade's column in the north-east, and proceeded by way of Carlisle, Preston and Manchester, where, at the end of November, he was able to raise a regiment that turned out to be England's sole contribution to the cause. Derby was reached on 4 December, but at that point Charles was reluctantly persuaded of the folly of proceeding further into hostile country. Besides Wade, far to the rear, Cumberland, with a second army, was now on his flank, and each of these had more men than he had. Sulky and bitter, the Prince began his retreat, a manoeuvre that was executed as rapidly and skilfully as the advance. It was marked by one sharp skirmish at Clifton, in Westmorland, which served to check the pursuit.

Back in Scotland, with ultimate defeat now inevitable, the Jacobites staved off the fatal day by drawing reinforcements of men from the Highlands and of money and clothing from the Lowland towns. They numbered some 9,000 when, in a confused fight at Falkirk on 17 January 1746, they beat back an equal force commanded by General Hawley. By February delaying tactics would no longer serve, and the Prince withdrew towards Inverness, which, with Fort Augustus, fell to his troops. Slowly and deliberately, Cumberland, who had trained his soldiers to meet the wild Highland charge, advanced from Edinburgh. The climax came on 16 April, when the Highlanders, exhausted after a fruitless night march that was intended to surprise the enemy, were totally crushed at the battle of Culloden. The clansmen dispersed and the rising was over, though five months elapsed before the fugitive Prince, having endured many hardships and narrow escapes, boarded a ship for France (20 September).

'Bonnie Prince Charlie' appears in Jacobite song and legend as a figure of romance and chivalry – 'Will ye no' come back again?' – but in real life he was of less heroic stature; demanding all from his faithful followers, he gave them little in return beyond an inspiring name, and he fled from Culloden, instead of dying, sword in hand, at the head of his brave Highlanders. The true heroes of the rebellion were the ordinary Highland soldiers, who, whether as volunteers or virtually conscripts, marched, fought and died valiantly for a doomed cause.[1] And, when the great adventure was over, not one of them was tempted to betray the prince with the huge price on his head, though many must have known of his whereabouts. Instead, they endured persecution at the hands of 'Butcher Cumberland' and his troopers.

As after the 'Fifteen, the government found it convenient to conduct trials of the prisoners in England rather than Scotland, where convictions would have been hard to get. The humbler rebels were dealt with in London, Carlisle and York. Most of the magnates had made good their escape, and over forty of them were attainted by statute in their absence, but Lords Kilmarnock, Balmerino and Lovat (hypocritical to the end) were executed. A rich haul of forfeited estates was handed over to Commissioners, who were instructed to expend the revenues for the improvement of Highland industries, farming, forestry and schools.[2]

In 1747, too, Parliament abolished heritable jurisdictions and so snapped the feudal ties that had for centuries bound tenant to landlord in many parts of Scotland. In doing so, the English legislators, who were not well informed about Scottish conditions, may have felt they were cutting at the roots of sedition and rebellion, but this was hardly the case. The feudal order prevailed in the Lowlands but only on the fringes of the Highlands, and it was great nobles like Argyll, Queensberry, Montrose, Gordon, Atholl and Morton who lost their baronial rights and, with them, their hereditary standing and their claim on the loyalty of their dependents. In the remote central and western Highlands, where Jacobitism had flourished, the power of the chiefs

[1] For one thing, it was doomed because, while help from France was essential for its success, no outside help was in fact possible in view of the British navy's command of the sea.

[2] For an account of the Commissioners' activities, see *infra*, pp. 153-5.

was patriarchal, not feudal – personal rather than legal and territorial. In the end, *their* authority wilted before the advance of a 'money economy' and not by dint of any statute.

By mid-century, Jacobitism was a mere sentiment, a far-off memory, the theme of many a plaintive song; and even those who were ready to pledge 'the King over the water' knew in their hearts it was best that he should stay there. England, twice frightened by serious rebellions, could hardly be expected to understand this, and she distrusted Scotland deeply after the 'Forty-five. The Highlands were disarmed; the tartan was proscribed as the garb of sedition (1746-82); the suggestion to enrol Highland soldiers (under English colonels) was rejected; and, when England got a militia to meet the threat of French invasion (1757), Scotland was refused one. It was William Pitt, the great war minister, who discarded these short-sighted views and sanctioned the levying of Highland regiments, which gave Britain valuable service in the Seven Years War (1756-63). Then, indeed, Scotsmen distinguished themselves among the generals, the admirals and the ambassadors; by the close of George II's reign (1760), Scotland had fully accepted the Union and was ready to play her part in the Empire.

CHAPTER VII

Black Cattle and Virginia Tobacco

IN THE course of the seventeenth century, as we have seen in an earlier chapter,[1] many Scotsmen had come to realise that the national economy was backward and unprofitable, and they had tried to inject a spirit of progress and enterprise into industry and commerce. Though the judgment of these early 'planners' was sound and their intentions praiseworthy, their actual achievements cannot be called impressive. The most ambitious of all the century's schemes – that of the 'Darien Company' – came to unparalleled disaster at its close.[2] Poverty still barred the way to economic advance.

The eighteenth century brought a change, and, during the reigns of Queen Anne and the first two Georges (1702-60), new men and money, new ideas and methods, introduced a breath of fresh life into the processes of producing and distributing goods and wealth. Not that the innovations amounted to a 'revolution': that term is more properly applied to what happened after 1760. The reforms of the early part of the century were gradual and limited; still, they did prepare the way for the wide and rapid advances of the true 'Industrial Revolution'. They may, indeed, be regarded as the necessary prelude to that dramatic change, for which they set the stage; and their 'action' falls into four 'scenes' or 'episodes', turning on agriculture, the linen industry, foreign commerce, and banking.

At the opening of the century the Scottish farmer still clung stubbornly, even superstitiously, to the laborious and unproductive ways of his forebears. His inability to make a decent living from the land proclaimed itself to the traveller in the very appearance of the countryside – the gaunt expanses of treeless waste, the many marshes, peat-bogs and patches of whin and broom, the open, unfenced fields, some of them climbing up the stony hillsides (where the 'dry-field' was preferred to the water-logged 'carse-lands'), the long, narrow strips or 'rigs' of plough-land separated by weed-covered 'baulks'. Crops were poor, farm animals were stunted, and life was hard and insecure even in normal times; but, when famine stalked the land, as it did in

[1] See *supra*, chap. iii.
[2] See *supra*, pp. 48-9.

the 'Seven Ill Years' (1695-1702),[1] nothing could save thousands of country folk from starvation and death.

Soon, however, Scottish nobles, lairds and farmers, in increasing numbers, were recognising that much of this poverty and austerity was due to ignorance and might be avoided. They learned that, with proper care, ordinary lands could provide a decent livelihood for the working farmer – and higher rent-rolls for the progressive landlord. Some of those who had visited other lands (perhaps while completing their education with a 'grand tour') were aware, for example, that good crops were regularly obtained from regions like East Anglia and Holland as a result of the farmer's attention to the matter of drainage – essential for all land, doubly essential in flat lands, liable to disastrous flooding. Others again had become acquainted with the merits of planned afforestation: they were convinced that trees, properly selected and planted, could help agriculture by binding the soil and serving as wind-breaks. What was needed, they believed, for successful farming was exact knowledge of such topics as the nature and functions of various soils, the suitability of different crops, and the use of machines and artificial aids to promote productivity; moreover, the will to apply that knowledge must be present. Both the knowledge and the will came to Scotland at this time, for two main reasons. First, the Union with England pointed the way; and, next, the work of Scotland's own 'improvers' led the advance.

When the Union of 1707 made trade 'free and equal' between the two countries, the pastoral farmers and the cattle dealers of Scotland found that the demand from the south for their beasts was greatly enlarged. Already before the Union both Highland and Lowland drovers had been accustomed to undertake the long journey to the English markets, and now the trade became a lucrative one: England could absorb all the cattle that were offered. Obviously, however, the animals should be healthy and well-fed to attract high prices. To ensure this, they must have proper winter-feed. The old diet of, say, straw and heather-mash meant skinny beasts, which with the long trek south would become thinner and weaker still, so that, requiring in any case to be fattened in England before slaughter, they would command very poor prices. Better winter feed would mean fatter beasts and higher prices. The solution to the problem of winter-feed

[1] Also known as 'King William's dear years', these were a succession of exceptionally bad seasons, when cold and damp summers, followed by early frosts, blighted and ruined the crops.

was found in the cultivation of turnips as a field-crop, and this practice spread rapidly in the early part of the century.

Cattle-rearing was thus one of the first branches to receive a stimulus from the effects of Union; about the year 1730 as many as 30,000 beasts were being sold at the great cattle market of Crieff. This trade brought to the landowners and large farmers a welcome flow of capital which was often laid out on the betterment of the farms. The indirect benefits were even more important. Turnips are a root-crop, and their cultivation in many fields formerly devoted to unending grain-crops (oats and barley) meant that, willy-nilly, the farmer was adopting a simple form of crop-rotation. His eyes were opened to what was possible and desirable in the way of varying, from season to season the produce of the soil.

Potatoes, another root-crop, were introduced about the year 1724; by 1740, in the face of much local prejudice, they were being grown on a fairly large scale in the Lowlands, though a further period of twenty years elapsed before they were generally adopted in the Highlands and the north. Yet another innovation brought in sown grasses and clovers; one of the pioneers, Thomas, sixth earl of Haddington (1680-1735),[1] was planting rye grass and clover on his East Lothian estate as early as 1708. By mid-century the more progressive farmers were alternating artificial grasses (having a yield three times as great as that of natural grass) with grain and other crops.

Rotation of crops was perhaps the greatest single advance made towards scientific agriculture during the period, but there were many others. New ideas were being discussed and tried out – the draining of boggy land by ditches, the restoration of strength to exhausted soil by means of fallow (a rest-year), the application of limes and manures, and the practice of hoeing and drilling. Enterprising nobles and lairds strove to shake the countryman out of his lethargy. One such was Andrew Fletcher of Saltoun (1655-1716), who, retiring from politics in disgust after the Union, devoted himself to agriculture. Impressed by what he had seen of Dutch machines for stripping the husks from barley and turning it into 'pot-barley', he sent a mill-wright, James Meikle, to Holland in 1710 to examine this device; soon after the Saltoun barley-mill – for long the only one in Britain – was producing its well-known pot-barley.[2] At Saltoun, too, a little after

[1] Besides being a practical agriculturist, Haddington wrote a treatise on forestry, which was published some time after his death.

[2] The old-fashioned alternative was to make bruised (or 'knockit') and partially husked 'bere' by means of 'knocking stones'.

Fletcher's death, the same Meikle introduced the use of fanners for winnowing corn (instead of relying on natural breezes).

A few miles to the west of Saltoun, and still in East Lothian, lay the estate of the Cockburns of Ormiston, another family that was keenly interested in making the most of its property. Adam, Lord Ormiston[1] (1656-1735), was one of the first landlords to give his tenants long leases (to induce them to undertake improvements in their own interest) and to enclose his fields (with stone dykes or walls). His son, John (1679-1758), was a member of parliament from 1707 to 1741, but even from London he kept in touch with the management of his estate by sending his gardener detailed instructions as to the trees to be planted and the vegetables to be grown. Around Dunkeld, in Perthshire, from the 1720s, the Dukes of Atholl busied themselves with planting out larches, which, in the course of the next half-century, were to run to many millions of trees and to cover thousands of acres. Yet another reforming landlord was Sir Archibald Grant of Monymusk, in Aberdeenshire (1696-1778), who, by correspondence or in person, directed the work of enclosing and planting his property. A statement dated 11 August 1733 shows no fewer than 66,842 trees in the garden and nurseries of Monymusk, all planted within the past twelve years; ash, hornbeam and plane predominated, but there were also substantial numbers of thorn, birch, elm and apple, and smaller quantities of chestnut, lime and beech, of plum, walnut, filbert and holly trees.[2]

It was men like these who, in 1723, came together to form the Society of Improvers in the Knowledge of Agriculture in Scotland.[3] The words 'improver' and 'improvement' were much in the thoughts of the eighteenth-century landed proprietor; to him, indeed, the term 'unimproved', when applied to land, was a challenge and a reproach. The Society served as a clearing-house for ideas on scientific farming. It encouraged the granting of long leases, the study of crop-rotations in relation to soils, the planting of trees, the drainage of marshes, the adoption of new crops, the enclosure of wastes and unprofitable 'commonties', and the promotion of mechanical inventions. It did invaluable work in the diffusion of knowledge, the pooling of experiences, and the solution of problems.

By 1760 the improvements were bringing undeniable benefits –

[1] His title was a life-peerage, granted to him as one of the supreme judges of Scotland: he was Lord Justice-Clerk under Queen Anne.

[2] See *Monymusk Papers* (Scottish History Society, 1945), p. 124.

[3] This body was the forerunner of the Highland and Agricultural Society (1784) and many small local bodies.

greater profits, higher rent-rolls, increased wages and more pleasing 'policies'.[1] But the advances were uneven. Midlothian, East Lothian and Berwickshire showed the reforms at their best; in the east, from Fife to Moray, as in the west country, there were patches of improved farming; and in the Highlands the crofters had hardly begun to change their wasteful, ancestral ways. The opposition to change was often dour and savage. The peasants were unwilling to give up their 'common' rights of pasturing their stock, gathering whin or rush, and quarrying stones. In 1724 the 'Levellers' of Galloway, fearing that the new enclosures threatened their way of life, rose and threw down the 'dykes'. Elsewhere, given free saplings to plant, some tenants refused them or even uprooted young trees, in the belief that they impoverished the soil, stole the sunshine and gave cover to destructive birds. Or again, they argued, why use good land to raise turnips for beasts, when it might grow corn for men? At Monymusk, we are told, 'Grant had often to scold his tenants and on many occasions he used his authority in the Baron Court to punish them for obstructing his efforts and destroying his plantations and dykes'.[2] Ignorance and prejudice were bitter enemies to progress, but time was on the side of the improvers, and better farming methods slowly but surely took root in one district after another.

Turning from agriculture to industry, we find that the first impacts of the Union on Scottish industries were disappointing. The woollen fabrics woven north of the Tweed could not compete with England's finer products. Higher salt duties made difficulties for the herring fishers and curers, already hampered by the fierce rivalry of the Dutch. The steep malt tax, threatened in 1713 and imposed in 1725, hit the brewing of ale and beer, then the ordinary beverages of high and low. Traders hated the strict collection of customs and excise duties. George I's reign was, therefore, well advanced before the expected advantages of the Union began to show themselves.

The first of the domestic industries to benefit was the making of linen cloth. In the late seventeenth and early eighteenth centuries both linen yarn, spun by housewives on the spinning wheel that could be found in almost every house, and coarse linen cloth, worked by weavers on their own hand-looms, were being produced in sufficient

[1] This was the term lovingly applied by landlords to the carefully tended or 'improved' parts of their estates.

[2] Quoted from H. Hamilton, *Life and Labour on an Aberdeenshire Estate* (Third Spalding Club, 1946), xxviii.

quantities to permit substantial exports to England. Some of the flax was grown in small patches on the farms or alongside the corn-fields of the villagers and town-dwellers; and more was imported by merchants trading with the Baltic ports. Even before the Union, the Scots Parliament did what it could to foster the industry by ordering the use of linen shrouds for burials and by forbidding the export of linen yarn.[1]

Marked progress began in 1727, when Parliament set up the Board of Trustees for Manufactures and gave them the duty of spending the accumulated funds of the second 'Equivalent' promised to Scotland by the Treaty of 1707.[2] Since none of these moneys had been laid out, the Board had £6,000 per annum at their disposal. They applied £2,650 to the linen industry, a like sum to the herring fisheries, and the balance of £700 to coarse woollen manufactures; but it is clear that linen profited most from their activities. Another statute of 1727 laid down standard lengths and breadths of linen cloth, and one of the Board's main functions was to inspect all cloth before sale and to stamp that which complied with the approved standards. In addition, the Board awarded premiums for the growth of flax and hemp,[3] and prizes for the weaving of fine cloth; they introduced machines for the preparatory processes of scutching and heckling,[4] promoted the use of new and improved looms, and encouraged the setting up of bleachfields.

Other bodies endeavoured to advance linen manufactures. The Convention of Royal Burghs frequently petitioned Parliament on behalf of the industry. Parliament itself helped by voting bounties for exported linen in the 1740s. The British Linen Company, established in 1746, gave financial assistance through local agencies and warehouses for the collection and distribution of yarn and cloth. The Commissioners for the Forfeited Estates, appointed in 1752 to receive and expend rents from the estates of the forfeited Jacobites, tried to foster Highland welfare in a variety of ways, including the foundation of spinning schools and the encouragement of home weaving.[5] The industry did not, however, take deep root in the Highlands, nor was it of much importance in the prosperous southern farming region. Over 90 per cent of the production, indeed, came from five counties – Forfar,

[1] See *supra*, p. 31. [2] See *supra*, p. 53.

[3] A coarser fibre that was especially suitable for the making of ropes and canvas.

[4] Scutching involved the cleaning and dusting of the flax fibres by beating; heckling (or hackling) was the process of combing and teasing out the fibres before spinning.

[5] For other activities of the Commissioners, see *infra*, pp. 153-5.

Fife and Perth in the east, and Lanark and Renfrew in the west.

The growth of the linen trade is indicated by the rise in the annual output of stamped cloth after the institution of the Board of Trustees:–

Year	*Thousands of Yards*
1728	2,184
1740	4,610
1750	7,573
1760	11,748

This remarkable increase meant that linen became 'big business'. The basic processes of spinning and weaving remained in the hands of the 'domestic' worker, using his (or her) own implements in cottage or farm-house, but flax had to be imported in large quantities by men with capital, while the sale of linen yarn and the purchase and marketing of finished cloth also called for the financial magnate. Moreover, large bleachfields, utilising the advances of chemical science, as well as scutching and heckling mills, were being set up almost from the start of the Board's operations, and all of these needed money for building and maintenance. Thus, in the linen industry, the capitalist (often called 'intaker' or 'manufacturer') appeared on the scene long before there were any spinning or weaving mills.

The 'free and equal trade' of the Union was not an immediate or unmixed blessing. The smaller ports on the east coast were, indeed, hard hit, since they had neither the larger ships required for ocean voyages nor the dredged channels, breakwaters, piers and quays that such vessels demanded. Most of them declined, leaving the merchants of the larger seaports, such as Leith, Dundee and Aberdeen, to serve the traditional trade routes to Norway, the Baltic, the Netherlands and France. In the west it was a different story. Glasgow and its smaller rival, Greenock, now found themselves on the right side of the map, well situated for commerce with the colonies of North America and the West Indies. Their merchants were able to seize their opportunities and to challenge the dominant position hitherto held by the traders of Bristol and London.

Atlantic commerce brought rich rewards. Sugar, molasses and rum, raw cotton and mahogany, found eager buyers and made quick profits. But much the most valuable of American commodities was the tobacco of Virginia and Carolina, which was in great demand in all the countries of Europe. Only Britain could supply fashionable society's craving for tobacco and snuff, and the Navigation Acts (by prohibiting the 'carrying trade' of foreign shipping) favoured the home ports.

Until 1718 the Glasgow merchants chartered English vessels for the colonial trade, but thereafter they used their own ships. Instead of the fifteen ocean-going Glasgow vessels of 1692, the Clyde had sixty-seven in 1735, one-third of them trading with the colonies; and later the rate of growth was even faster. Nearly 4,200,000 pounds of tobacco were brought into the Clyde in 1724, of which over three million pounds were re-exported; but this was merely the beginning, for within half a century the quantity had increased tenfold, while the proportion re-exported became even higher. This rapid development brought about a change in the character of the trade. Competition between the different ports was so fierce that it no longer sufficed for a skipper to buy his cargo on the spot or to barter Scottish goods for the tobacco: from about 1740 the merchants had to have resident agents in the colonies, to negotiate for whole crops in advance. It was a highly speculative trade and, being based on a state-imposed monopoly, a wholly artificial one. The Glasgow merchants, playing by the rules of this strange game of commerce (and, in the view of their English rivals, using some dubious tricks of their own), overhauled and eventually passed those of London and Bristol.

The tobacco trade stimulated Scottish manufactures in general and the export trades in particular. The outgoing vessels, instead of proceeding in ballast, took cargoes of linen cloth, of the linen tape (or incles) of Glasgow, of the linen thread and silk gauze of Paisley, of gloves, hats, boots and glass-ware, all of which found a ready market in the colonies. Industrial progress was aided in another way, since familiarity with tropical or sub-tropical products (apart from tobacco) might suggest new processes. Thus, Greenock's sugar-refining business sprang from the West Indies trade. Thus, too, imported cotton was woven experimentally, by itself or in combination, as the weft or 'woof', with a linen warp; such were the beginnings of what was later a great industry.

Above all, the profits of Transatlantic trade were spectacularly high: two or three successful voyages could make a man's fortune. Even more than the improving landlords and the linen manufacturers, the 'tobacco lords', as they were called, were men of wealth. Money began to circulate freely, and the effects were felt far afield – among the coach-builders of Edinburgh, the delft-makers of Leith, the granite-cutters of Aberdeen. The amassing of riches also had its importance for the future: it was necessary, if Scotland were to play its part in the coming Industrial Revolution, that it should have its enterprising capitalists.

In all this stirring of new economic life, the provision of banking services was an essential feature. For a whole generation after its foundation in 1695,[1] the Bank of Scotland had the field to itself. Feeling its way by trial and error, it set up branches, in 1696, at Glasgow, Dundee, Montrose and Aberdeen; the attempt, however, failed, the project was abandoned,[2] and the bank remained an Edinburgh institution. With coin in short supply, its notes passed as currency, as people trusted the bank's promise to redeem them for cash 'on demand'. Sometimes, as in 1704, adverse rumours sapped this public confidence, but the bank survived the 'runs' on its resources. It did not, as yet, accept deposits of money, though it would make loans on bond to substantial customers.

In 1727, when the 'Old Bank' directors were suspected of Jacobite sympathies, the Royal Bank of Scotland was instituted by charter, with strong government support. The two banks were keen rivals for public support and at times started 'whispering campaigns' to instigate runs on each other's supplies of cash. As a defensive measure, they soon adopted the 'optional clause', whereby they promised to repay notes either on demand or within six months, with interest, at the option of the bank. This clause, which was to be widely used and abused before it was declared illegal in 1765, was a retrograde step, since it shook public trust in the banks.

A more creditable measure that was put into effect by both banks by 1730 was the granting of cash credits, permitting a customer of good character, vouched for by two or three reputable friends, to obtain an advance of money (on which he paid interest) for what was judged a sound business enterprise. Before long, too, both banks were accepting deposits from clients, who could feel sure that their funds were in safe hands and were meanwhile earning interest. The issue of bank notes, the offer of cash credits and the readiness to accept deposits greatly helped all those who were striving, in town and country, on land and at sea, to achieve prosperity for the nation and for themselves.

One class of business that was not touched by the 'chartered' banks was that of negotiating 'bills of exchange'.[3] Advances of

[1] See *supra*, p. 31.

[2] A second attempt, in 1731, also failed.

[3] These were written undertakings, exchanged between merchants, by which a purchaser promised to pay, at a future date, for goods bought.

money could be obtained by the holders of such bills before their 'due date' at the cost of a proportionate deduction – whence the transaction was known as 'discounting' the bills. There was scope here for the part-time banker, and many merchants took up this profitable line along with ordinary shop-keeping. One of the earliest and greatest of private bankers or discounting houses was John Coutts and Company, founded in 1723; in an Edinburgh flat that served also as the family dwelling-house, this famous firm carried on the sale of cloth and wine, kept watch on corn prices and trade fluctuations, and conducted its banking business. It was the forerunner of numerous small firms of merchant-bankers throughout the country.

The last fifteen years of George II's reign witnessed two notable advances. As we have seen, the British Linen Company, established in 1746, concerned itself with such matters as the import of flax for sale to the spinners, the purchase of spun yarn for sale to the weavers, and the maintenance of warehouses and bleachfields. The scope of its financial dealings, however, soon led it to issue its own notes and, in effect, took it into banking. Other interests became less important and were given up by 1763. Thus, almost by accident, the British Linen became not only a bank, but a central bank with ready-made local branches (formerly local agencies); in this respect, it was a pioneer.

The other development of the period concerns the founding of true local banks, that is, companies without an Edinburgh connection and dealing only in money, not in merchandise. This step, despite the real needs of the smaller towns, was rendered difficult by the opposition of the chartered banks in Edinburgh; these combined, for example, to bring down an Aberdeen project in 1749. In January 1750, however, the Ship Bank opened its doors in Glasgow, and in November of the same year the Glasgow Arms Bank was founded.[1] It was natural that the hustling and growing commercial city of the west should be the home of Scotland's first successful local banks. Both the Ship and the Glasgow Arms had the backing of partnerships of substantial merchant-citizens, many of whom had served, or were to serve, as provost of the city. Although no other provincial town followed suit during George II's reign, the two Glasgow banks had pointed a way that was to be followed by many others in the next decade.

[1] These two banks took their names from the emblems engraved on their notes.

CHAPTER VIII

Social Stability in Town and Country

WHEN WE consider the long stretch of time between the Union of the Crowns and the death of George II, we cannot fail to be impressed by the rapid, numerous and massive changes in affairs of Church and State. The Crown by turns triumphant and humiliated, Parliament depressed to the status of little more than a 'rubber-stamp' and then exalted as a nearly sovereign assembly, Episcopacy alternately restored and abolished – these are among the landmarks of Scotland's road under the later Stuarts and the earlier Hanoverians. Industry and commerce, though gravely hampered by antiquated notions of privilege and monopoly, did undergo some dramatic changes: apart from the grandiose and over-blown Darien Scheme,[1] real progress was made in such matters as the planting of trees, the raising of black cattle for sale in England, the importation and refinement of sugar, and the shipment of cargoes of tobacco. If now we turn to the ordinary living conditions of the people, their homes and furnishings, their food, drink and dress, their travels and pastimes, their pleasures and afflictions, we are struck by the relative stability of society on the farms and in the towns.

This lack of violent change applies to all that we can learn about the total number and the distribution of the inhabitants of Scotland. In the year 1755 Dr Alexander Webster, a leading member of the Church of Scotland, drew up the results of a diligent inquiry which he had carried out, with the aid of his fellow-clergymen, into the population of the country; this was, incidentally, one of the very earliest attempts of its kind in the world. The total reached by Webster was 1,265,380, and, while his reckonings have some elements of guess-work, there is little doubt that his final calculation came very near the mark. Thus the Scottish population at the middle of the eighteenth century was just a quarter of what it was at the middle of the twentieth century: the really big changes have occurred since Webster's day. The previous century and a half present a sharp contrast. It is true that, in the absence of any earlier 'census' or even any reliable contemporary estimate, we cannot approach certainty; but all the indica-

[1] See *supra*, pp. 48-9.

tions[1] point to a fairly stable population during our period. Working backwards, therefore, from 1755, we might reasonably guess the Scottish total in 1707 at about 1,100,000 and this in turn would lead us to suppose that in 1603 it would be in the range 800,000-900,000.

More significant than Webster's total of the inhabitants is his evidence for their distribution throughout town and country. His figures for the four largest towns are[2]:–

Edinburgh (including Canongate and Leith)	57,220
Glasgow (without Gorbals)	23,546
Aberdeen (including Old Aberdeen)	15,433
Dundee	12,477

All the other Scottish towns (headed by Inverness, Perth and Dunfermline) had fewer than 10,000 inhabitants – fewer, that is to say, than there are today in Elgin or Montrose, in Rothesay or Troon. So, too, we notice a much more even spread, then than now, between county and county. Only Perth (with 120,116) reached six figures. Lanarkshire (then including Glasgow) had 81,726 inhabitants, and Fife very nearly as many, while Argyll's total was 66,286 and that of Ross (without Cromarty) 42,921. Thus, between 1603 and 1760, the population picture is one of quite small towns, a fairly evenly, though by no means thickly, peopled countryside, and a gentle and gradual increase in total numbers[3] over the whole period. The country-dwellers continued greatly to outnumber the townsfolk – probably by about five-to-one in the early part of the seventeenth century, and by four-to-one in the first half of the eighteenth century. The term 'country life' must therefore be understood to apply at this time to by far the greater part of the nation.

As we have seen,[4] the low state of agriculture and the poor returns to the farmer were reflected in the scenes that met the eye of the traveller in rural Scotland – open fields straggling up the hillsides,

[1] For example, we have fairly 'firm' figures from the seventeenth century for a few towns, e.g. Dunfermline, Aberdeen, Glasgow, Hawick, Kelso and Paisley; it is noteworthy that, though these were all flourishing places, where some increase in numbers is to be expected, there is nothing to suggest rapid growth in any of them at this time.

[2] Webster's figures in each case refer to *the parish*; that is, they include, besides actual town-dwellers, some who lived in the rural parts immediately adjoining each town.

[3] The sharpest rise was that of Glasgow, from fifth to second place among all towns; it is said to have had 7,644 inhabitants in 1610, and 12,766 in 1707.

[4] Cf. *supra*, p. 67.

undrained marshes and bogs, large expanses of whin, broom and rush, but few trees. Moreover, these conditions endured over wide areas well into the eighteenth century, for the 'improvements', real and valuable as they were, applied only to certain favoured parts of the Lowlands and were everywhere liable to encounter fierce and ignorant or superstitious resistance. By and large, the sight of the cultivated districts brought anything but pleasure to the beholder, while the remote glens, rugged slopes and cloud-capped bens of the Highlands filled him with horror and distaste rather than the admiration that is accorded them today. The countryside was to be passed through as quickly as one's horse would allow. Travel, indeed, was confined to what was unavoidable: roads were rough, narrow, uneven, and muddy or stony, and inns, despite the many statutes that called for their proper maintenance, were poor, mean and frequently filthy. A journey was an adventure and something of an ordeal: lucky the man who found, at the close of day, relief and welcome in the home of a friend or kinsman.

Life was hard and stern in the country, and the scarcity of money was everywhere apparent. Many a laird's total revenue fell short of £100 a year, and much of what he claimed might be debts of doubtful worth; such money as could be collected had to be used sparingly. Wages were thus modest. In Cromwellian times, the Earl of Wemyss, a wealthy nobleman, kept a household of seventeen persons, of whom the chaplain got £16 13s. 4d. sterling a year and the countess's lady-in-waiting (or lady's maid, as we should say) had £10, while the other servants, male and female, indoor and outdoor, received annual wages ranging from £5 down to £1 (paid to each of three washerwomen). Prices of commodities were likewise low. In the reign of Charles II, the household expenses of Sir John Lauder of Fountainhall, an eminent lawyer and judge, included £2 16s. 8d. for a cow, 17s. for a 'great Bible', 10s. for black lace to trim a gown, other 10s. for linen to make shirts, 3s. 3d. for a pair of shoes, 2s. 6d. for a pair of gloves, 1s. 6d. for a wooden chair, 1s. to the tailor for mending clothes, and 6d. to the barber.[1]

The signs of general poverty were to be seen in the houses of both high and low. The noble might live in a castle, the laird in a baronial

[1] For these details, see J. G. Fyfe, *Scottish Diaries and Memoirs, 1550-1746*, pp. 126-7, 202-3 (where the sums are mostly in Scots money, worth one-twelfth of sterling). Most servants, besides wages, had 'gains' in kind, such as a cloak, a coat, or a pair of shoes, while the farm-worker got meal or clothing.

tower or in one of the two-storeyed mansions that came in late in the seventeenth century, but it was an uncommonly prosperous farmer who could afford anything better than the two-roomed cottage of his forebears. Again, the laird had uncarpeted wooden floors in most rooms, the farmer had bare earth or trampled rush or heather, but all alike suffered from cold, damp and draughts, or else from peat-smoke. Deal tables and benches were to be found in most houses, as were box-beds (fitted with doors that enclosed them tightly), though some country gentlemen owned a curtained and canopied 'four-poster'. It was, however, at a 'flitting' that the austere simplicity of life showed itself at its clearest and starkest. When a tenant removed, he often took with him, along with his household gear, the beams and rafters of his roof, so that the incomer, as his first job, had to fit and thatch the roof over his head. Thus, as late as 1705, the baron-court of Urie, in Kincardine, forbade departing tenants to 'pull down any of their house-walls more than frees the timber' of the roofs. Even here, however, the old way was now falling into disrepute, for in 1712 the same court decreed that thatch was not to be removed at a flitting, but that, instead, the roof-timbers of the house and the out-buildings should be offered for sale at a fair price to the new tenant.

Food in the country was plain and, if wholesome, decidedly monotonous. Breakfast was taken about eight o'clock, after several hours of field-work, dinner at or soon after midday, and supper in the evening. At each of these meals the staple fare comprised oat-cakes, bannocks or barley-bread, porridge or gruel, and kail, or vegetable broth. Fresh meat was not to be had between November and May, for the cattle, half-starved during winter, were unfit for slaughter; instead, a salted carcase, known as the 'mart' because it had been killed about Martinmas (11 November), served the family for several months.[1] Mutton, often boiled in the broth, was not uncommon, while near the coast or a good fishing river white fish, salmon or herring were cheap and plentiful. Home-brewed ale was the drink of the ordinary country-dweller, but the laird drank much French wine, shipped from Bordeaux; coffee and tea (costing 25s. a pound at the time of the Union) were rare luxuries. Milk and butter were of low quality and were regarded as poor man's food: the cottar or 'girseman', keeping perhaps only one cow, could afford these, but not much else beyond meal.

Then as now, there was a wide gap between the best and the worst

[1] The need to disguise the 'high' taste of ageing meat explains the demand for salt, pepper, cloves and other strong seasonings and spices.

in the land. As it happens, we have the dietary tables for Glasgow's town hospital, founded in 1733,[1] and for the poor-house at Ayr in 1756.[2] In each of these institutions, both breakfast and supper consisted of oatmeal pottage with ale or milk, while midday dinner comprised broth and bread, the only variety being provided by the addition thereto of meat or fish or butter or cheese (but one only of these). At the other end of the social scale was such a family as that of Murray of Ochtertyre, in central Perthshire, whose household account books have survived for the years 1737-39.[3] Soups, meat, fish, poultry, vegetables and fruits were abundant and varied on their well-laden tables, as were custards, tarts, pancakes and fritters; like many another laird, too, Ochtertyre had plenty of hares and rabbits, of venison and pigeons,[4] and of such game birds as grouse, black-cock, woodcock, moorfowl, plover and partridge. By any standards, the Ochtertyre fare was rich and substantial.

Similar contrasts might be noted in respect of dress. Fashionable lords and ladies would don, if only for special occasions, fine silks and linens, lace and brocade, perfumes and jewels, but for everyday wear coarse home-spun woollens, grey or black, satisfied all classes – woollen shirts, hose and cloaks for the men, woollen or worsted petticoats and gaily coloured plaids for the women.[5] In privacy, too, gentlemen laid aside their wigs, which were apt to be hot and uncomfortable, and covered their shaved heads with a cap; an old and worn night-gown was a favourite garment for lounging indoors. From about 1730, when they 'walked abroad', they carried a cane instead of a sword. Laird or minister might wear a black hat, but the common headgear of the Lowlander was the blue 'Kilmarnock bonnet'. In the Highlands, plaids and hose, hand-woven and dyed, perhaps in contrasting colours to give a 'checked' effect, were the forerunners of the tartan kilt and trews; it was the Jacobite risings, especially the

[1] This was really an alms-house, for aged or infirm paupers, and not a medical institution.

[2] See T. Ferguson, *The Dawn of Scottish Social Welfare* (1948), p. 33, and H. Hamilton, *History of the Homeland* (1947), p. 79.

[3] They were published by the Scottish History Society in 1907.

[4] As readers of *Waverley* (chap. viii) will know, the 'doo-cot', or pigeon-loft, a customary feature of a 'country seat', supplied many birds for the laird's table, but the pigeons angered the farmers by eating their grain.

[5] Many a kirk session inveighed against the women's habit of totally covering their heads with their plaids in time of sermon, but the plaid remained in favour, despite all that the ministers could say about it, until about the middle of the eighteenth century.

'Forty-five, and also the enlisting of many Highland regiments in the late eighteenth century, that gave Highland dress its popular and romantic appeal in its modern form. In the Lowlands, meanwhile, the cloth required for shirt-lengths, plaidings and blankets was woven from the wool of the farmer's own sheep by a village webster (or weaver); a travelling tailor, paid a few pence a day and given his board and lodging while he worked, made up the cloth into garments.

Knowing no better, the peasant wore his clothes in all weathers and seldom thought of changing them; thus, wind, frost and rain outdoors, and smoke, draughts, dirt and damp clothing indoors, took toll of his health. His mode of life might make him a victim of rheumatism; work in the marshy, undrained fields could bring on shivering fits of ague[1]; and, ignorant of the real dangers of dirt, he was often laid low by smallpox. The old proverbial saying, 'The clartier the cosier', tells us much about the home conditions, the personal habits and the mistaken ideas of the old-time countryman. His interests could not be wide, for field-work usually occupied the whole of his daylight hours, and the reading-matter (of such few country-dwellers as could read) would not stretch far beyond the Bible, and an occasional chap-book or collection of ballads. Rural holidays were few – Fastern's E'en in February,[2] Beltane or May-day, and Hallowmas or All Saints (1 November). Most farmers attended a fair once or twice in the year; Communion services, held twice or four times a year, brought large gatherings, while weddings and funerals were occasions for bucolic fun and for rude plenty in food and drink. Pagan superstitions lived on in this Christian land, with its tales of fairies, witches[3] and demons, of charms and the evil eye; a farmer, after praying in church for rain or sunshine, might go to a wishing-well to make doubly sure of good crops!

It is easy, however, for any age to scoff at the shortcomings of an earlier and simpler time. The country-dweller of that period, along

[1] Known in Britain from the fourteenth century as a form of malarial fever, ague was given, in 1743, the 'new-fangled' Italian name of 'influenza'; the word suggests men's belief that the illness was due to the adverse 'influences' of the heavenly bodies upon the human lot: see Ferguson, *op. cit.*, pp. 130-2.

[2] Fastern's E'en, or Shrove Tuesday, fell on the day before Ash Wednesday (when Lent began); it was thus the seventh Tuesday before Easter.

[3] Witchcraft trials took place in the sixteenth century, they were very common in Scotland (as in other lands) during the seventeenth century, and, though infrequent, they continued into the eighteenth century. The last Scottish witch to be tried, condemned and burnt was an old woman of Dornoch, who perished in 1722 for having turned her daughter into a pony and having her shod by the Devil!

with all his failings and afflictions, had some assets denied to the more sophisticated Scot of the twentieth century. The country air was pure and fresh, the rivers ran clear and were full of salmon, while the farmer knew that, if he had hardships to bear, he shared them with all his neighbours, from the laird to the cottar. No class barrier separated man from man, for, in a harsh climate and often on a poor soil, nature itself forced all of them to live in kindly companionship.

Edinburgh during our period enjoyed an absolute primacy among Scottish towns. First in commerce and first in craftsmanship, although bereft of the presence of royalty from 1603, it was, until the Union of 1707, the meeting-place of the Scots Parliament; it was there that the General Assembly, after its reinstatement in 1690, invariably met; and it was there that the supreme law-courts, the Court of Session and the Court of Justiciary, were always held. Declared to be a city, as we have seen,[1] in 1633, Edinburgh was the favourite haunt of the nobles and the more ambitious lairds – the place in which they maintained their town houses. Its long lead over its nearest rivals is indicated in the 'stent-roll', or tax-roll, of the royal burghs, which, adjusted from time to time by the Convention, reflected the relative wealth, size and importance of the chief towns. In 1603 Edinburgh paid more than the next three burghs taken together, and very nearly as much as the next four, while at the close of our period it was actually assessed higher than the next four on the roll.[2] Thus Edinburgh not only maintained, but improved, its dominant position among the Scottish burghs. Its population probably doubled during the period – from about 30,000 in 1603 to about 60,000 by 1760.

On the other hand, the capital grew hardly at all in area. It continued to cling to the high ridge running from the Castle in the west to Holyrood in the east – that is, to the High Street and Canongate, which constituted the 'royal mile', and to the Cowgate, the Grassmarket, and the many 'vennels', closes and wynds branching off from them. The fall of the land to the north, where lay the Nor' Loch, was very steep, but to the south the slopes were gentler though still noticeable. The citizens had some 'elbow-room' for expansion, but they had accustomed themselves to the idea that their city was confined

[1] See *supra*, p. 8.

[2] The stent-roll, as revised in 1597, fixed Edinburgh at £28 15s. out of every £100; Dundee at £10 15s.; Aberdeen, £8; Perth, £6 3s. 4d.; and Glasgow, £4 10s. The adjustment made in 1730, valid at the end of the period, put Edinburgh at £34 10s.; Glasgow at £19 10s.; Aberdeen, £5 18s.; Dundee, £4 18s.; and Perth, £3 8s. See *Records of the Convention of Royal Burghs*, i, 10; v, 507.

within its historic limits, which were marked by the town walls, and especially by the so-called 'Flodden wall', which had been built in the period 1514-60 and extended to the south-west in the seventeenth century. Hence they were unwilling, rather than strictly unable, to build outwards, so that the increasing congestion of the time impelled them to build upwards. The tall 'lands' and tenements, some of them having six, eight, ten or more storeys, came to be packed with residents: in 1697, we are told, 'there were turned-up beds in nearly all the best rooms' of the houses of Edinburgh.

Sheer pressure of population, in conjunction with the upward expansion, explains many of the features of Edinburgh life in the seventeenth and eighteenth centuries. Class distinction and social snobbery could not flourish when rich and poor, well-born and humble, shared the same 'close' and the same house. Differentiation was vertical rather than horizontal. In the high 'lands', the lower floors, being noisy and too near the offensive smells of the street, were left to the merchants, craftsmen and booth-holders; the middle floors might contain lawyers, judges and even nobles; but the top storeys, with their long, steep stairs, were occupied by the city's poorest – chimney-sweeps, it might be, or water-caddies, porters or day-labourers. Living quarters being so cramped, it was found convenient to hold meetings for social or business purposes in the numerous taverns of the city. The narrow, uneven and ill-paved streets held two special hazards: with no public lighting, they were dangerous after dark, and, at any hour of the day, household refuse and slops might be emptied out of the windows to the traditional warning-cry (which reminds us of the French influence on old-time Scotland) of 'Gardyloo' (*Gardez l'eau*).

While natives and strangers alike railed against life's discomforts in these thronging streets, it is clear that they exercised a tremendous pull on the people of Scotland, and that all who could do so loved to visit or stay in the capital, which had colour, gaiety and pageantry. Food and drink were varied and plentiful; besides the staples of the country – barley-broth and salt-beef, ale and claret – there was abundance of fowls and cockie-leekie, collops and mutton, sheep's head and haggis, as well as delicacies like roast goose, oysters and crab-pies. Nor was such fare costly. When Alexander Carlyle was a student at Edinburgh in 1742, he and his fellows had 'a very good dinner' at 4d. a head, including 'broth and beef, and a roast and potatoes every day, with fish three or four times a week, and all the small beer that was called for till the cloth was removed'. Apart from the delights of the table, the young and active could enjoy golf, tennis and archery in or near Edinburgh, music and dancing were available, and, for the sporting members of society, cock-fighting and horse-racing.[1] After the Restoration, strolling players presented their dramas in the streets or the purlieus of Holyrood.

Above all, Edinburgh was the town in which royalty – a rare sight in Scotland after 1603 – might be on view. James VI and I was here in 1617, Charles I came for his Scottish coronation in 1633, and again, in a desperate effort to build up a royalist party, in 1641, while Charles II spent the summer of 1650 in his Scottish capital, before Cromwell had gathered his forces for a final assault on the northern kingdom. Between 1660 and 1707, however, pageantry meant the 'riding of Parliament', when the great officers of state, lords, barons and burgesses, each arrayed in the rich attire proper to his rank, rode in solemn procession from Holyrood to the Parliament House for the formal meeting of the three Estates. All of this ceased in 1707, and thereafter the citizens had to be content with the more sombre spectacle of the Lord High Commissioner riding up 'the royal mile' for the opening of the General Assembly of the Church.

The other towns, though much poorer and smaller, took their cue from Edinburgh. The Campbells of Argyll had their 'ludging' in Stirling, and the Campbells of Loudoun their 'hall' in Ayr. St Andrews had seen its magnificent cathedral and priory fall into ruins, but its three colleges were still occupied by masters and students. At Glasgow the cathedral had fortunately been preserved, and the numerous churches, broad streets and pleasant buildings of the western city were always admired by visitors. Aberdeen and Dundee were flourishing centres of trade. In these towns, as in the lesser burghs of the kingdom substantial, stone-built houses with slate roofs, nestling next to mere cottages, often had a charm of their own, with their crow-stepped gables, small turrets at the corners, and solid 'fore-stairs' jutting straight out into the street; especially attractive was the 'Old College' of Glasgow, built on the High Street mainly between 1632 and 1660.

In all the towns, however, the wooden galleries fronting the houses and the many thatched roofs made fire an ever-present menace. Dunfermline was devastated in 1624, Glasgow in 1652 and again in 1677, Kelso in 1684. Local regulations imposed severe penalties upon careless conduct and dangerous trades, such as the use of baking-ovens

[1] Leith races were instituted in 1665, with two silver cups as prizes.

or the making of candles, in densely peopled tenements. Parliament itself, in 1681, ordered the removal of all thatched roofs in Edinburgh, Glasgow, Aberdeen, Dundee and Stirling, and their replacement by slate or tile; but thatch, as the readiest and cheapest of roofing materials, lingered on into the nineteenth century even in the larger towns. No more effective was the statute of 1698 (largely inspired by the fire hazard) forbidding new buildings in Edinburgh above the height of five storeys.

If fire was the chief threat to the life of the community, the greatest risk to its health and well-being lay in the almost universal indifference to sanitation and ordinary cleanliness. The town-dweller was often a crofter, with a kailyard or a back-garden, and perhaps a small, arable holding, and he valued, as fertiliser, the dung-heap piled up on the street before his house. The custom was known to be injurious as well as unseemly, and the burgh records abound with decrees for the removal of all 'middingis' off the principal streets. Little, however, was achieved in the way of effective reform. The middens remained, and so did the loose swine, roaming the streets and rooting among the rubbish and filth. As late as 1725, the *fuilyie* (street-garbage) of Leith was 'rouped' (or let by auction) for five years for the sum of £121 10s., the 'tacksman', or lessee, undertaking, in return for this fertiliser, to keep the streets clean.

Urban conditions for long permitted and encouraged the ravages of epidemics and filth-diseases. Much the worst of these had been the bubonic plague, which, known in Scotland as 'the pest', was liable to visit the land, and especially the chief towns, at least once in every twenty years or so. Not only did it survive into the seventeenth century: it was particularly virulent in the years 1644-48, and it was responsible in a year for far more deaths than Montrose and his Covenanting opponents taken together. It would die down in one locality only to flare up in another. At the first rumour of its presence, the town council would order the closing and barricading of the town's ports (or gates), the doubling of the watch by day and night, and the repair of the back-dykes (which might offer easy access to strangers). Men from out of town were closely questioned, diseased or suspected persons were isolated in wooden huts on 'the muir' outside the town, unclean clothing was destroyed, and infected premises were treated by specially appointed 'clengers' (or cleaners). Those who broke the rules or failed to report the sickness were liable to the death penalty. At such times life was grim indeed, for the ordinary routine was utterly dislocated: for example, Glasgow University was dispersed in 1645, St Andrews in 1647. Despite all precautions, casualties remained high. In 1645, six out of Stirling's town council of twenty-one members, who had been active in combatting the infection, themselves died of it, while Aberdeen suffered 1,600 deaths in 1647-48 – that is, about one-fifth of the inhabitants. Leith, the main port for sea-going ships, was the most vulnerable of all: in the terrible year 1645, no fewer than 2,421 persons are said to have died of the pest in six months – fully half of the town's population. In 1665-66, the year of 'the Great Plague' in the south, the Scottish Privy Council forbade all traffic with London and other affected parts of England; for once, the restriction was completely successful, and no one died of the pest north of the Tweed. The year 1648 thus marks for Scotland the end of a dread scourge.

In the eighteenth century smallpox, the worst of the epidemics, was apt to be deadly among children. In two years (1740-42), we are told, over 2,700 persons, mostly children, died at Edinburgh. Inoculation against this disease began towards the close of our period, and was in fairly general use after 1745, but, whether from ignorance or carelessness, the ravages continued. Poverty, bad housing, overcrowding and inadequate food might lead to sickness and fevers, but the kirk sessions were able to do little more than relieve the urgent needs of the lame, the halt and the blind; for the ordinary poor, victims, it might be, of famine, unemployment or other misfortune, there was only charity, well-meaning but haphazard. And, though the beginnings of medical advance are to be noted in the seventeenth century,[1] physicians and surgeons were as yet neither numerous nor highly skilled. Hospitals, too, had been founded in the larger towns in the seventeenth century – George Heriot's in Edinburgh, John Cowane's in Stirling, and George and Thomas Hutchesons' in Glasgow – but these were really alms-houses for the respectable poor, and especially for orphans and the aged.[2] Institutional medicine began only with the foundation of Edinburgh Royal Infirmary in 1729, followed by that of Aberdeen in 1742; by 1760, medical science was still in its infancy.

Though living conditions were in many ways backward if stable during our period, some signs of social progress can yet be noted. The leaders of society were wealthier after 1603 than their forebears had been, and nobles, enriched by grants of Church lands, became courtiers

[1] Cf. *supra*, p. 41.
[2] This was true, too, of Glasgow's town hospital, as to which see *supra*, p. 81.

or politicians instead of warriors, spending their money on elegant living rather than the upkeep of great, armed followings. Burgesses, too, waxed richer from trade, crafts, private banking or money-lending. Lawyers and even clergymen inclined more to finery and luxuries; though the Covenanters lived simply and austerely, regarding as vain and sinful the indulgence of the natural appetites, the Episcopalians and, after 1690, some Presbyterians saw no harm in enjoying the good things in life. Moreover, the influence of London, a city that was now familiar to the travelled Scot, further favoured the growth of refined ways, in male dress, for example, as well as in female fashion.

The changes of the period 1603-50 were most marked in the homes of the well-to-do. The 'great hall' of castle or tower became the family dining-room, furnished with a dining-table instead of boards on trestles and with chairs in place of forms. Pewter plates and drinking stoups were still in use, but silver dishes were also fairly common. The kitchen was removed as far as possible from the living quarters, the bedrooms were given separate access, and those who could afford them had a drawing-room, a parlour and a study. Carpets, rugs, dressers and aumries (cabinets) were to be found in all the better homes, and other signs of rank or prosperity were such purely decorative items as carved wooden panelling, needlework covers and embroidered cushions.

The second half of the seventeenth century, despite the civil and religious strife of the times, saw a greater urge towards novelties and niceties, and here the lead was taken by Edinburgh, especially after the Restoration. Among the newer tradesmen now able to make a living in the capital were a gunsmith, a watchmaker, an engraver, a bookbinder, several surgical and marine instrument makers, a tobacco cutter, silk weavers and French perfumers. From 1675, a water-supply was piped in from Comiston, and the same year saw the importation of London's newest vogue – the coffee-house.[1] To mark yet another fashionable fad, periwig-makers were admitted as burgesses in 1677 and 1678, for shaved heads and periwigs were now deemed more correct than the long, curled hair affected by men in Charles I's time.[2] Bath-houses, with stoves for heating the water, were set up in Canongate in 1686. Hackney coaches had begun to ply in Edinburgh in 1673, but

[1] Tea and coffee had been introduced to England by the East India Company about 1660.

[2] The change was at least partly due to considerations of hygiene, for it was very hard to keep the long hair of the Cavalier 'dandies' clean and wholesome.

the *Burgh Records* of 19 October 1687 introduce another novelty: sedan-chairs, borne by two strong men 'in handsome liveries', were available for the use of the nobility, ladies, persons of quality and the sick and infirm, and could easily pass through narrow closes and wynds, 'wher coaches could not goe'.

Edinburgh led, and other towns followed at a distance. The youth of Edinburgh were playing billiards by 1659, and those of Glasgow and Aberdeen by about 1670. The town green of Dunfermline was being fenced off from 1666, for recreation instead of common pasturage. Glasgow, exploiting its trade with the West Indies, was sending rum and sugar to the other towns from 1681. And, as before, the houses of the leaders of local society everywhere reflected the changing tastes of the time: characteristic of the Restoration period are the cabinets and chests of drawers, elaborately ornamented with inlays, veneers and mother-of-pearl devices.

During the first sixty years of the eighteenth century the means of transport showed some modest advances. Stage-coaches were running between Edinburgh and Leith from 1702. Coach-building, however, got its start in Scotland only in 1738, when John Home went to London for his training; returning to Edinburgh with the necessary skill as well as the equipment, he set up an efficient coach-making plant. The Edinburgh-Glasgow stage-coach, taking twelve hours for the forty-six-mile journey, began in 1749,[1] but, until after the close of the period, the traveller to or from London had to choose between the rigours of riding horse-back and the great expense of a private or hired carriage.

In other ways the reigns of Queen Anne and the first two Georges saw an enrichment of social life in Edinburgh, which is all the more surprising in that it was feared that, with the extinction of the separate Parliament, the glory and gaiety of the capital would vanish. In fact quite the opposite occurred, and the citizens found ever new methods of spending their time and their money. The tavern, the coffee-house, the social club and the newspaper[2] catered to their craving for luxurious or civilised living. On their tables china and glass, sometimes of fine workmanship, began to displace the old-fashioned pewter vessels. With the price of ale increased after the Malt Tax of 1725, men partook more heavily of claret and brandy from France, port from Portugal, and whisky from the Highlands, while the ladies now served tea at

[1] See Hugo Arnot, *History of Edinburgh* (1779), p. 599, and H. G. Graham, *Social Life of Scotland in the Eighteenth Century* (1936 edition), p. 41.

[2] For the rise of the newspaper, see *supra*, p. 43, and *infra*, p. 114.

their four o'clock parties. Ordinary folk still dined at midday, but fashionable people put off their dinner-hour from one to two o'clock, and then (just before 1760) to three or even four in the afternoon. In matters of dress, English broad-cloth, muslins, silks and fine linens were preferred to home-spun woollens, and plaids went out of favour with women about 1750. Subscription balls, known as 'assemblies', were held from 1710, while a musical society flourished from 1728. Golf took firm root in 1735 with the institution of the Edinburgh Burgess Club, followed in 1744 by the Honourable Company of Edinburgh.

Even in this expansive age, however, the theatre had a long, uphill struggle. It is true that James VII, while still Duke of York and commissioner in Scotland for his brother, Charles II, had maintained a company of players at Holyroodhouse. In March 1682, influenced no doubt by the royal example, the town council of Edinburgh had gone so far as to allow the building of a timber house or stage in the High Street, but later that year it must have repented, for, on the complaint of the inhabitants that their children, apprentices and servants were wasting their time by daily frequenting the plays and public shows, it ordered the demolition of the structure. For a full generation after the Revolution, all dramatic performances were under a cloud in Scotland, but strolling players were again to be seen in Edinburgh from the accession of George II, despite the fact that town council, university and parliament itself frowned on their activities. The stricter Presbyterians thoroughly disapproved of their appearances. Thus, in 1728, Robert Wodrow deplored the visit of certain English 'players, comedians and strollers, come down to fill up our cup of sin'; in his view, they got 'too much encouragement', so that 'a vast deal of money, in this time of scarcity', was wasted on them. But public taste was slowly changing in these matters, and in 1746 a theatre or playhouse was built in the Canongate. The final acceptance of the theatre by the populace of Edinburgh came in 1756 with the presentation of John Home's tragedy of *Douglas*, for, when respectable ministers of the Church of Scotland were involved, it could no longer be held to be a public duty to denounce the stage.[1]

Not very long after the Union, Glasgow also had its newspapers, its concerts and its assemblies, while its Highland Society started in 1727 and its Literary Society in 1755. Alexander Carlyle, coming on from Edinburgh in 1743 to continue his studies, found Glasgow a

[1] See *infra*, p. 112.

pleasant enough spot: at a weekly meeting in a tavern, he tells us, a discussion was arranged, 'we drank a little punch after our beefsteaks and pancakes, and the expense never exceeded 1s. 6d., seldom 1s.' For the theatre, on the other hand, the going was really rough. Robert Wodrow applauded Glasgow's hostile response to the English strollers in 1728, when *The Beggars' Opera* brought them such small audiences that they 'got not so much as to pay their musick'. The first playhouse – little more than a wooden shed erected in 1752 near the cathedral – had a brief life, being demolished in the next year.[1] And yet a new liveliness was noticeable in the western city about mid-century. The East Port, in the Gallowgate, and the West Port, in the Trongate, as symbols of a vanishing past and obstructions to traffic, were removed in 1749, to be replaced by Glasgow's two most famous hostelries – the Saracen's Head (1755), the terminus for the Edinburgh coach, and the Black Bull (1760), the favourite meeting-place of the Highlanders.[2]

Aberdeen, too, had its musical society from 1748, and St Andrews its golfing society, which, founded in 1754, was later, under the name of the 'Royal and Ancient', to become the foremost golf club in the world. The new modes in dress, table-ware, food and drink, the new tastes for later dinners, social gatherings, dancing and recreation, were spreading outwards from the capital by the 1750s, but the major changes were not to come until the reign of George III.

[1] It was said that George Whitefield, the English revivalist, then on a visit to the city, incited a fanatical mob to attack the building as being the devil's work, but the preacher himself denied the story.

[2] See 'Senex' [Robert Reid] and others, *Glasgow Past and Present* (1884), VOL. I, pp. 71, 81-2.

CHAPTER IX

The Church Divided

THE OUTLINES of a solution to the problem of the relations between Church and State had been worked out, as we have seen, as part of 'the Revolution settlement': the ecclesiastical questions that agitated men's minds were too important to be left out of the politicians' considerations. Episcopacy, compromised by its association with Stuart autocracy, had been abolished, the Presbyterian order had been restored in the Church of Scotland, the Westminster Confession of Faith had been adopted as its main 'standard', the rights of lay patrons had been set aside in favour of the heritors and elders of each parish, and the General Assembly had been revived. The covenants had, however, been quietly dropped, to the chagrin of the 'Cameronians', who refused to have anything to do with a Kirk deemed to be unworthy of Scotland's Protestant heritage. On the other side, it had been made possible for Episcopalian pastors to retain their livings simply by taking an oath of allegiance to the Crown; but, if they would not conform to this extent, they too were to be cast out into the wilderness.[1]

In this sensible and temperate way, issues that were as much political as religious had been disposed of, and the determination of these matters left the Church of Scotland in a strong central position, and yet broad enough to appeal to the great majority of the nation. But there remained a number of points of domestic interest, which had to be decided for the Kirk by Parliament or by its own General Assembly.

In 1690, by one of the lesser statutes of the Revolution settlement, the Yule vacance (or Christmas holiday) was forbidden to be observed in any law court, on the ground that this had proved in the past to be a hindrance and interruption to the course of justice; actually, to the stricter Presbyterians, any celebration of Christmas savoured of Popery. If this measure suggests fanaticism, another that was passed at the same time points in the opposite direction. All earlier Acts imposing civil penalties after sentence of excommunication were abolished, so that the clergy lost their power of passing effective

[1] See *supra*, pp. 45-6.

judgment (possibly in a tyrannical way) on their fellow-men for their lapses from moral conduct or from due religious observances. Yet a statute of 1693 reaffirmed the general duty of the civil magistrates to support the censures of the Kirk with the force of their authority. Within the Church itself these minor reforms were completed in 1697 by the 'Barrier Act', which provided that any desired legislation must first be proposed to the General Assembly as an 'overture' and, if approved by it, sent down to all the presbyteries for their consideration; only if a majority of these supported the overture did it come before the next Assembly for final sanction. This procedure was designed as a safeguard against a rash, pliant, misguided or unrepresentative assembly, and was intended to ensure the truly democratic character of the Kirk's legislation.

A real difficulty arose in those years over the duty of naming the date and the place of the next meeting of the General Assembly. King William, though he made no pretence to rule by divine right, regarded this duty as part of his prerogative, but the Presbyterian ministers thought that they themselves had 'ane spirituall intrinsick power from Jesus Christ, the only Head of His Church, to meet in Assemblies'. A serious conflict threatened in 1692 and again in 1694, but by 1695 a reasonable working agreement had been reached: the king, through his commissioner, would summon an Assembly every year at a suitable time and place, and the ministers would not press the argument about their 'intrinsic power'. Since that time an Assembly has met every year, with the commissioner as the crown's representative. From 1704 onwards the expedient of a 'double declaration' was adopted, whereby the dissolution of one Assembly and the appointment of the next were announced first by the moderator and then by the commissioner; they had, of course, agreed on the date beforehand.[1]

Most of the credit for the wisdom and good sense shown by Crown and Kirk at this stage belongs to William Carstares, who was chaplain to William of Orange, accompanied him on his historic voyage to England in 1688, and remained as his chief adviser on all Scottish affairs. His opinions and his judgment were so sound and balanced, so far removed from extreme views, that the king was glad to follow them.[2] His influence and renown stood correspondingly high in

[1] This procedure held good until 1927, when it was slightly modified; since that date, the commissioner has merely noted the Assembly's own arrangements for its next meeting and has then, in the sovereign's name, bidden it farewell.

[2] 'I know him', said the king, 'to be a truly honest man.'

Scotland. Four times he was chosen moderator of the General Assembly, and from 1703 he held the important post of principal of Edinburgh University. Had Queen Anne been as ready as King William to consult him and to heed his suggestions, the affairs of the Church of Scotland might have run a smoother course during her reign. As it was, the part that he played in the years 1706-07 in safeguarding 'the true Protestant religion . . . with the worship, discipline and government of this Church . . . unalterably secured', and, on the strength of that guarantee, in inducing the Kirk to support the Union, shows him as an ecclesiastical statesman of the highest order.

The three Acts of 1712,[1] passed at the instigation of the Scottish nobles and the English Tories, caused deep distress to Carstares and his fellow-Presbyterians. The Yule Vacance Act, reversing the abolition, in 1690, of the Christmas vacation in the law-courts, was a mere pinprick, a frivolous measure designed to offend the Presbyterian masses, who regarded the restoration of this statutory holiday as a concession to Episcopalian or Romanist sentiment. Much more obnoxious were the other two statutes, the Toleration Act and the Patronage Act.

The Toleration Act, openly Anglican in inspiration and passed by an administration that was behaving intolerantly towards the English dissenters, was especially detested on account of the events that had led up to it. James Greenshields, an Episcopal pastor, had started services in Edinburgh in 1709, using the Anglican prayer-book. For this he had been deprived by the presbytery and, on refusing to submit, imprisoned by the civil magistrates. His appeal to the Court of Session was rejected, but the House of Lords sustained his further appeal, finding the magistrates in default and liable for costs (March 1711). To many Scots this decision confirmed their worst fears of the dangers of allowing appeals from Scottish law-courts to the House of Lords,[2] for it seemed to them dreadful that an alien tribunal should reverse the solemn decision of their highest courts in a matter of such moment as conformity of worship and the rights of the established Church. To the Anglicans, however, forming the great majority in Parliament, the Greenshields case carried a totally different moral: they were appalled at the disabilities imposed on their co-religionists in Scotland, where Episcopalians were actually 'dissenters'. This, they felt, was a grievance that had to be put right, or at least mitigated, as soon as occasion arose.

[1] Cf. *supra*, pp. 55-6. [2] Cf. *supra*, p. 53 and n. 1.

The opportunity came in February 1712, when the Toleration Act was passed by the united Parliament against the utmost endeavours of Carstares and his friends, who had gone to London to try to halt its progress. The Act sanctioned Episcopalian worship in Scotland, but it went much further, by imposing on pastors, Presbyterian as well as Episcopalian, the obligation to take the oath of allegiance (to the reigning monarch, who must belong to the Church of England) and of abjuration (of the exiled Stuarts). It was thus almost equally distasteful to both groups: the ministers of the Kirk were required to give their countenance to the Anglican faith of their sovereign, while the Episcopalian clergymen were ordered to renounce their Jacobite hopes. In both camps the extremists refused to take the oath, whether from Covenanting or from Jacobite scruples. Petty as these disputes may seem, in contrast to the great and good principle of toleration, the Act aroused bitter resentment. It threatened, indeed, to bring about a schism in the Kirk between the 'Jurants' and 'Non-jurants', those who accepted and those who rejected the oath; but an Act of 1719 removed this source of trouble by modifying the form of the oath.[1]

In the long run, much the greatest damage was done by the third statute of 1712, the Patronage Act, though it was not received at the time with such a storm of abuse as was the Toleration Act. The right of the individual lay patrons to appoint ministers to vacant charges was reaffirmed, to the exclusion of the heritors and elders who had been empowered to do so in 1690. Some arguments can be advanced in favour of this measure. It was to be expected that nobles, lairds and other enlightened patrons would nominate cultured and well qualified clergymen. It was hoped that the landowners, given this stake in the presbyterian system, would return to a Kirk which they had largely forsaken (for most of them favoured episcopacy). Many Scots, born and bred in a feudal society, approved this frankly aristocratic method of appointment, which had a long history behind it. In any case, the patron's power of nominating a new pastor would often be (as indeed it was) exercised agreeably to the wishes of the congregation. And yet, when every allowance is made, it remains true that the Act was, and was clearly seen to be, a breach of the very spirit

[1] The 1712 oath had obliged the swearer to support the Protestant succession, as settled in two named statutes of the parliament of England, the Bill of Rights, 1689, and the Act of Settlement, 1701, which contained the stipulation that the sovereign must be in communion with the Church of England. The 1719 oath referred simply to 'the Succession of the Crown in the Heirs of the Body of the late Princess Sophia . . . being Protestants', without mentioning any legislation on the subject.

(even more than the letter[1]) of the Treaty of Union; that it was passed in a mood compounded of levity and mischief[2]; and that it was the cause, for well over a century, of bitterness, conflict and schism in the Kirk.

With the accession of the house of Hanover in August 1714 a new phase opened for the Church of Scotland. The fear of a Romanist revival or an Episcopal restoration had passed away, and the days of conventicles and martyrdoms, of torture or deportation, were happily over. The Kirk was secure; it was now the Church 'as by law established', adhering to 'the reformed religion presently professed within this realm'. But its security had been gained at some cost to itself. The dropping of the Covenants, besides driving the Cameronians out of the Church, had created in the south-west – in Lanarkshire, Ayrshire and Dumfriesshire – a pool of religious discontent, a nucleus of critics of the existing establishment. In the north-east, from Angus round to Banff, the Episcopalians were especially numerous, and there were also groups of them spread elsewhere throughout the country, and particularly in the land-owning class. Still hankering after a Jacobite triumph, which might restore their system, they had not yet severed all connection with the national church. It is said that in 1707 no fewer than 165 Episcopalian clergymen were living in the manses of the Kirk, conducting parochial services and drawing their stipends.

For this and other reasons, the man-power problems of the Church were formidable. After their years of persecution under Charles II and James VII, the Presbyterians could not at once produce the hundreds of trained clergymen needed for the pulpits of the Church. A generation passed after the Revolution before the gaps could be filled with new men, properly qualified and duly ordained. Thus the Kirk, as it faced the challenge of a new age, could rightly claim to be the church of the people, but already it was something less than the church of all the people.

Some of the more evangelical of the Scots divines were now grieving over the lapses of their brethren from the true reformed faith, and in

[1] It might also be argued that the failure to carry out one clause of the Act of 1690 (which allowed each patron the sum of 600 merks, or £400 Scots, for the surrender of his right) had already vitiated that statute in respect of almost all the parishes of Scotland, so that its very validity was now (in 1712) in question; but this thesis smacks of special pleading.

[2] The chief trouble-maker, George Lockhart of Carnwath, an outright Jacobite, went so far as to propose that the old revenues of the bishoprics be devoted to the maintenance of the episcopalian clergymen who had withdrawn from the Church of Scotland. The Queen herself intervened to dissuade him from this extreme folly.

1718 one of their number, Thomas Boston, minister of Ettrick, in Selkirkshire, reissued an English Puritan treatise of 1645, entitled *The Marrow of Modern Divinity*. He and those who thought with him felt that this little book had valuable lessons for their own time, but others judged it to contain errors and heresies. The 'Marrow Controversy' agitated the Church for several years, and led the General Assembly to rebuke the 'Marrow Men' in 1720 and again in 1722; but these men, dubbed 'the twelve Apostles' from their number, defied all their critics' censures.

At the opposite pole from the 'Marrow Men' stood John Simson, professor of divinity at Glasgow University. His fault, it was found, lay in leaning towards the 'Arian' heresy of denying the separate divinity of Christ. After his students had been questioned over his lectures, the Assembly, in 1727, suspended him from teaching duties and, two years later, made this suspension perpetual (which had the curious effect of securing him his stipend, while forbidding him to perform any duties in return). Thus, with a fine nose for smelling out unorthodox opinions to right and to left, the Kirk tried to pick its delicate way through the thickets of Christian belief and practice.

The authority of the Church had been questioned in these debates, but the great attack was to come over the issue of lay patronage. That law, though it had been on the statute-book for twenty years, had not been rigorously carried out. Often enough a patron had left the choice of minister to the local people, while in other cases his nominee had been refused and he had been unable or unwilling to enforce compliance. Moreover, there was doubt as to just when a patron's right must be regarded as lapsed, and also, in that event, as to just who acquired the right of nomination in his place.[1] On the whole, the local difficulties were not acute so long as there were more parishes in need of ministers than ministers in search of parishes. By 1732, however, it was felt that the time had come to settle some of the doubtful points.

The General Assembly of that year passed an Act which declared that, if the patron failed to present a minister to a vacancy, the heritors and elders (or, in a burghal charge, the town council and elders) should give 'the call' for the approval of the congregation. This may seem a sensible and practical measure, and something of a 'half-way house' between the Acts of 1690 and 1712 (abolishing and restoring lay patron-

[1] Some adhered to the Act of 1649, which had affirmed 'popular election', i.e. by the male heads of families in the congregation, while others followed the Act of 1690, which gave the right to the heritors and elders only.

age), or even a laudable attempt to 'make the best of a bad job'. To the evangelicals of that day, however, it appeared as a gross betrayal of the true faith, partly because it recognised, if only as a necessary evil, the law of patronage (against which, now and for long after, the Assembly solemnly protested every year), and partly because the call by heritors and elders was preferred to popular election. The new measure was bitterly opposed by the 'Popular' party, among whom none was more outspoken than Ebenezer Erskine, a former 'Non-jurant' and 'Marrow Man', now minister of the West kirk of Stirling.

Erskine preached and wrote tirelessly against the Assembly's legislation, denouncing his fellow-ministers, the patrons, the heritors and elders alike. He was rebuked, but he and three other ministers protested against such censure in May 1733, and adhered to their former opinions. Refusing to submit to suspension or to any other form of Assembly discipline, the four, in November, formally 'seceded', or withdrew from the fellowship of their 'uncovenanted' brethren. At Gairney bridge, near Kinross, on 6 December, they declared that they had formed themselves into 'the Associate Presbytery', with Erskine as their moderator. Such was 'the Original Secession'.

Even yet many within the Church hoped to avoid a final break, and the Assembly, in a lenient or repentant mood, was most reluctant to proceed to extremes. The Seceders, on the other hand, were encouraged by the accession of other ministers, including Ralph Erskine of Dunfermline, Ebenezer's brother, and by the formation of small bodies of Seceders in other congregations. Thus fortified, they paid no heed to the Assembly's numerous appeals to return to the fold. Seven years passed before the Church was driven to depose the seceding brethren (May 1740).

The law of patronage, and the Assembly's efforts to steer a middle course between the decrees of the Parliament in London and the wishes of the people of Scotland, were the occasion, but perhaps not the ultimate cause, of the Secession. We can learn much from the two 'Testimonies' issued by the Associate Presbytery. In the first (November 1733), the brethren rebuked 'the lordly and magisterial power' of their opponents for persecuting 'the flock and heritage of God' – which came close to outright defiance of ecclesiastical authority. In the second (December 1736), their range was wider, for they deplored almost all that had happened in the Kirk in their time – the failure to renew the Covenants or to assert the divine right of Presbytery, the toleration of 'Episcopal hirelings', the uncovenanted union with England, the 'yoke' of patronage, the Yule holidays in the courts, the condemnation of *The Marrow*, alongside the failure to excommunicate Professor Simson, the sanctioning of such sinful activities as assemblies and balls, and the repeal of the statutes against witchcraft. The long catalogue suggests that the Seceders could not have found contentment within the eighteenth-century Kirk, whatever the mode of appointing ministers. For them the times were out of joint, and they had to testify against what seemed the prevailing errors.

There was much in the conduct of the Seceders which shows that they actively enjoyed the martyr's crown that they eagerly sought; they were deaf to the scriptural injunction, 'Be not righteous over much' (Ecclesiastes, 7:16). And yet their old-fashioned faith and their refusal to renounce the Covenants, no less than their upright lives, appealed to the people, as is plain from their rapid increase in numbers. By 1737 they had eight congregations, each with its own pastor, and by 1744 they were reorganised as the Associate Synod, with three presbyteries (Dunfermline, Edinburgh and Glasgow).

Soon the Seceders were themselves split by a new secession. Debate arose among them over the question of the 'burgess oath', which required new burgesses in certain burghs to swear to uphold 'the true Protestant religion presently professed within this realm'. This religious 'test' dated back to Reformation times and was intended to exclude Roman Catholics. Some Seceders thought it a mere matter of form, but to others it was sinful to promise to maintain the faith which was 'presently professed', for that was the faith of the church they had just left. The two groups, known as Burghers and Antiburghers, could not agree on a course of action; the former held a slight majority, but the minority, after prolonged wrangles, withdrew in April 1747 to form their own church, which they eventually called the General Associate Synod. In August 1748 they went so far as to depose from the ministry their late colleagues of the Associate (or Burgher) Synod. This internal schism was termed 'the Breach', and three generations were to come and go before it was healed.

Other events of the time show that many Scots Presbyterians were disturbed about the laxity, as it seemed to them, of the established church. One of these critics was John Glass, minister of Tealing, near Dundee, whose views, then deemed 'peculiar', might now be labelled 'advanced', for they stressed the purely spiritual or 'voluntary' nature of religion and worship, the rights of private conscience, and the sinfulness of the Covenants. He revived certain practices of the early Christians, and, from his frequent communions and simple 'love-feasts' (in which the broth of the country-folk was often used), his followers were dubbed 'Kailites', though they were better known in the eighteenth and nineteenth centuries as 'Glassites' or (after Glass's son-in-law) as 'Sandemanians'.

Again, in 1741, George Whitefield, the famous English Methodist, made a deep impression on his Scottish listeners. Quite independently of him, William McCulloch, the minister of Cambuslang, in Lanarkshire, started a great 'revival' of religion among his parishioners in February 1742, but before long Whitefield and others joined him in 'the Cambuslang wark'. The climax came on 15 August with a mass communion, which brought together some 30,000 people and was long remembered for its remarkable outbursts of preaching, praying and singing, of shouting, trembling and swooning, of demonstrations of joy by the converted and of repentance by the sinners.

In 1743, too, the 'Society men' or 'Cameronians', who had been following their lone path, generally without ministers to lead them, found two clergymen to their way of thinking, and established the 'Reformed Presbytery'. Dedicated with the utmost fervour to the truth and continuing value of the Covenants, these Presbyterian dissenters formed a tiny but very durable group.

Meanwhile, the Church of Scotland, little affected by these varied movements, was itself changing its outlook in a changing world. Patrons became bolder in presenting clergymen to vacant benefices, and the ministers, more and more of whom were themselves the nominees of patrons, were less ready to oppose unpopular 'intrusions'. Contrasting attitudes now showed themselves towards the law of patronage: the 'Moderates' began to view it as an aid to discipline and good order in the Church, but the 'Evangelical' or 'Popular' party still denounced and resisted it at every turn. While, therefore, the latter attached much importance to the Assembly's annual protest against the grievance of patronage, the former began to regard it as a customary survival, a mere matter of form.

By mid-century, or very soon after, the Moderates, closely associated with Scottish achievements in literature and philosophy, in education and the arts, were in the ascendant, and the General Assembly, far from sympathising with local opponents of patronage, was resolved to make an example of one of them. The choice fell on Thomas Gillespie, minister of Carnock in West Fife, who, with four others, had stood forth against an unwanted nominee at Inverkeithing. He was deposed in May 1752, accepted his fate with good-will and resignation, gave up his church, manse and stipend, and organised his own independent congregation, with a meeting-house in Dunfermline. A few years later, constantly denied readmission to the Church, he and his flock were joined by new groups formed, with their ministers, at Jedburgh and at Colinsburgh (in East Fife). These three congregations came together in October 1761 to constitute the 'Presbytery of Relief' – offering relief, that is to say, to pastors and worshippers from the heavy burden of patronage. The Church had suffered its second major secession.

By the close of our period the Moderates were carrying all before them. New leaders were coming to the fore and making their mark both inside and outside the Church – William Robertson and Hugh Blair, John Home and Alexander Carlyle. Proud of their standing in polite society, on good terms with the nobility and gentry, they were fluent speakers and ready writers, seeing no evil in ease and comfort, in dining and wining, in dancing and the theatre. Their 'lukewarm' faith, however, and what was called their 'mere morality' did not appeal to all their humbler parishioners, many of whom were turning away from the Church of Scotland to the Seceders, who with their simpler services and stricter faith seemed closer to the church of their fathers. A price was being exacted for the triumph of the Moderates.

If the Presbyterians had their troubles and conflicts at this time, for the two other major sects within the nation it was an age of deep suffering and sorrow. We have seen that, while many of the Episcopal clergymen were deprived after the Revolution, others took the oaths of allegiance in 1693 or 1695, and were able to retain their livings[1]; and we have also seen that, as late as 1707, such conforming pastors were said to number as many as 165.[2] To a man, of course, the bishops were, in the language of the day, 'Non-jurors'. While they made, for some time, no attempt to exercise diocesan functions, they remained in being chiefly for the purpose of consecrating new pastors for the small congregations, with their meeting-houses, which had to be set up as, one by one, the parishes of the establishment were filled by Presbyterians.

In 1705, when only five Scots bishops were left, they raised two others to the episcopal dignity – an example that was followed in later promotions. The Episcopalians naturally welcomed the Toleration Act of 1712, though their stricter members deplored the accompanying

[1] See *supra*, p. 46. [2] See *supra*, p. 96.

oath of abjuration. They had their brief hour of royal favour, and then their involvement in the Jacobite cause in 1715 brought a new wave of suppression. Some thirty-six clergymen in the diocese of Aberdeen were deprived of their livings, while an Act of 1719 ordered the closing of their meeting-houses unless the pastor prayed for King George.

In the 1720s the Episcopal Church (for it must now be regarded as a distinct and separate body[1]) was, like the Church of Scotland, troubled by dissension. Certain of its members favoured 'the Usages', but others, including the College of Bishops, opposed them as being ritualistic or even Romish; these usages included prayers for the dead, the mixing of water with the communion wine, and an invocation to the Holy Ghost. The controversy did not finally split the church, which, prior to 1745, enjoyed a fairly peaceful spell of life. It is reckoned that, with 130 pastors, it could at this time claim about half of the Scottish nobility, as well as a large measure of truly popular support in the north-east.

Renewed afflictions, more severe than any that had gone before, followed the failure of the 'Forty-five, for the constant devotion of the Scots Episcopalians to the exiled Stuarts cost their church the sympathy and protection of the Church of England, which was now staunchly Hanoverian. The statute of 1719, just mentioned, was reaffirmed with increased rigour, and, on top of that, all Episcopal pastors were required to be ordained only by an English or Irish bishop – not a Scottish one. These measures constituted a grievous blow, which badly shook the church. Though many nobles and lairds still adhered, the clergy, thoroughly discouraged, became fewer and fewer, while numerous members of the middle and lower classes, who had formerly worshipped with them, now joined the establishment. The Episcopalians, unwavering in their attachment to the Jacobite cause, were, largely because of that policy, at a low ebb by 1760.

Adherents to a man of the fallen dynasty, and deeply embroiled in all the risings, the Roman Catholics could expect no toleration in such a Protestant state as Scotland. If their fortunes did not decline steeply during the period, the reason was that they could scarcely have been lower at its opening. In fact, their numbers did fall off somewhat.

[1] The nineteenth century Episcopalian historian, George Grub, dates the separate existence of his Church from the year 1720, when, on the death of Bishop Rose, of Edinburgh, the last of the pre-Revolution prelates, the device was adopted of appointing John Fullarton to the see of Edinburgh and the office of 'Primus', or presiding bishop – a course that also was followed in later times. See G. Grub, *The Ecclesiastical History of Scotland* (1861), VOL. III, pp. 379-84.

It is estimated that, having flourished under James VII's rule, they amounted at the Revolution to about 50,000, or 5 per cent of the whole population. This figure dropped to around 40,000 by 1745, and a further decrease followed Culloden, which entailed slaughter, persecution and some emigration. In his unofficial census of 1755, Webster gave separate entries for those of the Romanist faith. Most of these lived in an area forming a broad band across north central Scotland, and were distributed among four shires, namely, Aberdeen, 2,288; Banff, 3,150; Inverness, 5,664; and Argyll, 4,329. All other counties fell short of 1,000, and even of 400, and the Scottish total was 16,490. Since these figures probably refer to communicants only, and since they may be slightly imperfect,[1] we should in all probability reckon the total Roman Catholic population at the close of our period as about 33,000, or 2·6 per cent of the whole.

Proscribed as it was, the Roman community was, for the first time since the Reformation, organised after a fashion. Thomas Nicholson was appointed vicar-apostolic for Scotland and consecrated bishop in 1694,[2] and in 1700 he divided the country into districts, with a missioner assigned to each. In 1703 there were, under Nicholson's charge, thirty-three clergymen – seventeen secular priests and sixteen 'regulars', including in all seven Irish. In 1731 two vicariates, each under its 'bishop', were formed, one for the north, or Highlands, and the other for the south, or Lowlands. Thenceforth the ministrations of the Romanist clergy could be conducted in a systematic way, though still forbidden by law.

[1] E.g. there were 'nil returns' from thirteen counties, and in these, or some of them, though the numbers would admittedly be small, it is certain that there must have been some who professed the Romanist faith.

[2] The request for this appointment had been made to Rome in 1687, when James VII's toleration was being enjoyed.

CHAPTER X

The Dawn of the Enlightenment

THE REVOLUTION, the Union and the Hanoverian succession, marking the passage from the seventeenth to the eighteenth century, afforded a greater degree of security from strife, promoted the peaceful pursuits of commerce and industry, and favoured a gentler and more comfortable mode of living. These improvements in turn rendered possible, along with increased wealth and leisure, an advance in education, literature and the arts; and this advance was itself helped by the fact that religion no longer dominated men's minds. The reigns of Queen Anne and the first two Georges accordingly yield a record of progress that is interrupted to a surprisingly small degree by the 'Fifteen and the 'Forty-five, large as these events may loom in the eyes of posterity.

Improvement in the schools was steady but very slow. No legislation concerning them was passed during the period, so that the statutory limits of the parish schoolmaster's annual stipend remained as they had been fixed by the Act of 1696 – roughly £5 11s. sterling as a minimum and £11 2s. as a maximum. In other respects too – the scholar's fees, the subjects taught and the master's additional emoluments – the practices of the seventeenth century, already described,[1] persisted into the eighteenth. For teachers and pupils alike, life was hard and austere. Single-room schools, damp, cold and draughty, were the rule, generally with earth-floors and often without desks. In many a village any building or odd room that happened to be available – the church itself perhaps, or a barn or stable – was made to serve the purpose, for heritors were reluctant to 'stent' themselves and the other parishioners as the Act required. And yet some advance is to be observed: according to a 'memorial' (or memorandum, as we should say) presented by the parish schoolmasters in 1748, their average annual income from all sources was then about £11 – little enough, but rather more than the bare statutory scale would suggest, even when allowance is made for their fee-revenue.

It was in the Highlands – far from the centres of wealth and trade, with large, scattered parishes, few roads, and Gaelic-speaking inhabitants who were as likely as not to be Episcopalians or Roman

[1] See *supra*, pp. 36-7.

Catholics – that the difficulties confronting an educational system based on Presbyterianism were truly daunting. There was little hope of the Highland parishes, from their own meagre resources, emulating the work of those of the Lowlands; and, in fact, very few of them had schools of any kind in 1700. A special problem demanded a special remedy, and it came in 1709, when there was founded the Society in Scotland for Propagating Christian Knowledge.[1] Supported by the subscriptions of nobles, judges, clergymen and others in England as well as Scotland, it was separate from the Church of Scotland, but enjoyed the help and sympathy of the General Assembly. Its object was to set up schools, and to appoint and pay schoolmasters, in those parts of the Highlands and Islands where the need was greatest. The task was boldly tackled, and by 1732 schools had been established in 109 parishes. A second charter empowered the Society, in 1738, to start spinning schools for girls, who were also to be taught to read. Thenceforth both sides of the work went on together. It was hampered by the old dislike of the Lowlander for the Gaelic (or 'Irish', as he scornfully called it) of the Highlander, but by 1758 this prejudice had been overcome to the extent that the Psalms and New Testament were published in a Gaelic translation. And the Society's efforts were helped, after 1752, by the labours of the Commissioners for the Forfeited Estates.[2]

In some of the better parish schools, a devoted teacher would, as before, prepare the talented boy for the university, but that function, in general, fell to the burgh or grammar schools, with their sustained, relentless 'drilling' in Latin. Henry Mackenzie, for example, attended Edinburgh High School from 1752 until 1757, when he was between the ages of seven and twelve. For four years he was in the class of one of the four assistant masters – for the grammar school followed a system similar to that of the university regents – and here he read mainly Virgil, Cicero and Horace; the fifth year he spent in the rector's class, studying Livy to improve his skill in Latin prose. School hours now ran from seven to nine, from ten to twelve, and from two to four, allowing breaks for breakfast and dinner.

Edinburgh's case was typical, though its curriculum was on the severe side; the grammar school as a rule needed four masters to do its work properly. From time to time, and in different places, some

[1] This is not to be confused with another body known as the 'S.P.C.K.' – the Society for Promoting Christian Knowledge, an Anglican body set up in 1699, for the establishment in England of charity schools, parish libraries and other Anglican institutions.

[2] See *infra*, pp. 153-5.

attempt was made to teach other subjects, such as Greek or French,[1] geography or drawing, while there were also increasing numbers of private teachers in these and similar branches. About mid-century, however, the idea was gaining ground that these intermittent efforts were not enough, and that systematic instruction in matters other than Latin language and literature should be offered, especially to the children of well-to-do townsfolk. Hence arose the 'academy', intended to supplement, rather than to rival, the work of the grammar school by providing for the 'modern' side of education. The academy was usually an endowed school, supported by the town council and a number of private subscribers, and charged fees as high as, or higher than, those of the grammar school. Its courses might include mathematics, physics, geography, mensuration, navigation and book-keeping. Scotland's first school of the new type dates to the close of our period: Perth Academy was founded in 1760.

Some of the private schools in the towns were for girls, but in general little provision was made for their education. We do hear of girls' schools, under the charge of a sewing-mistress, at Brechin (1722), Stirling (1726), Arbroath (1735), Forres (1736) and Wigtown (1757). Exceptionally, the schoolmistress at Dumfries taught pastry-making as well as sewing and embroidery (1719), while the Glasgow mistress gave instruction in the spinning of flax into yarn fine enough to make thread or cambric (1727). Elsewhere, no doubt, even more modest 'schools' for girls existed from time to time, without leaving behind a record of their work.

While progress at the schools was thus limited though real, the reforms at the universities were fundamental and sweeping. They began with the abolition of the antiquated and often denounced system of 'rotating regents', and the substitution therefor of 'fixed' professorships, which allowed specialists to give instruction in the branches in which they were expert. Attempts at change along these lines had been made in the seventeenth and early eighteenth centuries, but the reform was completed at Edinburgh in 1708 and at Glasgow in 1727; in each case the four regents gave way to professors of Greek, Logic, Moral Philosophy and Natural Philosophy. Chairs of Mathematics and Humanity (Latin) were already in being at both these centres, so that full provision was now made for the basic 'arts' or 'philosophy'

[1] French is known to have been taught long before our period in such larger towns as Edinburgh and Aberdeen, and there is record of instruction in that language at Haddington in 1731 and at Stirling in 1755.

course. The change from regencies to professorships was made at St Andrews in 1747 and at Marischal College, Aberdeen, in 1753. (King's College, Old Aberdeen, clung to the old rule until 1798.)

Theological and legal studies were meanwhile promoted by means of old, revived, or entirely new chairs in Divinity, Hebrew and Ecclesiastical History, and (at Edinburgh) in Civil Law, Public Law and Scots Law, but it was in medical teaching that the greatest advance took place. There were professorships of Medicine, real or nominal, at all the universities during the seventeenth century, and these were the starting-points for the later developments. By 1726 Edinburgh had set up a full Faculty of Medicine, with chairs of Botany, Medicine, Anatomy, Chemistry and Midwifery, and its famous Infirmary was started three years later. Though it was in competition with the 'extra-mural' Colleges of Surgeons and of Physicians, which leaned rather to practical training, the Edinburgh faculty was the first university 'school' of medicine in Britain, equipped to impart to students the whole existing range of medical theory and knowledge.

One further innovation was the necessary prelude to the eighteenth-century advances. The traditional Latin 'dictates' or 'prelections' were often not clearly understood by the students, despite the work of the grammar schools, and it was a notable triumph for common-sense when lectures in English displaced them. At Glasgow, Francis Hutcheson is recorded as having been, about the year 1730, among the first to take up the new mode. Though some old-fashioned teachers adhered for a time to their formal Latin readings, the change was before long generally adopted throughout the universities. This cleared the way for the use of newer text-books, and the antiquated Dutch commentators began to yield place to such 'moderns' as Newton in physics and Locke in philosophy.

With their structure and methods thus overhauled and reformed, the Scottish universities entered on a period of expansion and distinction. Edinburgh in particular, profiting from the fruitful principalship of William Carstares (1703-15), won renown for the brilliant gifts of its leading professors. The chair of Mathematics was filled by James Gregory ('the second') of the celebrated Aberdeen family, until his death in 1725, and thereafter by the equally talented Colin McLaurin.[1] Patrick Cuming brought lustre as professor of Divinity

[1] Of McLaurin one of his students, Alexander Carlyle, wrote, 'He made mathematics a fashionable study, which was felt afterwards in the war that followed in 1743, when nine-tenths of the engineers of the army were Scottish officers.'

(1737-62), as did John Stevenson during his long tenure of the chair of Logic (1730-75).

In medical education Edinburgh's success was outstanding. Alexander Monro, the first of three generations of men of the same name who were to hold the same chair in succession over a period of 126 years, was professor of Anatomy from 1720 to 1758, while William Cullen came over in 1755 from the Glasgow chair of Medicine to teach in Edinburgh (as his successor, Joseph Black, was to do in 1766). They and their colleagues built up Edinburgh's academic fame to the point where it became almost essential for the aspiring physician in England, Ireland or the colonies, as well as in Scotland, to undergo part of his training there.

Taking second place in medical studies, Glasgow outstripped Edinburgh in one branch – that of moral philosophy. As occupants of that chair, Francis Hutcheson (1731-46) and Adam Smith (1752-64) drew students from far afield by the high repute of their lectures. Their contemporary, Robert Simson, the mathematician,[1] who had another very long tenure (1711-61), won lasting fame as an Euclidean scholar: McLaurin was one of his many able disciples. James Moor, professor of Greek from 1746 to 1774, was the most eminent of Glasgow's classicists. At Aberdeen three more members of the Gregory family – father and two sons – successively held the post of 'mediciner', or professor of Medicine, at King's College (1725-73), where Thomas Reid, yet to make his mark in philosophy, was a most impressive and influential regent (1751-64).

The melancholy exception to the tale of achievement is supplied by St Andrews, which, stripped of its former glory as Scotland's ecclesiastical capital, was now sunk in apathy and decay. Daniel Defoe, in 1727, found St Salvator's College 'in its declining state and looking into its grave'. By the 1740s the University's top-heavy structure of three separate colleges for a total student-body ranging between 100 and 150 could no longer be justified. A partial solution was found in 1747, when St Salvator's and St Leonard's were combined as the United College, and the opportunity was taken to replace an excessive number of regents by six professors.

The most noteworthy building project of the period was the construction, begun in 1722, of houses for Glasgow's principal and its

[1] He is not to be confused with his uncle, John Simson, professor of Divinity from 1708 to 1740, who fell foul of the General Assembly for his unusual theological views: see *supra*, p. 97.

twelve professors: these formed a third quadrangle to complete the graceful Old College. For the students here and at Edinburgh, the reverse process held good: the days of 'living-in' were numbered, for it was impossible to accommodate in college chambers the 300 and upward youths who now sought courses in each of these cities. The practice of college residence was abandoned early in the eighteenth century, and students instead found lodgings in town, though for long the well-to-do were accustomed to board in the professors' houses. 'Living-in' was also abandoned at Marischal College by 1755, but it lingered on at King's College and at St Andrews into the early nineteenth century.

Along with residence in chambers, the old obligation to speak only in Latin, even in conversation, was dropped, as was the use of student censors to report the conduct of their fellows to the masters. One result of giving up the regent system was far from satisfactory. These men had been tutors, responsible for the whole education of their young charges, and, when they went, the students tended to pick and choose the courses that appealed to them, and not to trouble about graduation. A degree was not really essential for advancement; what mattered more was the favour of a wealthy patron, who could smooth the path for a talented youth.

The universities were now making a rich contribution to the cultural life of the nation. This is well exemplified in the career of Thomas Ruddiman (1674-1757). A Banffshire farmer's son, educated at his parish school and at King's College, Aberdeen, he became in turn schoolmaster, printer and librarian. His *Rudiments of the Latin Tongue* (1714) was, during much of the eighteenth and nineteenth centuries, the standard text-book in the grammar schools, his edition of the complete works of George Buchanan, in two large folio volumes (1714-15), is a marvel of delightful and legible typography, while he also published, in 1739, James Anderson's magnificent *Diplomata et Numismata Scotiae*, with beautifully clear engravings of charters and coins illustrative of Scottish history. Another aspect of this matter appears in the double achievement of the Foulis brothers, Robert (1707-76) and Andrew (1712-75), in starting a university press at Glasgow in 1743, whence issued a series of classical texts equally admired for their elegance and their accuracy, and in setting up their Academy of the Fine Arts within the Old College in 1754, with instruction in painting, engraving and sculpture. If financial success eluded this ambitious venture, complete triumph was to attend the arrangement whereby, in 1757, James Watt of Greenock, then in his twenty-second year, became mathematical instrument maker to the university and was given a workshop and lodgings in the college. He owed much to the friendly interest of Robert Dick, professor of Natural Philosophy, and Joseph Black, then professor of Anatomy; and much of consequence for Scotland and the world was to flow from the researches which his opportunities permitted.

Scottish prose of the period 1700-60 shows a markedly practical strain. This is apparent at the outset in the essays and speeches of Andrew Fletcher of Saltoun, which belong to the years 1698-1704 and contain, in their clear and direct pungency, more than a hint of the style of the great English masters of the time, Steele and Addison. Fletcher is best remembered for his reference to the 'very wise man' who 'believed if a man were permitted to make all the ballads he need not care who should make the laws of a nation'. His works are inspired by the patriotic sentiments and the political aims that governed his life.

It is again in keeping with the Scottish tradition that much attention should be given to historical writings. The Presbyterian view of what was then 'modern' history is presented by Robert Wodrow in his *History of the Sufferings of the Church of Scotland from the Restoration to the Revolution* (1721-22). On the other side of the fence stood Bishop Robert Keith, whose *History of the Affairs of the Church and State of Scotland* (1734) presents an Episcopalian account of the Reformation, while his *Catalogue of the Bishops of Scotland down to the Year 1688* (1755) is still of interest to scholars. Father Thomas Innes, a Roman Catholic priest, completes this trio with his *Critical Essay on the Ancient Inhabitants of . . . Scotland* (1729). Apart from their equally strong religious bias, all three are notable for the close attention they paid to original sources.

Practicality, too, is the keynote of the writings of one whose intellectual attainments were held in the highest regard by his contemporaries – Henry Home, who in 1752 became a judge under the title of Lord Kames. Best known to lawyers today for a series, beginning in 1728, of *Decisions of the Court of Session*, and for his *Principles of the Law of Scotland* (1754) and other legal works, he had a wider reputation in his own day. His *Essays on the Principles of Morality and Natural Religion* (1751) were his first offering in the field that, above all others, delighted the best minds in Glasgow and Edinburgh at mid-century – that of philosophy. But the philosophers of the time were realists: it was useful knowledge that they sought to expound.

As early as 1725 Francis Hutcheson[1] had published his *Inquiry into the Original of our Ideas of Beauty and Virtue*, and several other books came later, though he is now ranked higher as teacher than as writer. Not so David Hume, the great sceptic and free-thinker of the age, whose *Treatise of Human Nature* (1739-40) was the first of half a dozen works that he published on philosophical subjects during the reign of George II. The pronounced strain of atheism in his thinking, while it intrigued those who were like-minded, was a challenge to the divines and a scandal to many simple folk. His famous *Essay on Miracles* (1748), for example, closes with this passage:–

> We may conclude that the *Christian Religion* not only was at first attended with miracles, but even at this day cannot be believed by any reasonable person without one. Mere reason is insufficient to convince us of its veracity; and whoever is moved by *Faith* to assent to it is conscious of a continued miracle in his own person, which subjects all the principles of his understanding, and gives him a determination to believe what is most contrary to custom and experience.

Hutcheson's pupil, and a successor of his in Glasgow, was Adam Smith, whose 'prentice hand' may be seen in the fine phrases, philosophic disquisition and clear analysis of his *Theory of Moral Sentiments*, published in 1759.

Next to philosophy, the taste of the age ran to history. The year 1754 brought the first volume of Hume's *History of England*, to be followed by four others and so completed in 1761. Tory and royalist, averse to all popular movements aimed against good order and established authority, Hume was yet aware, as few historians then were, of the significance of social progress and changing customs. His book retained its popularity for many generations, and, both during and after his own lifetime, was reissued, often with added chapters by other hands,[2] in numerous editions. In 1759 William Robertson published his *History of Scotland*, covering the reigns of Queen Mary and of James VI down to 1603. Couched in calm, sensible and yet polished prose, free from passion or prejudice, and based on a study of first-hand evidence, his book was, like Hume's, an instantaneous success: thirteen editions were called for before his death in 1793 and even more after it.

[1] Though born in North Ireland, he was Scottish by descent and also by choice, spending much of his life in Glasgow.

[2] The favourite of these 'continuations', running from 1688 to 1760, was that of Tobias Smollett (shortly to be noticed); Smollett had already issued his own *Compleat History of England* (1757-58).

In 1760 Smith and Robertson were in their prime, with much of their best work yet to come, while Hume was busy on his *History* and even Lord Kames, then sixty-four years of age, had many fruitful years before him. Yet the age of 'polite letters' had already arrived. The Edinburgh *literati* had their Select Society, started in 1754 by Allan Ramsay, the younger (soon to be noticed); here the brightest wits of the day discussed topics ranging from passing political questions to the eternal verities. Again, the presentation of John Home's tragedy of *Douglas* on the Edinburgh stage in 1756 marks a milestone in the nation's cultural progress. Though the play had far less merit than was then thought, its author and its chief sponsors were clergymen, and yet they escaped with the lightest of censures from the Church for their 'frivolous' conduct. The event was rightly hailed as a victory for good sense and for 'Moderatism', a proof that the theatre was now respectable, and a sign that there was nothing sinful in decent amusement and the temperate enjoyment of leisure.

In England, meanwhile, Tobias Smollett had written his novels *Roderick Random* (1748) and *Peregrine Pickle* (1751), but these works link him rather with the world of Fielding, Richardson and Sterne than with his native Scotland. Smollett, like several other lettered Scots of his day, made sallies into English verse. The most talented of this small company was James Thomson, who wrote a lively pastoral poem, *The Seasons* (1726-30), and is even better known as the author of *Rule Britannia* (1740). Such works have little connection with any Scottish cult or tradition, and find their rightful place in the context of English literature.

The stream of Scottish vernacular poetry had become, as we have seen,[1] a mere trickle in the seventeenth century, and it might have been expected to dry up altogether in the rarefied atmosphere of the 'polite' philosophers and historians of the early Hanoverian age. The matter turned out quite otherwise, and the revival of interest and achievement in Scots dialect verse is one of the surprising features of the eighteenth century. In the initial phase of this truly popular movement, three names are outstanding. James Watson came first, with his *Choice Collection of Comic and Serious Scots Poems* (1706-11), including pieces as old as *Christis Kirk on the Green*, seventeenth-century verse like that of the Sempills, and a few contemporary poems. Among the last was 'Bonny Heck', recounting the dying words of a greyhound in the six-line 'Habbie Simson' metre, which was to be

[1] See *supra*, p. 42.

Burns's favourite. Its author was William Hamilton of Gilbertfield, who, in 1722, published an edition of Blind Harry's 'Wallace', which, in due time, was to be one of the sources of Burns's poetic and patriotic inspiration.

Hamilton carried on with Allan Ramsay (1686-1758), the third and most important of the group, an exchange of sprightly 'epistles' in the six-line metre, and here again we detect a foreshadowing of Burns, for this type of poetic exercise was to attract him, impelling him to emulate and excel the work of his predecessors. Ramsay was highly praised for *The Gentle Shepherd* (1725), a pastoral which, though graced with pleasant scenes of Scottish rural life, owes more to English models. It is what he did for vernacular poetry that is of deep significance. A wig-maker and bookseller,[1] he was one of Edinburgh's 'characters', hitting off, in satires or elegies, in comic poems or lampoons, the personalities and episodes of the colourful street and tavern life of the capital. In the *Evergreen* (1724), he reissued many poems of Henryson, Dunbar and other largely forgotten 'makars'. His *Tea-table Miscellany* (1724-32) is a collection of Scots songs, some old, some new, and some adapted or re-written, Ramsay himself being the author of many of them. His realism and his warm human sympathies, his caustic wit and his lyrical gift, marking him as a true forerunner of Burns, are seen at their best in 'Bessy Bell and Mary Gray', in 'This is no my ain House', in 'For the Sake of Somebody', and in the 'Elegy on Maggy Johnstoun' (a well-known ale-wife), from which this stanza is taken –

> When we were wearied at the gowff
> Then Maggy Johnstoun's was our howff; [*meeting-place*
> Now a' our gamesters may sit dowff, [*gloomy*
> Wi' hearts like leid;
> Death wi' his rung rax'd her a yowff [*fetched her a blow*
> And sae she deid.

The 'Forty-five rising made a strong appeal to the song-writers of Scotland, but its hopes and fears were only to be enshrined in many lovely lyrics long after the events had become a cherished memory. The one well-known Jacobite song that belongs to the time of the rebellion is 'Hey, Johnnie Cope, are ye waukin' yet?', a bantering skit

[1] It was in his bookshop that he started, in 1725, the first circulating library in Scotland. Passing through various hands and increasing to over 30,000 volumes, this library was used by many of Edinburgh's literary lights of the time and survived into the nineteenth century.

on the tardy tactics of the Hanoverian general at Prestonpans; it was composed by Adam Skirving, a farmer of the neighbourhood.

In another direction the rising had some immediate literary results. The poetry of the Gael had hitherto belonged to Irish rather than Scottish letters, but the separation of Scots Gaelic from the Irish or Erse language was now complete, and the Jacobite cause engaged the interest of the Highland bards. In 1751 appeared the first literary work to be printed in Gaelic, the intensely patriotic and martial verse of the Jacobite, Alexander Macdonald. A little time passed before the appearance of the collected poems of Duncan Ban MacIntyre (1768), including satires and elegies, love-songs and vivid descriptions of Highland scenery. Though he had fought with the government forces, some of his work was tinged with Jacobite sentiment. Another strain, that of the belated impact on Gaeldom of the Protestant faith and teaching, appears in Dugald Buchanan's hymns, which, published in 1767, were very popular in the north and were often reprinted and translated. The third quarter of the century thus saw the flowering of Gaelic culture as a further element in a many-sided literary renaissance.

Most of the newspapers of the period were weekly publications, though the more daring ventures were bi-weekly or tri-weekly. Many, indeed the great majority, of the projects were short-lived. There was, for example, a *Courant* at Edinburgh in 1705, which ran for fifteen years, and another at Glasgow in 1715, which lasted for only six months; some had even briefer runs. Four papers, however, made their mark and each survived for more than a century. The *Edinburgh Evening Courant*, unconnected with the similar titles of the time, began in 1718 and the *Caledonian Mercury* in 1720.[1] The *Glasgow Journal* was launched in 1741, and in 1760 it absorbed yet another *Courant*, which had been started in the western city in 1745. The *Aberdeen Journal*, beginning in 1747, was destined to be the longest liver of all, for it is still with us as the *Press and Journal*.

The record of the magazines was not dissimilar. The careers of the *Tatler* (1711) and the *Edinburgh Review* (1755) were very short, but one periodical showed real hardihood. This was the *Scots Magazine*, started in January 1739 as a monthly, each issue usually extending to forty-eight pages and priced at sixpence. Its scope is indicated in the wording of the title-page of the first volume: '. . . containing a General View of the Religion, Politicks, Entertainment, &c. in Great

[1] The *Mercury* was for some time printed and published by Thomas Ruddiman, already mentioned (*supra*, p. 109).

Britain, and a Succint Account of Publick Affairs, Foreign and Domestick, for the Year MDCCXXXIX'. With its prose and verse, its essays and reports, its extracts from and reviews of books, it fulfilled the promise of its title reasonably well and became an established literary institution. Its bound volumes, forming a vast array, are now a valuable source of information on all aspects of life in the eighteenth century.

Scottish ability has never been so pronounced in the arts as in letters, but a few minor achievements belong to our period. In architecture, the link between the seventeenth and eighteenth centuries is supplied by the stately pile of Hopetoun House, in West Lothian, which was begun in 1698 from the design of Sir William Bruce, the re-builder of Holyroodhouse, and was later completed, to a modified plan, by William Adam, who was to hand on to his gifted sons his taste for the 'Palladian' style in country mansions.

Sir John Medina, a Spanish portrait-painter who had settled in Edinburgh, was still at work in the first decade of the new century. His follower, William Aikman (1682-1731), after observing the fashion of an extended tour of the Continent, came back resolved to try to do for Scotland what Sir Godfrey Kneller had done for England. His many portraits of literary and political leaders were highly regarded in his own day, though it is unfortunately true that lack of demand at home impelled him to leave Edinburgh for London in 1723. He was followed in his turn by Allan Ramsay, the son of the poet (1713-84). After the customary period of training in London and Rome, young Ramsay, between 1740 and 1756, devoted himself to the making of likenesses of such of the lords and ladies, judges and lairds, as were willing to commission his brush; but he, too, responded to the lure of London, where he became a fashionable portraitist and a special favourite of George III. His portraits of Duncan Forbes, the third Duke of Argyll, the famous Earl of Bute, Flora Macdonald, Gibbon, Hume and Rousseau are among his better-known works; but his departure for the south left Scotland, for all its acknowledged leadership in polite literature, an almost barren field in respect of the fine arts.

CHAPTER XI

The Reign of George III

THE ACCESSION of George III in October 1760 brought to the throne the first of the Hanoverian line who could be called a native rather than a German monarch: 'I glory', he said, 'in the name of Britain', and he meant what he said. The event opened a new era for Scotland. The testing-time of the union of the two countries was past, and no issue was now likely to divide them. In the international sense, too, Great Britain presented a solid front, and Scotland was beginning to take a real share in the burdens – especially the military burdens – of Empire. In the Seven Years War (1756-63), Highland regiments were serving with distinction; among them, Fraser's Highlanders fought with particular gallantry in the Quebec campaign of 1759. Here James Murray (later to be governor of Canada) was brigadier in Wolfe's army, and his successor in command. Another Scot, Admiral Sir James Douglas, captured Dominica, in the West Indies, in 1761.

Political and military unity, it is safe to say, had been achieved by 1760, and the amalgamation of the two states was an accepted condition of public life. But a true union of hearts and minds had yet to be reached. Mutual suspicion, inherited from centuries of hostility and confirmed by recent civil strife, had bred misunderstanding between the nations. To the Londoner, the Scot was not only poor, backward and rude: he was also a Jacobite, open or concealed. To the Scotsman, the 'auld enemy' was rich and arrogant, cruel and heartless. The best men in each nation were superior to such vulgar notions, but popular prejudice died hard on both sides of the border.

The political changes of the early years of the new reign were to fan the flames of reciprocal distrust. The great English war minister, William Pitt, 'the architect of victory', was at the height of his power and fame. Leaving the old Duke of Newcastle as nominal head of the government and director of the party machine, he attended to affairs of state and the conduct of the war. But George III was determined to rule as well as to reign, and this meant some abridgment of the powers of the Whig magnates. For this purpose the king's chosen instrument was John Stuart, third Earl of Bute (1713-92), who had been his tutor and was now his political adviser; he was a Tory of the new stamp, perfectly loyal to the house of Hanover.

It was mainly through the king's influence that Bute entered the cabinet in March 1761, as one of the secretaries of state (Pitt being the other). Convinced that the time had come to make a just and profitable peace with France, Bute induced some of his colleagues, partly by argument, partly by intrigue, to adopt his policy. The resignation of Pitt, who thought that Britain ought to fight on, in October 1761, followed by that of Newcastle in May 1762, left Bute as unchallenged head of the ministry. His premiership lasted for less than a year, but in that period he accomplished the king's twin aims of breaking the solidarity of the Whigs and ending the war. The Treaty of Paris (February 1763), transferring from France Canada and many island colonies, adding Florida to the North American dominions, and strengthening the British hold in India, was a reasonable enough settlement, but even better terms might have been secured, and some concessions avoided, by a firmer stand in the negotiations. The common people undoubtedly thought so, and they believed that the true champion of British interests was Pitt, who had been sacrificed, and not Bute, who had taken his place by devious means and for unworthy ends.

The fury of the ordinary Englishman, and particularly of the Londoner, spread from Bute to all his fellow-countrymen, and the Scots acquired an evil name as servile, miserly, treacherous and corrupt. Now, Bute had many friends and clients, hangers-on and job-seekers, while London itself was often the goal of the ambitious Scot, whether he sought professional advancement or commercial profit. The presence in the capital of such people was apt to draw upon them the jeers and taunts of the mob. Bute's coach was attacked on the street and even Scottish serving officers were exposed to public insults. Moreover, the northern nation was still not allowed a militia for its defence, though it is fair to add that opinion in Scotland itself was divided when the proposal was revived in 1762,[1] some objecting to it on the ground of expense and some for its bad effect on the supply of labour. In London two rascally agitators, John Wilkes and Charles Churchill, did their utmost to increase popular hatred of 'the grasping Scot', who was held in lower esteem in the years 1761-75 than ever before or since.

[1] The Act of 1757 had applied to England alone, and a similar bill for Scotland had been defeated in 1760, before the death of George II.

After Bute came a series of English prime ministers and purely English cabinets: from 1763, no Scotsman served in the successive administrations of Grenville, Rockingham, Chatham, Grafton and North, until, in October 1779, David Murray, Viscount Stormont and later earl of Mansfield, became a secretary of state. Admittedly, Bute was supposed to exercise a sinister 'backstairs influence' long after his withdrawal from office, but this gossip ceased to have any truth after 1765. In the middle of this period of Scottish eclipse occurred a famous lawsuit which shows Anglo-Scottish relations in a strange light.

Archibald, first and last duke of Douglas, had died childless in 1761; his title died with him, but his vast estates were a tempting prize for the lucky claimant. In 1746 his sister, Lady Jane Douglas, then in her forty-ninth year, had privately married John Stewart (later Sir John Stewart of Grandtully). In 1748, when she was over fifty years of age, she had given birth, at Paris and in obscure circumstances, to twin sons, one of whom had died. The estates were now (in 1761) claimed on behalf of the surviving son, Stewart Douglas. His mother's demise had occurred in 1753, his father died in 1764, and the romantic marriage and the orphan's claim caught the public fancy. The Douglas name was popular in Scotland, that of Hamilton was not, and, if the boy's suit failed, the estates would pass to the Duke of Hamilton. The Court of Session was sharply divided over the protracted 'Douglas cause', and in July 1767 gave its verdict, by the casting vote of Lord President Dundas, against the boy. The judges known to have favoured (as it seemed) the Hamilton interest were in danger from the violent temper of the Edinburgh mob. The appeal was taken to the House of Lords, who, in February 1769, reversed the Scottish court's decision, to the exuberant delight of the people of Edinburgh. 'Mr Douglas'[1] was a popular hero, the Hamilton faction was curbed, and the truth had prevailed, all thanks to the House of Lords – a very different picture from the outcome of the Greenshields case sixty years earlier.[2]

In the world of politics, the king was still determined to break the power of the Whigs and, by means of his own followers, 'the king's friends', to direct the government himself. When, in 1770, his most dependable servant in Parliament, Lord North, became prime minister, George III had gone far to attain this end. In overseas matters,

[1] He had no claim to the title and never was a Scots peer, though in 1790 he became a peer of Great Britain as Lord Douglas of Douglas.

[2] See *supra*, p. 94.

meanwhile, most of the politicians were agreed that the American colonists should help to defray imperial costs. Their contribution was to be exacted, even if this meant driving them into rebellion, and this is precisely what happened in 1775 as the climax to a series of foolish mistakes and tragic misunderstandings. Though these domestic and colonial policies drew forth much opposition at home, it was remarked that very little of this stemmed from 'North Britain', where both George III's personal rule and the war against the colonists were popular.

Scotland's contribution to the military forces in the war of 1775-83 was greater than in the previous conflict. Six complete regiments of Highlanders[1] were enrolled in the years 1777-78. Among the Scots commanders overseas, Sir Charles Douglas relieved Quebec in 1776, Sir Hector Munro captured Pondicherry in India in 1778, and Sir George Eliott won fame by his heroic defence of Gibraltar for over three years (1779-82). The hazards of war came uncomfortably close when John Paul Jones, an American naval officer born in Scotland, raided the Kirkcudbrightshire coast in 1778 and threatened a descent on the shores of the Firth of Forth in 1779. Despite such dangers, several fresh proposals to form a Scottish militia were again rejected, though three regiments of 'fencibles' were raised for home defence in case of invasion.

The attitude of the Scottish M.P.s to the line of conduct of the king and Lord North remained much less hostile than that of their English colleagues, whose resistance to royal dictation reached its peak in April 1780, when John Dunning put forward his famous resolution, that 'the influence of the Crown has increased, is increasing, and ought to be diminished'. In an angry mood, the House of Commons passed the motion by 233 votes to 215 (a large muster for a division in those days), but only 7 Scots were in the majority, 23 were against Dunning's move, and the remaining 15 were absent. Clearly there were many 'king's friends' among the 45 members from beyond Tweed.

The reasons for Scotland's ready acquiescence in the king's plans for directing the affairs of both parliament and colonies are to be sought in the system of 'management'. Until his death in 1761, Archibald, third duke of Argyll, had 'managed' Scotland, and from that date until 1765 Bute (who was Argyll's nephew) wielded control,

[1] Included among them were the Highland Light Infantry (originally called Macleod's Highlanders) and the first formation of the Seaforth Highlanders.

in or out of office. In the next phase, while no immediate successor of like calibre appeared, the chief influence rested with the lord advocate of the day, who generally saw to it that the Scots members clung together and voted as a bloc. In the elections of 1774 Midlothian returned Henry Dundas, a member of a well-known legal family. With his appointment next year as lord advocate the way was open for the classic example of Scottish 'manager'.

The defective workings of the political machine in Scotland, partly inherited from the pre-1707 constitution, partly induced by the parliamentary union itself, became acute and glaring in the reign of George III, causing general apathy or cynicism towards the questions of the day. In the counties the franchise, as settled in 1681,[1] was confined to those entitled to hold in chief from the Crown land worth £400 Scots (£33 6s. 8d. sterling) per annum. In the eighteenth century the lawyers had discovered and the courts had agreed that a qualification to vote could be created by the conveyance, say to a kinsman or friend, of the bare title or 'superiority' of land of the stipulated value, without giving actual possession or use of the land. In this way, especially in the years 1770-90, large numbers of 'parchment barons' were given 'fictitious votes' in order to augment the voting power and political influence of a landowning family. Even with such additions, the county electorate was not large. In 1788 Ayr had 220 shire voters, Fife 188, Aberdeen 158, and the rest smaller numbers, down to Clackmannan with 16, Bute with 12, and Cromarty with only 6. In all Scotland there were 2,624 qualified electors, and very nearly half of them were 'parchment barons'; they thus formed a body of men who, by reason of their numbers and composition, readily lent themselves to intrigue and 'management'.

Of the royal burghs, Edinburgh alone returned its own member, the other sixty-five being grouped in fourteen districts of burghs. Here the objections were twofold. The towns that were not royal burghs were excluded from the burghal franchise, and merged instead in their shires; and among them were some growing and flourishing places, like Leith, Paisley, Greenock, Kilmarnock and Falkirk. Secondly, in the royal burghs only the magistrates and councillors had any say in the choice of the members, and the town councils were self-elective and indeed self-perpetuating. Their numbers varied between a dozen in the smaller burghs and just over thirty in Edinburgh and Glasgow, and averaged not much more than twenty. Hence there

[1] See *supra*, p. 17.

were some 1,400 men in all Scotland with a share in the burgh franchise.

In the shires the political game of 'making interest' was played according to its rules. In general, no money actually changed hands, but an astute politician, known to have influence 'at court', gathered support by undertaking to use state patronage in favour of the voter – rewarding him, for example, or his son or nephew, with a commission in the army or navy, or perhaps a post in the customs or excise, or a clerkship in the East India Company. By faithfully observing his unwritten (or even unspoken) promise, the politician remained sure of a loyal local following. In the burghs the methods were cruder. The bailies and councillors could be, and indeed expected to be, bribed. Even such an admirable candidate as George Dempster of Dunnichen, a good landlord and a good patriot, had to pay, it is said, £10,000 in 1761 for his election by the Perth burghs, and his political debts were a crippling burden throughout his life.

In this tangled domain of tacit understandings and customary rewards, Dundas moved with skill and confidence. The fall of North in 1782 made way for a number of short-lived ministries and for the acknowledgment of American independence in the Treaty of Versailles (September 1783). Amid the confusion of parliamentary politics, Dundas chose wisely by espousing the cause of William Pitt, the second son of the great war minister, then in his twenty-fifth year. Dundas's control over the Scottish members, and his influence with the peers, were invaluable to young Pitt, whose administration, starting in December 1783, was at first shaky, though it was to last for over 17 years. Dundas was given the treasurership of the navy, a lucrative office which he had already held for a short time. While not yet in the cabinet, he was, as acknowledged 'manager' of Scotland and as Pitt's able lieutenant, a powerful figure in the political world.

Although Pitt and Dundas were later to be labelled 'Tories', this was not true of their early careers. From 1780 there was much talk in England of parliamentary reform, and Pitt was one of the chief spokesmen of this cause. In 1782 and again in 1783, while in opposition, he put proposals for reform before the Commons, and in 1785, as prime minister, he introduced a bill which would have disfranchised some of the decayed boroughs of England and brought in some of the larger and newer towns. Defeated on each occasion, he gave up the project. In 1775 Dundas had spoken in favour of rejecting fictitious shire votes, but he, too, changed his mind later on such matters.

Radical opinions were meanwhile gaining ground in Scotland

generally. Many of the weavers were known to be of an independent cast of mind; the seceders were accustomed to question the basis of authority in church and state; the American struggle for freedom had its sympathisers on this side of the Atlantic; and the English reform movements had some impact north of the Tweed. There was agitation among the voters in certain shires between 1783 and 1790, though little was achieved, and some Scots were advocating reform of the burgh franchise from 1782. From 1784 attention was mainly directed to the abuses of municipal government, including the domination or open seizure of the burgh magistracies by local peers, collusive sales of the common lands, and fraudulent contracts for burgh works. Opposed by the town councils, the Convention of Royal Burghs, and the ministry in London, the reformers were yet able to induce the English Whig, Richard Brinsley Sheridan, to champion their views in Parliament. From 1787 Sheridan presented petitions and motions in favour of popular elections for the Scottish town councils, but the delaying tactics of Dundas put off a decision from year to year. Finally, in 1793, the project, along with every other idea of reform, was set aside in view of the situation in France.

From its start on 14 July 1789, the French Revolution stimulated progressive movements elsewhere and was greeted with enthusiasm by all reformers. Letters of congratulation were sent to France, political clubs became lively and meetings were frequent and spirited. The Society of Friends of the People, already at work in England, spread into Scotland in the summer of 1792. Its modest aims included annual parliaments and manhood suffrage, and its members were mostly law-abiding and orderly, but its activities were confused with those of more extreme societies. When, on 1 February 1793, just eleven days after the execution of Louis XVI, the French republic declared war on Britain, reform came to be viewed as akin to sedition or treason. Men of property feared that the rising tide of democracy, if not checked, would, in the French manner, sweep away the admirable British constitution.

By this time Dundas, having become home secretary in 1791, was virtually undisputed master of Scotland. The landed families felt obliged to him for past favours, in the shape of posts, pensions and promotions. He was popular despite his blustering ways and his reputation as an intriguer. He had even contrived to endear himself to the Highland chiefs by restoring the forfeited estates in 1784.[1]

[1] See *infra*, p. 155.

'King Harry the Ninth' was determined to show no leniency to Whig or radical critics of the régime: the 'Dundas despotism' was to be the government's retort to the French 'reign of terror'. In this resolve he had the full support of the law and especially of the notorious Lord Braxfield, the lord justice clerk, who presided over farcical trials and pronounced savage sentences with undisguised glee. In the autumn of 1793 the two chief victims, Thomas Muir, a lawyer, and Thomas Fyshe Palmer, a clergyman, were sentenced to transportation for fourteen and seven years respectively.[1]

Repression continued in the next two years. Three more offenders were transported and one was executed, but the extremists still spoke wildly of arming the people and setting up a republic. The English Habeas Corpus Act was suspended in 1794, as was the similar Scottish statute of 1701 'against Wrongous Imprisonment'. The legal definitions of 'treasonable practices' and 'seditious meetings' were extended in 1795. From 1797 the place of the 'Friends of the People' was taken by the less respectable 'United Scotsmen', in alliance with the avowed rebels of the 'United Irishmen'.[2] The leader of this new radical movement, George Mealmaker, a Dundee weaver, was transported for fourteen years and the society, suppressed in 1799, dwindled and disappeared from view.

For home defence against the threat of French invasion, seven regiments of 'fencibles' were formed in 1793, while from 1794 'volunteers', including 'yeomanry' (or cavalry), were ready to relieve the regular troops if required; Burns at Dumfries and Scott at Edinburgh were among these volunteers. In 1797, a greater effort being called for, a Scots militia was at long last authorised to be raised by ballot. Opposition to this measure of conscription turned on the fear that, once enrolled, militiamen might be posted for foreign service, and on the resentment caused by the exemption of the volunteers from the ballot; the latter, since they had to provide their own equipment, were drawn from the wealthier citizens. Riots broke out, and, in suppressing the disturbance at Tranent, the soldiers killed eleven men. Four further sentences of transportation were imposed and the Militia Act was reluctantly accepted by the sullen masses.

[1] Transportation, involving the hazards and afflictions of the long voyage to Australia, was often regarded as akin to a slow death sentence.

[2] The aims of the United Irishmen were to co-operate with the French for the establishment of a republic, and the United Scotsmen, many of whom were actually Irish, formed small secret societies bound by oath to pursue the same conspiratorial objectives.

The nation shared fully in the trials and triumphs of the war, the fifth Anglo-French conflict of the century. From 1794 the military effort was directed, with by no means uniform success, by Dundas as secretary of state for war. Once more a large number of Scottish regiments were raised, and to this recruiting drive are to be ascribed the beginnings of the Camerons (1793), the Gordons (1794) and the Argyll and Sutherland Highlanders (1794 and 1800). Overseas, the initial assault that led to the first capture of the Dutch colony of Cape of Good Hope in 1795 was headed by two Scotsmen, Vice-Admiral George Keith Elphinstone and Major-General Sir James Craig, and the core of their force was supplied by a battalion of the 78th regiment (the Ross-shire Buffs, later the Seaforths). Among other Scottish commanders in the field were Admiral Adam Duncan, the victor of Camperdown in 1797, and Sir Ralph Abercromby, who finally defeated the French army in Egypt at Alexandria in 1801. Peace came in March 1802 with the Treaty of Amiens, but it was recognised as being simply a breathing-space between wars.

The tone of political life changed with the new century. Republican agitators, drilling secretly with pikes to be ready to surprise Edinburgh castle, gave way to more respectable reformers. The Whigs had suffered eclipse during the years of repression, but they were again putting the reasoned case for constitutional reform. Their leaders were Henry Erskine and Francis Jeffrey, two sober and intelligent lawyers; the former had publicly protested against the arbitrary legislation of 1795, and had been deposed from the deanship of the faculty of advocates. In 1802 the Scottish Whigs founded the *Edinburgh Review*, a periodical which put equal stress on political aims and literary grace, and which exercised great influence in the direction of progress and rational change.

The war broke out again in May 1803, to last for eleven years and to be the longest in British history. Pitt, out of office since 1801, was recalled as premier in May 1804, and Dundas, now Viscount Melville, served under him as first lord of the admiralty. He was as strong as ever in Scotland, and his many friends were astounded and shocked when the House of Commons, in April 1805, censured him[1] for having misapplied public funds while acting as treasurer of the navy. He immediately resigned his office and faced impeachment. In June 1806, after fifteen days of trial, the House of Lords acquitted him of

[1] The votes were equal – 216 on each side – and the motion to censure was carried by the Speaker's casting vote.

all charges. This news was joyfully received in Scotland, where many hastened to celebrate with public dinners and congratulations to their hero, but his political reputation was gone and he did not again seek office, though his popularity remained high. The evidence suggests that he had acted with culpable negligence, but without fraudulent intent.

Pitt's death in January 1806 caused the break-up of his administration and the formation of 'the ministry of all the talents', mainly Whig but partly Tory; it was noted for its abolition of the slave trade in March 1807 and it was followed by a further long period of Tory rule (1807-30). The main concern was the conduct of the war against Napoleon, who had been declared Emperor in May 1804. The military forces deployed against him were large, Britain's contribution was substantial as well as steady, and the Scottish contingents naturally played a big part, especially in the Peninsular War and the final campaign of 1815. The charge of the Scots Greys at Waterloo to the cry of 'Scotland for Ever', with men of the Gordons clinging to their legs or stirrups, is one of the army's epic legends, and more Scottish regiments show 'Waterloo' among their battle honours than do not.[1] Among the generals of the time were Sir David Baird, the second captor of Cape of Good Hope (1806), and Sir John Moore, the hero of the famous retreat to Corunna (1809).

Melville died in 1811 and his son, Robert Dundas, who had already held minor offices, succeeded to the peerage and also became unofficial 'manager' of Scotland, though with powers greatly reduced from those enjoyed by his father at his height. Next year the second Viscount got his father's old office of first lord of the admiralty, and he held it throughout Liverpool's long ministry (1812-27). Slowly, however, the Whigs were gaining ground. The return of peace on Napoleon's first abdication in 1814 made possible an enormous gathering in Edinburgh for the purpose of petitioning against West Indian slavery; this was, in the words of Henry Cockburn, the Whig lawyer, 'the first assembly of the people for a public object that had occurred here for about twenty years'. In February 1816 an avowedly political meeting, to petition Parliament against the income tax, was held in the same city. In January 1817 the *Scotsman*, a newspaper that was

[1] It is shown by these two regiments, and also by the Scots Guards, the Royal Scots, the Black Watch, the H.L.I. (since 1958 the Royal Highland Fusiliers) and the Camerons (who, as this book goes to press, are being amalgamated with the Seaforths as the Queen's Own Highlanders).

both respectable and Whig, started weekly publication; it soon had a large circulation and acquired authority as the voice of reform. And from 1819 the cause of burgh reform was again being advocated, in a manner to be examined later.[1]

The demands now being made for annual parliaments and universal suffrage were sincere, but much of the discontent sprang from lack of work and lack of bread, for the last four years of George III's reign were clouded by scarcity and unemployment, post-war depression and social unrest. There were rumours of the starving masses drilling and taking unlawful oaths, and measures were passed in 1817, and again in 1819, to suppress seditious meetings, the possession of arms, and irregular military exercises. At the trials of the time, in contrast to the days of Muir and Palmer, the new generation of able Whig lawyers defended the accused with such success that light sentences were imposed, oi the charges were dismissed or dropped. Towards the close of 1819 there was special fear of disturbances by the Glasgow weavers, and elaborate military precautions were taken in Edinburgh and elsewhere to deal with the 'Radical War' and (to quote Cockburn again) to meet 'an army much talked of but never seen'. It had still to be seen (though the rumours persisted) when, on 29 January 1820, the old king died in the sixtieth year of his reign, the longest thus far recorded in Scottish, English or British history.

[1] See *infra*, chap. xvii, especially pp. 188-91.

CHAPTER XII

The Start of the Industrial Revolution

IN THE year 1759 two Englishmen, John Roebuck and Samuel Garbett, and one Scot, William Cadell, formed a partnership and started to build an ironworks at Carron, near Falkirk, some 2½ miles from the Firth of Forth. And in that year an Act of Parliament empowered the town council of Glasgow to cleanse, enlarge and improve the channel of the river Clyde. Though the significance of the date and of the events did not at once impress itself, we can now see that they serve, better perhaps than any others, to mark the first stirrings of a vast and protracted economic change that was going to transform the country and the people, their work, their play and their mode of life.

The very term 'Industrial Revolution' did not come into use until long after the time we are considering,[1] and is indeed open to the criticism that, when examined in detail, the changes involved are seen to have been gradual, widespread and cumulative – in a word, they were evolutionary. Far from being localised or datable, they have been, are being, or will be adopted in all parts of the world, for they amount simply to the application of scientific knowledge to every branch of economic activity – in the words of the economist, to the production, distribution and exchange of goods – with the emphasis laid on the use of machines to perform work for man.

Despite its world-wide reach, it can truly be said that the Industrial Revolution took its rise in England, which had, in the eighteenth century, many advantages over other countries. England enjoyed internal peace, along with such a degree of civic freedom as to favour the growth of a spirit of progress. Her skilled craftsmen formed a pool of intelligent workers from whose midst inventors were likely to spring. She had accumulated mercantile wealth, ready for investment, and she had both colonial resources and easy access to tropical products. Coal and iron, vital for the new age, were to hand, while her very lack of timber stimulated the quest for other fuels. No rival could match

[1] The term first came into general use with the publication in 1884 of Arnold Toynbee's *Lectures on the Industrial Revolution in England*, but it had been devised some fifty years earlier by the French economist, Jerome A. Blanqui. The term itself was something of a challenge by the new kind of 'economic' historian to the 'academic' historian, with his abiding interest in purely 'political' revolutions.

these varied assets, so that, by about 1750, England led the way with a clear start over all others.

Scotland shared some of these advantages, but not all. She had ample mineral deposits, water power and (since 1707) trading opportunities, but she lacked expert craftsmanship and investment capital. Yet foreign workers could be and had been brought in to impart their skills to the natives, while, as we have seen,[1] fortunes were being made from improved farming, the domestic linen trade and the shipment of tobacco. Her great human asset was the wide diffusion of education among the people, which made them adaptable workers and good learners. Thus, while Scotland's full entry to the Industrial Revolution was inevitably later than that of England, the time-lag was not long – say, about one generation (1750-83).

There was steady progress between 1759 and 1822 in some branches, notably agriculture, linen-making, the coal and iron industries, and banking; but other branches received, from time to time, such a stimulus as almost to justify the term 'revolutionary'. One such critical period was the 1780s, when the new and partially mechanised cotton industry took firm root, road transport was greatly speeded up, and commercial enterprise was given a fresh direction, while the canals that were to become prime carriers were nearing completion. Another forward surge came in 1812 with the harnessing of steam-power, the outstanding technical achievement of the age, for the propulsion of ships. Hence the picture of the first phase of the Industrial Revolution presents a background of sustained but gradual advance, and, in the foreground, a few dramatic leaps and onward plunges that changed the pace and course of economic progress.

Agriculture, still the leading 'industry', engaged, at the close of our period (1822), about one-third of the population. High profits and increased rent-rolls now depended on the adoption of the newer techniques – the enclosing, drilling and draining of fields, the fallow year, the cultivation of turnips, potatoes, artificial grasses and clover, the use of lime and manures, the orderly breeding and feeding of stock, and the employment of the best available implements. The whole temper of the age inclined the landowner towards these accepted rules of good husbandry, which a farmer could neglect only to his own loss. To call any land 'unimproved' now beyond a doubt implied a grave reproach, but to reclaim the waste justified a little boasting. Thus George Dempster, the Angus laird, wrote in 1793: 'The best crop of

[1] See *supra*, chap. vii.

barley, not bear, in this parish is now in the stook on the summit of the hill of Dunnichen 750 feet above the level of the sea.'

Certain developments helped to promote the agrarian reforms. About 1764 James Small of Berwickshire perfected a 'swing' or 'chain' plough.[1] Lighter and shorter than the cumbersome old 'Scotch plough', it had a narrow, tapering head that cut and turned the soil with half the effort, and it could be managed by one man with two horses (instead of three men with ten or twelve oxen). Though the Scotch plough was still used in heavy, strong soils, Small's model was preferred for the cleaner fields of the 'improved' estates. A later refinement was that of the all-iron plough, while the threshing machine, invented in 1786 by Andrew Meikle, millwright of Dunbar, before long displaced the flail. Again, the Entail Act of 1770 made it easier for landlords to give their tenants long leases and, with them, a sense of security that might induce them to undertake costly works. For the benefit of the industrious farmer, too, the Highland and Agricultural Society, founded in 1784, 'pooled' the latest information on agrarian improvements.

The politics of the time seemed to favour the farming interest. The French wars, especially that of 1803-14, assured the market for farm produce by making foreign imports scarce and dear by reason of the shipping hazards. It was profitable as well as patriotic to grow grain and raise beef, so that in the year 1814 as many as 140,000 acres were under wheat. The return of peace looked like ending this 'protected' market, but the farmer was saved, in his own view, from this threat by the new Corn Law of 1815,[2] which forbade the importation of foreign corn unless and until the home price reached the high level of 80s. a quarter.[3] In the unreformed Parliament the landowning interest was strongly represented, and this measure, devised and retained against protests, obliged the growing mass of townsfolk to buy dear bread and so to sustain the home farmer against his overseas competitors.

Despite the war-time urge to grow grain, farmers in each area did tend to concentrate on what suited soil and climate. Berwickshire and

[1] Two earlier models, the Rutherglen plough (*c.* 1743) and the Leith plough (*c.* 1748), had embodied some of the principles on which Small worked.

[2] The earlier Corn Laws had been less effective in keeping down imports, or keeping up domestic prices, than had simple war-time scarcity of victuals. The farmer then hardly needed Parliament's 'protection'.

[3] Lower levels were fixed for grains other than wheat, namely, 53s. for rye, pease and beans, 40s. for barley, and 27s. for oats.

the Lothians had the large cornfields that bespoke the prosperous farmer. The north-east, from Angus round to Caithness, with harder soil and harsher climate, did best with mixed farming, while the south-west inclined more to dairy-farming and stock-breeding. In the highlands the old ways lingered on most stubbornly. A survey of the Breadalbane estates at Lochtayside in 1769 showed farming in its primitive form – teams of plough-oxen owned communally, outfield that ought to have been ploughed up, wet lands that needed draining, long treks for man and beast between disjoined 'rigs'. Yet from 1762 sheep-rearing was spreading from the southern uplands to the highland counties, and by 1800 the sheep were to be found everywhere in the north. The Inverness wool fair, set up in 1817, attracted buyers from the south and from Yorkshire. The traditional trade in black cattle also flourished. Over the drove roads from the north and west they came in their thousands to the great cattle fair at Crieff or to the 'tryst' at Falkirk, while many others set out from Galloway for England. It is reckoned that, by 1800, as many as 100,000 cattle found their way each year over the border.

The linen industry made steady progress throughout the period. As before,[1] the rate of growth is best indicated in the annual records of the quantity of cloth stamped for sale by the officials of the Board of Trustees for Manufactures:–

Year	*Thousands of Yards*
1760	11,748
1770	13,050
1790	18,092
1800	24,236
1822	36,269

(*Note.* From 1822 the official stamping of cloth was discontinued.)

Thus the total output was more than three times as great at the close of the period as at its start. Despite this expansion, the industry retained its 'domestic' character, for, while the preparatory and finishing processes of heckling[2] and bleaching were carried out in mills and on large bleachfields, the basic work of spinning and weaving was still done by hand. Machine-spinning presented problems that for long baffled the inventor, as the sticky fibre of the flax made it unsuitable for the rough machines of the day, whereas the hand-spinner could delicately sort out the gummy strands and prevent them breaking.

[1] See *supra*, p. 73. [2] See *supra*, p. 72, n. 4.

The few spinning mills set up at this time were mainly experimental and not very important, while the weaver worked his hand-loom in his own cottage. The 'manufacturer' or capitalist nevertheless really controlled the industry, often importing flax and sometimes spun yarn, and financing the work of both spinner and weaver.

The distribution of the linen industry throughout Scotland is significant; the figures for the different counties in the year 1782 are as follows:–

County	*Output: Thousands of Yards*	*Value: Thousands of Pounds*
Forfar	6,742	177
Fife	2,361	90
Perth	1,700	81
Renfrew	1,577	167
Lanark	1,572	166
Rest of Scotland	1,397	94
Total	15,349	775

Thus the industry was concentrated in three eastern counties (with over 70 per cent of the total output) and two western counties (with over 20 per cent), and all others were far behind. The linen cloth produced in the whole country averaged out at a fraction over 1s. a yard, but the differences between east and west in respect of values were striking. For Renfrew and Lanark the figure was above 2s. 1d. a yard, for Perthshire it was just over 11d., for Fife about 9d. and for Forfarshire not much more than 6d. The different kinds of cloth produced explain these divergencies. Dundee and the surrounding parts were concerned mainly in the production of coarse cloths, brown linens and Osnaburghs, suitable for packing, sacking and rough jobs, whereas the weavers of Glasgow and Paisley specialised in fine fabrics, such as lawns, cambrics, incles (linen tape) and gauze.

The skill, experience and adaptability of the western weavers constituted one reason for the change in the 1780s from linen to cotton; another was the suitability of the Clyde valley area, with its damp climate, for the new processes; and yet another was the readiness of the western merchants to switch to a new and promising line of business. Some of these men had already risen to affluence as linen-masters, and others had made their fortunes from commerce with North America; but the willingness of masters and men would not have availed without the creations of the Lancashire inventors, James Hargreaves, who built his spinning-jenny about 1765, Richard Arkwright, who patented the water-frame in 1769, and Samuel Crompton, who made his spinning-mule in 1779.[1] The frame and the mule, at first driven by water-power, so increased the output of cotton yarn that the weaver could obtain all that he needed, and the application of steam-power to the mule from about 1792 speeded up production still more. The mechanisation of the complex process of weaving was slow. In England Edmund Cartwright made a primitive power-loom in 1787, but Scottish industrialists took it up in a small way only from 1807. The hand-loom weaver, commanding weekly wages of 25s. or 30s. during the war, was in a strong position, with the machine just beginning to threaten his livelihood towards the close of the period.

The first small cotton-spinning mill began work at Rothesay in 1779, and it was followed by others at Neilston, Johnstone, East Kilbride, Glasgow, Deanston and Stanley (the last two in Perthshire). Cotton, especially fine muslin, soon became fashionable for articles of dress, male and female, but the undoubted success of the industry dates from David Dale's New Lanark mills, opened in 1786, utilising water from the Falls of Clyde, and before long employing 1,334 workers. By 1800 the west had virtually abandoned linen[2] for cotton, which became (after agriculture) Scotland's premier industry; by 1814 the value of its annual output was very nearly £7,000,000, while linen stood at £1,775,000. Of the 120 cotton mills in all Scotland at that

[1] The jenny was operated by a single worker, but, instead of spinning one thread at a time (as was the case with the hand-wheel), it could spin six or seven together, and later on this number was very greatly extended. It produced only soft yarn, suitable for the weft, so that the warp threads, requiring more strength, had still to be spun on the wheel at this stage. Arkwright's frame made use of rollers to draw out the strands (or 'rovings') before they passed to the spindles to get the twist that gave them their strength. The coarse yarn that came from the frame was stout enough to serve as warp, and this fact made possible the speedy manufacture of all-cotton fabrics. The mule was so-named because, combining the principles of both the jenny and the frame, it was held to be a 'cross-bred' device. It yielded yarn that, being fine as well as strong, was suitable for use as both warp and weft. Whereas the cheap and simple jenny could be worked by spinners in their own cottages, the frame and the mule, being bigger, costlier and power-driven, really pre-supposed the mill. Though the mule was favoured in the newer and larger mills, the frame was retained for some purposes, and especially for the yarn required for very fine fabrics: it had the advantage of being less subject to vibration than the steam-driven mule. For these and other details, cf. T. S. Ashton, *The Industrial Revolution* (Home Univ. Lib., 1948), pp. 70-4.

[2] By 1822 the linen cloth stamped in Renfrewshire and Lanarkshire had dwindled to 48,554 yards.

time, a few were located in remote parts, but the great majority were in Lanarkshire and Renfrewshire. Financial control was centred in Glasgow and Paisley, for the weavers, though still for the most part working in their own cottages, lived largely by piece-work done for the owners of the spinning-mills or else for yarn importers and 'manufacturers'.

Just as linen had stimulated the development of bleachfields, so cotton promoted the growth of other branches. It was for the dyeing of cotton that George MacIntosh and David Dale engaged M. Papillon, of Rouen, to start the 'Turkey red' process at Dalmarnock, near Glasgow, in 1785. Other profitable 'off-shoot' industries were calico-making and calico-printing. Meanwhile, the hand-knitting of stockings, traditional in the Aberdeenshire villages and farms, flourished until, about 1800, stocking-frames came into use at Hawick. The ancient woollen industry of the Borders itself received an impetus from the setting-up of spinning mills, early in the nineteenth century, at Galashiels and Hawick. Before 1820 the tide of economic change had submerged most of the small rural industries that were by-employments in the old-fashioned agriculture: the spinning, weaving and knitting that had once occupied the spare time of the farmer's family had moved into the towns, with their factories and their wage-earners.

Though the first phase of the Industrial Revolution was emphatically the age of textiles, other branches recorded advances that were full of meaning for the future. James Watt's discovery, in 1765, of the principle of the separate condenser gave us, in effect, the steam engine, perhaps the basic invention of modern times. In 1784 the Englishman Henry Cort evolved new methods of puddling and of rolling wrought or 'malleable' iron – that is, iron that could be 'hammered' or shaped into any required form.[1] And in 1801 another Scot, David Mushet, showed the value of Lanarkshire's rich deposits of blackband ironstone, an ore with a high coal content and so capable of economic smelting.

Epoch-making as these developments were, the coal and iron industries were still on a modest scale at this time. Growth there was, but it was slow. Coal-mining was helped by the use of stationary steam-engines for pumping water and raising coal. In a different

[1] Cort's process involved re-heating with coke the pig iron (the primary product of the furnaces), then stirring it with iron rods and pressing it between iron rollers, to remove the carbon and impurities that would otherwise have rendered it so brittle as to be nearly unusable. This invention released the forge-masters, who produced the wrought iron, from dependence on charcoal as a fuel.

way, it became a respectable occupation when Acts of Parliament of 1775 and 1799 freed the colliers from their semi-servile state, for the law had previously held that they were 'astricted' or tied to their place of work. New pits were now opened near Edinburgh and Glasgow, where domestic as well as industrial demand was rising, and in Fife, Lanarkshire and Ayrshire. It is estimated that by 1814 some 2½ million tons were being raised and consumed. With a labour force of perhaps 40,000[1] in 1821, it was reckoned the fourth largest industry, coming after agriculture, cotton and linen.

For some time after 1759 the cast-iron products of the Carron works were typical of the Scottish industry. From 1761 these included guns and, from 1778, the famous light cannon, which, as 'carronades', earned world-wide repute. From the start, too, Carron was casting pots and pans, ploughs and spades, grates and stoves, railings and gates. From 1779 Carron's achievement prompted the establishment of other works further west, including Wilsontown, the Clyde works, and Omoa (all in Lanarkshire), and Muirkirk in Ayrshire; Calder and Shotts works followed at the opening of the nineteenth century. The industry was, however, still classed as 'secondary' in 1814, when the pig iron output was valued at only £229,320 – little more than one-eighth of that of linen, and less than one-thirtieth of that of cotton.

Prosperity came in a modest way to the lesser trades of the country, including paper-making and printing at Edinburgh, chemicals and soap-making at Glasgow, sugar-refining at Greenock, rope-making at Gourock, and, diffused more widely, leather manufacture and shoe-making, earthenware and glass-blowing, ironmongery and haberdashery, brewing and distilling, bakery and confectionery. The fisheries also advanced, but this subject, relating more particularly to the Highlands, is reserved for treatment in a later chapter.[2]

The revolution in transport is as remarkable as that in industry. On the roads, the old method of 'statute labour' was largely superseded by the new device of road-tolls, which were collected, at toll-gates or turn-pikes at intervals along the route, from all highway users and spent on the construction, upkeep and repair of the roads. Each individual 'line of road' had its own 'turnpike trust', a committee of local officials and gentry, and hundreds of these were set up by statute

[1] Reliable figures are unobtainable, but Sir John Sinclair reckoned that 13,160 families (equal to 50,500 persons) were employed in all Scotland's mines and quarries; many women and children would be included in this total.

[2] See *infra*, chap. xiv, especially pp. 155-6, 159.

during our period. They did much to improve the actual roads, while newly acquired industrial skills led to better, lighter and faster coaches and carriages. About 1780, too, occurred a great development of the system of posts and stages, providing regular stopping-places with fresh re-mounts. In 1786 the journey by stage-coach between Edinburgh and London was reduced to sixty hours; from Glasgow to London needed only sixty-five hours by 1788; and by the end of the century six hours sufficed between Edinburgh and Glasgow. In 1787, it is recorded, a Glasgow mercer received goods from London within six days of ordering them by letter – a truly astounding performance in terms solely of horse transport.

In the Highlands the improvements came mostly after 1803, when the Highland Commission for Roads and Bridges was set up, with the famous Scottish engineer, Thomas Telford, in charge of the work. By 1821 885 miles of 'parliamentary roads', as these new highways were called (to distinguish them from the earlier 'military roads'), had been built, and no fewer than 1,117 bridges had been provided in the difficult country that had to be traversed. By 1806 Perth and Inverness, the termini of the principal Highland route, were connected by stage-coach, the journey of 115 miles taking two days. The year 1811 saw Aberdeen and Inverness linked up, and by 1819 the system – conveying mails and passengers regularly and reliably – was carried to the extremity of the kingdom with a service to Tain, Wick and Thurso.

Our period covers the projection and completion of the Scottish canals, which were of limited usefulness by reason of the hilly surface of the land. The first two, the Forth and Clyde canal and the Monkland canal, were authorised in 1768 and 1770, and both were completed, after long delays, in 1790. The former stretched thirty-five miles from Grangemouth on the Forth to Bowling on the Clyde, with a three-mile 'cut' to Port Dundas, just north of Glasgow, where it linked with the Monkland canal, running eastward some twelve miles to Faskine, beside Airdrie. The Monkland's main function was to bring coals cheaply and speedily to Glasgow, while the Forth and Clyde was used for such bulky cargoes as grain and flour (westward) and coal and machinery (eastward). The Crinan canal, joining Loch Fyne to the sea over a nine-mile route, was completed in 1801, and it was followed in 1807 by an eighteen-mile waterway connecting Aberdeen and Inverurie. In 1811 an ambitious project, that of linking Glasgow overland with Ardrossan, was carried as far as Johnstone, about eleven miles from its Glasgow terminus, but it was never taken any further.[1] The year 1822 brought the opening of Scotland's last two canals – the Union, thirty-one and a half miles in length and connecting Edinburgh with Falkirk and so, by the Forth and Clyde, with Glasgow and the west; and the Caledonian, following a sixty-mile route through the Great Glen from Inverness to Loch Linnhe, and requiring only twenty-two miles of 'cut'. For about a generation these seven canals were highly serviceable, the busier of them earning large profits from both freight and passenger traffic.

In the long run the deepening of the Clyde was to produce an artificial waterway (for such it became) more important than all the canals taken together. The first Act, in 1759, had little effect beyond drawing attention to the troublesome presence of shallows in the channel, with only fifteen to eighteen inches of water at low tide, and it remained for the engineer, John Golborne,[2] in 1768 to suggest the true remedy – the building of jetties to contract the channel, which could then be deepened by dredging and by the scouring action of the tide. A second Act, in 1770, authorised works along these lines, to secure a depth of seven feet, and this was achieved by 1775, while a third Act, in 1809, aimed at nine feet (at low water), and this too was soon reached. Glasgow thus became a real sea-port, able to take ocean-going vessels.

The outstanding engineering triumph of the time was the harnessing of Watt's great invention for the propulsion of ships. The forerunners were William Symington's experimental *Charlotte Dundas* (1802) and the American Robert Fulton's *Clermont* (1807), but it was the launching of Henry Bell's *Comet* on the Clyde in 1812 that led to the enthusiastic adoption of steam-power, first for river work, then for coastal trips, and next for short-sea voyages. By 1823 no fewer than ninety-five steamers had been built in Scotland, seventy-two of them on the Clyde. A new industry, as well as a new form of transport, had been born.

Meanwhile, without benefit of steam, deep-sea commerce flourished,

[1] The local proprietor, the twelfth Earl of Eglinton, had grandiose plans for developing Ardrossan as the port of Glasgow, with a canal connection. Harbour works began in 1806, and Ardrossan did become a busy coal port, but the difficult terrain of the Renfrewshire hills forced the abandonment of the projected 'through' canal.

[2] He was one of several eminent engineers engaged from time to time on this work; among the others were John Smeaton (in 1755), James Watt (in 1769), John Rennie (from 1799) and Thomas Telford (from 1806).

though it had received one sharp set-back and had changed its character. After 1760 the tobacco trade expanded, to reach new heights in the 1770s. It was still a re-export traffic. Out of 46 million pounds brought to the Clyde in 1771, very nearly 44 millions went out again – to Bordeaux, Morlaix, Havre, Dunkirk and other French towns; to Rotterdam (the biggest customer of all); to Hamburg and Bremen; to Dublin and Cork; and, in smaller amounts, to various ports on the shores of the Baltic and the Mediterranean. Glasgow had now pushed far ahead of Bristol and London, for, out of a total British import of some 90,000 hogsheads in 1772, no less than 49,000 came to the Clyde. John Glassford, the leading Glasgow merchant of his day, is said to have owned twenty-five ships and to have traded for the vast sum of £500,000 a year. The 'tobacco lords', like London's 'nabobs' of the East Indian trade, were rich and often arrogant merchant princes, strutting the streets in their costly finery and beckoning to lesser men to approach and speak. But 'the bubble burst' with the outbreak of the American war, for the import of tobacco dropped to 7½ million pounds in 1776, and to 295,000 pounds in 1777. Many bankruptcies followed, and the trade, dependent on the old Navigation Laws, never returned, for, after the peace of 1783, the Americans naturally conducted their own commerce with Europe. But fortunes had already been made, and the enterprising merchants, seeking promising new outlets for their capital, helped above all to finance the cotton industry.

Commercial recovery came quickly from 1783, when the Glasgow Chamber of Commerce, the first in Britain, was founded. Cargoes of raw cotton went some way to make up the loss of the tobacco trade, while Greenock's intake of West Indian sugar mounted steadily. The east coast trade expanded without violent change, but with an increasing tendency in favour of the larger ports, Leith, Dundee and Aberdeen. Interruptions came with the French wars, and in the later 1790s the sugar ships bound for the Clyde were peculiarly vulnerable to enemy privateers. Despite these hazards, Scottish shipping improved year by year in both numbers and tonnage. By 1800 there were 2,155 ships, of an average size of 75 tons, showing a twenty-fold expansion since the Union; in 1820 there were 2,851 and the average tonnage was 95·9. Hence the impetus towards larger harbours with deeper approaches; hence, too, the work of the Northern Lighthouse Commissioners, set up in 1786, in lighting the headlands and making them guides rather than dangers for navigators.

The steep rise in the country's wealth was reflected in corresponding increases among such tradesmen as fleshers and bakers, tailors and innkeepers.[1] It is some indication of the numbers involved that, when the Glasgow volunteers were reconstituted after the resumption of the French war in 1803, one of the eight battalions of infantry was supplied by the grocers, who formed a smart body of 600 men. So, too, with banking, which was vital for economic progress. A measure of state regulation came in 1765, when Parliament forbade two growing abuses, the 'optional clause'[2] and the issue of notes of less value than £1 (for 'scrip' was being given out for ridiculously small sums); this statute made for responsible banking practice. Again, war-time conditions led in 1797 to the suspension of cash payments throughout Britain, which meant a departure from the 'gold standard' but caused little trouble in Scotland, where the people took happily to 'paper money'.

For the most part, however, Scottish banking evolved at this time in response to commercial needs, without government intervention. All but one of the new banks are to be classed as 'local', the exception being the Commercial Bank of Scotland, established in 1810. Thus, Glasgow got the Thistle Bank in 1761 and the Merchant in 1769. Banks were founded at Dundee and Ayr in 1763, and these examples were followed in the next half-century by many other provincial towns, including Perth, Dumfries, Aberdeen, Stirling, Greenock, Falkirk and Paisley. Most of the local banks were managed on sound principles, but two of them came to grief: the 'Ayr Bank' (properly Douglas, Heron and Company) failed through unwise speculation in 1772, causing much distress throughout Scotland, and the Glasgow Arms Bank was an unlucky victim of the financial panic of 1793. Private banking, meanwhile, and the mixture of financial and mercantile interests declined, and opinion favoured a broad base for banks that were banks and nothing else. As one aspect of this trend, branch-banking (in which the British Linen Company had taken the lead) became the settled policy of the Bank of Scotland from 1774, and of the Royal Bank from 1783. Yet a new type of small-scale, local banking began in 1810, when the Rev. Henry Duncan set up the first savings bank, ready to accept small deposits from working men and women, at Ruthwell, in Dumfriesshire. The savings movement at once became popular and spread rapidly through the country.

[1] This last-named increase was deplored by the ministers as having a corrupting effect on the people; cf. *infra*, pp. 147, 157.

[2] See *supra*, p. 75.

The true pioneers of the Industrial Revolution were the skilled engineers and the dedicated scientists, and of these Scotland produced not a few – Watt and Golborne, Rennie and Telford, Mushet and Bell. But, granted their inventions and new processes, there was need too for the men with commercial vision and enterprise, with trust in their judgment, a share of good luck, and willingness to invest in new projects. The versatility of such men is amazing to anyone used to the more settled conditions of a later age. Thus, by turns or concurrently, David Dale was linen merchant, bank agent, cotton master, town councillor and bailie, a manager of the Infirmary, a road expert and a lay pastor.[1] One of his partners in a cotton factory on a picturesque site at Spinningdale, in Sutherland, was 'honest George' Dempster, the Angus improver, a respected if unorthodox member of Parliament, a promoter of fisheries and lighthouses, and the inventor of early forms of both ice-packing and central heating. Another outstanding cotton magnate at the close of the century was Kirkman Finlay, head of the firm of James Finlay and Company, owners (then, as now) of the mills of Deanston (Perthshire) and Catrine (Ayrshire); besides being lord provost of Glasgow, the local M.P. and rector of the University, he sent Glasgow's first trading ship to India (1816) and also, much later (1834), started commerce between the Clyde and China. To such bold *entrepreneurs* the Industrial Revolution owed much.

[1] He belonged to a small sect, the 'Old Scotch Independents', whose meeting-house, provided by a Glasgow candlemaker, was dubbed 'the Candle Kirk'.

CHAPTER XIII

Lowland Society in the Textile Age

THE TOTAL population of Scotland had been estimated by Alexander Webster in 1755 to be 1,265,380. By 1801, according to the first official census, it had grown to 1,608,420, and the figure in 1821 was 2,091,521. In the first forty-six years of this period, therefore, the increase was just over a quarter, while the next increase – also slightly over a quarter – occurred in as short a time as twenty years: the rate of growth, that is to say, was more than doubled after 1801. For the whole sixty-six years the increment works out at 65·4 per cent, or very nearly two-thirds.

Each of the thirty-three counties showed an increase over the entire period, but there were wide variations between their rates of growth. Leaving aside the mainly Highland shires (for consideration in the next chapter), we note that certain Lowland shires lagged far behind others in population-growth, including the following four, the 'slowest' of all[1]:–

County	*1755*	*1801*	*1821*
Haddington	29,709	29,986	35,127
Linlithgow	16,829	17,844	22,685
Peebles	8,908	8,735	10,046
Roxburgh	34,704	33,721	40,892

The contrast with the four fastest growing shires is sharp, for each of these more than doubled its inhabitants during the period:–

County	*1755*	*1801*	*1821*
Ayr	59,009	84,207	127,299
Edinburgh	90,412	122,597	191,514
Lanark	81,726	147,692	244,387
Renfrew	26,645	78,501	112,175

Economic causes account for these differences. The slow-growing shires were mainly concerned with farming, were as yet little touched by the newer industries, and had no large towns. In the counties of

[1] If we were to include the northern counties, three of them would belong to this 'slow-growing' group – Kincardine, Banff and Elgin. It is noteworthy that none of these three is truly Highland in character and that all of them are (and were) in the farming sense much superior to their Highland neighbours.

the second group the cotton trade was flourishing and the rising coal industry had taken firm root, while they contained Scotland's three largest towns besides others that were forging ahead. The population movements of the time were, indeed, mostly a matter of urban growth, and the figures for the bigger towns, or rather for the urban parishes,[1] are even more impressive than those for the counties:–

Parishes	*1755*	*1801*	*1821*
Glasgow	27,451	77,385	147,043
Edinburgh	52,720	82,560	138,235
Paisley	6,799	31,179	47,003
Aberdeen	15,730	27,519	44,796
Dundee	12,477	26,084	30,575
Greenock	3,858	17,458	22,088
Kilmarnock	4,403	8,079	12,769
Falkirk	3,932	8,838	11,536

Rapid growth was thus the characteristic of the two chief cities (with Glasgow overtaking and passing Edinburgh), of the major seaports and of the towns that were deeply involved in the early phase of the Industrial Revolution. Most astonishing is the advance of Paisley, the home of textile experimentation, to third place, ahead of both Aberdeen and Dundee, which had long been rivals for that position.

A gentler and more manageable, though still substantial, increase was recorded by the old county towns, the secondary seaports and the linen centres:–

Parishes	*1755*	*1801*	*1821*
Perth	9,019	14,878	19,068
Dumfries	4,517	7,288	11,052
Montrose	4,150	7,975	10,338
Ayr	2,914	5,492	7,455
Stirling	3,951	5,271	7,113

The position in the towns of this group is well summed up in the statement made in 1791 by the minister of Ayr: 'Upon the whole, the inhabitants have been increasing sensibly, though not rapidly, for more than 30 years past'.

While settled urban communities were thus expanding, some

[1] At this time the parish was the basic unit for census purposes, and the parish statistics are more precise and reliable than the purely burghal figures. In the above table, Glasgow is taken as including the Barony and (from 1801) Gorbals, Edinburgh includes Leith, Paisley covers both Paisley and the Abbey parishes, and Aberdeen comprises both St Nicholas and Old Machar parishes, i.e. it includes Old Aberdeen.

others were called into being for the first time – built, so to speak, from the ground up. Planned from the start by progressive landlords or textile mill-owners, these new villages, some of them destined to grow into towns, were a feature of the 'rage for improvement'. Grangemouth, on the Firth of Forth, was definitely 'begun' in 1777 and soon attracted trade as both a canal port and a seaport. About the same time, Letham, in Forfarshire, was laid out as a linen spinning and weaving village; Johnstone, in Renfrewshire, made its mark as a cotton centre; and Larkhall, in Lanarkshire, was based on weaving and mining. In other cases new life was infused into decayed hamlets; Longforgan, in Perthshire, was revived by the adoption of linen weaving, Blantyre, in Lanarkshire, by ironstone mining and the cotton trade, and New Langholm, in Dumfriesshire, first by cotton and later by woollen manufactures. Most remarkable among such places, Airdrie, a market town with perhaps 1,200 inhabitants at the start of the period, was so stimulated by a combination of the cotton, coal and iron industries that, by 1821 (when it became a burgh), it had a population of 4,862.[1]

Meanwhile, in the rural Lowlands, wherever farming was reasonably prosperous – and this was fairly general at this time – population was stable or increasing slightly. Thus Haddington, a good farming county, advanced, as we have seen, from 29,709 in 1755 to 35,127 in 1821. Its neighbour, Berwick, with an equally sound reputation in agriculture, rose from 23,987 to 33,385 during the same period. It is true that there was some exodus from country to town, for scientific farming brought savings in man-power through the use of the machine. Yet the people in the 'improved' districts did not simply suffer diminution in numbers through loss of farm-work: the position was much more complex than that. The higher standard of living created a demand for the labours of all sorts of 'marginal' workers, such as blacksmiths, wheelwrights, joiners, masons, slaters, ditchers and dykers, while each little village had its shopkeepers and innkeepers. Not all the displaced farm labourers had to drift into the towns in search of a living. On the large farms, moreover, gangs of seasonal workers were needed, especially at harvest-time. Many of these came from the Highlands, but others were recruited locally. For one reason or another, despite much disturbance of the traditional ways of life, the Lowland counties as a whole were able to retain their population.

[1] And Airdrie's subsequent growth was to be even more remarkable – to 6,594 in 1831 and to 12,418 in 1841.

Nevertheless, even a steady rural population, alongside a rapid urban increase, argues a shift from country to town, and it is clear that, on balance, the 'natural increase' of the population – the excess of births over deaths – was showing itself mainly in the towns. By 1821 the 'agricultural class' was reckoned as forming only one-half of all the 'productive classes' and less than thirty-eight per cent of the total population. The hope of regular work and good wages beckoned the countryman townward, while the fear of rural unemployment disposed him to follow his hopes. If he stayed behind, he must face the competition of others, notably Highlanders and Irishmen, who were prepared to work for low wages. For the most part, these were migrant workers, spending the summer or the harvest season in south Scotland and returning home with what they had saved. As yet, few of the Irish had come to stay: their great period of settlement was to come after 1820. There was, however, a continual 'seepage' throughout the period of young and hardy Highlanders into the towns and villages lying nearest to the Highland line. Glasgow and Dundee already had substantial Highland 'colonies', while the minister of Greenock stated, in the *Old Statistical Account* (1792), that one might walk the High Street of that town from end to end and hear only Gaelic being spoken!

The rise in wages that accompanied the increased production of wealth benefited most members of the community. The day-labourer got 7d. or 8d. in 1765, but by 1815 he was making 1s. 8d., while an expert workman such as a mason got double those wages. By 1770 the ploughman was being paid £2 each half-year; by 1800 the figure had risen to £5 and by 1815 to as much as £10, though a slight reduction followed the coming of peace, when wages ranged between £7 and £9. Over the same period the wages of women-servants on the farms rose from 13s. 4d. to £3-£4 in the half-year.[1] War-time profits and high wages loosened social ties and tended to make the bond between master and servant purely a cash one, instead of the old relationship based on personal loyalty and personal services. There was now room for the 'self-made' man.

Every aspect of social life was affected by the economic changes of the time. Improved agriculture meant better and more varied food.[2] The advance of the textile and allied industries brought within reach

[1] These figures are taken from George Robertson, *Rural Recollections* (1827).

[2] The last *general* famine in Scotland occurred in the winter of 1782-83, though much *local* suffering was to be caused by the potato failures of 1837 and 1846.

linen shirts, silk and cotton dresses, hats, shoes and gloves. Progress in iron-smelting and in ironmongery provided grates, pots and pans, and the newer household plenishings also included delft, china and glass. Foreign luxuries, like sugar, lemons, oranges, rum, brandy and snuff, found their way into the well-to-do houses. A high malt-duty reduced the demand for ale and, very gradually, tea began to win favour. The constant French wars made claret an 'unpatriotic' drink and enhanced the popularity of port (for Portugal was traditionally an ally). And, finally, the continuing dominance of the 'Moderate' party in the Church[1] had the effect of weakening the disapproval, on Puritanical grounds, of the theatre, dancing, card-playing ('the devil's beuks') and sports.

It was in Edinburgh that the fashionable life of society was to be seen at its gayest and most colourful. The reigns of the first two Georges had witnessed many advances in the arts and graces of living, but the capital had remained within its narrow, historic bounds.[2] Now, under George III, it burst out of these bounds and spread in all directions, though old customs died hard: as late as 1769, there were two dukes, sixteen earls, and many lords and judges living in the high, cramped 'lands' of the Canongate, and yet change was already in the air. The removal in 1764 of the Nether Bow port, dividing the High street from the Canongate, signalised a sharp break with the past. In 1767 the first new house appeared among the farmlands beyond the 'Lang dykes', the road that was soon to be renamed Princes street. At the east end of that street the Theatre Royal was built in 1769 and the Register House in 1774. Developments now came rapidly, and Princes street was soon followed by Queen street and George street to the north. St Andrew's square was laid out in 1778 at the east end of George street, and that gracious thoroughfare was given a fitting western terminal with the completion, in 1800, of Charlotte square, the loveliest in all Edinburgh. The 'new town' was an architect's triumph.

The uneven surface of the city posed for the planners the problem of linking different levels across deep chasms or down sharp declivities. One solution was the building, in 1772, of the North bridge, connecting old town and new town at their eastern ends, and providing a line of street that was continued southward, to span the low-lying Cowgate, with the opening in 1788 of the South bridge. To the west, following a different design, work began in 1781 on 'the Earthen Mound', a

[1] See *infra*, chap. xvi. [2] See *supra*, pp. 83-4.

steep drive-way made from the rubble derived from the feverish building of the time. To the south-east, beyond the spot where, from 1789, Edinburgh's new College buildings were going up,[1] George square offered another centre of gracious living.[2] By the end of the century the new town was the favoured residential area, while the High street, Canongate and their purlieus, abandoned to the poorer inhabitants, were already showing signs of decay and dilapidation.

It was in this altered physical setting that the capital reached its peak of achievement in arts, letters and life.[3] At the taverns and coffee-houses, in the meetings of clubs and societies, food was abundant, wine flowed freely and wit sparkled. The leaders of fashion took up the latest London fads and the newest pastimes. As early as 1761 the novelty of sea-bathing had become known, for the *Courant* of 30 May of that year advertised 'a proper house on wheels, with horse and servants', to be hired for one shilling from the Royal Oak inn at Leith. From about 1763 oyster-cellars in the Cowgate were drawing in well-to-do customers. The theatre became so generally accepted that in 1784, when the great actress Mrs Siddons came to town, the General Assembly, in the words of the diarist Alexander Carlyle, 'was obliged to fix all its important business for the alternate days when she did not act, as all the younger members, clergy as well as laity, took their stations in the theatre on those days by three in the afternoon'.

As the reign of George III wore on, some old landmarks passed away. Sedan chairs, formerly favoured by ladies, and powdered hair, the hall-mark of the gentleman, both went out of fashion. In the early years of the nineteenth century, the City Guard, described by Lord Cockburn[4] as 'all old, hard-featured, red-nosed veterans', gave way to a proper police force, while the extended supply of piped water put a stop to the wearisome labours of the water-caddies, climbing the steep stairs to sell their little casks, filled from the wells, at a penny each. Yet much that was good lived on: though Cockburn asserts that swearing and drunkenness were too prevalent among gentlemen, he also states that in 1811 'society and literature adorned each other . . . and . . . we still retained more native talent and reputation than could be found in any other town in the empire, except London'.

[1] See *infra*, p. 166.

[2] No. 25 was the home of Walter Scott from his birth in 1776 until the year 1797.

[3] See *infra*, chap. xv.

[4] His *Memorials of his Time* and his *Journals* give us our best picture of early nineteenth century social life, just as Carlyle's *Autobiography* does for the mid-eighteenth century.

Glasgow's physical growth was extremely rapid. In the west end, 'Cow lone' became Queen street and was quickly built up, as was Jamaica street, which, leading to the new bridge (1772), recalls the West Indies trade on which fortunes were now based.[1] The additions to the western city lacked the architectural grace of Edinburgh's 'new town' and yet some of its former beauty survived for a time, so that John Gibson, the local historian, could quite truthfully write in 1777, 'Every stranger is charmed with the appearance of Glasgow'. Social and convivial groups flourished – the Gaelic Club, the Board of Green Cloth (for card-playing), the Grog Club and many others. A second theatre, opened in 1764, was destroyed by fire in 1780, but a third, built in 1782, had a longer life. Nine lamps, set up in 1780 on the south side of the Trongate, represent the city's first venture in public lighting; a little later, sedan chairs were giving way to hackney coaches. We read[2] of 'salt-water quarters' (or holiday homes down the firth of Clyde) being taken up by Glasgow merchants in the years 1778-82 at Rothesay, Dunoon and Largs, while, in the early years of the nineteenth century, David Dale and Kirkman Finlay sought seclusion and quiet in country mansions.

On the south bank of the Clyde, meanwhile, the fashionable new suburb of Gorbals was being laid out in the 1780s and 1790s, and after 1800 Woodside, in the west end, was developed with rather more haste than plan. By this stage, indeed, the city's growth was so hectic that little time or thought was devoted to the housing of its teeming masses, and the central streets and lanes (deserted, like those of Edinburgh, by 'the quality') were being transformed into congested slum tenements, in which Highlanders, Irish and others of the poorest inhabitants lived in squalor and poverty.

The changes elsewhere in Scotland, if less dramatic, were still noteworthy. They include some good planning of streets and squares, a few pleasing town halls and spired churches. The new uses of leisure are brought out by the writers of the *Old Statistical Account*, in the 1790s – hunting at Dumfries, golf at Perth, card-parties and dancing at Montrose – while many towns had their masonic lodges, weavers' societies and lending libraries. As city ideas and modes spread afield,

[1] Glasgow also has Virginia street, commemorating the tobacco trade. With these might be compared Antigua street and India place, in Edinburgh, and Baltic street and Jamaica street, in Leith.

[2] In *Glasgow Past and Present* (3 volumes, 1884), which, compiled by 'Senex' [Robert Reid] and others, is our best source for the life and manners of the western city from the 1770s on.

pewter gave way to china and glass, the spinet to the piano, and the dinner-hour was put back in fashionable homes from three o'clock to four, and then to five. The country gentry now preferred roomier and lighter classical styles of building to the austere and old-fashioned baronial tower, and wall-paper, clocks and mirrors were to be seen in farm-houses.

Tea-drinking, becoming a national habit, was deplored by many writers, but even worse, in the eyes of the ministers, was the multiplication of inns and dram-shops, which, they thought, debauched and debased ordinary men. Before the end of the century, Dunblane had forty-one ale-houses and inns, St Andrews forty-eight, Dunbar forty-six and Stirling sixty-eight, though these towns were all short of 5,000 in population.[1] Despite the strictures of the clergy, the number of licensed premises rose steadily throughout the period, and intemperance became a widespread vice.

If the lower orders indulged, often to excess, in whisky-drinking, while their betters partook copiously of wine and brandy, of rum punches and toddies, the daily fare of the bulk of the people changed but slowly with the passing years. In the words of a petition of 1774, 'it is a well-known fact that oat meal is the capital article of food among the lower people of Scotland'. The boys and girls employed at Dale's 'model' mill of New Lanark (opened in 1786) got oatmeal porridge at breakfast and supper, with milk in season and at other times with 'swats' (beer and molasses). Midday dinner comprised barley-broth, with beef or cheese in turn, or sometimes herring in winter and fresh butter in summer, and always either potatoes or barley-bread. Thus the main addition at this time to the traditional homely fare consisted of potatoes and herring; meat and cheese were much rarer than in England, while wheat-bread and tea, though gaining favour, were still costly enough to be regarded as luxuries.

Housing ills now began to result from the migration of country folk into the older and poorer quarters of the cities and towns, whither they brought their rural habits and ideas. The one- and two-roomed country cottage might be a fitting and healthy, if humble, abode, but, transferred to a crowded urban site, the same accommodation could be degrading and (in the absence of sanitary conveniences) dangerous to health and life. And it must be remembered that it had been

[1] Of Dunfermline, a larger place with 101 ale-houses, the minister wrote, 'The general use of whisky is arrived at an alarming height among many in the lower ranks of life.'

customary, even for substantial citizens, to live in small flats giving on to a common 'close' in a high tenement. The scene was thus set for the spread of the slums in the already densely populated towns, for the early nineteenth-century attitude to housing needs was often harshly unsympathetic. The houses of two rooms (including the kitchen), allowed to each schoolmaster by an Act of 1803,[1] were denounced by some as 'palaces for dominies'. Again, in 1818, Dr Robert Graham, visiting Glasgow's foul tenements, found little to distinguish the cellars for pigs or cows from those for human beings, and saw one apartment, measuring twelve feet by less than five, which had held six people, sick with fever, in the past two days.

The late eighteenth-century changes had mixed effects on the national standards of health. Ague, or malarial fever, yielded before the agrarian improvements, including drainage, and inoculation gave some protection against smallpox, the cause of fearful mortality among children, though the real preventive measure, vaccination, came only in 1801. Rheumatism, on the other hand, was as virulent as ever and consumption was increasing, while Sir John Sinclair, the great statistician of the time, believed that farm-work was healthful, but that the long hours of labour in the cotton mills were harmful to men, women and children. It was after 1800 that urban congestion, filthy streets and insanitary houses began to take a heavy toll among the poorer townsfolk. From 1818 typhus and other fevers were a deadly menace, and temporary fever hospitals were set up in Glasgow and Edinburgh to deal with many hundreds of victims. By the close of the reign of George III, the social consequences of the Industrial Revolution were showing themselves in an ugly light.

The problem of poor relief became more pressing in the early years of the nineteenth century than it had formerly been. The legislation of the sixteenth and seventeenth centuries, on which the system rested, had made permissive (but not compulsory) both the levying of assessments (the poor's rate) and the provision of 'correction houses' for the employment of idle vagabonds, but there were in fact very few workhouses in Scotland, while, by 1800, only ninety-two parishes, or one in ten, had assessments for the poor. Instead, from church-door collections and any other available revenues, the heritors and kirk sessions doled out quarterly pittances of a few shillings to the infirm poor of the parish. This voluntary method worked fairly well in a stable and mainly rural population, and, for the rest, a dozen or two

[1] See *infra*, pp. 163-4.

'licensed beggars', with official 'leaden tokens' or badges, were allowed to make periodic rounds in certain districts and to get what they could from the neighbours' charity.

By 1800 the nature of the problem was changing. It was not now a matter of crop failure causing distress among country folk: it was the townsfolk who suffered most from trade depression and mass unemployment. War-time work and wages were uncertain, but poverty and want became acute after 1815. By 1820 one person in forty was a pauper, and the average annual cost of his upkeep was £2 11s. 8d., of which the greater part still came from the 'voluntary' charity of the Church. Thus, with each decade that passed, the social challenge of pauperism became more urgent.

For the paupers things were bad, but for other outcasts of society – the sick, the insane and the criminal – they were worse. Infirmaries or hospitals were opened at Glasgow in 1794, at Dundee in 1798, and a little later at Paisley and Greenock,[1] but beds, medical attention and medicines were all inadequate, especially during epidemics. The first lunatic asylum in Scotland was established at Montrose in 1782, and others followed at Aberdeen (1800), Edinburgh (1813), Glasgow (1814) and Dundee (1820), but they were poorly equipped and little, beyond physical confinement, was done for the patients. For the custody of debtors, delinquents and criminals there were in 1818 five 'bridewells'[2] and eighty-two common gaols, most of them dark and filthy dens, without drainage or ventilation; a common rate of maintenance for the prisoners was 6d. a day. Not for such unfortunates (many of them victims of poverty and ignorance, others of intemperance) were the glittering triumphs of the Industrial Revolution.

[1] Edinburgh and Aberdeen already had their infirmaries: see *supra*, p. 87.

[2] These were penitentiaries or reformatory prisons, and were named from the hospital of Bridewell (i.e. the well of St Bride or Bridget) in London, which was used as a workhouse or 'house of correction' for rogues, vagabonds and all who were regarded as wilfully unemployed.

CHAPTER XIV

The Highlands after the 'Forty-five

IN THE century that followed the decisive battle of Culloden, the differences between Lowland and Highland Scotland were sharply accentuated and became a standing challenge to the unity and progress of the nation. Economic change had transformed life and work in the English-speaking parts, but the impact on the Highlands was weak, intermittent and patchy. Clinging to their traditional ways, loyal to their ancestral chiefs, and deeply attached to the Gaelic language and culture, the natives of the northern regions resisted or ignored the alien improvements that were generally welcomed in the south, and so formed a 'Celtic fringe', which defied the attempts of statesmen, economists and churchmen to bring them into line with their Lowland neighbours.

For this purpose we cannot simply regard as 'Highland' those parts of Scotland that lie beyond the 'Highland line', the geological fault which runs from the vicinity of Dumbarton in the south-west to that of Stonehaven in the north-east. The maritime counties from Kincardine round to Nairn, the narrow coastal strip north of Inverness, and the counties of Caithness, Orkney and Shetland, must all be distinguished from the main mountainous mass of northern Scotland. In the social and economic sense (and in several others) we must equate the Scottish Highlands with the whole or the greater part of the shires of Perth, Argyll, Inverness, Ross and Sutherland, including the Western Isles from Islay up to Lewis.

Delimited in this way, the Highland region constitutes almost exactly half[1] the area of all Scotland, but much the largest part of it is uninhabitable and even unusable by man, with the arable averaging ten per cent in many districts and dropping as low as one per cent in some. Despite their physical disabilities, the five counties maintained, at the start of the period, nearly a quarter of the inhabitants of Scotland,[2] so that they were already over-populated in terms of the resources of

[1] The modern land area of the five counties (including, instead of Ross, the slightly larger united shire of Ross and Cromarty) is 14,932 square miles, while that of Scotland is 29,795 square miles.

[2] Webster's enumeration of 1755 gives them 309,560 inhabitants (or, including Cromarty with Ross, 314,823) out of a Scottish total of 1,265,380.

the land. To maintain these large numbers, with war and pillage now ruled out, the meagre produce of the soil – the oats and bere painfully extracted from the scattered runrig holdings – had to be supplemented from other sources. Around the coasts and in the islands fishing, for herring, cod and ling, brought an addition to the food supplies, if not to the cash reserves, of many localities. There was some trade in the parts with easy access to the Lowlands, in timber, horses, cheese and butter, while the distilling of whisky was beginning to be profitable; but the central support of the Highland economy, the main 'cash crop', so to speak, comprised the rearing of small, black cattle for ultimate sale in the markets of the south.[1] There was ample summer pasture in the hills, and it was the money derived from cattle sales at Crieff or Falkirk that enabled the peasant to meet his rent and to import the commodities that could not be produced at home – extra meal, iron, timber, sailcloth, ropes and salt.

The enforced peace that came to the Highlands from 1746 had the effect of transforming the clan chiefs from leaders of men into owners of land. Like landowners elsewhere, they developed a taste for luxurious living and craved French wines, imported fruits and spices, finery in dress, silverware and costly furnishings. With only their rents to live on,[2] and burdened with estates that might be large, but were seldom productive, they soon ran into debt.

Below the landowner in the social scale came the tacksman, forming a class peculiar to the Highlands. The tacksman was a cousin or near kinsman of the chief, renting a substantial part of the latter's estate by 'tack' or lease, collecting rents from the tillers of the soil as sub-tenants, and paying a part thereof to the chief as his own rent. The tacksman was a gentleman and had formerly served the chief in a military capacity as one of the captains of the clan; cherishing this blood relationship, he stood apart from the mere peasantry.

Far beneath the tacksmen came the peasant-farmers, who might be joint-tenants, holding a farm in groups of from two to eight, or who might occupy lowlier stations in the community, as crofters, cottagers, cottars or farm servants, each with a tiny holding, a mere plot of arable and enough pasture for a few cattle or sheep. The scarcity of good land and the pressure upon it of a dense population kept the individual holdings small – as little as five acres for a tenant-farmer, perhaps from

[1] Cf. *supra*, pp. 25, 68-9, 130.

[2] And it should be remembered that many rents were still paid in kind – including, at the lowest level, a few scraggy fowls.

one to three acres for a cottar. Minute sub-division of holdings was, and remained, the only way to avoid landlessness, which threatened starvation among those living so close to the soil. Cultivation was less by the plough than by the *cas chrom*, the cutting spade or foot-plough, which brought a high yield for hard toil; laborious as was this method, it suited an infertile land, where only labour was plentiful.

Besides cattle, sheep were reared in small numbers for their wool and their mutton, and horses were bred for ploughing in the better farming districts,[1] as well as for transport. Oatmeal was the basis of the traditional diet, but some barley-bread was used along with oat-cakes or porridge. Beef was scarce, even mutton was eaten mainly by tacksmen or substantial tenants, but herring and milk were commoner. Clothing consisted mainly of woollens, home-spun, home-woven and home-dyed, perhaps in vari-coloured checks,[2] and raw-hide brogues were also a local product, though some linen garments were imported.

The so-called 'black houses' of the Highlands, without either glass or slate, were built by the peasant's own hands from undressed stone, rough timber, turf and heather. Carts, too, were almost unknown, their function being served by sledges, creels and baskets, while, so far as possible, both farming and fishing implements were made from local materials by local labour. For all but a handful, life in the Highlands was harsh, plain and exacting, with no surplus for comforts or niceties, and with a slender margin of safety from famine and want. Yet, though there was no movement between classes and no hope of the peasant bettering his lot, society was held together by common beliefs and mutual loyalties, by the bond of fears and sufferings shared by all.

Highland conditions lagged far behind those of the Lowlands and the gap widened with the passing years. Most of the interest of Highland history in the century after 1746 turns on the efforts that were made to close or narrow that gap, and to confer on the clansmen (sought or unsought) the benefits of the progress achieved in the south. In part those efforts represent official policy and are embodied in acts of parliament, but in part they came from the spontaneous and unaided enterprise of many individuals – the reaction of Highlanders and of

[1] They were used four to each plough – the old heavy, wooden 'Scotch plough', with three or four men in charge.

[2] Though 'Highland dress' was proscribed from 1746 to 1782, the distinctive tartans of the clans evolved in the eighteenth and nineteenth centuries. Cf. *supra*, pp. 60-1, 66, 81-2.

outsiders to the opportunities of making a new kind of living beyond the Highland line.

First and foremost among the public attempts of the time to stimulate prosperity and advance welfare in the Highlands were those of the Commissioners for the Forfeited Estates. They were not quite the earliest of their kind, for there had been some fifty forfeitures after the 1715 rebellion. At that time, however, the government had delegated to others the task of administering the chiefs' properties, with results that had been far from satisfactory. For one thing, the net balance accruing to the Exchequer, after all claims and expenses had been met, had amounted only to £1,107. For another, scope had been given to purely speculative bodies, such as the York Buildings Company, which had purchased estates in order to make a commercial profit out of them by sundry developments, including the exploitation of mineral resources.[1] Realising that the former policy had been mistaken, and that serious efforts must be made to ameliorate the lot of the ordinary clansman, the authorities adopted a different attitude to the estates, some forty in number, that were forfeited after the 'Forty-five.

The 'Vesting Act' of 1747 formally transferred title to the estates to the crown, while the 'Annexing Act' of 1752 provided for the payment of creditors and the management of the annexed properties. Rents and profits were to be applied to 'the better civilising and improving the Highlands' as well as to 'preventing disorders there for the future'. The rents of fourteen specified estates, including the large domains of Lovat, Lochiel, Cromarty and Keppoch, were to help to promote the Protestant faith, good government, industry, manufactures, and loyalty to the king. The Commissioners were empowered to grant leases, to appoint factors and clerks, to erect schools and prisons, and to provide instruction in agriculture and industry.

The twenty-eight Commissioners were mostly Scots (Lord Kames usually acting as chairman) with a few Englishmen added; many of them, as members of the Board of Trustees for Manufactures, had already striven to improve industrial conditions in the Lowlands,[2]

[1] One curious survival from these miscarried plans is the tiny hamlet of New York, on the shores of Loch Awe, where there was formerly a station of the company. As late as 1764 the estates still held by the company (by then bankrupt) – those of the Panmure, Seaforth and Marischal families – were sold back to the heirs of the former owners. (The company had originally been formed for the purpose of supplying London with water, but, failing in that project, had turned to other fields of investment, including the forfeited estates.)

[2] See *supra*, pp. 72-3.

and now hoped to extend the good work to the Highlands. Before they had even made a start, however, their plans were hampered by a gory episode which illustrates one aspect of the deplorable conditions they were to combat.

Most clansmen on the forfeited estates regarded their exiled chiefs as martyrs and continued to send them their customary rents, so that, with the government factor also demanding payment, many were burdened with double rent, and in this case it was the factor, not the forfeited chief, who was deemed the oppressor. One such factor was Colin Campbell of Glenure, who managed the forfeited estate of the Stewarts of Ardshiel, in the Appin district of Argyll. He had fallen foul of the tenants and it was no doubt one of 'these Barbarians' (as he called them) that fatally shot him, near Ballachulish, on 15 May 1752, on the eve of the date fixed for the eviction of many Jacobite tenants. The suspect, Allan Breck Stewart, made his escape, but James Stewart, half-brother of the chief of the sept, was seized, tried, condemned and hanged for the deed. 'The Appin murder' remains a historic mystery, for the evidence, as we have it today, is inconclusive. All that is clear is that the murder was the outcome of a clan feud, that the trial was held at Inveraray before the Duke of Argyll as justice-general, and that, with eleven of the fifteen jurymen being of the name of Campbell, the accused's chances of a fair trial were not bright.[1]

The Commissioners' work began with detailed agricultural surveys and went on to positive measures to overcome the congestion and poverty that afflicted the estates. Long leases (up to forty-one years) were granted and guidance was given on the improved methods of farming, including drainage, enclosures, fallow, crop rotation, potato cultivation and winter fodder. Encouragement was given to the linen industry, and attempts were made, in conjunction with the Board of Trustees, to induce Lowland workers to come north and impart their skills to the natives. Education was fostered as an aid to industry. At Rannoch, for example, the pupils were taught reading and writing in the forenoon, and the boys did farm-work in the afternoon, while the girls learned spinning and sewing from the schoolmaster's wife. At Stornoway more than 400 girls had been taught spinning by 1765, and at New Tarbat, in Easter Ross, no fewer than 900 girls and 150 boys had been given instruction, during a period of nine years, in spinning, weaving and other crafts.

Again, many Highland boys were sent as apprentices to Lowland

[1] The story is immortalised in Robert Louis Stevenson's famous novel, *Kidnapped.*

farmers, spinners, weavers and dyers, so that they might return as skilled workers. A few churches were erected to supplement the parochial system in remote parts. Generous grants were made for the building of roads, bridges and harbours. At the Peace of 1763, discharged soldiers and sailors were given bounties to settle, as labourers or fishermen, on the forfeited estates, though this part of the Commissioners' schemes had little lasting result.

In 1784 the prime minister, William Pitt the younger, and Henry Dundas, then lord advocate, decided that the time had come to restore the estates, at a fair price, to the heirs of the old owners, and this was done by an Act passed that year. The transaction was applauded in Scotland and brought the Exchequer over £90,000, so that, long after this time, further grants were made for various purposes, including the payment of schoolmasters (through the S.S.P.C.K.), the construction of bridges, harbours and canals, and the completion of the Register House in Edinburgh.[1] But the main work had been rounded off in 1784 with the departure of the factors and the return of the chiefs. Though some of their plans did not quite come off, the Commissioners had attempted much and achieved something towards the economic advancement and the social betterment of a large Highland area.

Among other public agencies striving for similar ends was the Highland and Agricultural Society, founded in 1784 in the interest of improved farming, but even more important was the British Fisheries Society, which from 1786 directed its energies to the promotion of fishing, especially along the west coast, where (in contrast to the east) fishing was a matter of subsistence rather than of commerce. The crofter or cottar, using small boats and crude, home-made nets, fished for his family's use, for the high cost of salt, transport difficulties and the absence of ports and market-towns made it almost impossible to develop any steady trade. The eastern waters, on the other hand, had long attracted the Dutch, with their large boats and proper curing techniques, and from 1750 the government in London, hoping to combat this competition, offered bounties, based on tonnage, for all fishing 'busses': these were decked boats of twenty tons and upwards, with equipment up to the official standard. The bounty system helped the east coast men, the boatmen from the Clyde, and those who fished

[1] Other grants helped to promote the mapping of the Highlands, and in addition surveys were made for possible canals, and valuable reports were produced on the mineral, botanical and other resources of the region.

the waters of Loch Long and Loch Fyne, in Argyll, but it did little for the remote communities of the north-west, which clung to their small-scale, unremunerative practices.

The British Fisheries Society's aim was therefore to establish 'stations' along this coast to provide for the curing, packing and marketing of herring. The three places selected were Tobermory, in Mull, Ullapool, on Loch Broom, and Lochbay, in Skye, but, though much time, thought and capital were given to these ventures, none of them really succeeded. Tobermory became a busy little harbour, with some trade and some boat-building, Ullapool grew into a sizeable village and Lochbay into a crofting township, but the fishing depot was still to seek, and the west coast fishermen adhered to their uneconomic, ancestral ways.

In its next scheme, however, the Society scored a brilliant success. In the years 1806-11 it built a new harbour just south of Wick and laid out a new suburb called Pulteneytown, which came to overshadow the old royal burgh and to be a thriving fishing port – absorbing and giving new life to the town of Wick. From about 1814 Wick and, to a lesser degree, Helmsdale, in Sutherland, shared in the general advance of the herring fisheries, which brought prosperity to the north-eastern ports, as far as Peterhead; and yet, in the north-west, where progress was most needed, the Society, with the best intentions, had achieved next to nothing.

During our period, indeed, the silent operation of economic laws had more effect than parliamentary enactments; in particular, the life and work of the ordinary Highlander were profoundly affected by four outstanding new developments – potato culture, sheep rearing, the kelp industry and seasonal labour.[1]

The agrarian improvements had a mixed reception in the north of Scotland. In the south-eastern portion of the region, comprising Highland Perthshire, South and Mid Argyll, and East Inverness (as also in the north-eastern coastal strip), holdings were enlarged in the approved fashion: the substitution of compact farms for runrig strips was deliberately adopted, on the Duke of Argyll's orders, in Tiree in 1776, and the process spread into fairly general use by about 1820. Thus many middle-class farmers, with farms up to or beyond 150 acres, paid rents of £20-£100 a year, and the wage-earning labourers

[1] For much of what follows reference may be made to Malcolm Gray, *The Highland Economy, 1750-1850* (1957), an admirable and dispassionate study of a theme that has too often been charged with emotion in the past.

often tilled their own small holdings. Turnips, potatoes and grasses were sown, as well as oats, barley and a little wheat, lime was used as fertiliser, and the iron plough was nearly universal. Sheep farms were mostly of moderate size and other stock were carefully bred and reared.

There were artisans in such towns and villages as Kenmore and Killin, Oban and Kingussie, commerce was brisk at Campbeltown, and fishing as a speciality prospered at Tarbert, as it did in the north-east ports. Here and there dairy-farming, the sale of eggs and potatoes, distilling, linen-spinning, the cutting of timber and, above all, the traditional cattle trade served to diversify the economy. In one way or another the peasant had modest but fairly adequate cash resources.

Social conditions in the nearer Highlands approximated to those of the Lowlands. Houses were built of hewn timber, dressed stone, slate and glass, coal was beginning to displace peat, clothing depended more on imported cotton and woollens than on the old home-spun fabrics. Towards the close of the period, tea and sugar were finding their way into humble homes. Tea-drinking was for long denounced, but excessive whisky-drinking was the main social vice of the whole Highland area. Almost to a man, the clergy deplored the large number of inns and dram-shops that tempted the poor into debauchery – 'seminaries of vice and idleness', as they were called by the minister of Kirkhill, near Inverness (1792).

Beyond the Great Glen, the pattern of life and work was very different. While farmers of the middle rank were few, the holdings of the numerous crofters and cottars remained miserably small, and even these were sometimes shared by several families; congestion was specially acute in the crofter-fisher settlements.

Of all the improvements so enthusiastically taken up by southern farmers, only two made any deep impression on the north-western mainland and islands. The first was the cultivation of the potato, which seemed ideally suited to a region with surplus labour and little arable, since it gave a very high yield to the acre. In the late eighteenth century the new crop gained favour rapidly, displacing oats and bere from many fields, and, long before 1846, half or more of the sown land in most parts was given over to it. Here and there the light plough came into use, but many crofters, without money but with plenty of time on their hands, adhered to the 'spade husbandry' of the *cas chrom*. In the popular diet, dairy produce and even oatmeal became rarer than the standard potato and herring.

The second major change of the period was the adoption of commercial sheep-rearing. Unlike the potato, the sheep did not fit naturally into the Highland economy: introduced from the south by external capital, and sometimes with external labour, it depended on the profits to be made from large-scale operations. Many of the sheep-walks supported several thousand animals and rented for £100, £200, or more. They filled up the empty hill lands first, but then, especially after 1800, they encroached on the already slender supply of arable, so that the sheep-farmers, requiring land cleared of tenants and able to offer tempting rents to debt-ridden landowners, were the cause of families being removed and finally of whole glens being denuded of inhabitants. The climax came in the decade 1811-20 with the notorious Sutherland clearances, when the evicted tenants were re-settled in new crofter-fisher communities along the coast; their savage treatment left bitter memories that were to endure for generations.

Sheep-rearing, it is true, created some employment, but the shepherds formed a small class of skilled men, better off on the whole than the crofters. For the latter the coming of the sheep meant loss of both arable[1] and pasture[2] lands, but its effect was different in the two sections of the Highlands. Distress was not too severe in Perthshire and the south-east, for the dispossessed tenants could be absorbed either locally (with farming relatively prosperous) or by easy migration to the nearby Lowlands. On the north-western seaboard, however, and in the islands, there was little chance of alternative employment, and yet there was a strong disinclination to emigrate, so that the existing congestion was intensified on an ever sparser allowance of tillage.

For a time it seemed that salvation would come from the kelp industry. North-west Scotland yielded plentiful supplies of sea-weed, which need only be collected and burnt in simple kilns to produce the alkaline substances required for the manufacture of soap and glass. Protected by duties imposed on foreign commodities like barilla and potash, and favoured after 1793 by the difficulties of war-time trade, the kelp industry grew rapidly from about 1750 to reach its peak in 1810. Kelp was a particularly valuable 'cash-crop' in North and South Uist and the other Outer Isles, and it also flourished in Skye, in the

[1] It is reckoned that, over the entire 'crofting' counties, something like one-fifth of the arable went out of cultivation because of the sheep-walks, probably as much as one-fourth in Sutherland, and an even higher proportion in certain parishes.

[2] The intensified grazing of hill lands by sheep led to the rapid spread of bracken, an unprofitable and indeed injurious form of vegetation.

Argyll islands, along the adjacent mainland coast, and in Orkney. At its height it fetched £20 a ton, but the landlords were able to skim the cream off a lucrative trade, so that the peasants became, in effect, piece-work wage-earners making, in a good year, £8 by really hard labour.

The long-term effects of the rise of kelp were not good, for small holdings were further sub-divided to accommodate the landless labourers who swarmed to the main kelping areas and so increased the over-population. Moreover, prices fell after 1810, still more with the freeing of trade on the return of peace in 1815, and yet again with the reduction of tariff duties in the early 1820s. The price of kelp dropped to £7 by 1825 and to £3 by 1834, and production fell off sharply, though it did not cease: in the Outer Hebrides, despite reduced profits, it remained as the tenant's chief source of cash, and consequently the landlord's chief hope of rents being paid.

Seasonal labour away from home was another money-maker for the Highlander. The Lowland farms needed extra hands at harvest-time, and bands of hardy Highland youths repaired thither until, about 1820, they were displaced by migrant hordes of equally strong and even poorer Irish labourers. Attention then turned rather to the north-eastern fishing ports, where, during the six-week herring season in late summer, they could expect to make perhaps £3 or £4 (and so pay the rent).

The pattern of the economy was thus a complex one, but from 1815 to 1846 the trend was generally downward. One by one the marginal activities that promised to save the land-hungry peasant from penury failed him. Fishing prospered only locally and spasmodically, kelp ultimately declined into insignificance, and linen-spinning, defeated by Baltic competition, had nearly disappeared by 1840. Even the long-established cattle trade was no longer what it had been, for prices tumbled from their 1810 peak of £6 to about £3 10s. in the 1830s. Sheep-rearing made large profits for a few wealthy men but impoverished the many. And in the poorest districts the welfare and indeed the life of the community came to depend on a single crop – potatoes.

The poverty of the tenants was transmitted to the landlords, whose rent-rolls might double between 1750 and 1790 and double again by 1815, but whose debts, induced by their princely aspirations, kept ahead of their revenues, so that insolvency was almost inevitable when market prices collapsed. Not only were the tenants unable to pay any rent: they also required, by way of charity, work or meal – or both. Embarrassed beyond endurance, most of the Highland proprietors, between 1820 and 1846, had to sell their ancestral estates in whole or in part.[1] The belief grew steadily, among both the remaining old proprietors and the new owners, that clearances and emigration offered the only remedy for economic ills, the only hope of a contented and prosperous community. By 1846, even kindly and humane proprietors were being impelled towards this policy of despair.[2]

The population returns of the period illustrate the tendencies which we have been considering. The five predominantly Highland counties[3] increased from Webster's estimate of 314,823 in 1755 to 358,967 in 1801, and to 436,094 in 1841. It is true that, in relation to Scotland as a whole, the five counties declined from nearly a quarter in 1755 to just over a fifth in 1801 and to almost a sixth in 1841; still, their positive growth in numbers – without assistance from industry, the great stimulator of population – was impressive. The detailed figures are as follows:–

	1755	*1801*	*1841*
Argyll	66,286	81,277	97,371
Inverness	59,563	72,672	97,799
Perth	120,116	125,583	137,457
Ross (with Cromarty)	48,084	56,318	78,685
Sutherland	20,774	23,117	24,782

It is noteworthy that the fastest rate of growth was shown by Inverness and Ross (sharing the Western Isles) and the slowest by Perth. Moreover, both Argyll and Perth reached their peak figures in 1831 and thereafter declined; Inverness attained its maximum in 1841, while this point was not to be reached by Ross (and Cromarty) or by Sutherland until 1851.

The contrast between the nearer and the more distant Highlands is more clearly apparent from the parish figures. The returns for the Outer Hebrides and the north-west coast include the following statistics:

[1] The noble families of Argyll, Breadalbane and Sutherland, it is true, retained their ancient heritages, but they were exceptions.

[2] The impact of Scottish and Highland emigration on overseas lands is considered *infra*, chap. xix.

[3] Although Ross and Cromarty were separate shires until their formal union in 1891, they were taken together for many purposes (including the census) long before that date, and, since separate totals are unobtainable or unreliable, joint totals are given in these figures and in the table that follows.

	1755	*1801*	*1841*
Harris	1,969	2,996	4,429
Lochs (Lewis)	1,267	1,875	3,653
North Uist	1,909	3,010	4,428
South Uist	2,209	4,595	7,333
Applecross (Ross)	835	1,896	2,861
Lochbroom (Ross)	2,211	3,533	4,799

In each case the number of the inhabitants more than doubled during the period and the rate of increase was always greater than that of Scotland as a whole.

The south-eastern Highlands yield statistics that indicate a stable or declining population; among the returns for the more mountainous parishes of Argyll and Perthshire these may be taken as fairly typical:–

	1755	*1801*	*1841*
Inveraray	2,751	2,051	2,285
Inverchaolain	944	626	699
Balquhidder	1,592	1,377	871
Blair Atholl	3,257	2,848	2,231
Dull	5,748	4,055	3,811
Fortingall	3,859	3,875	2,740

The census returns confirm the impressions derived from other sources. Potato cultivation, large-scale sheep-farming, the rise and decline of kelp, the fluctuating fisheries, the advance and retreat of the cattle trade, seasonal and migratory labour, evictions and emigration – each in turn affected life and work in the Highlands; but the increasing congestion of the north-west, alongside the diminishing population of the nearer Highlands, was basically due to a different attitude to the problem of surplus labour. As the agrarian reforms spread in Perthshire and Argyll, the dispossessed and the unemployed left their homes to seek a new life, especially in Glasgow or the neighbouring shires of Lanark, Renfrew, Dumbarton or Ayr, if not overseas. In the north-western coastal and insular areas, on the other hand, agricultural progress was limited, and the inhabitants, reluctant to leave their ancestral homes, stayed where they were, to eke out a life of toilsome poverty, to intensify the over-population of a barren land, and to create social problems of the utmost gravity.

CHAPTER XV

'The Athenian Age'

IN THE years that lay between the accession of George III in 1760 and the death of Sir Walter Scott in 1832, Scotland forged ahead in the realms of scholarship and learning, of imaginative writing and creative art. Her universities were everywhere admired, her poets, novelists and artists were lauded, her philosophers and historians gained the respectful attention of civilised peoples, and the books and magazines that issued from her presses influenced opinion and judgment throughout the world. The stir and bustle of cultural life centred in Edinburgh, which, though no longer in the political sense a capital city, was hailed, in the enthusiastic language of the 'Age of Enlightenment', as 'the Athens of the North'.

The broad base of the intellectual, literary and scientific achievements of the time was provided by a system of elementary education which, with many gaps and defects, was a credit to the nation, for at long last the Knoxian ideal of a school in every parish was within sight of realisation. A petition put forward in 1782 on behalf of the schoolmasters gave their average annual income as about £13 sterling, and, if this hardly represents affluence, it does show an advance from the 1748 figure of £11. The document, moreover, professed to speak for the teachers in the 900 parish schools of Scotland, and this suggests that only a few dozen parishes were at this date without a school.[1]

Educational progress came without benefit of parliamentary assistance, for the legislators contented themselves with giving a general blessing to the work (at which we have already glanced[2]) of the Society for Propagating Christian Knowledge and of the Commissioners for the Forfeited Estates; an Act of 1786, for example, transferred some of the balances accumulated by the Commissioners to the Society, for the furtherance of its schemes. The statutory stipend of the parochial schoolmasters remained as in 1696, ranging between £5 11s. 1d. (100 merks) and £11 2s. 2d. (200 merks) a year.

[1] When the *Old Statistical Account* was compiled in the years 1791-99, it was based on a total of 938 parishes in all Scotland.

[2] See *supra*, pp. 104-5, 153-5.

For the 1790s the evidence of the *Old Statistical Account* shows conditions varying widely from parish to parish, with many a dominie still facing hardship, discouragement and sheer penury. At Kilmuir Easter, in Ross, only the minimum stipend was paid and this, eked out by scholars' fees and other emoluments, was 'not sufficient to provide the teacher with the common necessaries of life'. The two schools in Lundie and Foulis, Perthshire, seem to have been in an even worse state, for each teacher had but £40 Scots (£3 6s. 8d. sterling) a year, so that changes were frequent; this was also true of Glassford, Lanarkshire, where the school had seen five changes in six years. To supplement an inadequate income, the schoolmaster at Glenholm, Peeblesshire, kept a shop, while those of Strathmartin, Forfarshire, were wont to act as land-measurers or auctioneers.

Devoted men were ready to face all handicaps and to do their best for their pupils. At Campsie, Stirlingshire, the village schoolmaster chose 'to accept the office upon the bare emolument of the school wages' (that is, the scholars' fees), and at Kirkmichael, in Perthshire, there were also voluntary teachers for the remote parts. All the children in Anstruther Wester, Fife, without exception, were taught to read English,[1] while adults, ashamed of their lack of earlier schooling, shared the children's lessons at some of the schools.[2] By the 1790s there were only five parishes in all Scotland without a school, and five others without a school-house.[3]

The system undoubtedly had weaknesses as well as good points, and it was probably Sir John Sinclair's insistence upon the teachers' needs that led Parliament, in 1803, to pass the Parochial Schoolmasters Act. The minimum annual stipend was raised from 100 to 300 merks (£16 13s. 4d. sterling) and the maximum from 200 to 400 merks (£22 4s. 5d.); if grain or meal were paid as salary (as it sometimes was), this was to be reckoned at 200 merks a chalder.[4] The heritors must provide a commodious schoolhouse and a house for the schoolmaster of not more 'than two apartments including the kitchen', as well as a quarter-acre garden. Where two teachers were required (as

[1] Sir John Sinclair stated in 1818 that all the adults of Stewarton (Ayrshire) and Fordyce (Banff) could read.

[2] This was recorded of Renfrew and of Newburgh (Fife): see *Old Statistical Account*, VOL. II, p. 169; VOL. VIII, p. 188.

[3] See Sinclair, *Analysis of the Statistical Account of Scotland* (1825-26), VOL. II, p. 92, note †.

[4] The chalder was a very large measure, containing sixteen bolls, the boll being nearly equal to six bushels by the modern measure.

in large parishes), a salary of 600 merks (or three chalders of oatmeal) might be split between them.[1] Most enlightened and far-sighted of the clauses of the statute was that which provided for adjustments to be made in the stipends after each period of twenty-five years, in accordance with the prevailing money values as settled in the 'fiars prices'.[2] The schoolmasters reaped the benefit of this legislation in 1828, when their maximum annual stipend was raised to £34 4s. 4d.[3] With fee-revenue that might be as low as £10 a year or as high as £50, and with other customary perquisites, the parish teachers, if still far from well-paid, had much more security by the close of our period than had formerly been their lot.

The work of the parochial schools was supplemented by that of the 'Society' schools, which grew to a total of 264 by 1818, apart from 107 spinning and sewing schools for girls. Moreover, the special problems of the cities and big towns were now being tackled through the co-operation of the kirk sessions of the different charges into which these populous centres came to be split, and eventually over 100 such 'sessional' schools were helping to keep the poor and ragged children of Edinburgh, Glasgow and other towns off the streets. Then, in May 1824, the General Assembly began to establish and finance additional schools in large and ill-served parishes, especially in the Highland area, and these 'Assembly' schools in time numbered about 200.

Thus reinforced, the parish schools served the nation tolerably well, giving most of the boys and some of the girls[4] instruction in reading, writing and simple arithmetic, and, at their best (and this is particularly true of Aberdeenshire and the north-east), teaching the 'lad o' pairts' Latin and even Greek, and so preparing him for the university. But the parish system no longer stood alone, for the Seceders, the Relief Church and the Episcopalians all had their own schools, while the Roman Catholics re-entered the field from the opening of their first school at Glasgow in 1817.

During this period many of the burgh schools were still wedded

[1] In such cases the main school remained the 'parish school', while the second one was known as a 'side school'.

[2] The fiars prices (of the different grains) were 'struck' or fixed for each county every year at a meeting of the sheriff court, after evidence had been heard about local prices from all interested parties. This old practice is still followed.

[3] A second review ought to have been held in 1853, but this was not done and the clause was allowed to lapse; the Act itself was superseded by the legislation of 1861. See *infra*, p. 269.

[4] Many parish and burgh schools were now 'co-educational'.

to the purely classical tradition, as we know from the bitter testimony of Henry Cockburn, who attended Edinburgh High School between the ages of eight and fourteen (1787-93), devoting six hours each weekday for four years[1] to the drudgery of elementary Latin before going on to two pleasanter years of Greek and advanced Latin under the rector. Just before his time, Robert Reid attended the Glasgow Grammar School from his ninth until his thirteenth year (1782-86). His school hours in summer were from seven till nine, from ten till twelve, and from one till three, in winter only from nine till twelve and from one till three, but in winter the boys worked on Saturday forenoons, whereas Saturdays in summer were 'play-days'. The quarterly fees were raised in Reid's time from 5s. to 7s. 6d., while long after this, in 1815, Greek was added to the school's curriculum, a fifth class was instituted, and the fees were raised to 10s. 6d. a quarter.

It was the widespread reaction against exclusively classical studies that created the demand for academies, and the Scottish pioneer of 'modern' education, Perth Academy (1760),[2] was followed by many others, including Dundee (1786),[3] Inverness (1788), Elgin (1801), Dumfries (1804) and Edinburgh (1824). There was plenty of room for both types of school, which in some places co-existed in friendly rivalry, and elsewhere entered local unions. To our period also belong two famous privately endowed schools, now known as Dollar Academy (1818) and Madras College, St Andrews (1831), as well as Scotland's first 'public' school in the English sense – Loretto, in Edinburgh (1829).

Evening classes for adults and mechanics' institutes – both stressing 'practical knowledge' – were popular in the early years of the nineteenth century. So, too, were 'Anderson's Institution', set up for the behoof of Glasgow's working men under the will of the able but cantankerous professor of natural philosophy, John Anderson (1726-96),[4] and the Edinburgh School of Arts, founded in 1821.[5] At the other end of the

[1] During these four years, says Cockburn, though he thought himself well enough prepared for each lesson, 'there were probably not ten days in which I was not flogged, at least once'.

[2] Cf. *supra*, p. 106.

[3] Later incorporated in what became Dundee High School.

[4] Expressly designed as an up-to-date rival to the 'Old College', it did indeed offer serious competition in many fields of science and learning, and developed, on the one hand, into the Anderson College of Medicine (absorbed by the University in 1947) and, on the other, into what is now the Royal College of Science and Technology. The West of Scotland Agricultural College (1889) also evolved in the main from one of its departments.

[5] It developed into the Heriot-Watt College (1885).

educational scale, infant schools were being organised in the late 1820s by the reformers, Robert Owen and David Stow, and it was as an adjunct to his infant school at Glasgow that the latter was to develop the first 'normal school' for the training of teachers.[1] The national picture is completed with a miscellany of Sunday schools, charity schools connected with hospitals, and 'adventure' schools, varying in quality but generally of low calibre, often lasting for only a few years, but helping in a small way to fill the educational gaps.

For the universities it was a time of steady advance and expansion. Edinburgh College, finding its quarters cramped and inconvenient, moved to graceful new buildings at what came to be known as the Old Quadrangle, started in 1789 according to the design of Robert Adam but completed only in 1834 on a modified plan drawn up by William Henry Playfair. With over 1,000[2] students and 30 professors by the close of the period, it easily led the others; Glasgow had over 800 students and 19 professors, and numbers were smaller at Aberdeen and St Andrews.[3] With the abandonment of 'common tables' at St Andrews in 1820, the last link was severed with the old practice of college residence, and in all four centres the students were now accustomed to live in town lodgings.

The start of classes had been put back from October to November, and the end of the session was advanced from May to April. At Aberdeen, with its classical renown, its exacting standards, and the strong local preference for graduate teachers, it was usual for the students to complete their degrees, but graduation in arts was less common at Glasgow, even less so in Edinburgh, and almost unknown at St Andrews. In divinity, law and medicine the granting of degrees was irregular and open to abuse, for the payment of fees was often regarded as more important than the passing of any test, and at the worst the honour was simply bought and sold.

One of the best features of the universities was their retention of the policy of the 'open door' to the poor student, who, if he had the talent, could pass from burgh or parish school to his chosen college, frequently with the aid of a bursary, which, even if it were £10 a year or less, was a great help, for living expenses were low. We know, for example, that Duncan Dewar, an arts and divinity student at St Andrews

[1] See *infra*, p. 270.

[2] Its numbers were very much larger during and just after the Napoleonic wars (with their demands for doctors and surgeons), rising to a peak of over 2,000.

[3] In 1826 St Andrews as a whole and the two Aberdeen colleges each had over 300 students, but numbers had generally been far below this figure during the period.

between 1819 and 1827, spent about £14 a year on rent and food, coal, candles and oil, books and clothes, and such refinements as hats and gloves, snuff, sweets and whisky; and, though he had to be careful in his spending, he was not among the very poorest.[1] In 1827, also, the principal of Edinburgh University told of one student, then taking arts, whose outlay over the 24-week session for room-rent, fire and three meals a day came to but £8 2s.; and he asserted that a few highly exceptional youths spent even less.[2] Such cases were extreme: on the whole the Edinburgh and Glasgow students paid £15 a year or more to live and learn, while those at the other two centres could manage on rather less than that sum.

This was the homely, austere background against which the Scottish universities attained eminence in the world of learning. Brilliant teachers of youth were to be found in classics and philosophy, in divinity, law and medicine, and in such newer disciplines as astronomy, agriculture and natural history. Aberdeen's fame was fostered by Thomas Reid, the spokesman of 'the Scottish' or 'common sense' school of philosophy, by the theologian and critic, George Campbell, and by the philosopher-poet, James Beattie. St Andrews, if something of an academic backwater, had a poet of genius among her students in Robert Fergusson, but her brightest ornament was the great Church leader, Thomas Chalmers, both an alumnus and a professor of the university.[3] Glasgow (with Thomas Campbell as *its* student-poet) had a galaxy of inspiring teachers, including (apart from Reid, who came from Aberdeen, and Black and Hope, who went to Edinburgh) William Leechman in divinity, John Millar in law, James Moor and Sir Daniel Sandford in Greek, and John Anderson ('Jolly Jack Phosphorus'), who delighted the townsfolk with his experiments in physics and came to loathe his colleagues.

But it was Edinburgh University, of which William Robertson became principal in 1762, that won the highest renown at this epoch. Such was the fame of its medical school that prospective physicians flocked to it from all parts: American youths, for example, came in numbers to attend the lectures and demonstrations of William Cullen in medicine and Joseph Black in chemistry, and to take back with them across the Atlantic the enthusiasm and verve of their student

[1] See *Duncan Dewar's Accounts* (edited by Sir Peter Scott Lang, 1926).

[2] See Sir Alexander Grant, *Story of the University of Edinburgh* (1884), VOL. II, p. 488.

[3] George Hill and George Cook, successive leaders of the Moderates (who opposed Chalmers's policies), were also both St Andrews men: cf. *infra*, p. 178.

days, and the resolve to do what they could for their own land along similar lines of medical education.[1] Other great names of the time were those of James Gregory and W. P. Alison in medicine, Charles Hope in chemistry, the popular preacher, Hugh Blair, first incumbent of the chair of 'rhetoric and belles lettres',[2] Andrew Dalzel in Greek, John Robison and John Playfair in natural philosophy, and Macvey Napier, of conveyancing. Above all, the chair of moral philosophy alone was occupied in succession by four men of rare and varied genius – Adam Ferguson, Reid's ablest disciple Dugald Stewart, Thomas Brown and John Wilson ('Christopher North').[3]

It is true that some of the professors leaned to 'eloquence', to silver-tongued oratory, rather than to pure scholarship, and yet posterity has endorsed Adam Smith's verdict of 1785, that Edinburgh University was better than 'any other Society of the kind I ever knew'. Room for criticism there was, but of administration rather than teaching. The Edinburgh professors were becoming restive under town council control, especially over such academic matters as the medical curriculum, but a law-suit of 1825 went against 'the Toun's College'. At Glasgow the incumbents of the older chairs denied their 'junior' colleagues any real share in government and finance. There were scandals over the award of honorary degrees at St Andrews, and there was needless duplication of effort between Aberdeen's two colleges. With a view to tidying up these and other defects, a royal commission, appointed in 1826, collected much useful information and reported in 1830, but its suggestions were not adopted at this stage, when Parliament's energies were directed to matters of political reform.[4]

The justly high repute of its university was one reason for acclaiming Edinburgh as 'the Athens of the North', and the other was the fact that most of the leading poets and philosophers, historians and journalists, painters and architects, gravitated to the congenial setting of 'Auld Reekie', with its *salons*, its learned societies, its convivial inns and genteel coffee-houses. University scholarship and general culture went hand in hand: never had their common interest in polite letters and the advancement of the arts been stronger.

[1] One of them, Dr Benjamin Rush, wrote, 'methinks I see the place of my nativity [Philadelphia] becoming the *Edinburgh of America*': L. H. Butterfield (ed.), *Letters of Benjamin Rush* (1951), VOL. I, p. 29.

[2] This chair, founded in 1762, was really the forerunner of the chair of English literature, and the earliest of its kind.

[3] For his writings, see *infra*, p. 171.

[4] The commission's proposals did, however, form the basis of the reforms instituted in 1858 (e.g. the university court); cf. *infra*, pp. 270-1.

Now, as before,[1] it was in philosophy and history that the educated reader most delighted. Many a lesser light propounded his system of logic, ethics and metaphysics, but the primacy rested with Thomas Reid, whose *Inquiry into the Human Mind* (1764) clearly sets forth the views of the 'common sense' school and rejects the sweeping scepticism of Hume. Reid's work held its place for a full half-century and is still highly regarded, but it was as a by-product, so to speak, of philosophical thought that Adam Smith produced, in his *Inquiry into the Nature and Causes of the Wealth of Nations* (1776), one of the literary classics of all time and the 'foundation charter' of the new science of political economy. Owing something to Francis Hutcheson and to his French forerunners, Smith was yet a great and original thinker, and generations of believers in the merits of 'free trade' were to draw inspiration from his words:–

> The property which every man has in his own labour, as it is the original foundation of all other property, so it is the most sacred and inviolable. The patrimony of a poor man lies in the strength and dexterity of his hands; and to hinder him from employing this . . . in what manner he thinks proper without injury to his neighbour . . . is a manifest encroachment upon the just liberty both of the workman and of those who might be disposed to employ him. As it hinders the one from working at what he thinks proper, so it hinders the others from employing whom they think proper.

Among the historians William Robertson enhanced his fame with his *Reign of the Emperor Charles V* (1769) and his *History of America* (1777); Adam Ferguson's *Essay on Civil Society* (1766) and *History . . . of the Roman Republic* (1782) each ran to many editions; John Millar, by virtue of his *Historical View of the English Government* (1786), is deemed one of the pioneers of 'constitutional' studies; and Thomas McCrie, in his *Life of John Knox* (1812) and *Life of Andrew Melville* (1819), blended historical scholarship with Presbyterian orthodoxy. In the field of biography, indeed, as a branch of English literature, pre-eminence belongs to James Boswell, with his *Life of Samuel Johnson* (1791), and to John Gibson Lockhart, whose *Life of Burns* appeared in 1828, though his masterly *Life of Sir Walter Scott* naturally falls outside our period (1837-38). The diarist, too, another sub-class of the historian, is well exemplified for us by Alexander Carlyle and Henry Cockburn, whose works have been cited for the light they cast on their times. Less concerned with literary graces than the amassing of facts, the 'working' historians of the age included David Dalrymple,

[1] See *supra*, pp. 110-11.

Lord Hailes, who based his *Annals of Scotland* (1776-79) solidly on the original sources, and George Chalmers, whose *Caledonia* (1807-24) proves him to be Scotland's most industrious antiquary. To this epoch, moreover, belongs the *Statistical Account of Scotland*,[1] drawn up by the parish ministers in the years 1791-99 and giving us indispensable information on all aspects of the life of the time, while the monumental project of the *Acts of the Parliaments of Scotland* was launched by its first editor, Thomas Thomson, in 1814.[2]

With so much erudition in the air, with the nation thirsting for enlightenment, it is not surprising that close attention was paid to the means for the diffusion of knowledge. The first edition of no less a work than the *Encyclopaedia Britannica* was published at Edinburgh, in three volumes, in 1771 by the naturalist, antiquary and printer, William Smellie. In the early years of the nineteenth century, circulating libraries, philosophical societies and literary clubs were active in stimulating the quest for culture, while, a little later, the Bannatyne Club at Edinburgh (from 1823) and the Maitland Club at Glasgow (from 1828) were publishing, for the behoof of scholars, texts of historical worth or literary interest.

A greater impact on the masses was that of the newspaper. The *Glasgow Herald* (first called the *Advertiser*) began in 1783, the *Kelso Border Mail* in 1797, the *Dundee Advertiser* in 1801 and the *Dundee Courier* in 1816,[3] the *Ayr Advertiser* in 1803, the *Montrose Review* in 1811, and, perhaps most influential of all as a chief organ of Whig opinion, the *Scotsman* in 1817. Many others followed, at Inverness, Stirling, Cupar, Elgin, Perth and elsewhere, and by the close of the period most of the larger towns and their neighbourhoods were served by at least one weekly newspaper, which, by way of a 'reading circle' of subscribers, reached the intelligent artisan as well as the person of means and education.

The dissemination of cultural views, rather than political news, was promoted by the rise of the periodical review. The old *Scots Magazine*[4] survived until 1817, and several other ventures were made in this field in the later eighteenth century.[5] In 1802 appeared the

[1] It is known as the *Old Statistical Account*, to distinguish it from the similar *New Statistical Account* (1834-45); a further series, the *Third Statistical Account*, began in 1951 with the volume on *Ayrshire* and is in course of publication.

[2] It was completed, in thirteen very large volumes, in 1875.

[3] These two were amalgamated in 1926.

[4] See *supra*, pp. 114-15.

[5] The *Edinburgh Review* (half-yearly, only in 1755); the *Weekly Magazine* (1768-84); and the *Edinburgh Magazine and Review* (monthly, 1773-76).

first of three new periodicals that quickly established themselves in favour and esteem: this was the *Edinburgh Review*, issued by the city's leading publisher, Archibald Constable, and advocating the Whig cause in politics and the 'Moderate' side in the Church, though literary criticism was its chief interest. Its contributors – Francis Jeffrey, Sydney Smith, Francis Horner and Henry Brougham – were a formidable group of 'social lions' and arbiters of taste, but the Tories (and Evangelicals) had their spokesmen too, including Professor John Wilson, James Hogg ('the Ettrick Shepherd'), Walter Scott and J. G. Lockhart, who were resolved to reply in kind to the challenge of the *Edinburgh*. The *Quarterly Review* began in 1809, but the truly effective retort came with *Blackwood's Magazine*, launched in 1817 by Constable's chief rival, William Blackwood. The *Edinburgh* and *Blackwood's* subsisted partly by sheer literary merit and partly by the heat and fury engendered by their mutual antagonism. In addition, *Blackwood's* relied for much of its appeal on the *Noctes Ambrosianae*, a long drawn-out (1822-35) series of imaginary dialogues, placed at a hostelry run by one Ambrose, ranging over every topic of interest to mankind, and very highly thought of in their own day.[1] Support for such publications necessarily came from the educated classes, but in 1832 appeared *Chambers's Edinburgh Journal*, which (in weekly numbers, costing 1½d. each) dispensed to the masses instruction and amusement of a humbler kind: it was the first really successful medium of cheap, popular culture.

If this was the heyday of the polite literature of philosophy, history and criticism, imaginative writing was at an even higher level. The year of Scott's birth, 1771, saw the appearance of Tobias Smollett's best work, *Humphry Clinker*, and also of Henry Mackenzie's *The Man of Feeling*, highly praised in its day as a 'novel of sentiment'. The year 1808 brought *The Cottagers of Glenburnie*, by Elizabeth Hamilton, while Susan Ferrier wrote three novels, *Marriage* (1818), *The Inheritance* (1824) and *Destiny* (1831). Each of these works contains realistic descriptions of Scottish scenes and family life, but the best of Scott's contemporaries as a novelist was John Galt (1779-1839), whose *Ayrshire Legatees* (1820-21), *Annals of the Parish* (1821), *The Provost* (1822) and *The Entail* (1823) vividly re-create the characters and conditions of urban and rural life in the author's own time.

The poetry of Robert Fergusson (1750-74), as of Allan Ramsay,

[1] The principal author of the *Noctes* was Wilson ('Christopher North'), but Hogg, Lockhart and others also had a hand in some of the numbers.

clearly foreshadows that of Burns. A more introspective man than his great successor, with a weaker physique and an even readier tendency to drown his sorrows in drink, Fergusson, despite his tragically early death, left a remarkable series of satirical vignettes – mostly in the six-line stanza – of Edinburgh life, including 'Leith Races', 'Hallow Fair', 'Auld Reekie' and 'The Daft Days'; his work, and his alone, might easily be mistaken for that of the master:–

> Now mirk December's dowie face [*drooping*
> Glowrs owre the rigs wi' sour grimace
> While, thro' his *minimum* of space,
> The blear-ey'd sun,
> Wi' blinkin' light and stealing pace,
> His race doth run.

Not a few writers of this epoch are remembered for one or two well-loved Scots songs, among them John Skinner for 'Tullochgorum', Lady Anne Barnard for 'Auld Robin Gray', Allan Cunningham for 'John Grumlie', Robert Tannahill for 'Jessie, the Flower o' Dunblane' and 'The Bonnie Wood o' Craigielea', and James Hogg not so much for his prose works[1] as for 'Cam' ye by Athole' or 'When the Kye comes hame'. A greater contribution was made to vernacular literature by Caroline, Lady Nairne (1766-1845), whose lilting or rollicking songs rank next after those of Burns in public favour – 'The Laird o' Cockpen', 'The Land o' the Leal', 'Caller Herrin'', 'Charlie is my Darling', 'Will ye no come back again?', 'The Hundred Pipers' and 'The Rowan Tree'.

In an entirely different vein, James Macpherson (1736-96) won European fame for his alleged 'translations' from the Gaelic epic poet Ossian (*Fingal*, 1762, and *Temora*, 1763); the 'Ossianic' controversy raged fiercely during his lifetime and has never quite died out, but it is thought nowadays that Macpherson freely adapted and re-cast traditional legends from the Highlands, and that 'impostor' is too harsh a term for this wayward Celtic pioneer of the romantic movement. A generation later, it was another Scot, Thomas Campbell (1777-1844), who wrote the best-known of the patriotic and martial verse of the Napoleonic age.

Thus, even without Burns and Scott, 'the Athenian age' produced much creative literature of distinction, but its renown, of course, rests

[1] And yet modern critical opinion is highly favourable to his macabre study, *The Private Memoirs and Confessions of a Justified Sinner* (1824).

chiefly on the fact that it covers the careers of Scotland's two greatest writers of all time. Robert Burns (1759-96), though born to a struggling Ayrshire farmer, was well-read, especially in the poetry of his Scottish predecessors; from them he inherited much – a variety of metres (his favourite six-line stanza, the nine-line stanza of 'Christis Kirk on the Green', the fourteen-line stanza of 'The Cherry and the Slae', the heroic and octosyllabic couplets), the tunes of dozens of old folk-songs, the taste for homely descriptions of nature and country life, and the cult of the love-song, the drinking song and ecclesiastical satire. But on all his work he impressed the stamp of his own genius, and generations of simple Scots, at home and abroad, have turned to him for solace, for amusement, for the joy of recapturing something of their own youth. Among his songs, 'Duncan Gray', 'Scots Wha Hae', 'Comin' thro' the Rye', 'Ca' the Yowes to the Knowes' and 'The Lea Rig' have an undying appeal; of his lyrical and narrative verse, 'Tam Samson's Elegy', 'The Jolly Beggars', 'Tam o' Shanter' and 'The Twa Dogs' are as truly 'Scottish' in feeling as anything in our literature; never has religious hypocrisy been more trenchantly exposed than in 'The Ordination', 'Holy Willie's Prayer' and 'Address to the Unco Guid'. The range of his moods is as wide as human nature itself, extending from the solemnity of these lines (in 'To a Mouse'):–

Still thou art blest, compared wi' me!
The present only toucheth thee:
But och! I backward cast my e'e
    On prospects drear!
An' forward, tho' I canna see,
    I guess an' fear!

– to the festive gaiety of Hallowe'en:–

Wi' mony sangs, an' friendly cracks,
    I wat they didna weary; [*I know*
And unco tales, and funnie jokes –
    Their sports were cheap and cheery:
Till butter'd sow'ns,[1] wi' fragrant lunt, [*steam*
    Set a' their gabs a-steerin'; [*stirring*
Syne, wi' a social glass o' strunt [*liquor*
    They parted aff careerin'
        Fu' blythe that night.

[1] Sowens or sowans was a light paste or pudding made from oatmeal dust or bran, slightly soured or fermented by steeping in water, and best eaten with milk.

While Burns's life reached its premature close mainly by reason of ill-health, complicated, but not caused, by his addiction to drink, the career of Sir Walter Scott (1771-1832), after attaining the dizziest heights of fame and popularity, was clouded over by the failure of Constable's publishing business in 1826, for, as an active partner, Scott was too proud and honourable to seek relief in bankruptcy, and chose, at the cost of his health and happiness, to devote his last six years to the superhuman task of paying off his creditors by the work of his pen. Heroic in his life as in his works, he left to posterity a mass of writings which (apart from many historical[1] and miscellaneous books) places him with the world's great authors on three counts. First, in *The Minstrelsy of the Scottish Border* (1802-3), he rescued age-old ballads from threatened oblivion, refining, adjusting and completing them with loving care, and yet retaining the authentic voice of the past, as in the bitter cry of reproach (against the merciless James V) in 'Johnie Armstrong':-

> To seik het water beneith cauld ice,
> Surely it is a greit follie –
> I have asked grace at a graceless face,
> But there is nane for my men and me.

Secondly, his original verse, especially 'The Lay of the Last Minstrel' (1805), 'Marmion' (1808) and 'The Lady of the Lake' (1810), provides moving narratives woven imaginatively around episodes that had fired Scott's feeling for the national history; no passage is better known than the Flodden battle-scene:-

> But yet, though thick the shafts as snow,
> Though charging knights like whirlwinds go,
> Though bill-men ply the ghastly blow,
> Unbroken was the ring;
> The stubborn spear-men still made good
> Their dark impenetrable wood,
> Each stepping where his comrade stood
> The instant that he fell.

Thirdly, from 1814 until 1831 there appeared (at a rate of one, two or even three a year, besides many other works) the matchless series of the Waverley novels, known and admired the world over – both the

[1] Most notable among these are the *Tales of a Grandfather* (3 series, 1827-29), forming a connected history of Scotland for the use of the young; on adults as well as children the influence of the *Tales*, in presenting the traditional and romantic record of the nation's past, has been enormous.

romantic tales of chivalry and war in distant lands, like *Ivanhoe*, *The Betrothed* and *The Talisman*, and the even better stories with a Scottish setting, in which Scott moved with the easy familiarity of the expert, particularly *Waverley* itself, *Guy Mannering*, *The Antiquary*, *Old Mortality*, *Rob Roy* and *The Heart of Midlothian*.

'The Wizard of the North', though he had his human failings – vanity in his life, prosiness in his writings – also had personal courage, true patriotism and literary genius in full measure, and, when he died in 1832 (before discharging all his debts, but having so wrought as to ensure that all creditors would ultimately be paid in full), Scotland and mankind were the poorer for his passing.

It is fortunate that 'the Athenian age' of letters and learning had its worthy artist. With the great and regrettable exception of Burns, the distinguished men and women of the time are imperishably recorded on the glowing canvases of Scotland's pre-eminent portrait painter: Sir Henry Raeburn (1756-1823) left us vivid and colourful likenesses of Scott and Viscount Melville, Sir John Sinclair and Dugald Stewart, judges like Lord Braxfield and Lord Newton, Highland chiefs like Macdonell of Glengarry and The Macnab, attractive women like Mrs Scott Moncrieff and Mrs William Urquhart. And a younger contemporary, Sir David Wilkie (1785-1841), won extraordinary popularity with his delineations of common scenes of domestic and village life – 'Pitlessie Fair', 'The Blind Fiddler', 'Rent Day', 'Village Festival', 'The Penny Wedding', 'Blind Man's Buff' and others, which found their way, as coloured prints, into many humble Scottish homes.

During this remarkable epoch, moreover, architecture flourished as never before. Robert Adam (1728-92) designed the Register House, Charlotte square and the original buildings of the University in Edinburgh, the Royal Infirmary in Glasgow, Culzean castle (Ayrshire) and other rural mansions, but neither he nor his brother William confined his attention to Scotland: Sion house in Middlesex, Portland place, Lansdowne house and the Adelphi, all in London, besides many country houses, attest the appeal of their talents and taste to English patrons. In this respect they were typical of their time, for, in art as in science, Scotsmen went forth to find work, fame and fortune in England and on the Continent. Outstanding among such voluntary exiles was James Watt, the mechanical genius of the age (1736-1819), but there were many more – William and John Hunter, among the leaders of London's medical fraternity in the first part of George III's reign,[1] James Hutton (1726-97), 'the first great British geologist', William Murdock[2] (1754-1839), the pioneer of gas lighting[3] and author of 'the earliest practical essay on the subject', Sir Robert Strange (1721-92), who, as a line engraver, was 'in the very first European rank',[4] Gavin Hamilton (1730-97), the Lanark painter who became an expert excavator of Roman antiquities, and James Tassie from Pollokshaws (1735-99), the exquisite worker in enamels, seals and cameos, whose portrait-medallions brought him high renown as an original artist.

If there was a sneer, there was also some truth, in Voltaire's comment, made at the start of the period (1762) – 'it is from Scotland that we receive rules of taste in all the arts – from the epic poem to gardening'.

[1] It is to William Hunter (1718-83) that Glasgow University is indebted for the Hunterian museum, incorporating the varied and valuable collections made and bequeathed by him.

[2] He changed his name to this spelling to accommodate his English associates who were unable to cope with the guttural 'ch'.

[3] He arranged the illuminations at Soho to celebrate the Peace of Amiens in March 1802.

[4] The last three quotations are all taken from the *Dictionary of National Biography*.

CHAPTER XVI

Dissent and Disruption

THE CLOSE connection between learning, literature and religion during the 'Age of Enlightenment' is perfectly symbolised in the career of William Robertson, historian, principal of Edinburgh University, and acknowledged leader, from 1762, of the Moderate party in the Church of Scotland.[1] It was by his direction and advice that, for nearly two decades, the affairs of the General Assembly were guided, and his voice was always in favour of legality, respectability and tolerance. He and his friends, such as Alexander Carlyle and Hugh Blair, put the stamp of their own reasonable and civilised views on the ecclesiastical polity of their time, and, to a large extent, disarmed the opposition of the Popular or Evangelical party. To the latter group, indeed, belonged Alexander Webster, the ingenious author of the unofficial census of 1755, but its ablest spokesman, John Witherspoon, left Scotland in 1768 to become a great president of the College of New Jersey and thus to lay the foundations of the famous institution now known as Princeton University. Sir Henry Moncreiff[2] was elected moderator in 1785, and for over twenty years he led the Evangelicals, but during much of the time the Moderates had things their own way.

The sharpest conflict between the Church parties still, and for long after, arose over the issue of lay patronage. To the Moderate majority patronage was the law of the land, and the Church must admit any minister who was lawfully presented and was qualified in life and doctrine: only if the presentee were a loose liver or of unsound faith could he be rejected by the presbytery. The remedy, in their view, lay with the Church itself, for did it not license every candidate for the ministry? It was therefore incompetent for a presbytery (in defiance of the General Assembly as well as of Parliament) to refuse a valid presentation by a patron: licence and presentation must automatically be followed by ordination, and the 'call' by the congregation (which the Popular party regarded as essential) was but an empty form, little more than a convenience, or at best a sign of good will

[1] See *supra*, pp. 101, 111.

[2] He was a Perthshire baronet and one of several of his line ordained to the ministry; he later added his wife's name to his own, to become Sir Henry Moncreiff Wellwood.

from the laity. Robertson and his friends, indeed, went so far as to maintain that patronage had helped to sustain good order in the Church and had raised the quality of the clergy. They may even have thought privately of the seceders as forming a useful safety-valve for discontent among Presbyterians, rather than as a reproach to the policy that had driven them out.

The toleration of communions other than the Presbyterian was a cardinal point with Principal Robertson, who had no doubt that the penal laws against the Roman Catholics were a stain on the record of a humane and civilised society. In England the Romanists were relieved in 1778 of their civic disabilities,[1] so that thenceforth they could, as citizens, inherit property (though they could not yet vote or hold political office). The intention was to apply the reform to Scotland in 1779, but early that year 'no-Popery' riots in Edinburgh and Glasgow showed that popular sentiment was strongly against the change. The government bowed to the storm and abandoned its proposal, while the General Assembly declared repeal of the penal laws to be inexpedient and dangerous.

In 1780 Robertson gave up the leadership of the Moderates, to be succeeded by another university dignitary, George Hill, a professor at St Andrews, soon to become principal of St Mary's College there[2]; but the change brought no difference in church polity. The logical conclusion of the tendencies of the time came in 1784, when the General Assembly dropped the annual protest against patronage – a protest, it is true, that had degenerated into a routine item of business; still, the decision showed that the Moderates no longer felt lay patronage to be a grievance to be got rid of as soon as opportunity offered.

Towards the close of the century the defects of the parochial organisation of the Church were giving concern to its leaders. The 938 parishes, each as a rule provided with one church and one minister, no longer corresponded to the population-pattern, for, while certain country districts were losing their inhabitants, some of the larger towns were growing at an alarming rate, and a number of entirely new communities were springing up. It was difficult for the Church to extend its services efficiently into such new centres, since the parish was a

[1] The change was not effected without controversy and disturbance, for London witnessed in 1780 destructive riots led by a deranged Scotsman of noble birth, Lord George Gordon.

[2] He was in turn (1819) to be succeeded in the leadership of the Moderates by his nephew and biographer, George Cook, who likewise became a professor at St Andrews.

legal entity, and any radical change, such as the establishment of a *quoad sacra* parish,[1] involved legal proceedings which might be protracted and costly,[2] and would almost certainly demand increased contributions (to meet the charges for the new ministerial stipend and the upkeep of the new church and manse) from the heritors. The easier and cheaper method was to set up 'chapels of ease' to serve the new communities, and a regular plan to this end[3] was adopted by the Assembly in 1798, but that body was quite unwilling to provide relief by this device for a congregation that was merely burdened by an unpopular presentee. The problem had thus been posed but not finally settled, and indeed each year that passed rendered more challenging the needs of the 'churchless' masses of the Industrial Revolution.

Another difficulty arose over the stipends, which had last been systematically reviewed in the reign of Charles I, and which had failed to keep pace with the rise in prices and wages. By the mid-eighteenth century, the average annual stipend was £52, but many ministers got only £30 or £40, and some as little as £20. An all-round increase was badly overdue, but the stumbling-block was again the reluctance of the heritors to undertake any additional outlays. For this reason a proposal for a general augmentation had to be dropped in 1793, and another unsolved, and acute, problem was carried over into the nineteenth century.

The very virtues of the Moderates – their urbanity, their scholarly interests, their tolerance towards other men's creeds – were apt to cut them off from ordinary people, many of whom were now turning away from such remote and superior pastors to the simpler and humbler ministers of the Popular party within the Church, or of the seceders without. The steady growth of Presbyterian dissent, mainly by reason of departures from the Church of Scotland of members displeased with an individual minister forced upon them by a patron, or dissatisfied with the whole bearing of the Moderate leaders, is a striking feature of the times. By 1773 there were 190 dissenting congregations in Scotland, and they were thought to have as many as 100,000 ad-

[1] When a division of a civil parish (or parish *quoad civilia*) is set aside as a separate unit for ecclesiastical purposes only, it is called a parish *quoad sacra*; a parish that is still undivided for both civil and ecclesiastical purposes is a parish *quoad omnia*.

[2] Since 1707 the jurisdiction of the Commissioners (or Court) of Teinds had been vested in the Court of Session, the highest civil court in the land, before which litigation was liable to be expensive. Cf. *supra*, p. 7, n. 2.

[3] The erection of new chapels was to be sanctioned by the Assembly after full inquiry and report by the presbytery concerned.

herents; by 1800 their popular support was reckoned at 150,000 (or about 15 per cent of the total adult population). Even if some allowance be made for exaggeration in these figures, the threat was serious enough to reflect on the claim of the establishment to be a truly national church. Not that all was plain sailing for the seceders: they too had their conflicts, most notably in 1782, when the 'Lifter' controversy – a dispute as to whether the minister should 'lift' the Communion elements before or after the consecrating prayer – looked like sundering the Anti-burgher synod, though the split was healed before very long.

The Scottish Episcopalians continued to labour under the civil disabilities imposed in 1746,[1] but, persecuted as they were, they had a triumph in November 1784, when, at Aberdeen, four of their bishops consecrated Samuel Seabury as bishop of Connecticut and so transmitted the apostolic succession to the Protestant Episcopal Church in the United States. The death of Prince Charles in 1788 released them from their strange loyalty to the exiled (and Roman Catholic) Stuarts and at last allowed them to offer prayers – some of them, it is true, with misgivings – for King George; and the penal laws against them were repealed in 1792. The members of the Roman Church in Scotland, thwarted in 1779, had longer to wait for emancipation, but at least their priests had the benefit, from 1793, of a small government subsidy to alleviate their indigence.[2] Their numbers are thought to have undergone a further contraction at this time – from some 33,000 (or 2·6 per cent of the total population) about 1760 to 30,000 (or 1·8 per cent) in 1800.

While no revolutionary changes occurred before the end of the century, its closing years saw the stirrings of a new spirit that was destined, within a generation, to transform the religious life of the nation. The long 'reign of the Moderates' was by no means over, but from this time onwards the balance began slowly to swing towards their opponents. Thomas Chalmers (1780-1847), licensed in 1799, and Andrew Thomson (1779-1831), who qualified soon after, were to put fresh heart into the Popular party, just when the Moderates were becoming more noted for complacency, caution and excessive legality than for the scholarly qualities that had formerly been their main characteristics.

From outside the fold, at this time, there came a challenge to the Church in the informal meetings conducted by the brothers Robert

[1] See *supra*, p. 102.

[2] This financial assistance was arranged by Dundas in an utterly secret manner.

and James Haldane. Though cold-shouldered or denounced by the Presbyterians, the Haldanes, from 1797, were setting up independent chapels or tabernacles and starting Sunday schools, and this year marks the foundation of what became the Congregational Union of Scotland. The General Assembly expressed concern in 1799 about such 'vagrant teachers and Sunday schools', excluded from its parochial charges or chapels any who were not licensed for its own ministry, and even denied their right to preach. This Act was clearly aimed against the Haldanes and their associates, but the Congregationalists survived and gathered more and more adherents.

Meanwhile, a 'new light' dawned among the Seceders, which led them to reconsider the old Presbyterian tenet that it was the duty of the civil magistrate to maintain the true faith; many of them came to reject this view, to regard the Covenants as mistaken, and to hold that religion should be 'voluntary' – a matter for the individual conscience and not for the state. The Associate (or Burgher) Synod,[1] unable to compose this dispute, split into the New Light Burghers, who, being in a majority, retained the name of the Associate Synod, and the Old Light (or 'Auld Licht') minority, who were numerous enough to form before long their own Original Associate Synod. A similar schism occurred within the Anti-burghers in 1806, the New Light majority keeping the title of General Associate Synod, while the Old Lights in this case took the style of Constitutional Associate Presbytery.

A period of sixty years had thus brought a fourfold division among the Seceders, and yet such was the vigour of Presbyterian dissent that all four branches flourished and increased[2]: not only that, but the way was prepared for a series of cross-unions among them. In 1820 the Associate Synod (New Light Burghers) combined with a majority of the General Associate Synod (New Light Anti-burghers) to form the United Associate Synod of the Secession Church; popularly known as the United Secession, this body, much the largest among the dissenters, stood forth as the champion of 'voluntaryism'. The non-uniting minority of the General Associate Synod, calling themselves 'Protesters', chose instead, in 1827, to throw in their lot with the Constitutional Associate Presbytery and to form with it the Associate Synod of Original Seceders. By these changes, the four branches of

[1] See *supra*, p. 99.

[2] Dr Thomas McCrie (1772-1835), the biographer of Knox and Melville, and in his day the most distinguished of Seceders, belonged to the smallest and most extreme branch, the Constitutional Associate Presbytery; cf. *supra*, p. 169.

THE ORIGINAL SECESSION:

DIVISIONS AND UNIONS, 1747-1842

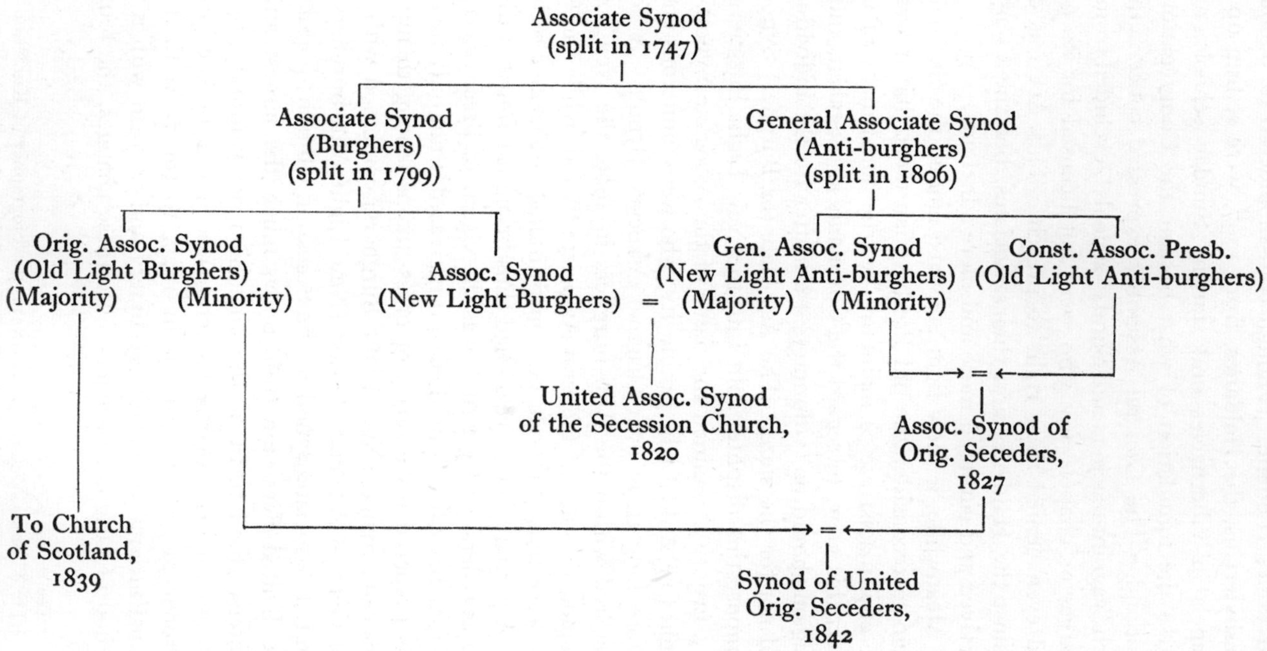

the Original Secession were reduced to three, each of which enjoyed a fair measure of public support. (See table on facing page.)

For the ministers of the Church of Scotland the year 1810 brought the long-sought augmentation of stipends, when Parliament set aside a sum of £10,000 a year from the public revenue for the purpose of raising the emoluments (in money or kind) in each parish to a minimum of £150. The clergymen rightly welcomed the relief thus afforded them from material cares, but it is pertinent to note the economic and social consequences of the change. Only recently (in 1803) had the annual salary of the parish schoolmaster been increased to a *maximum* of £22 4s. 5d., and, while it is true that he might receive a substantial sum from the scholars' fees, he was probably still somewhat underpaid. Not so the minister: even on the minimum stipend he was comfortably placed, and many livings were, or came to be, far above the minimum. The danger was that the minister would align himself with the county gentry on equal terms, lose 'the common touch' and suffer by comparison with the simple, austere life of the dissenting pastor (to whom £100 a year might be a fond dream). The relative affluence and the class interests of the established clergy had their bearing on what was to follow.

In the opening decades of the nineteenth century the Church was agitated by certain spiritual and social causes which proved sharply controversial. Sabbath schools were for long regarded with distrust as being alien and therefore vaguely threatening to the traditional order: they might put dangerous thoughts and aspirations into the minds of the children of the poor. 'Church extension', the campaign to carry religious services into the newer towns and the raw suburbs created by the Industrial Revolution, also aroused misgivings, since it cut across the existing parochial organisation, which was deemed basic and essential. The Moderates' abhorrence of 'enthusiasm' spread to foreign missions, and from 1796 projects to evangelise the heathen, though advocated by the Popular party, were opposed as unnecessary or absurd. Not until 1824 did the General Assembly make a move in the direction of approval, so that Alexander Duff was able to leave for India in 1829 as the first missionary of the Church of Scotland, to found a mission school at Calcutta in the next year.

In the eyes of the champions of an evangelical faith, the spiritual and material wretchedness of the times, and especially the grinding poverty of the great cities, were a challenge to the powers of religion. While many were coming to believe that compulsory assessments for poor relief were the only solution to this problem, others held that the ancestral way of neighbourly and voluntary charity agreed best with true Christian fellowship. Among the latter was Thomas Chalmers, now in the forefront as a preacher and writer. To prove to the world that the voluntary system, properly applied, could still work in the most trying conditions, he took charge in succession of two of Glasgow's poorest parishes, the Tron and St John's, where, with a band of devoted helpers, he did much to relieve and elevate the neediest inhabitants (1815-23). Whether his work would have stood the test of time is doubtful, for he gave it up to take a chair at St Andrews in 1823, whence he went on to Edinburgh in 1828.

In 1833, at long last, the reign of the Moderates came to an end, for the Evangelicals then secured, and thereafter retained, a majority in the General Assembly, while their intellectual and spiritual superiority was even more marked than their numerical advantage. In no sense could their opponents match the zeal and ability of Chalmers or of his lieutenants, David Welsh, Thomas Guthrie and Robert Candlish. Their advent to power, and their determination to achieve in the Church a reform akin to that which had been made in the State in 1832, brought on 'the Ten Years' Conflict' (1833-43), a sustained struggle to amend the ecclesiastical establishment by the introduction of a large measure of freedom from political and judicial control.

The Assembly of 1834 passed two Acts which virtually gave notice of its intention fundamentally to alter the existing state connection. It was declared by the Veto Act 'that no pastor shall be intruded[1] on any congregation contrary to the will of the people', that is, 'if the major part of the male heads of families . . . shall disapprove' of him: the law of patronage was to be subject to a simple congregational veto. The Chapel Act provided that all ministers settled in chapels of ease should be members of the church courts, with the full rights of parish ministers, and with territorial districts (hitherto denied to them) now assigned to them: by this enactment the Church assumed the right to amend its own constitution without reference to Parliament or Court of Session (acting as the Court of Teinds).[2]

The first trial of strength occurred at Auchterarder, in Perthshire, and led to prolonged litigation (1834-39), since the presentee, after

[1] The conflict is often styled 'the non-intrusion controversy'.

[2] Church politics – apart from the constitutional issue – were involved in this measure, for the chapel ministers were known to favour the Popular party, and their admission to parity of status would increase that party's power. For the Court's jurisdiction, cf. *supra*, p. 7, n. 2, and p. 179.

objection by the congregation and rejection by the presbytery, had recourse, along with the patron, to the Court of Session, which ultimately found the presbytery's action to be illegal, and this verdict was confirmed, on appeal, by the House of Lords. Meanwhile, a different situation had developed at Lethendy (East Perthshire), where the patron, bowing to the presbytery of Dunkeld's disapproval of his first presentee, made a second nomination, which was acceptable; but the first presentee complained to the Court of Session, which thereafter censured the presbytery (1837-39). Marnoch, in Banffshire, supplied yet another pattern of behaviour, for here, after a rejected presentee had successfully invoked the aid of the Court of Session, the presbytery of Strathbogie became sharply split, the majority being ready to enforce the law of patronage, but the minority abiding by the terms of the Veto Act. While the General Assembly denounced and eventually deposed the majority, the Court supported them and actually forbade any of the minority to sit in the Assembly (1837-42). The impasse was complete: Dr Cook and the Moderates could not get the Veto Act annulled because they were outnumbered, Dr Chalmers and the Evangelicals would not hear of compromise, and all endeavours to persuade the government in London to alter the law of patronage failed.

While the conflict was moving to its climax, the Popular party received a further accession of strength in 1839, when the greater part of the Original Associate Synod (Old Light Burghers), sympathising warmly in the struggle against patronage and finding no good reason for remaining outside the reawakened Church of Scotland, rejoined it. Some of the members of the sect, however, refused to follow this course, and combined instead, in 1842, with the Antiburghers (who had already come together in 1827) to form the Synod of United Original Seceders.

A sharper edge was given to the non-intrusion cause by the foundation, in 1840, of the bi-weekly Evangelical newspaper, *The Witness*, under the able and militant editorship of Hugh Miller.[1] The years 1840 and 1841 passed without any middle way being found by the Assembly, while the accession to power of the Conservatives, under Sir Robert Peel, in August 1841, made no difference as regards Parliament's unwillingness to intervene. In May 1842, moved by what it deemed 'the illegal encroachments of the Court of Session', the Assembly, in the document known as the Claim of Right, protested against these 'invasions', reaffirmed the liberties of the Kirk, and

[1] See *infra*, p. 273.

suggested either that these be maintained or that all should 'endure resignedly the loss of the temporal benefits of an establishment'. These words were, and were intended to be, prophetic.

The winter months brought no relief. Government and Parliament refused to act, and the Court of Session, having several times declared against the Veto Act, now found equally against the Chapel Act, by rejecting as unlawful a proposal to assign a part of the parish of Stewarton, in Ayrshire, to a Seceder minister who had come in by way of the union of 1839 (January 1843). In May 1843 the Assembly met, with the Evangelicals firmly resolved to carry out their plans 'for separating, in an orderly way, from the establishment'. Having read out a long protest, Dr Welsh, the moderator, followed by Chalmers, Candlish and a host of colleagues, solemnly left the meeting and proceeded with calm dignity to form the Free Church of Scotland. Some 450 ministers 'came out' at the Disruption – rather fewer than the Evangelicals hoped, rather more than the Moderates expected, and, all in all, much the largest breach ever suffered by the Kirk. The tragedy – for, despite all the enthusiasm, courage and self-sacrifice involved, such it was – might possibly have been averted, had the Popular party been more patient, or the Court of Session less legalistic, or, perhaps most important, the government more sympathetic and accommodating; as it was, no one was prepared to yield an inch for the sake of a negotiated settlement, and the unhappy strife pursued its course to its deplorable end.

Almost coincident in time with the Disruption was a minor breakaway from the main body of Presbyterian dissent. The Rev. James Morison left the United Secession Church in 1841 in protest against a rigid insistence on the doctrine of salvation for 'the elect' only, instead of for all men, and in 1843 he and other 'Morisonians', as they were commonly called, formed the Evangelical Union.

The Scottish Episcopal Church took an important step in 1804, in pursuance of an undertaking given in 1792 in return for the abrogation of the penal statutes.[1] The bishops and clergy assented, and promised to subscribe, to the Thirty-nine Articles of the Church of England, thereby aligning their doctrine and worship with that of the Anglicans and, in consequence, moving further away from the principles that they had once held in common with the Presbyterians. These Articles thenceforth served as the standard 'test' of the Episcopalian faith in Scotland, and this requirement, together with acceptance

[1] See *supra*, p. 180.

of the royal supremacy, was reaffirmed in 1811. Apart from this major change of polity, the period was uneventful for the Episcopalians.

For the Roman Catholics, by contrast, it was a time of rapid and significant development. 'Catholic emancipation' had been advocated for fifty years by reformers throughout Britain and Ireland when, in 1829, the Tory administration of Wellington and Peel induced Parliament to accept the change, so that thenceforth adherents of the Romanist faith became full citizens, eligible for political office. Within Scotland the character of the Roman Catholic community was now being profoundly modified as a result of the large-scale immigration of Irish labourers and their families, especially from the 1820s onwards.[1] By 1827, when the church was reorganised in three vicariates-apostolic (the western, eastern and northern) instead of two, it is estimated that the 30,000 Romanists (mostly native) of 1800 (amounting to but 1·8 per cent of the population) had increased to 70,000 (or 3·0 per cent), of whom some 25,000 were in the Glasgow district alone. By 1841 the number of Irish-born inhabitants of Scotland had swollen to 126,300, or 4·8 per cent of the total; and, although this figure is not to be equated with the Roman Catholic population (for there were both native Romanists and Irish Protestant immigrants), it does suggest the substantial influx into Lowland Scotland, which was still to grow immensely but was already, towards the close of our period, beginning to cause alarm to the champions of the Protestant faith.

[1] But the first 'Irish Catholic' church had been set up (in Paisley) as early as 1808, and there were Romanist schools in Glasgow from 1817.

CHAPTER XVII

The Beginnings of Reform

IN THE middle of the reign of George III there had been some agitation for the reform of both Parliament and the burghs, but the demands then made, although reasonable in themselves, lost their appeal when they could be denounced as seditious or revolutionary claims for the violent overthrow of an admirable and free constitution, and they were effectively silenced by the outbreak of the Reign of Terror in France in 1793.[1] From about 1800, accordingly, the Whigs, urged on, and frequently embarrassed, by their radical allies, had an uphill fight to reinstate reform as a respectable and practicable cause, and a full generation was to pass before Parliament could be induced to make the changes that had become long overdue. A narrow franchise and close corporations suited the Tory party, and, indeed, made possible its almost unbroken tenure of power, so that it needed more than the exposure of the evils of England's rotten boroughs and Scotland's record of magisterial misdeeds to persuade the government of the day to amend a system which, corrupt as it might be, was basic to its own existence.

It was politics, then, that linked the two causes, which might otherwise have been considered separately; for, whereas parliamentary reform called for a major readjustment of the balance of forces within the state – a shift of power away from the privileged and propertied classes – burgh reform, though asserted by its advocates to be the more urgent of the two, was a matter of correcting a large number of varied and often petty abuses, and could therefore be tackled piecemeal (always provided that the ministry allowed Parliament to take the necessary action). Thus, while the electoral changes had to await the full triumph of liberal ideals in the body politic, some advances, small enough when viewed in isolation, and yet of good augury for the future, were actually achieved in the field of municipal government.

The burgh constitutions were open to criticism on various grounds. First, in the absence of any central check on revenue and expenditure or of an effective audit of the accounts, the magistrates and councillors were quite irresponsible, and it was notorious that they had so abused their position that, by fraudulent sales (often to themselves, their

[1] See *supra*, pp. 122-3.

families, or their friends) of common lands and rents, by refraining from taxation and by reckless borrowing, they had alienated the 'patrimony' of many burghs and brought them (despite the high level of urban prosperity) to the brink of insolvency. Secondly, the powers of the burghs, even if conscientiously used, were archaic and utterly unsuited to the needs of the factory age: in particular, they were inadequate or wholly lacking in respect of 'watching', lighting, cleansing and water supply. Thirdly, the creation of new burghs, badly needed by reason of the growth of new industrial centres, seaports and suburbs, was cumbersome and difficult: additions to the sixty-six royal burghs (still legally possessing the monopoly of trade) had been ruled out altogether by the Union, while there was doubt as to whether the status and rights of a burgh of barony were worth the trouble and expense of erection and maintenance.[1] Finally – and this was the hard core of the problem – the town councils of the royal burghs were self-perpetuating bodies, answerable to no one but themselves and forming a close oligarchy, while burgess-ship itself was kept within narrow limits by the raising of the charges exacted from guild brethren, craftsmen and burgesses.

The first tentative moves in the direction of burgh reform may be seen in the passing of local 'police acts' or in the granting of charters conveying 'police' powers: 'police' at this time, and throughout most of the nineteenth century, meant the right and duty of administering such branches of government as lighting, paving, street-cleaning, water supply, drainage, taxation for all these purposes, and sometimes, but not always, 'watching' (which came near to the modern meaning of 'police'). The police statutes of Glasgow (1800) and Edinburgh (1805) showed the way for the smaller towns, a substantial number of which followed suit, including old burghs like Paisley (1806), Kilmarnock (1810), Peterhead (1820), Alloa (1822) and Dundee (1831); new creations like Airdrie (1821), Bathgate (1824) and Kilsyth (1826);

[1] The Act of 1747 abolishing heritable jurisdictions (see *supra*, pp. 65-6) had drawn a distinction between burghs with an independent constitution and burghs wholly dependent upon their superior, granting the former the powers of a royal burgh, but restricting the latter to a quite petty jurisdiction. It remained for the Court of Session to determine whether or not any given burgh of barony was to be deemed independent for the purposes of the Act – a question of serious import to the greater burghs. Kilmarnock's right was vindicated in 1771, but judgment was found against Greenock in 1794 (when repression was at its height), although its case was similar to that of Kilmarnock; Hawick, an exceptionally strong municipality, was able to establish its independent status in 1805. The stigma of inferiority could, it is clear, be gravely prejudicial to an 'unlucky' burgh of barony.

and suburban burghs like Calton (then outside Glasgow, 1817), Gorbals (1823), Anderston (1824) and Leith (1827). These new or renewed municipalities acquired a 'police' establishment more in keeping with current requirements, and a few of them (Airdrie being an outstanding example) obtained positively liberal constitutions.

Meanwhile, a possible line of attack on the close corporations developed from 1817. The elections of councillors at Montrose in 1815 and 1816 were found to have been irregular (vacancies having been filled by ballot) and were set aside as invalid by the Court of Session. A fresh election by poll of all the burgesses was ordered – a device which had last been generally adopted in 1689 to rid the municipalities of King James's Romanist nominees, and since then occasionally, in exceptional circumstances. The opportunity was now taken to allow the whole body of burgesses of Montrose a continuing interest in the annual elections, and this small local gain was enough to arouse the reformers' hopes that, in this indirect manner, the odious practice of self-election might be discarded. In alarm at such a prospect, the Tory ministry closed its ranks and refused to authorise further local polls, even when asked by the councillors themselves. The scandal was blatant, but at least attention was drawn to the need for municipal reform.

In 1819, to the surprise and delight of reformers everywhere, the opposition persuaded the Commons to appoint a committee of inquiry into the affairs of the burghs. Even more astonishing was the result, for, after investigating the financial position of Edinburgh, Aberdeen, Dundee and Dunfermline, the committee found that all four were in effect bankrupt. Aberdeen was the most flagrant sinner: having got an Act of Parliament in 1810 sanctioning a large loan for the building of new docks, it had borrowed and spent £127,000, but had not got the docks. Less inquisitive committees were appointed in 1820 and 1821, and Parliament finally, in 1822, passed an Act providing for the submission of burgh accounts to the Scottish Exchequer,[1] and their challenge by any interested burgess. In the words, however, of the Municipal Corporations Commissioners in 1835, 'the provisions of the Act have proved nearly useless', for complaints were dismissed by the court when burgesses, to prove their standing, produced their 'burgess tickets', documents that were fully acceptable in any Scottish court,

[1] This Act represented a return to the principle of an Act of the Scottish Parliament passed in 1535, which likewise had been quite ineffective: see *supra*, VOL. I, p. 238.

but were now rejected as mere copies.[1] The reformers' hopes were again blasted, the Tories were willing to incur the odium of defending a system that was manifestly evil and corrupt, but the day of reform could not be indefinitely postponed.

The short reign of George IV (1820-30), though it saw an unbroken succession of Tory ministries (Liverpool, Canning, Goderich and Wellington), was in reality a period of preparation for the inevitable changes. The Tories themselves introduced a few minor reforms, including Peel's reorganisation of the London police force, the removal of the death penalty for lesser offences, the abrogation of the Navigation Acts, and the emancipation of the Roman Catholics.

For Scotland the reign opened with the rumoured 'Radical War' still pending.[2] Having conceived a grandiose but visionary project for a provisional government to follow a general strike, the Glasgow Radicals on 5 April 1820 sent a small armed contingent to rouse the Carron workers and, after a brief skirmish at Bonnymuir with the cavalry, the rioters were dispersed. Minor disturbances at Glasgow and Greenock completed the story of the 'Radical War', which brought twenty-four death sentences but only three actual hangings. The extremists thus suffered discomfiture and discredit: not so the Whigs, who held a large and enthusiastic meeting in December of that year to petition the king for the removal of his ministers.

The event of the reign that made the deepest impression on contemporary Scotland had nothing to do with reform movements. This was the king's visit in 1822, which marked the first time for 171 years that a reigning monarch had been in Scotland. George IV arrived at Leith by royal yacht on 14 August and next day proceeded to Edinburgh through cheering throngs, while banners waved and the castle guns sounded a salute. He took up residence at Dalkeith palace, but came frequently to Edinburgh, to worship, to dine and to hold receptions. Sir Walter Scott, as royalist, patriot and the country's leading citizen, was a kind of universal master of ceremonies. The king's sojourn, lasting a fortnight and bringing colour and pageantry back to Edinburgh and Holyrood, was a rousing success and was long remembered with pleasure by the people of Scotland.

On the inception of Canning's administration in April 1827, no successor to the second Viscount Melville was named as 'manager' for

[1] The 'ticket' was an extract from the council records, certified by the town clerk as authentic. The Court held that, *by English law*, this was inadmissible as evidence so long as the principal record existed.

[2] See *supra*, p. 126.

Scotland, and that unofficial post disappeared; instead, the home secretary, advised and assisted by the lord advocate, was made responsible for Scottish affairs. While this procedure, in view of the home secretary's heavy duties as an essentially English minister, was far from satisfactory, it was to endure for nearly sixty years, and its adoption marks the end of an era.

One further change of a non-controversial kind was consummated just before the end of the reign. By an Act of 1808, the Court of Session had been reconstituted in two divisions, the first comprising the Lord President and seven other lords, the second the Lord Justice Clerk and six lords. In 1830, as part of a general reorganisation of the British law-courts in the interests of economy and efficiency, the Court was ordered to be reduced from fifteen to thirteen lords, eight of them forming the Inner House of two divisions – the first under the Lord President, the second under the Lord Justice Clerk – and the five junior lords sitting in the Outer House, hearing cases as single 'lords ordinary' and referring difficult matters, or allowing appeals, to one of the divisions of the Inner House (or to a 'full bench' of both divisions). The occasion was taken to curtail the number of courts and judges: for example, the office of judge admiral disappeared, the jurisdiction of the Scottish admiralty court in maritime cases going to the Court of Session and the sheriff courts, while the Court of Exchequer was reduced from three 'barons' to one,[1] and the sinecure post of Lord Justice General was to cease with the existing incumbent (the duke of Montrose) and be merged with the office of Lord President.

George IV, dying in June 1830, was succeeded by his brother, William IV (1830-37), Parliament was dissolved, the general election brought a decisive shift of power in favour of the Whigs, and a new ministry, pledged to reform, took office under Earl Grey in November, with Jeffrey as lord advocate and Cockburn as solicitor-general in charge of Scottish business. The prolonged struggle for the reform bills, English, Scottish and Irish (March 1831-July 1832), was marked by a government defeat in the Commons, a dissolution and another general election in May 1831, the return of a more strongly Whig house, the Lords' resistance and a futile Tory attempt to form a ministry, and finally, before enactment, the 'threat' to create by royal prerogative sufficient new peers to ensure an acquiescent upper chamber. In Scotland, as elsewhere, the conflict was followed with unflagging

[1] The Court came to an end in 1856, its jurisdiction being taken over by the Court of Session.

interest; the country, says Cockburn, was 'in a most excited and uncomfortable state, but disgraced by no violence. . . . Nobody who did not see it could believe the orderly joy with which the people have received their emancipation'.

The Scottish Act, passed on 17 July 1832, followed the lines of the English statute. The narrow and archaic county franchise and the electoral rights of the irresponsible town councils were alike abrogated, the vote going to the £10 householders in the burghs, the £10 proprietors and £50 occupiers in the shires. Scotland gained eight new seats, to make 53 members out of an unchanged total of 658 commoners.[1] The shires were still to have 30 members, but the alternate representation and disfranchisement of the smaller counties[2] gave way to the 'pairing' of shires for the return of one shared member – Clackmannan and Kinross, Elgin and Nairn, Ross and Cromarty. The eight new seats all went to the cities and burghs. Edinburgh got a second member, while Glasgow, also with two M.P.s, and Dundee, Aberdeen and Perth, each with one, were taken out of their districts as separate constituencies. A new class of non-royal or (as they came to be called) 'parliamentary' burghs was created, of which Paisley and Greenock each got their own member, and eleven others, including Leith, Falkirk and Kilmarnock, were distributed among the districts of burghs, rearranged in composition though unaltered in total at 14.[3] In contrast

[1] To the 513 English and Welsh and 45 Scottish members of 1707 had been added 100 Irish M.P.s under the Irish Act of Union of 1800. The new house was to comprise 500 members for England and Wales, 53 for Scotland and 105 for Ireland.

[2] See *supra*, p. 54.

[3] The details are as under (with the head burgh named first in each district and the 'parliamentary' burghs italicised):–

Wick, Kirkwall, Dornoch, Tain, Dingwall, *Cromarty*;
Inverness, Fortrose, Nairn, Forres;
Elgin, Cullen, Banff, *Peterhead*, Inverurie, Kintore;
Montrose, Inverbervie, Brechin, Forfar, Arbroath;
St Andrews, Cupar, Crail, Kilrenny, Anstruther Easter, Anstruther Wester, Pittenweem;
Kirkcaldy, Dysart, Kinghorn, Burntisland;
Stirling, Culross, Inverkeithing, Dunfermline, Queensferry;
Falkirk, Linlithgow, *Airdrie*, *Hamilton*, Lanark;
Leith, *Portobello*, *Musselburgh*;
Kilmarnock, Rutherglen, Renfrew, Dumbarton, *Port Glasgow*;
Ayr, Irvine, Campbeltown, Inveraray, *Oban*;
Dumfries, Annan, Lochmaben, Sanquhar, Kirkcudbright;
Haddington, North Berwick, Dunbar, Lauder, Jedburgh;
Wigtown, Stranraer, Whithorn, New Galloway.

For the arrangements made in 1654 and 1707, with which the above list may be compared, see *supra*, p. 15, n. 2, and p. 54, n. 1.

to England (where 143 members were taken from the smaller towns and allocated elsewhere) only three of the Scottish royal burghs (Peebles, Selkirk and Rothesay) were merged in their respective shires.[1] The treatment of Scotland differed, too, from that of England in that university representation was refused, whereas Oxford and Cambridge each continued to elect two members.[2]

The Scottish Reform Act, though a moderate measure, corrected the worst abuses of the old system. The new voters were the shopkeepers and the better-off artisans in the burghs, and the substantial farmers in the shires. If, to the resentment of the Radicals, the mass of the workers remained voteless, the transfer of political power to the middle class was a real advance, for, instead of well under 5,000 electors, there were now well over 60,000. Moreover, the fairer allocation of the seats reflected the changed and changing distribution of the population, especially the growing concentrations in the main cities and the rise to importance of towns of the second rank, headed by Paisley and Greenock. Thus the will of the people, stifled under the 'management', could at last express itself. True, the grant of eight additional seats was a belated and half-hearted gesture towards rectifying the under-representation of 1707: a just balance had still to be struck, since Scotland, with over one-sixth of the population of England and Wales,[3] had only between one-ninth and one-tenth of the members.

The political consequences of the first Reform Act were immediate, extensive and enduring. Down to the year 1830 the Tories had invariably held a majority of the forty-five seats, and the Scots M.P.s had usually been noted as staunch ministerialists, often of uncritical or subservient temper.[4] The very breath of reform was enough to transform the situation, even on the old franchise: with some eight gains, the Whigs won twenty-four Scottish seats in the election of May 1831, against twenty-one for the Tories. The first contest under

[1] Each of these shires was so small as to be threatened with 'pairing' with another shire, and the preferred alternative was to throw in the county town with the county and so to create a total electorate worthy of its own member.

[2] One cogent argument against Scottish university representation was the relative infrequency of graduation – for the graduates would naturally be the voters. Cf. *supra*, p. 166.

[3] The census figures in 1831 were 2,364,386 and 13,896,797. To put it another way, each of Scotland's 53 seats corresponded to an average quota of 44,611 inhabitants, each of the 500 for England and Wales to only 27,793. (The case of Ireland, with a population of 7,767,401 in 1831, was even more striking.)

[4] It is noteworthy, too, that, in his ministry of 1828-30, Wellington had from first to last five Scottish colleagues – Lords Aberdeen, Melville and Rosslyn, Sir George Murray and Charles Grant (later Lord Glenelg).

the new régime, held at the end of 1832, gave the Whigs forty-three Scottish seats, the Tories only ten, and this result set the tone of political life for the rest of the century. The Liberals, as the Whigs soon began to call themselves, never failed (whatever might happen in England) to carry Scotland; the Conservatives, as Peel's moderate Tories now preferred to style themselves, had to be content as the minority party.

With the Liberal administration returned to power and enjoying massive Scottish support, the long-desired burgh reform could not be further delayed: it was in the nature of a logical sequel that self-election, discarded for the choosing of M.P.s, should likewise be abandoned as the basic principle of municipal government. As it happened, the existence of nearly standard burgh 'setts' or constitutions made the reformers' task very much easier in Scotland than it was in England, with its great variety of local customs and tenures, and this difference explains the enactment of the Scottish reforms in 1833 and the delay in England until 1835 for the corresponding statute. In the interval royal commissions were appointed to inquire into the municipal corporations of both countries, but, whereas the English commission's labours were the indispensable prelude to complex legislation, the Scottish reports are mainly of historical interest, for the essential changes had already been made.[1]

These changes were embodied in three statutes of 1833, of which two were quite straightforward, conferring on the £10 householders the right of electing the town councils in the sixty-six royal burghs (with certain exceptions[2]) and in the thirteen parliamentary burghs. The annual elections were to begin in November 1833, and one-third of the councillors were to retire each year, so that the elected would be continually responsive to the electors. For each parliamentary burgh a number of councillors, varying between six in Oban and sixteen in Paisley and Leith, was stipulated, but no change was made in the powers of either the royal or the parliamentary burghs.

The third statute of the series, less regarded at the time, was perhaps of greater significance for future developments. It authorised the £10 householders residing in a royal burgh or a burgh of barony, at a regularly convened meeting, to resolve to adopt a 'police system',

[1] Admittedly, the Scottish commissioners made recommendations for consequential reforms (e.g. unions of burghs, and extensions of boundaries), but their reports, general and local, are primarily archive material of the highest value.

[2] In nine small burghs, where the £10 householders were fewer than the existing councillors, the old method of the self-elective town council was meanwhile retained.

and to go on to choose 'commissioners of police', empowered to appoint police officers and to assess the inhabitants for the purposes of watching, lighting, paving, cleansing, water supply, drainage, scavenging, the prevention of infectious diseases and the removal of ruinous houses. It is noteworthy that the new terms 'police magistrate' and 'commissioners of police' came in place of the traditional provost, bailies and councillors, suspect through the misconduct of the close corporations. Moreover, though the councillors might, if elected as such, be commissioners, the only statutory limitation was that one-fifth of the new body must be chosen by the town council. It was *not* the existing burgh that became a 'police burgh', it was the residents therein who initiated the new local authority (with much wider powers than the old), so that a system of dual administration could come into being – one town maintaining, at the inhabitants' choice, two separate burghs.

The twin aims of the reformers had been achieved, and no further distinctively Scottish changes were made by Parliament during William IV's reign. That is not to suggest that the Scottish M.P.s lacked interest in the later phases of the reform era: on the other hand, political as well as humanitarian sentiment warmly favoured the great measures of 1833, the abolition of colonial slavery and the restriction of factory hours (which, of course, applied throughout Britain).[1] When Earl Grey, the reforming premier, retired from public life in 1834,[2] Edinburgh gave him a tremendous ovation and a memorable banquet, and, at the general election of 1835, the nation showed where it stood by returning thirty-eight Liberals and fifteen Conservatives. Yet, whereas Parliament in those years found time to attend to English banking, poor law, civil marriage and registration, to the East India Company's trading rights and to many troublesome aspects of Irish affairs, Scotland had no place in this part of the programme. William IV died in June 1837, to be succeeded by his youthful niece, Victoria, without even university reform, admitted by all to be urgently necessary,[3] having been undertaken. Much remained to be done during the new reign.

[1] Though the Act of 1833 disappointed the advocates of the ten hours day (which became law only in 1847), it was a useful measure, prohibiting the labour of children under nine in all textile mills, imposing an eight hours limit on those under thirteen, and a limit of sixty-nine hours a week on young persons under eighteen, and providing for whole-time inspectors.

[2] He was succeeded by Lord Melbourne, who held the premiership (apart from a Tory interlude under Peel, December 1834-April 1835) for the rest of the reign.

[3] Cf. *supra*, p. 168, and *infra*, pp. 270-1.

CHAPTER XVIII

The Expansion of Reform

QUEEN VICTORIA'S accession in June 1837, at the age of eighteen, initiated what was to be the longest reign in our history (1837-1901), outstripping that of her grandfather, George III, by over four years. (See table on p. 198.) It was also to be one of the most momentous of 'periods' in the record of mankind. For Britain at large the reign involved a sharp advance in material prosperity and a vast development of the overseas Empire (subjects to be considered in later chapters), as well as the matter of immediate concern to us here – the gradual, and in the long run close, approach to political democracy.

For Scotland the reign was the heyday of Liberalism.[1] Progressive opinion, liberated by the Reform Act, dominated the politics of the nation and ensured that, until 1900, the Liberals won every general election in Scotland. They formed, not so much a single political party in the twentieth-century sense,[2] as a loose confederacy of allied groups or individuals, ranging from the reactionary[3] to the radical and often engaging in internal strife both in Parliament and in the constituencies.[4] Their great strength lay in the urban middle classes enfranchised by the 1832 Act. The dissenters and evangelicals were Liberal almost to a man, as were, inevitably, the free traders, so that religion and economics buttressed the support of a political creed, giving it a moral and philosophical, as well as a secular, content. The Conservative appeal was much narrower, for the Tories, traditionally champions of the agricultural interest, were the spokesmen of the landlord and the farmer, who composed a section of the population

[1] The term 'Liberal' was now displacing 'Whig', which was confined (sometimes under the qualification 'Old Whig' or 'Reform Whig') to the right wing of the party – to those who thought the reforms of 1832 had gone far enough – while the Independent Liberals on the left shaded into the Radicals, both advocating further changes. So, too, 'Tory' was giving way to 'Conservative', though the older term never quite died out.

[2] It is true that, as the century wore on, party discipline and cohesion were tightened, but disunity returned over the Home Rule split in 1886.

[3] Some, like Lord Elcho, called themselves 'Liberal-Conservative'.

[4] It was not unknown for two or even three Liberals of varying political complexion to contest one burgh seat, and for the Conservative to finish at the foot of the poll.

which, it is important to remember, was shrinking with the increasing industrialisation of the country. The bias of the great majority of the nation was thus already towards the Liberal side, and, as the events of the reign unfolded, they served to confirm and strengthen this tendency.

In accordance with the prevailing constitutional practice,[1] the

THE MAIN ROYAL LINE FROM GEORGE III

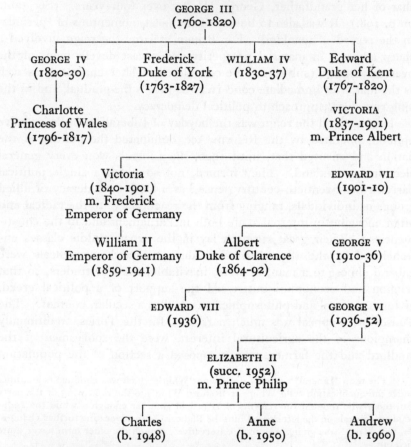

- GEORGE III (1760-1820)
  - GEORGE IV (1820-30)
    - Charlotte Princess of Wales (1796-1817)
  - Frederick Duke of York (1763-1827)
  - WILLIAM IV (1830-37)
  - Edward Duke of Kent (1767-1820)
    - VICTORIA (1837-1901) m. Prince Albert
      - Victoria (1840-1901) m. Frederick Emperor of Germany
        - William II Emperor of Germany (1859-1941)
      - EDWARD VII (1901-10)
        - Albert Duke of Clarence (1864-92)
        - GEORGE V (1910-36)
          - EDWARD VIII (1936)
          - GEORGE VI (1936-52)
            - ELIZABETH II (succ. 1952) m. Prince Philip
              - Charles (b. 1948)
              - Anne (b. 1950)
              - Andrew (b. 1960)

Note: Reigning kings and queens are in capitals, with their regnal years in brackets; for others the dates are those of birth and death.

[1] Queen Victoria was the last monarch whose succession was so observed: the two elections of 1910 bore no constitutional relationship to the death of Edward VII and the accession of George V.

accession of the new sovereign was followed by a dissolution of Parliament and a general election in August. Lord Melbourne's Whig ministry was returned to power for a further term, but its victory at the polls was obtained in a curious way. The Tory opposition actually carried England and Wales with a majority of some 20 seats, but, winning only 19 of the 53 Scottish seats, and faring even less well in Ireland,[1] they found themselves in a minority of about 34 in the Commons. It was not to be the only time that an English verdict was to be reversed in this manner.

Two extra-parliamentary movements attracted much attention at this epoch. The years 1836 and 1837 brought trade depression, severe unemployment and futile strikes, and the discontent of the British working-classes found expression in the People's Charter of 1837, demanding manhood suffrage, the secret ballot, equal electoral areas, annual parliaments, the cancellation of a property qualification for M.P.s, and payment of members. In 1839, after the preparation and rejection of a monster petition, the English agitation entered a phase of violence and decline, but then, under sensible and moderate leadership, Scottish Chartism flourished vigorously for a time as a native and idealistic philosophy, in which, besides the political aims of the charter, temperance or total abstinence, pacifism, the abolition of capital punishment and non-intrusion in ecclesiastical affairs were all stressed. Chartist churches and Chartist schools were set up and, between 1838 and 1843, three newspapers were published – *The True Scotsman* at Edinburgh, the *Chartist Circular* and the *Scottish Patriot* at Glasgow. From 1842, however, the impetus died away, and Chartism as such no longer had any distinctively Scottish character[2]; yet its claims continued to influence radical thought throughout Britain for two generations, until, indeed, with the exception of annual parliaments, all its political demands had been conceded.

As Chartism was the outcome of working-class desperation, the Anti-Corn-Law League was the mouthpiece of middle-class political arithmetic. From the first Scottish meeting, held in Edinburgh in January 1839, the League's denunciation of protective duties and 'dear bread' was warmly approved, and Duncan McLaren, an 'advanced' Independent Liberal, became the staunch ally of the English

[1] A majority of the Irish M.P.s sympathised with Daniel O'Connell, 'the Liberator', in his nationalist agitation for the repeal of the Union of 1800.

[2] The movement lingered on in Ireland, and came to an end with another huge (but not wholly genuine) 'petition' in 1848.

free traders, Cobden and Bright. As organiser and propagandist, McLaren rallied Scottish sentiment against the corn laws, though as yet neither the Old Whigs nor the Radicals[1] were committed to free trade.

The Melbourne government made the first tentative move towards reform in the shires, where financial control, and with it such responsibility for local affairs as existed, lay with the commissioners of supply, established in the seventeenth century for tax assessment and other purposes.[2] By two Acts of 1839, they were given charge (along with burgh magistrates) of the country's prisons, and they were empowered, but not required, to maintain a county police force, imposing and using to this end the old levy known as 'Rogue money'.[3]

The reward of Sir Robert Peel, who had been directing the Conservatives with sense and skill, came in 1841, when the general election gave his party a majority of over 70. In Scotland, too, it did unusually well, winning 22 seats – 20 in the shires, along with the Falkirk and Haddington districts of burghs – against the Liberals' 31. For Scotland the great event of the time was the Disruption of 1843, and Peel was roundly blamed by many Presbyterians for his failure to avert the tragedy.[4] Wherever the fault lay, the government had to take cognisance of the results of the schism in secular matters, for it had reduced the Kirk from a national to a sectarian body, unqualified to act as the sole dispenser of poor relief. An Act of 1845, accordingly, set up 'parochial boards of managers of the poor', comprising the greater heritors of each parish, magistrates of burghs (if any), representatives of kirk sessions, and members elected on a high property franchise (with a sliding scale of multiple votes for the larger properties). To them were entrusted the duties of keeping the poor's roll, fixing the amount of relief, making the assessment,[5] and building or enlarging poor-houses, in parishes with populations over 5,000, for the 'aged

[1] To the Radicals, aiming at purely 'political' and 'popular' reforms, the League was suspect as an essentially middle-class organisation, furthering the manufacturers' interest in cheap bread for the urban workers.

[2] Cf. *supra*, pp. 18, 36. They were individually named in each Act granting 'supply' until in 1798 their status became automatic, depending on the possession of £100 Scots (£8 6s. 8d.) of valued rent per annum.

[3] The disarming Act of 1725 had authorised the freeholders in each shire to raise this tax to defray the costs of 'apprehending, subsisting and prosecuting criminals', and the tax had been transferred in 1832 to the commissioners of supply.

[4] See *supra*, pp. 185-6.

[5] The practice, begun in 1663, of levying the rate half from owners, half from occupiers (*supra*, p. 18), was retained in the Act.

and other friendless impotent poor'; but, says the Act, 'nothing herein contained shall be held to confer a right to demand relief on able-bodied persons out of employment'. Central control and co-ordination went to the Board of Supervision in Edinburgh, with nine members serving *ex officio* or appointed by the Crown. Thus reform in its primary stages had reached the shire and the parish, as well as the burgh.

The agitation against the corn laws meanwhile proceeded briskly. In December 1843 Bright wrote approvingly to McLaren, 'The late meetings and all your printings must have saturated the Scotch mind with Free Trade doctrines'. His most brilliant *coup* was the convening of 801 ministers of the Secession, Relief and other evangelical Churches to denounce 'the sinfulness and injustice of the Corn Laws'. It was, in the end, the Irish potato famine of 1845-46, and the desperate need for cheap imported grain, that forced Peel's hand, but public opinion – not least in Scotland – had been fully prepared for the repeal of the corn laws before that step, inaugurating the era of free trade, was taken in May 1846.

Before its departure, Peel's cabinet put through Parliament an enactment that was really a footnote to centuries of Scottish history. The ancient privileges of merchants and craftsmen, involving monopolies, respectively, of foreign and wholesale trade, and of small-scale manufactures and petty retail trade,[1] had long since fallen, for the most part, into desuetude. From about the middle of the eighteenth century, for example, it had been legally impracticable for merchants to prosecute 'unfree traders' (since the courts would not enforce such archaic claims), while from 1751 the linen (and consequently the cotton) industries had been freed from craft restrictions. Now, in 1846, the exclusive rights of burgesses, merchants and craftsmen were all formally abrogated, so that, since that time, burgess-ship ('the freedom of the burgh') has been purely honorary, and bodies like the merchant guild and the incorporated trades have become social and charitable organisations, and nothing else.

The immediate defection of Peel's right-wing supporters, infuriated by his surrender to the free traders, and the splitting of the party into Protectionists and Peelites – the latter being closer in spirit to the Liberals, whom, indeed, they eventually joined – caused the downfall of their chief and the accession to office of the Whigs under Lord John Russell (1846-52). The next election, in August 1847, showed little change in the posture of affairs beyond reflecting the deep cleavage

[1] See *supra*, VOL. I, chap. xxiv.

among the Tories: in Scotland 14 of the 21 Conservative members returned were reckoned Peelites.

At mid-century one of the strongest sentiments in British public life was anti-Romanism, which, in 1845, had inspired an extraordinary uproar over Peel's innocuous project to recognise and permanently endow Maynooth College for the training of Irish priests; the Act was passed only with Liberal help and amid much popular misgiving. In Scotland, too, the grant of public moneys for such a purpose was denounced, partly from fear of undue Irish influence, partly from general 'voluntary' scruples over state endowments of religious institutions. In 1850, also, the cry of 'Papal aggression' (against the assumption of territorial titles by English Romanist bishops) sounded as heartily in Scotland (which was not affected) as in England.[1]

In contrast to these passionate exchanges, the two measures of burgh reform sponsored by the Russell ministry were entirely non-controversial. The right to adopt a police system was extended in 1847 to the non-royal parliamentary burghs, while the statute of 1850 known as Lock's Act gave it to 'populous places', certified by the sheriff to have over 1,200 inhabitants. The scope of police administration was widened to include the provision of public baths, control of lodging-houses, oversight of slaughter-houses, inspection of foodstuffs, and many another 'improvement'. Existing police burghs, as well as new ones, might adopt the 1850 Act. Moreover, the magistrates and councillors now became the police commissioners in all royal and parliamentary burghs having a police system, while in burghs of barony they could become commissioners only by vote of the householders. Lock's Act produced a substantial number of police burghs in the 1850s.

The year 1852 brought a minority Tory administration under Derby (February), followed by a coalition of Liberals and Peelites under Aberdeen[2] (December); the chancellorship of the exchequer in the former went to Disraeli, in the latter to Gladstone, the two men destined to be the outstanding politicians of the second half of the century. The general election held in August of that year brought only a minor shift in the balance of parties; the Liberals secured 33 Scottish seats, the Peelites 7, and the Conservatives 13.

The blend of the moral or philosophical and the severely practical

[1] Cf. *infra*, pp. 266-7.

[2] He was the first Scottish prime minister since Bute, in 1762-63 (*supra*, pp. 116-17).

in Scottish Liberalism shows itself in two campaigns of the time. The cause of temperance had for several decades engaged the interest of Christian reformers, for drunkenness was a besetting sin of all classes, not least the working men, and few barriers stood in the way of over-indulgence. When Duncan McLaren was lord provost of Edinburgh in 1852, the city magistrates punished Sunday offences more severely than those committed on week-days, and inn-keepers began to close their premises on 'the day of rest'. This local experiment had good results, and Parliament in 1853 accordingly passed the Forbes-Mackenzie Act for the control of licensed houses. Opening must not be before eight a.m. or closing after eleven p.m. (for nocturnal 'tippling' was a common vice), grocers were to have only an 'off-licence', and on Sundays public houses were to be shut, though hotels and inns might provide drink for residents or for *bona fide* travellers.[1] An improvement in standards of behaviour, and a diminution of clandestine 'nipping', flowed from this regulation of the drink trade.

Pacifism was the other cause that appealed strongly to British Liberals at this time. The country had been free of any major European conflict since Waterloo, but now the Crimean War, involving Britain with France and Turkey against Russia, was impending, and Scottish Liberals were prominent in the ranks of the 'Peace party', which included those who were totally opposed to war as a method of settling international disputes, those who deplored the high costs of armaments, and those who feared the baleful influence on public life of a military caste. Like other pacifist movements, however, this one did not long survive the actual outbreak of hostilities (March 1854).

The one Scottish reform undertaken by the Aberdeen cabinet was the compulsory registration of births, deaths and marriages; this duty had hitherto been discharged unsystematically and unevenly by the kirk sessions, and was entrusted by an Act of 1854 to the parochial boards in parishes and to town councils in burghs.[2] These bodies must appoint the registrar (normally still the session clerk), who was to render to the registrar general in Edinburgh all returns relating to vital statistics.

The ten years 1855-65 were occupied by the two Palmerston

[1] This exception was intended for the benefit of churchgoers seeking a meal and refreshment between forenoon and afternoon services and unable to return home for the purpose because of the distance involved – over three miles. The *bona fide* clause has been used in the twentieth century by other travellers, engaged in more secular pursuits.

[2] England's system of national registration had been created by an Act of 1836.

administrations, except for an interlude (February 1858 to June 1859) filled by another Derby-Disraeli minority government. It was a stirring epoch in foreign affairs, which were the veteran premier's main interest, but domestic politics were quiescent almost to the point of stagnation: it was notorious that Palmerston would not hear of parliamentary reform.[1] The elections of April 1857 and May 1859, confirming the general Liberal ascendancy, are chiefly memorable as marking the final absorption of the Peelites; on both occasions the Scottish electors returned thirty-eight Liberals and fifteen Conservatives.

The 'Palmerstonian truce' did witness the passage of three useful statutes for the improvement of local government in Scotland. In 1857 eight district boards of lunacy,[2] composed of members chosen from the commissioners of supply and burgh magistrates, were put in control of the asylums in their district. Another, and more important, Act of the same year rendered obligatory the power that had been permissive in 1839: commissioners of supply were compelled to establish, from March 1858, a county police force. Burghs without their own police establishment were to come within the county for this purpose, and further, while the Treasury would pay one-fourth of local police charges, this was not to apply to burghs of less than 5,000 population: this was the first step towards local amalgamations, the first hint that the smaller burghs would do well to throw in their lot with the county. In 1862 the statute known as Lindsay's Act lowered to 700 the minimum requirement for a 'populous place' aspiring to become a police burgh,[3] and at the same time imposed many new rules in matters of health, sanitation, drainage, water-supply and cleansing: the adoption of this Act was the favoured method for the creation of new police burghs in Victorian Scotland.

The manner of conducting Scottish business – through the already over-burdened home secretary and lord advocate – was now attracting critical attention: it was asserted that there were waste, irresponsibility and an inadequate share of the national revenue. So, too, in the wider context of parliamentary reform, Scotland's under-representation, it was held, should be rectified. The leading exponent of such

[1] Of other men's projects for reform, Russell's bill had been withdrawn in 1854, Disraeli's was defeated in 1859.

[2] The eight original 'districts' (ultimately increased to thirteen) were Inverness, Aberdeen, Perth, Edinburgh, Stirling, Glasgow, Renfrew and Dumfries. They were renamed district boards of control in 1913.

[3] Since the new burgh need not have its own police force, this enactment was not necessarily in conflict with what is said in the preceding sentence.

arguments, McLaren, was returned at the head of the Edinburgh poll in the summer of 1865, to become known at Westminster as 'member for Scotland'. This election, the last under the terms of the first Reform Act, sent the Liberals back with a comfortable majority, and Scotland was once again their happy hunting-ground, yielding them 42 seats to the Conservatives' 11.

The death of Palmerston in October 1865 opened the way for reform, but it was not to be accomplished by Russell, his successor in the Liberal leadership, whose franchise bill was defeated in June 1866. The government was replaced by a third Derby-Disraeli administration (June 1866 to December 1868[1]), which endeavoured to 'dish the Whigs' by bringing in and passing its own reform bill. In the course of the debates, McLaren made out a strong case for increasing the Scottish quota of M.P.s. Scotland, he showed, had between one-ninth and one-tenth of the population of the British isles, and contributed between one-eighth and one-ninth of the total taxation[2]; instead of 53 members out of 658, he contended, she should have 68. The government, however, may well have been more impressed by the fact that adding to the Scottish contingent meant adding to their opponents; in the end, 7 additional seats were given, making 60 in all out of an unchanged total of 658.

The second Reform Act (1867-68) greatly extended the electorate, the vote in Scotland going to rate-paying householders and £10-a-year lodgers in the burghs, and to £5 owners and £14 occupiers in the shires. Two of the seven additional seats were allocated to the shires, Aberdeen, Ayr and Lanark each being divided into two constituencies, while Peebles and Selkirk were joined as one; among the cities, Glasgow got a third member and Dundee a second, while a fifteenth district of burghs, that of Hawick,[3] came into being; and the two remaining members went to the universities – one to St Andrews and Edinburgh, the other to Glasgow and Aberdeen. Sensible enough in themselves, if partly inspired by a cynical party manoeuvre, the terms of the second Reform Act, bringing in many members of the working-class,

[1] Derby's resignation, because of failing health, in February 1868 left Disraeli as prime minister for the last ten months of the government's term.

[2] To put it another way, the yield of Scottish taxation, standing at £7,740,000 in 1868, was well above one-seventh of that of England, while her M.P.s were fewer than one-ninth.

[3] It comprised *Hawick*, *Galashiels*, and Selkirk, the first two being 'parliamentary' burghs, the third a royal burgh; for the fourteen existing districts, see *supra*, p. 193, n. 3.

at least in the towns, were a half-way house towards the complete change now favoured by the more advanced Liberals.

Under the Conservative administration, Parliament passed an important Public Health Act in 1867,[1] and gave recognition in 1868 to the growing stature of the commissioners of supply by authorising them to raise a 'county general assessment' in lieu of 'Rogue money', which was finally abolished.

The election of November 1868 swept Gladstone into power with a majority of 112, thanks to the Scottish and Irish votes: his party won 53 Scottish seats, including all the burghs, and yielded only 7 in the shires. Ecclesiastical business took up much time during his ministry, and one of its major achievements was the disestablishment in 1869 of the (Episcopal) Church of Ireland. Some of the Scottish dissenters would have welcomed a similar measure for Scotland, but the most fervent of them could scarcely claim that the cases were parallel. One small grievance, however – a mere pin-prick – was redressed in 1870, after exciting adverse comment for thirty-six years. The annuity-tax, levied from householders in Edinburgh and Montrose for the maintenance of the ministry of the Church of Scotland in these towns, was heartily detested as a symbol of servitude and an unjust imposition, and the annulling statute gave satisfaction, though for over a generation still to come disestablishment was to be advocated by Liberal dissenters.

For Scotland Gladstone's greatest service in his first ministry was the famous Act of 1872 making education compulsory to the age of thirteen, setting up school boards, to be elected in each parish and burgh by the £4 owners and occupiers, and bringing all the Presbyterian schools within the national system.[2] By another, and general, reform of that year, the secret ballot was introduced for all parliamentary and municipal elections.

The Liberal tide had spent its force by 1874 and it was a tired and disunited party that went to the polls in February of that year, when the Conservatives, for the first time since Peel's triumph of 1841, got a clear majority, amounting to 83, in the House of Commons. It was essentially an English victory, for in Ireland a strong Nationalist party had emerged, and in Scotland the Liberals retained 41 seats, while 16 of their opponents were successful in the shires and only three in the burghs (one in Glasgow, and the others in the Ayr and Wigtown districts).

[1] See *infra*, pp. 255-6.

[2] Cf. *infra*, p. 269.

If Disraeli's chief concern was with foreign and colonial commitments – the Suez canal, the Russo-Turkish war, the Congress of Berlin, the Zulu and Afghan campaigns – his term of office is still noteworthy for three Scottish enactments. First and foremost, church patronage was abolished in 1874, and henceforth presentations were to be made by the communicants and members of each congregation. Next, in 1877, prisons ceased to be a local responsibility and were transferred to the home secretary, assisted by a prisons commission. And the Roads and Bridges Act, 1878, abolished road tolls and the older practices – statute labour in the country, 'causeway mail' in the burghs – giving control to town councils in burghs with a population over 5,000 and elsewhere to county road trustees, comprising commissioners of supply and members elected by the ratepayers of rural parishes and by the town councils of the smaller burghs. The Act provided for a county road board as an executive committee and for district road committees within each county; for the first time the elective principle was given a part in the management of county affairs.

Once more the pendulum swung to the other side, Gladstone's rousing campaigns in Midlothian in November and December 1879 showed that the Conservatives had outlived their popularity, and the Liberals came back to power in April 1880, outnumbering Conservatives and Home Rulers; the Scottish verdict was the same as in 1868 – 53 Liberals to 7 Conservatives.

The second Gladstone administration (1880-85), undertook a minor reorganisation in 1882, when the Fishery Board for Scotland, comprising six Crown-appointed members and three sheriffs, took the place of the earlier Commissioners for the British White Herring Fishery.[1] The government's claim to fame, however, rested on the third Reform Act (1884-85), a bold and logical measure granting manhood suffrage in town and country alike. Since the reallocation of seats was strictly based on the distribution of population, Scotland, with an increased quota of 72 members out of 670, was at last justly represented. English boroughs and Scottish districts of burghs with fewer than 15,000 inhabitants were merged in their shires, and an upward limit of 50,000 was settled for one M.P., and of 165,000 for two, while it was laid down that no further double-member constituencies were to be created.

The redistribution scheme followed these general rules. Seven

[1] **Despite its name, this body, originally appointed in 1809, had been limited in jurisdiction to Scotland since 1869.**

additional seats went to the shires: Lanark, much the most populous of Scottish counties, got six members instead of two, and Fife, Perth and Renfrew were each split into two divisions. Among the cities, Glasgow was given seven members instead of three, Edinburgh four instead of two, and Aberdeen a second M.P.,[1] but the Haddington and Wigtown districts were suppressed,[2] to give a net gain of five burgh members. The Gladstonian reform, radical in its application to Scotland, was yet contrived with sufficient ingenuity to retain as many as possible of the traditional electoral units – individual burghs, districts of burghs, and above all single shires, of which no fewer than 19 each kept its own member despite all the changes.

In 1885 the agitation against the lack of proper ministerial arrangements for Scotland at last bore fruit in a bill, introduced by the earl of Rosebery,[3] for the appointment of a secretary for Scotland. Before the bill could become law, Gladstone, defeated on the budget, had given way to a 'caretaker' government under his opponent, Salisbury,[4] but the office was duly instituted as a cabinet post by the still Liberal house, its first incumbent being the duke of Richmond (August 1885). Though the various statutory boards (for poor law, lunacy, prisons and fisheries) retained their independence, it was understood that the Scottish secretary was to be a truly responsible minister; his staff became 'the Scottish Office' and he took charge (as nominal vice-president of the Privy Council committee) of the most important department – that of education. At long last, therefore, definite provision had been made for the conduct of Scottish business within the Union.

The year 1885 gives us an admirable vantage point for a retrospect of Scottish public life in the Victorian age. Parliamentary reform had been achieved with manhood suffrage and a fair distribution of seats; local government, it is true, required further attention, particularly at

[1] The new rule, cited above, meant that Aberdeen burgh became two divisions, each returning its M.P., whereas Dundee, Scotland's other two-member burgh, returned its M.P.s as a single constituency, each elector having two votes; this difference remained until 1948. Cf. *infra*, p. 319, n. 1.

[2] This left thirteen districts (twelve of the 1832 districts, plus the Hawick district, brought in in 1868). There were thus thirty-nine shire members, thirty-one burgh members and two university members.

[3] He had previously served Gladstone as under-secretary at the home office, with Scotland as his special charge, and in March 1885 he entered the cabinet as lord privy seal. Like the duke of Argyll, the other prominent Scottish Liberal peer of the time, he shared the general opinion of the need for a Scottish secretaryship.

[4] He had succeeded to the Conservative leadership in 1881, on the death of Disraeli (who had been created Earl of Beaconsfield in 1876).

county and parish level, but the later changes were largely consequential, since the principle of democratic control was now very generally accepted for all matters political. Henceforth 'reform' was bound to lose some of its magic as a rallying cry, and its place was to be taken by other and more compelling issues – Irish home rule, already troublesome and threatening to reach breaking-point, the cohesion of the Empire, and the shadows of world war. A new epoch was about to dawn.

For over half a century the Liberals had carried Scotland at every general election. Their smallest majority of Scottish seats (in 1841) was nine; thereafter it rose regularly, to reach 31 in 1865, and the larger electorates and more numerous seats under the second Reform Act increased the range of the Liberal margin to 22-46. The determining factor was the burgh vote, for all or almost all of the burghs returned Liberals at each election: sometimes they dropped one or two seats – at most, in 1874, three. At four successive elections from 1857 to 1868, they made a clean sweep of the burgh constituencies, and there were actually in 1885 more burgh seats with than without unbroken records of Liberal representation since 1832. Among the shires, one group, including most of the northern counties, was predominantly Liberal, another, with many southern seats, was mainly Conservative, and the third was fairly evenly divided. On the whole, there was little between the parties in the shire contests down to 1865, but from that date the advantage – sometimes the great advantage – lay with the Liberals.

The evil memory of the unreformed burgh corporations, the genuine national aspiration for a 'Christian democracy', the dissenters' distrust of authority and repression, the general adherence to free trade doctrines, and the influential support of the leading newspapers, the *Scotsman* and *Glasgow Herald*, combined to make Scottish Liberalism irresistible. This constant bias in Scottish politics, together with the Irish addiction to 'Repealer' or Nationalist principles, brought about the recurrent frustration of the English Tories, so that, as we have seen, only Peel in 1841 and Disraeli in 1874 were returned to Westminster with a clear Conservative majority, although, throughout the period, their party did as well at the polls in England as did their opponents. For better or worse, Victorian Scotland, despite its small size and (until 1885) its serious under-representation, played a large part in settling the 'colour' of British political life.

It would, however, be erroneous to depict the progress of reform between the accession of Victoria and the eve of the general election of December 1885 as a triumphant Liberal procession. During that period, Liberal or mainly Liberal ministries were in office for exactly twice as long a span of time as the Conservatives,[1] and yet the record shows that, of the twenty constitutional enactments relating to Scotland, twelve were passed under Liberal, eight under Conservative, governments.

[1] Whig, Liberal or Peelite-Liberal ministries were in office for thirty-two years and four months, Tory or Conservative for sixteen years and two months.

CHAPTER XIX

Scotland and the Empire

IN THE last quarter of the nineteenth century a new concept of Empire became an important element in British political life, and it is therefore fitting for us to glance back at the part hitherto played by Scotsmen in the settlement, development and defence of the overseas dominions.

As early as the seventeenth century, as we have seen, Scotland had undertaken certain colonial enterprises, partly on her own account – the grandiose Nova Scotia plan (1621) and the disastrous Darien scheme (1695-1700)[1] – and partly within the English 'plantations', especially in East New Jersey from 1682 onwards.[2] Again, in the eighteenth century, substantial numbers of Scots found new homes in Georgia, in North Carolina and in upper New York. These emigrants included many Highlanders, often Jacobite in politics and Roman Catholic in faith,[3] and after the Peace of Paris in 1763 the tide rose sharply: the disbanding of Highland regiments added a large quota of discharged soldiers, and the exodus was at a high level until the outbreak of war with the colonists in 1775.[4]

The 'old Empire', before its collapse in 1783, had provided Scotsmen with both commercial and military opportunities. Glasgow traders had made quick profits and amassed large fortunes,[5] generals and admirals had won renown, and many battalions, Highland and Lowland, had given distinguished service in the Seven Years War and the American War.[6] While the American plantations had been the most prosperous and attractive parts of the old Empire, the colonies that remained afforded scope alike for new trade-routes[7] and for new fields of military endeavour, to the extent that the historic Scottish regiments had all taken shape before Waterloo.[8] Settlement, too,

[1] See *supra*, pp. 6, 48-9. [2] *Supra*, pp. 20-1.

[3] Among them was Flora Macdonald, the romantic heroine who assisted the escape of Prince Charles Edward after Culloden. With her husband, Allan Macdonald of Kingsborough, she settled in North Carolina in 1774, and led a 'loyalist' (i.e. Hanoverian) rising, which was defeated at Cross Creek in 1776; they returned to Scotland in 1779.

[4] It is reckoned that between 20,000 and 25,000 Scots emigrants crossed the Atlantic between 1763 and 1775.

[5] See *supra*, pp. 74-5, 136-7. [6] *Supra*, pp. 66, 116, 119.

[7] *Supra*, pp. 137, 139. [8] *Supra*, pp. 119, 124, 125.

continued, Canada[1] now being favoured by the Scots emigrant, whether a solitary adventurer, an ambitious craftsman, a displaced crofter with his family, or a member of an entire community evicted during a Highland clearance.[2] In the north of Scotland, on the western seaboard and throughout the Hebrides, the emigrant ship became a common sight in the nineteenth century, making its call and eventually departing with hundreds of travellers, dejected or hopeful, bound for a new life across the ocean.

Most of the early Scots settlers chose one of the maritime provinces – Nova Scotia, Cape Breton Island or Prince Edward Island – but others found their way inland to Upper Canada (Ontario). Among those who promoted systematic emigration was Thomas Douglas, earl of Selkirk, who strove manfully – though final success eluded him – with the Red River settlement (1811-19), noteworthy as the beginning of Winnipeg and Manitoba; another was John Galt, the novelist,[3] who, as secretary of a land-purchasing company, founded the town of Guelph, Ontario (1827), in the midst of a rich agricultural district. Further afield a few intrepid Scots made their mark in this vast and virgin country. In 1789 a fur trader, Alexander MacKenzie from Stornoway, had explored the river that bears his name, following its course to the Arctic Ocean, and in 1795 he became the first man to cross the Rocky mountains and to reach the Pacific from eastern Canada; in the far west, too, the Fraser river recalls the daring of its explorer, Simon Fraser (1808).

Many Scottish families took the Gaelic language and culture with them, and their descendants cherished them through several generations, forming, so to speak, communities of exiles, dreaming of their old home in a strange and distant land. Others, again, threw themselves whole-heartedly into the public life of their adopted country. One such was William Lyon MacKenzie, who led a revolt of the discontented British settlers of Ontario in 1837; the rising, it is true, quickly collapsed, but it drew the attention of the Melbourne ministry to the grievances of the colonists and helped to bring about the grant of responsible government in 1840. The outstanding Canadian politician of the century was Sir John Alexander MacDonald of Glasgow (1815-91), the organiser and first premier of the self-governing

[1] Already, at the time of the American War, many loyalists, particularly in upper New York province, had been unwilling to remain in the United States and had moved in a body to Canada.

[2] Cf. *supra*, pp. 158, 160-1.

[3] See *supra*, p. 171.

dominion of Canada, created by the British North America Act, 1867. And it was another Scot, Donald Smith (later Lord Strathcona), who saw to the building and completion of the Canadian Pacific railway (1885), the country's vital line of communication.

To the development of Australia, a penal settlement, from 1788 to 1840, for political and criminal convicts, individual Scots made their contribution.[1] Between 1809 and 1825 the governorship of New South Wales was held in turn by two enlightened Scots, Lachlan MacQuarie and Sir Thomas Brisbane (for whom the capital of the state of Queensland was named), while the first truly successful trans-continental journey from south to north was made in 1862 by John McDouall Stuart. In New Zealand Scottish emigrants were more numerous, and Dunedin, the capital of Otago, was founded in 1848 by a group of members of the Free Church of Scotland, including the Rev. Thomas Burns, nephew of the poet.

India, too, had its notable Scottish proconsuls, among them the first earl of Minto, who, as governor-general from 1807 to 1813, pacified the country and gave it unaccustomed tranquillity; Mount-stuart Elphinstone, who, as governor of Bombay from 1819 to 1827, promoted the advancement of Indians; his contemporary in the governorship of Madras, Sir Thomas Munro, a recognised expert on Indian affairs; and, above all, James Ramsay, tenth earl and first marquis of Dalhousie, a vigorous if controversial governor-general (1848-56), who annexed Punjab, Lower Burma and Oudh, introduced the railway and the telegraph, and prohibited such native customs as 'suttee' or widow-burning.[2]

To Africa, still a largely unknown continent, with a British base in Cape of Good Hope[3] and a few scattered coastal settlements and naval stations, Scotland sent, not colonists, but explorers and missionaries. As early as 1768-72 James Bruce, 'Abyssinian Bruce', had discovered the source of the Blue Nile, while in 1795-99 Mungo Park, the Selkirk surgeon, explored the course of the Niger, only to perish on a second journey in 1806. Missionary work in the south began with Robert Moffat, who devoted the greater part of a long life (1795-1883) to the Christianising of Bechuanaland. His son-in-law, David Livingstone from Blantyre (1813-73), was perhaps the greatest explorer-missionary

[1] John MacArthur, the pioneer of the Australian wool and wine industries, though born in England, was, as his name indicates, of Scottish parentage.

[2] Dalhousie's critics felt that his zeal for expansion and reform was a main cause of the Indian Mutiny in 1857.

[3] For its two captures, see *supra*, pp. 124, 125.

of all time, locating the Zambesi river, Victoria falls and Lake Nyasa, lost to the world on his quest for the source of the Nile, found by Stanley in the climax to a fabulous adventure-tale (1871), battling through life against the horrible slave-trade, and deliberately staying on to die in the land to which he had given his heart.

In the field of higher education, again, the stamp of Scottish drive and inspiration made itself felt from McGill University, founded by James McGill, an emigrant from Glasgow, in 1821, to the University of Otago in Dunedin, the first to be set up in New Zealand (1869). And, just as organised medical teaching in America owed its rise in the eighteenth century to Scotland,[1] so the establishment of medical faculties in Canada during the nineteenth century was largely the work of Scottish or Scottish-trained doctors and surgeons.

The Scottish regiments, meanwhile, maintained their reputation for disciplined gallantry, both in the 'police actions' that occurred on the empire's fringes between Waterloo and mid-century and in the more serious wars that followed. At the battle of Balaclava, for example, it was the 93rd, or Sutherland Highlanders,[2] who formed 'the thin red line' that repelled the Russian cavalry, while the Scots Greys were part of the Heavy Brigade, whose charge, though less publicised, made more sense than the brave but foolish onrush of the Light Brigade (October 1854). The Highland Brigade was led by Sir Colin Campbell (later Lord Clyde), one of the few generals to emerge from the Crimean War with undiminished renown, and he acquired further fame as commander-in-chief in India during the mutiny (1857-58).

Despite all the varied activities overseas, the very being and meaning of Empire made little impact on home politics. Tories and Whigs, Scottish and English, were in substantial agreement in regarding the colonies as temporary dependencies, bound in due course to detach themselves from the mother country, as the United States had already done. Thus, while self-government was willingly enough granted to Canada from 1840 and to Australia (beginning with New South Wales) from 1843, this was done without enthusiasm, in the belief that it was simply a step towards inevitable separation. Few politicians thought

[1] Cf. *supra*, pp. 167-8.

[2] In 1881, on the completion of the reorganisation of the army in regiments, generally of two 'linked' battalions and each with its own recruiting district, the 93rd was united with the 91st (Argyllshire Highlanders) to form the Argyll and Sutherland Highlanders. As a result of this and other such changes, Scotland had, from 1881 to 1957, ten regiments of infantry, besides the Scots Guards and the Royal Scots Greys.

otherwise, but one of the exceptions was Disraeli, who, as early as 1866, was thinking and speaking of Britain as a world-wide sea-power, the centre of a maritime empire.

In his ministry of 1874-80 Disraeli strove to make the people conscious and proud of their imperial heritage. He annexed Fiji (1874) and Transvaal (1877), contrived the purchase of a controlling interest in the Suez canal (1875), had the Queen proclaimed Empress of India (1 January 1877), and sought to check Russian expansion in Afghanistan from 1878. He succeeded so well in his aim that, for the first time, the public began to think of the Empire as a trust – 'the white man's burden'. With the new imperialism, however, his rival Gladstone, essentially a fiscal expert, had small sympathy, and he showed his lack of interest during his second administration (1880-85) by granting the Boers virtual independence (1881),[1] by retreating from Afghanistan (1881),[2] and by abandoning – or so it seemed to many – Gordon to his fate at Khartum (1884-85).[3] These lapses go far to explain Gladstones' defeat and resignation in June 1885.

Pride of empire, while it put fresh heart into the Conservatives, gave added significance to the Irish question, which, ever vexatious, now threatened to split the Liberals. Parnell fanned the agitation for a separate all-Ireland parliament, and the position became critical as a result of the general election of December 1885, the first to be held under full manhood suffrage. The Liberals won exactly half the Commons seats, 335, the Conservatives 249 and the Irish Nationalists 86. The Scottish electors had stubbornly adhered to their habits by returning 62 Liberals and only 10 Conservatives: Glasgow's seven M.P.s were all Liberals, and indeed their opponents gained but one of the burgh seats (the Kilmarnock district). Clearly, England was veering more strongly towards Conservatism, and Gladstone was dependent on the Scottish and (more important for his policies) the Irish votes.

[1] The humiliation was the greater in that it followed a British defeat at Majuba hill (February 1881).

[2] In this case, withdrawal came after a British triumph – Roberts's epic march from Kabul to Kandahar in August 1880.

[3] Britain had intervened in Egypt in 1882, when Sir Garnet Wolseley defeated the fanatical followers of Arabi Pasha at Tel-el-Kebir and pacified the land. An even fiercer insurrection developed in Sudan under the Mahdi, and General Charles Gordon was sent out to arrange an orderly evacuation of the Egyptians; cooped up in Khartum, he withstood a siege of over ten months before being overwhelmed – with the relief force two days' journey distant. Gordon was revered as hero and martyr, and Gladstone was blamed for his tardy and half-hearted support.

Gladstone's third administration (February-July 1886), taken up as it was with Irish affairs, saw the passage of the Crofters' Holdings Act, designed to relieve the distress of the Highlands and Islands, where evictions for default of rent had produced some ugly scenes ('the Crofters' War'). The Act, introduced by Sir George Trevelyan, secretary for Scotland, provided for fair rents, security of tenure, the enlargement of holdings, compensation for improvements, and the cancellation of arrears.

The Irish demands evoked much sympathy from Scottish Liberals, many of whom, besides approving the Parnellite programme, favoured a general measure of devolution, whereby responsibility for 'local' affairs would go to 'local' parliaments in England, Scotland and Ireland (and perhaps also in Wales). The veteran Duncan McLaren advocated 'a measure of Home Rule which would apply equally to each of the three kingdoms, and have a tendency to unite them more and more in one friendly bond of brotherhood'. Although Scotland's grievances were greatly allayed in 1885 by the grant of adequate representation and the appointment of its own minister,[1] the Scottish Home Rule Association was instituted, with Liberal support, in 1886, and a mild form of propaganda for self-government thereafter persisted.

In Ireland the home rulers were in deadly earnest, and the Irish question now dominated British politics. Gladstone's announcement of his conversion alienated many of his own party, who saw in his bill (April 1886) a base surrender to intimidation, for the prime minister was evasive about a similar measure for Scotland, and McLaren wrote to his fellow-dissentient, Bright, 'If I had the health and strength which I possessed in Anti-Corn Law times, I would be prepared . . . "to testify" against the proposed injustice.' The bill was defeated in the Commons, and the breach in the Liberal ranks was serious and permanent: thousands of Liberal Unionists, as they were called, turned against their leader in Scotland (particularly in the towns) as in England, carrying with them into opposition the influential *Scotsman* and *Glasgow Herald*. In contrast to the new fervour for imperialism, Gladstonian separatism appeared unpatriotic and defeatist – 'little Englandism'.

The general election of July 1886, fought expressly on the home rule issue, revealed the extent of the damage. The Conservatives and Unionists outnumbered the Liberals and Irish Nationalists by 118, and, though the Liberals held Scotland, their margin was relatively

[1] See *supra*, pp. 207-8.

smaller than at any time since 1841: 43 constituencies returned Liberals, 17, including 8 burgh seats, Unionists, and 12 Conservatives. And the Unionists, while intending to maintain their separate identity, co-operated with, and ultimately merged in, the Conservative party,[1] just as, a generation earlier, the Peelites had combined with the Liberals.

The Salisbury administration (1886-92) made a sensible innovation in the realm of Scottish finance.[2] As McLaren had been well aware,[3] Victorian Scotland easily 'paid her way' as a partner in the union, contributing handsomely in taxation without receiving much in return: since France was thought of as the potential enemy, Germany as the friend, military barracks and naval dockyards were mostly located in the south,[4] so that Scotland benefited little from this substantial branch of the national expenditure. Now, in 1888, a Treasury calculation showed that 80 per cent of the United Kingdom revenue was derived from England and Wales, 11 per cent from Scotland, and 9 per cent from Ireland. Henceforth, the 'Goschen formula' (called after the Liberal Unionist chancellor of the exchequer) served as a 'ready reckoner' for the allocation of budgetary grants: Scotland claimed, and still claims, 11/80ths of any sum allowed to England and Wales, that is, 11/91sts of the total for Great Britain.[5]

Popularly elected county councils were set up in England in 1888, and the corresponding Scottish Act was passed in 1889.[6] To the new councils were transferred the varied functions of commissioners of supply, justices of peace and county road trustees, along with responsibility for police forces in all burghs with fewer than 7,000 inhabitants, and for the jurisdiction under the Public Health Acts formerly exercised by the parochial boards. A 'consolidated county rate' was to be levied for all county purposes. Complete autonomy was not, however, granted to the new bodies, for capital expenditure and police administra-

[1] The name 'Unionist' continued in general use for about half a century.

[2] Another minor but useful reform of the time was that whereby all thirteen judges of the Court of Session became also judges of the High Court of Justiciary (1887); thus the *personnel* of the supreme civil judicature became identical with that of the supreme criminal judicature.

[3] Cf. *supra*, p. 205.

[4] Exceptionally, the fortification of Inchkeith island, in the firth of Forth, was ordered by Disraeli and completed in 1881.

[5] The Treasury returns for the period 1891-1922 show that Scotland continued to pay approximately 11 per cent of the U.K. revenue, though Ireland's share dwindled sharply and England had to find correspondingly increased sums. Cf. *infra*, pp. 297-8.

[6] Unlike the town councillors (with one-third retiring each year after serving for three years), county councillors were, and are, elected *en masse* every third year.

tion were to be supervised in each county by a standing joint committee, comprising the sheriff as chairman, seven county councillors and seven commissioners of supply (retained for this purpose). In the larger counties district committees, including county councillors for the district and representatives of parochial boards and of any burghs within the district, were to act for the council in matters concerning roads and public health.

Besides instituting county councils, which promptly became the most potent of local authorities, the Act of 1889 provided for a tidying-up of the country's geographical divisions. Ross and Cromarty, already bracketed together for most purposes, were formally united as a shire, but Shetland was detached from Orkney and given the infelicitous name of 'Zetland' (though it remains 'Shetland' in popular parlance). Moreover, a boundary commission was appointed to adjust county, parish and burgh limits: historically, the sheriffdom or shire was an ill-defined administrative and judicial unit, the parish a purely ecclesiastical unit, and the burgh largely an economic unit, each of them without reference to the others. As the result of the commission's labours (1890-92), each burgh and (with rare exceptions) each parish was placed wholly within one county, all detached portions of parishes were suppressed, and the same was done with discontiguous portions of counties: for example, the district of Kincardine-on-Forth, comprising the parishes of Culross and Tulliallan, was transferred from Perthshire to Fife. The only anomaly of this kind that was left untouched was the detached part of Dunbartonshire, containing the parishes of Cumbernauld and Kirkintilloch.

Another step in local reform came with the Burgh Police Act of 1892, the longest Scottish statute of the century, consolidating previous legislation and adding some new items. 'Dual administration'[1] disappeared: henceforth each burgh must elect either town councillors or police commissioners – but not both. The size of the council was fixed in relation to the burgh's population, and discretion was given to appoint a 'stipendiary magistrate'[2] to sit with the 'lay magistrates' (or bailies).

Gladstone won the general election of July 1892 with a majority (including the Irish Nationalists) of 40 over the combined Conservatives and Unionists, carrying Scotland by 50 seats against 22 (11 Conserva-

[1] See *supra*, p. 196.

[2] That is, a paid professional judge, with legal training and qualifications equal to those of a sheriff-substitute.

tives and 11 Unionists). His second home rule bill, the *raison d'être* of his fourth administration, though passed by the Commons, was rejected by the Lords in September 1893, and, now in his eighty-fifth year, he resigned the premiership in the following March, to be succeeded by his brilliant but erratic lieutenant, Rosebery.[1] During his brief ministry, as might be expected, attention was paid to Scottish affairs. By an Act of 1894, parish councils, popularly elected every three years, took over poor relief and local rating from the parochial boards, and at the centre the Local Government Board displaced the Board of Supervision. Democracy[2] had finally triumphed in all three fields of local government – burgh, county and parish. In 1894, too, and again in 1895, Rosebery set up the 'Scottish Grand Committee', including all Scottish M.P.s, to take the committee stage of Scottish bills referred to it. This mild measure of devolution was a concession to the advocates of Scottish home rule: each year from 1889 to 1895 a motion was introduced for a separate Scottish parliament, and, while this was not taken very seriously by the members at large, it had many friends among Scottish Liberals.

Rosebery, himself something of an imperialist, had little sympathy with the ideals of the older Gladstonians – 'peace, retrenchment, reform' – and the party now entered upon a decade of divided counsels and declining fortunes. July 1895 brought a crushing defeat at the polls, when the opposition returned to power with a majority of 152 over Liberals and Irish Nationalists together. In Scotland the contest was closer than at any time since 1832: the Liberals held 39 seats, and the 33 that declared for their opponents included 14 burgh constituencies and the two university seats.

That the tide was indeed turning is clear from the warmth of Scotland's response to the full-blooded patriotism which marked the third ministry of the marquis of Salisbury (1895-1902). As the century drew to its close a series of stirring events focussed attention on the crown, the empire and the army: Joseph Chamberlain's imaginative handling of colonial affairs, the Queen's diamond jubilee in 1897, Kitchener's reconquest of the Sudan through his brilliant victory at Omdurman (1898), the Boer War (1899-1902), especially from the

[1] He was the third Scottish premier since the Union (the others being Bute and Aberdeen), but four of his successors in the next thirty years were to be Scotsmen – Balfour, Campbell-Bannerman, Bonar Law (actually born in Canada) and Ramsay MacDonald.

[2] The term must always be understood, in a Victorian context, as applicable to males only: 'Votes for Women' were still an unfailing source of hilarity.

early reverses to the relief of Mafeking in May 1900,[1] and the proclamation of the Commonwealth of Australia, the second great federation of self-governing dominions (1 January 1901).[2] In the midst of the Boer War,[3] with martial fervour at its height, the Salisbury cabinet had its mandate renewed at the 'khaki election' of September 1900, which is remarkable in that, while the Conservative majority over the whole United Kingdom was slightly reduced, that party improved on its 1895 record by winning Scotland by a margin of four seats. Included in the 38 successful candidates on the government side were all seven Glasgow M.P.s – a total reversal of the 1885 result. Even Orkney and Shetland, regarded as a safe Liberal seat, fell to the other party.

The longest reign in our history ended on 22 January 1901, when Edward VII succeeded to the throne. Peace was signed with the Boers on 31 May 1902, Transvaal and the Orange River Colony being annexed but given a form of representative government. In July 1902 Salisbury resigned office, and A. J. (afterwards Earl) Balfour became premier. The ten years of Conservative rule were not noteworthy for Scottish enactments, but two measures deserve mention. By the Town Councils Act, 1900, the term 'commissioners of police' was abolished, and all burghs were required to use the historic forms, provost, bailies and town councillors. In 1903, in recognition of its possible strategic importance in time of war, Scotland's first naval base was authorised and started at Rosyth in Fife,[4] and a permanent military camp was also planned, at Stobs in Roxburghshire.

Liberal disunion was still a cause of weakness at the close of the Boer War. Imperial sentiments were favoured by Rosebery and Asquith, and by the Liberal League, set up by the former in 1902, but the pacifist views of the Young Scots Society, organised in the same year, were shared by Sir Henry Campbell-Bannerman, who had had, since 1899, the difficult task of leading his party in the Commons. But their troubles were slight compared with those which afflicted the Conservatives from 1903, when Chamberlain resigned in order to devote all his efforts to a crusade for tariff reform and imperial preference.

[1] Though it was preceded by the reliefs of Kimberley and Ladysmith, and by the shattering of the main Boer forces at Paardeberg (all in February 1900), it was Mafeking that called forth such extravagant rejoicing as to add a new word to the language – 'mafficking'.

[2] The first governor-general was the earl (later the first marquis) of Linlithgow (1860-1908).

[3] All twelve Scottish regiments served during the war, besides companies of the different yeomanry formations.

[4] It proved to be of the utmost value during two world wars.

The free trade controversy crippled the government and Balfour's tenure of office was extremely unhappy, until, with by-elections running steadily against him, he resigned in December 1905. The election of January 1906 confirmed the 'caretaker' Liberal ministry in office, with a clear majority over all other parties.

The Scottish results in 1906 ran true to form in that 58 Liberals were elected against 12 Unionists, including only two from Glasgow instead of the seven of 1900, and these two free traders.[1] The novel feature was the return of Scotland's first two Labour M.P.s, for Dundee and the Blackfriars division of Glasgow. Nineteenth-century Liberal members had often acted as spokesmen for the working-class, and indeed on the left wing radicalism shaded into socialism: in 1886 R. B. Cunninghame Graham, an avowed socialist, won North-west Lanarkshire as a Liberal. From 1892, it is true, the Independent Labour party held a few seats on their own account, but these were all south of the Tweed. Even after 1906 the breach between Liberal and Labour was not complete: by a local understanding, Dundee's two seats were held, from 1906 to 1918, against Unionist opposition by one Liberal and one Labour candidate, the two parties tacitly refraining from 'cut-throat' competition. At the national level, however, any such concordat was disclaimed, for the Scottish Liberal Federation resolved in 1906 to oppose all socialist candidates at parliamentary elections.

Though perturbed by the continuing dissension between the imperialist and radical wings, the Liberal administrations of Campbell-Bannerman (1905-08) and Asquith (1908-15) held together and survived the two general elections of 1910 (January and December): the second of these was brought on by the acknowledged intention of the strongly Tory House of Lords to thwart the government's aims. The appeal to the country, though it reduced the Liberals to dependence on the support of the Irish Nationalists, could be taken as an endorsement of further reforms, including Irish home rule. The Scottish results showed little change, save that, from December 1910, alongside 58 Liberals and 11 Unionists, there was a third Labour M.P. (for West Fife).

The record of reforms achieved during those years, if it fell short of the ministry's programme, was impressive. Old age pensions were instituted in 1908, the Union of South Africa, the third great self-governing federal dominion, was formed in 1910, the Parliament Act

[1] The *Glasgow Herald*, while remaining Unionist, was for free trade.

of 1911 curtailed the Lords' veto to a two-years delaying power, cut down parliament's permissible life from seven to five years and started the payment of members, and a system of unemployment insurance was begun in 1912. Domestic politics were bedevilled in the years 1912-14 by the deep cleavage over Ireland: the government was resolved (not without misgivings) to grant home rule, but the peers fought the bill to the last ditch, while the Ulstermen and their British sympathisers threatened civil war. The final triumph of the Liberal policy was purely nominal: the home rule bill was passed in 1914, but, war having broken out with Germany, its operation was suspended for the duration of hostilities.

In its dealings with Scotland the government incurred both praise and criticism. It was proposed in 1906, for reasons of economy and lack of suitable accommodation, to remove to England the Royal Scots Greys, the country's only cavalry regiment, but the resultant outcry brought a change of mind and a decision to build Redford barracks, near Edinburgh. In 1907 the Scottish Grand Committee, which had lapsed under the Conservatives, was revived and transformed from a 'select' (or sessional) into a 'standing' (or permanent) committee. From 1909 the negotiations for a full church union ended talk of disestablishment, but home rule for Scotland was still being discussed: Parliament, it was claimed, was too busy or insufficiently interested to find time for such Scottish needs as temperance and land reforms. In June 1910, some 20 Liberal members constituted the Scottish Nationalist Committee, advocating self-government in domestic affairs. From time to time motions and bills got a sympathetic hearing, but because of the more pressing Irish problem they were always shelved; in 1912, however, the Commons went so far as to resolve that Scotland and Ireland should have equal treatment in any scheme of devolution.

To the pre-war years belong three Scottish enactments, each significant in its own way. Under the Small Landholders Act, 1911, the Board of Agriculture was set up in 1912 as a central institution for dealing with crofts and crofters, and the Scottish Land Court was established for hearing and determining cases arising in that connection. In 1913 the Highlands and Islands Medical Service, a pioneer state enterprise for the encouragement of general practice in remote, thinly peopled and unremunerative areas, was authorised, and the Temperance (Scotland) Act permitted 'local option' polls, whereby the electors in parishes or wards of burghs might control the sale of liquor by voting for 'No Change', 'Limitation of Licences', or 'No Licence'.

Postponed by the outbreak of war, these two statutes did not take effect until after its end.

Asquith's cabinet had thus done something for Scotland, but it was lukewarm about home rule for that country. In 1913, and again in 1914, time was refused for a Government of Scotland bill, which envisaged a Scottish executive, comprising the lord high commissioner and the revived privy council, and a legislature of 140 members to be returned by the existing constituencies without the universities, while 72 Scottish M.P.s were to continue to represent the nation in the imperial parliament. The Unionists may well have been right in asserting that there was no real popular demand for this measure and that it was merely an academic exercise in constitution-making; nevertheless, had Irish home rule gone into force in a legal and peaceful manner, consistency might have obliged the Liberals to set up a Scottish parliament in Edinburgh.

For the time being, however, both the Scottish and Irish questions were hushed as the war clouds gathered. The menace of German military ambition had overhung the whole period of Liberal rule, compelling even the pacifist ministers to acquiesce in the building of a large and costly navy, based on the all-big-gun *Dreadnought* (1906), and in the reorganisation of the army on a war-footing.[1] Several international crises were weathered, but the invasion of Belgium inevitably brought Britain to the side of France and Russia, in opposition to Germany and Austria-Hungary, and the declaration of war on 4 August 1914 ushered in a new and fateful era.

[1] Carried out by R. B. (later Viscount) Haldane as secretary of state for war, the sweeping reforms of 1906 and subsequent years created an expeditionary force organised in six divisions of infantry and one of cavalry (about 165,000 men), remodelled the reserves on a basis of preparedness, and transformed the old volunteers and yeomanry into the 'Territorial Army'. Haldane's new system was to prove its worth in the 1914 campaigns.

CHAPTER XX

The Countryside Changes its Face

DURING AND just after the Napoleonic wars, as we have seen,[1] agriculture, supporting perhaps a third of the people,[2] was still the primary 'industry' of Scotland. War-time prosperity, it is true, had vanished with the return of peace. The price of wheat tumbled from 126s. 6d. a quarter in 1812 to 44s. 7d. in 1822, and the post-war depression continued for some further years. The eventual recovery was due in part – and the farmers were inclined to credit it entirely – to the operation of the Corn Law, which ensured a market protected against cheap imported grain. The law was changed by Wellington's ministry in 1828 from an absolute prohibition of imports with the home price under 80s. to a sliding scale of duties, varying from 36s. 8d. when the quarter cost 50s., to 16s. 8d. at a price of 68s., and to 1s. at 73s. The rates were again modified by Peel in 1842, to 20s. at a home price of 51s., diminishing to 12s. at 60s. and to the old limit of 1s. at 73s.; but the Tories, and indeed many Whigs, resisted the demand for repeal until the Irish famine forced Peel, at the cost of his political career, to take the plunge into free trade in 1846.[3]

Far from taking his ease under the beneficent shelter of the Corn Laws, the Scots farmer brought a high degree of skill and ingenuity to his labours during the period 1822-46. While the earlier improvements – enclosed fields and long leases, rotation of crops and the use of fallow, light iron ploughs and the threshing machine (now often steam-driven) – spread to districts hitherto untouched, the progressive farmer took up the challenge of new ideas and new techniques. In 1823 James Smith, of Deanston in Kilmadock parish, Perthshire, started his system of 'thorough' drainage and deep ploughing, and before long his method was adopted with enthusiasm.[4] His success stimulated

[1] See *supra*, pp. 128-9.

[2] The census of 1821 returned 130,699 families as forming 'the agricultural class', and Sir John Sinclair, using the (perhaps high) allowance of six persons to a family, equated this to 784,194 persons, out of a total population of 2,091,521. But Sinclair's figure of course includes children of all ages, and the 'working' figure might be about 500,000, or one in four of the Scottish total.

[3] Cf. *supra*, p. 201.

[4] His *Remarks on Thorough Draining and Deep Ploughing* (1831) is one of the agrarian classics. His system involved parallel drains about thirty inches deep, lined in the bottom with stones and leading to a main cut along the lowest level of the field.

others to develop further improvements, including the costly but highly beneficial underground drainage of very wet lands by means of tiles. From 1825 crushed bone was being used as manure, to be followed from the 1840s by Peruvian guano and sundry chemical fertilisers. In 1828 the Rev. Patrick Bell from Forfarshire invented a reaping machine of great practical value. From 1837, too, experiments were afoot with the steam-plough, though its use was limited and the horse-plough remained the standard.

Better transport contributed materially to agricultural advance. By 1836 coastal steam-ships were carrying cattle from the north-east counties to the English markets,[1] and the rapid construction of the railways from the 1840s[2] made it easy to move feeding stuffs, fertilisers and farm produce from one part of the country to another.

If, in general, the 'Corn Law times' were marked by a slow climb towards prosperity, conditions varied greatly between one district and another. At one extreme were the farms and crofts of the north-west, with problems of survival to which some consideration has already been given (chap. xiv), and at the other were the large and fertile fields of the Lothians and south-east. Between them lay the dairy farms of the south-west, with Dunlop cheese as their best-known product, the historic orchards (now spreading to the flat lands) of the Clyde valley, the assorted agriculture, ranging from 'improved' to 'old-fashioned', of central Scotland, and the highly successful mixed arable and pastoral holdings of the north-east.

It was East Lothian that best exemplified 'high farming', the intensive cultivation of wheat and other grains, and of drill-sown turnips, which, along with oil-cake,[3] ensured the quality and value of its fat cattle. 'The markets', wrote George Robertson in *Rural Recollections* (1829), 'were kept full of the best beef the whole year round.' Robertson was a native of Lothian, but we have also the testimony of England's radical politician and agricultural expert, William Cobbett, who, after touring the Lothians in 1831, pronounced the farm-yards to be 'factories for making corn and meat, carried on

[1] And it was the new steamship connection between Kirkwall and Leith (started in 1833) that led to a gradual and beneficent change in the Orkneys. Those islands had been so backward, so poverty-stricken, that one farmer in 1796 had been criticised for raising his ploughman's wages from 7s. 6d. to 10s. a half year. Ready access to the southern markets made cattle-rearing worth-while, and Orkney cattle (and later poultry) came in time to enjoy a good reputation and to bring prosperity to the islands.

[2] These matters are discussed *infra*, chap. xxi.

[3] This rich and concentrated form of cattle-feed was made from crushed oil-bearing seeds, such as linseed (the seed of the flax plant), cotton-seed and rape-seed.

principally by the means of horses and machinery'. They were, indeed, capitalist enterprises, the average farm having from 300 to 500 acres,[1] and the best land renting for as much as £7 an acre. The tenant-farmer, leasing his land for perhaps twenty-one years, needed a large number of workers (including harvesters in the season), the best stock and machines available, and some familiarity with such matters as soil chemistry, zoology, botany and accountancy; thus equipped, he could expect to become a rich and respected member of the local community.

For the farm-workers, conditions were harder. The value of the yearly wages of the Lothian hinds, paid partly in money and partly in meal and other 'gains', might be reckoned to amount to £25 or even more,[2] while day-labourers got 1s. 6d. or 1s. 8d., and harvesters from 6s. to 10s. a week. Cobbett, used to English living standards, deplored the poky inconvenience of the married labourer's single-roomed cottage, and all observers recognised the temptations to slovenly or immoral lives offered by the 'bothy', the crude and primitive out-building set aside in some areas for unmarried ploughmen. James Hogg thought that the 'one amelioration' of the 'absolute slavery' of the rural workers was 'the liberty at each term of selling themselves to the highest bidder'. And, naturally, the farmers took on harvesters at the lowest wages that proved acceptable, whether they were native Lowlanders, Highland migrants, or the Irish who, from the 1820s, tended to displace the others from field-work, as from all other kinds of poorly paid labour. The chief change in the countryman's diet noted by the compilers of the *New Statistical Account* (1834-45) was the appearance of tea, sugar and wheaten bread, usually as part of the afternoon meal, even in the humblest cottages.

The fears of landlords and farmers that free trade spelt ruination were not realised, and in fact the period from 1846 to 1873 was one of general prosperity for Scottish agriculture. Many kinds of farm produce, after all, had never had the protection of the Corn Laws – potatoes, dairy produce, beef, mutton and wool – and, where wheat was a vital crop, as in the Lothians and Berwickshire, the farmers were resourceful enough to withstand adversity. Two other factors, both

[1] This is far above the average for arable farms elsewhere, which would range between 50 and 200 acres.

[2] Wages were rather less in other counties, e.g. £12-£18 in Stirling, £12-£16 in Ayrshire, £10-£14 in Perth, £14 in Aberdeen, and £9-£12 in Banff. In each case food (generally meal, potatoes and milk) and lodging were allowed in addition, so that £20 in all would be nearer the true total.

favourable to farming, were indeed vastly more potent than 'repeal'. One was the very rapid rise in the population of the towns, which added to the farmer's potential customers, and the other was the steady expansion of railway and steamship communications, which increasingly offered the means of feeding the urban masses. Agricultural machinery, too, was much improved, and the Great Exhibition of 1851, which included a display of American reapers, stimulated the mechanisation of farming processes. One consequence was a lessening of the need for harvest workers, and this in turn meant that after mid-century the Irish in Scotland mostly left the rural scene and became town-dwellers. Again, the cutting off of Russian wheat imports during the Crimean War (1854-56) gave a fillip to the domestic producer, whose harvests at that time found a ready market.

It is true that the economic advantage of the towns continued to lure young men and whole families from the country, and that fewer hands were required for cultivation as standards improved. Despite the strains and stresses of the period, however, it is also true that conditions in general were stable and flourishing. The large wheat-field was still typical of the south-east and eastern counties, but heavy yields of oats, barley, turnips and potatoes were also obtained throughout the land. Four native breeds of cattle acquired fame at this epoch. The 'black polls' or Aberdeen-Angus, the best beef producers, were raised in the north-east, from Forfar to Moray, and provided the English market with its favourite 'prime Scotch' beef. In the south-west the Ayrshire breed, supplying the finest dairy cows, was preferred, though the hardier Galloway herds were to be found on the hill pastures of that region. Highland cattle, delighting the artist's eye with their shaggy coats, noble heads and wide-flung horns, were at home in the glens and on the mountain-sides that were unsuited for less rugged beasts. It was estimated that more than a quarter of all the sheep in Britain belonged to Scotland, the Cheviot being bred in large numbers in the southern uplands and the Black-faced variety further north. Cross-breeding was, however, common with both cattle and sheep, so that English strains were represented in this way by the famous Shorthorn cattle and the Border-Leicester sheep.

For the 1860s, as for all subsequent decades, a number of official reports informs us in detail about the diets of rural workers.[1] Porridge, now taken with milk instead of ale, normally appeared at both breakfast

[1] See in particular H. Hamilton, *History of the Homeland* (1947), pp. 77-9, and T. Ferguson, *Scottish Social Welfare, 1864-1914* (1958), chap. v.

and supper, but, at one or other of these meals, it was often followed, and sometimes replaced, by tea with bread or oatcakes; potatoes, fish and milk, or else broth or peasemeal soup and bread, formed the usual midday dinner. Meat and cheese provided only occasional changes, though they were common on the farmer's own table, where they were shared by the young ploughmen boarding with him. The heaviest meat-eaters were said to be the shepherds, who were allowed the 'braxy' sheep or lambs (the victims of disease).

The halcyon days for the farmer came to an abrupt end in 1873, when, for various reasons, the 'great depression' began, to reach its depth in 1879 and to last, though with fluctuations and partial recoveries, until about 1894. A shortage of gold and some ill-advised speculation afflicted the international money markets, while at home agriculture, suffering from over-expansion and inflated rents, had to face a run of bad harvests from 1873. Worst of all, transport developments now told heavily against the British farmer. The railways of America enabled the wheat and meat of the plains to be rushed to the eastern seaports, and thence by fast steamship to the open markets of Britain. Freight costs were reduced to a fraction, imports of American wheat were doubled in twenty years, and the area under wheat in Britain was halved. At the same time or soon after, Irish butter and bacon, Dutch cheese, Danish dairy produce, Australian wool, New Zealand mutton and Argentine beef all benefited from cheap sea transport and free trade. Massive imports of foodstuffs suited the manufacturer and the town labourer, but the dawn of world-wide commerce had a shattering effect on the farmer. His wheat dropped from 56s. to 24s. a quarter, he could no longer afford the prevailing high rents, and, since only the most efficient of the arable holdings were viable economic units, marginal lands, optimisitically ploughed up in better times, passed out of cultivation.

To the winds of adversity Scotland, with a climate much less equable than that of her overseas competitors, was peculiarly vulnerable, and the great depression wrought a transformation in her agriculture. The extent of the change is shown by the acreage under wheat,[1] which stood at more than 260,000 in 1856, a year of stability and prosperity,

[1] Acreage returns and livestock numbers were collected and published by the Highland Society in the mid-1850s, and by the Board of Trade from 1866 on, but the mode of classifying and presenting these varied, so that the statistics are not strictly comparable; e.g., the earlier surveys excluded all details for small holdings and crofts, rented at under £20 per annum in the crofting counties and under £10 elsewhere.

declined to 45,000 in 1894, at the end of the depression, and recovered only to 60,500 in 1914. Other crops recorded merely minor fluctuations, but the acreage under permanent grass rose fairly steadily, and all categories of livestock increased in numbers, as the following figures indicate:–

	1856	*1894*	*1914*
		(thousands omitted)	
Horses	180	206	209
Cattle	967	1,202	1,215
Sheep	5,822	7,273	7,025[1]
Pigs	127	149	153

The new emphasis was upon animal husbandry, since a readier sale was found, under free trade conditions, for domestic meat and dairy produce than for home-grown grain. Moreover, the value for breeding purposes of the hardy native strains of cattle, the Aberdeen-Angus and the Galloway, was now appreciated by the ranchers of North America, so that the more astute Scottish farmers paid much attention to their pure-bred herds. From 1882 their best animals were fetching the unheard-of prices of 300, 400 or even 500 guineas, and shipments of prize cattle to Canada and the United States became a routine matter. As one new fashion set in, an old one died out: cattle-droving by way of the great Falkirk 'tryst', for the ultimate benefit of the English consumer, had continued throughout the first half of the nineteenth century, but the obvious advantages of the railway network put an end to the practice in the later decades of the century.[2] Dairy-farming techniques meanwhile progressed in the south-west: the Scottish Dairy Association was founded in 1884, and the farmers were quick to take advantage of such mechanical aids as cream separators and milking machines, and also of the townsfolk's craving for fresh milk, butter and cheese.

Thus the farmers struggled fairly successfully for survival in a violently competitive world, but it is noticeable that the growth of even the most flourishing branches did not keep pace with the increase of population, which, with industry booming, was particularly rapid at this time: there were fewer than 3,000,000 inhabitants of Scotland

[1] The net decrease in the total of sheep between 1894 and 1914 covers (*a*) a substantial increase in the numbers kept on the low-lying farms, and (*b*) a sharp decline in the numbers of sheep on the hill-grazings.

[2] Of special importance in this connection was the completion in 1880 of the line to Oban, after which droving fell off sharply; the last Falkirk tryst was held in 1901.

in 1856, but about 4,150,000 by 1894. Contracting in some directions, and only modestly expanding in others, agriculture sustained a relative decline in the scheme of things.

The impact of the great depression upon the Highlands was quite different, but no less momentous. The famine of 1846, if less serious in Scotland than in Ireland, had been devastating in its effects wherever the potato was cultivated intensively, as a means of feeding the excessively large numbers of people who were reluctant to leave their homes.[1] The drastic cure of evictions, to make way for sheep-walks, was still being applied here and there after 1850, but the more humane landlords tried to salvage the local economy by works of drainage and land reclamation, and by education in improved methods of farming. The most prominent reformers along such lines at mid-century were the Duke of Argyll in Tiree and James Matheson in Lewis, but it is significant that each of them was impelled in the end to persuade many of his tenants to emigrate, and so to relieve the intolerable congestion of these islands.

From 1852 the construction and use of Balmoral castle as a royal summer residence made deer-stalking and grouse-shooting fashionable sports, and suggested new ways of turning to account what had been barren and unprofitable lands. Then, in the 1870s, with the onset of the depression, sheep-farming suffered from the competition of fine Australian wool and New Zealand mutton. Many of the Highland grazings had meanwhile deteriorated from too much cropping and the exhausted lands could not carry as large flocks as before. The graziers were unable to pay high rents, so that, as leases expired, proprietors were ready to convert the grazings into deer forests or grouse moors and to let them to rich sporting tenants from the south. Admittedly, the land involved was mostly poor, but this seemingly anti-social development sharpened the edge of the resentment of the crofter, struggling to meet the rent of his tiny holding, or being deprived of it for failure to do so.

The smouldering anger of the peasantry burst into flame in 1882, when the 'Crofters' War' broke out in Skye, to spread to the Outer Isles and the western seaboard of the mainland. Attempts at eviction or arrest led to resistance and riots, which continued despite the appeals of the ministers and the physical exertions of the police, aided on occasion by gunboats and marines. A 'no rent' policy was widely adopted from Martinmas 1884, but already, in 1883, a royal com-

[1] Cf. *supra*, pp. 157, 159.

mission had been appointed to examine the crofters' plight and suggest remedies. The Napier commission's report was sympathetic and sensible, the government accepted its recommendations, and Parliament, in June 1886, passed the Crofters' Holdings Act, the main terms of which have been mentioned.[1] Though there were disturbances until 1888, the commissioners did good work, in the course of their statutory tours through the crofting counties, by settling disputes, granting compensation and alleviating hardships. Their visits and reports continued annually until 1913, by which time rent reductions aggregating 25 per cent and the cancellation of arrears up to 67 per cent had been arranged.

Another royal commission, appointed in 1892 and reporting in 1895, viewed the land question from a different angle. The 'Deer Forests commission', as it was called, tried to assess the feasibility of making a better use, either as arable or as hill pasture, of the immense tracts devoted to sheep grazings, deer forests and grouse moors. Their finding was that just over 1¾ million acres, nearly half lying in Inverness and Ross, were suitable for the creation of new crofts or medium-sized farms, or for the extension of existing holdings. Far more of the land thus scheduled was grazing rather than forest, and was usable, if at all, and then by a part-time crofter, as pastoral rather than arable land; and no terms were suggested for any such conversion. Still, academic exercise as this possibly was, it is significant that some 'economic potential' attached to an area not much less than one-tenth of Scotland. Suspicions of neglect and misuse lingered on and helped to inspire the legislation of 1911, by which the Board of Agriculture was empowered to create or extend small holdings, and the Land Court was instituted to adjudicate disputes concerning crofters.[2]

For Scottish agriculture in general, recovery came from the mid-1890s, partly because there was an upward swing of prices, partly because farming, though less widespread, was more efficient than formerly, and partly because the farmer tended to look for his profits to the production of perishable foodstuffs – beef, mutton, milk, butter, cheese and eggs. Not that the home market for such commodities was completely protected, for the advance of refrigeration had, so to speak, brought Australia, New Zealand and the Argentine to the housewife's doorstep. But, within its limits, Scottish farming in the pre-war years was again on a steady and prosperous basis.[3]

[1] See *supra*, p. 216. [2] Cf. *supra*, p. 222.
[3] And the application of science to farming techniques was carried further as a

The census reports illustrate the way in which agriculture's share in the national economy had contracted since Napoleonic times. The 500,000 persons engaged in agriculture, forestry and horticulture in 1821, forming about one in four of the population, had dwindled by 1861 to 350,000, or less than one in eight, and by 1911 to 200,000, or fewer than one in twenty. Of all the men and women classed as 'gainfully employed', nearly 26 per cent were engaged in farming and fishing in 1861, but only 11 per cent in 1911. Again, although the total population of Scotland more than doubled between 1821 and 1911 – rising from 2,091,521 to 4,760,103 – those counties which depended mainly on agriculture were actually losing inhabitants. Practically half of all the counties, sixteen out of thirty-three, had passed their peak at some point in the nineteenth century and were decreasing in population by the twentieth century:–

County	*Population*			
	In 1821	*At Peak*		*In 1911*
Argyll	97,316	(1831)	100,973	70,902
Banff	43,663	(1891)	64,190	61,402
Berwick	33,385	(1861)	36,613	29,643
Caithness	29,181	(1861)	41,111	32,010
Inverness	89,961	(1841)	97,799	87,272
Kinross	7,762	(1831)	9,072	7,527
Kirkcudbright	38,903	(1851)	43,121	38,367
Nairn	9,268	(1871)	10,225	9,319
Orkney	26,979	(1861)	32,395	25,897
Perth	138,247	(1831)	142,166	124,342
Ross and Cromarty	68,762	(1851)	82,707	77,364
Roxburgh	40,892	(1861)	54,119	47,192
Selkirk	6,637	(1891)	27,353	24,601
Sutherland	23,840	(1851)	25,518	20,179
Wigtown	33,240	(1851)	43,389	31,998
Zetland	26,145	(1861)	31,670	27,911

Rural depopulation thus afflicted all eight Highland or crofting counties, from Argyll to Zetland, and eight others, from Wigtown to Nairn, that might be termed Lowland. Emigration, the deer forests, the townward drift in search of employment or amenities, the use of such machines as the combined reaper and binder, the decay of village crafts – each had played some part in the process. By 1914, though

result of the work of the agricultural colleges at Glasgow (opened in 1900), Edinburgh (1901) and Aberdeen (1904).

wages had remained firm or even increased in the face of falling prices, while the work had been lightened and shortened by mechanisation, farm labour was hard to come by in most districts. This was deplored, not only by the farmers, but by those who felt that an unbalanced economy was a tragedy for the whole nation.

In a span of ninety years, the countryside had changed its face, the countryman had changed his ways. Hill pastures, rough grazings and woodlands had everywhere encroached on the farm-land, and, while fields were larger, corn-fields were fewer. The 'but-and-ben', with its kailyard and privy-midden, was still to be seen, but in many places it had given way to a substantial, two-storeyed farm-house, the centre of a cluster of neat buildings housing the stock, the grain and the varied implements of what was now a highly specialised industry. The married labourer's tiny cottage and, where it survived, the comfortless bothy[1] of the young ploughmen had changed less than most items in the rural scene. In the Western Isles, the worst type of 'black house' – a single room for man and beast, without window or chimney, soot-blackened and insanitary – had either disappeared or been transformed by enlargement and improvement into a properly lit and ventilated 'white house'.

In the seasonal cycle of the countryman's life there remained the occasions which combined serious business with rustic revelry – the 'feeing fairs' or hiring markets, when many a ploughman changed his master, the harvest-home, cattle-shows and ploughing-matches. Similarly, there were feasting and drinking at country funerals, and all joined in to dance to the fiddle at weddings. At Hallowe'en some of the kitchen and fireside games described by Burns lingered on; at Hogmanay (31 December) the 'guisers' (disguised mummers) presented their childish tableaux and recitations and begged for the customary gifts, while their elders went 'first-footing' their neighbours; but 'Handsel Monday' (the first Monday of the year) had mostly been replaced by New Year's day as the time for family reunions and presents, and 'Fastern's E'en' (Shrove Tuesday in England), when the boys had brought their fighting-cocks to school, was no longer recognised.

Many a reformer lamented the countryman's addiction to strong liquor on all special occasions, but to others there was more cause for disapproval in the changes in his ordinary diet. The consumption of porridge and oatcakes, of milk and potatoes, had been fostered by the

[1] The bothy system still prevailed in the eastern and north-eastern counties, but in the south, where it had never been prominent, it was scarcely to be found by 1914.

payment of wages in kind, but that was a waning practice by the first decade of the twentieth century. While meat and cheese were in commoner use than formerly, tea, baker's bread, scones, butter and jam were almost universal, and tea was, in the eyes of the commentators, the villain of the piece. The more remote country-dwellers, especially in parts of the Highlands and Islands, clung to their traditional broth, porridge and milk, but elsewhere, according to the testimony of medical observers, the innumerable cups of strong, black tea were undermining old and healthy habits, ruining digestions, and causing anaemia, headaches and nervous disorders.

CHAPTER XXI

The Ascendancy of Heavy Industry

THE FIRST phase of the Industrial Revolution, lasting into the third decade of the nineteenth century, had seen the mechanisation of cotton-spinning, and the capitalist organisation of the smaller-scale, and still largely manual, operations of linen-spinning, weaving and coal-mining; iron-working, ship-building and engineering were as yet minor elements in the economy. For a generation cotton kept its lead among Scottish industries, but thereafter the position was transformed by the upsurge into first place of the varied but allied branches of metallurgy.

The fact that cotton maintained its status, instead of improving upon it, meant, in the burgeoning economy of an expanding population, a relative decline. Of the 192 cotton mills in 1838, employing 35,600 workers, 107 were in Lanarkshire, 52 in Renfrewshire; Glasgow had 98 of them and Paisley 41. By 1856 the mills numbered only 152, but they were rather larger on average, for their labour force was 34,700. Linen gave employment in 1838 to 17,900 workers in 183 mills, more than half of which were in Forfarshire (96) and another quarter in Fife (46). The 112 woollen mills at the same date were much smaller, with 5,100 workers, and they were also spread more diffusely through the counties, with 24 in Clackmannan, 18 in Ayr, 17 in Roxburgh, 15 in Selkirk, and diminished numbers elsewhere. In round numbers, therefore, the average cotton mill employed some 200 workers, the linen mill 100, and the woollen mill 50.

In textiles generally the machine only gradually displaced the manual worker. The power-loom was adopted by most cotton-masters in the 1830s and 1840s, and, in one of the grimmest tragedies of the factory age, the hand-loom cotton weaver was slowly but inexorably 'squeezed out'. By 1838 his weekly earnings might be as low as 4s. 6d., and even the fancy muslin weavers could only command wages that ranged between 6s. and 9s. 6d. As regards the linen branch, machine-spinning was taken up in the years 1825-35, but power-loom weaving only about 1860, when again the depressed hand-loom weaver faced starvation wages and ultimate unemployment. The specialist workers fared better: in 1838 the woollen weavers of

Galashiels and Hawick, the carpet-makers of Kilmarnock and Glasgow, and the sailcloth-workers of Port Glasgow and Leith, made between 10s. and 15s. a week, and sometimes more. From 1833, the Dundee mills were changing progressively to the manufacture of jute, the cheapest of packing and wrapping fabrics, and from 1847 Kirkcaldy turned largely to the making of linoleum, while Dunfermline's table-linen enhanced its good repute; each of these branches prospered.

The most exotic product of the time was the Paisley shawl, woven entirely by hand in imitation of Oriental embroidery. With a warp of a composite yarn called 'Cashmere' (wool spun around a silk core), which was dyed beforehand, and a weft of fine Tibetan wool or worsted,[1] the shawl was woven, of six or seven colours, in an intricate pattern of conventional geometrical designs intermixed perhaps with flowers and leaves, and always with the characteristic 'pine' *motif*, which was practically its hall-mark.[2] It was of two kinds – the 'filled', 'harness' or winter shawl, ten or twelve feet in length, and the simpler summer shawl, about five feet square, with a solid centre of red, black, white or green, and the pattern only around the edges – and from the 1840s was usually reversible, with the same design appearing front and back, in interchanged colours. An article of luxury and fashion costing around £20, it was held in high regard for weddings, and the shawl trade lasted, with fluctuations and depressions, from 1820 until, soon after 1870, the competition of attractive printed shawls from the English Midlands killed it. Arduous as was his toil and finicking his product, the Paisley weaver was a true, creative craftsman, making a brave if futile gesture of defiance against the all-conquering machine.

As heavy industry developed, each branch became more closely bound up with all the others. Geography and geology determined their location in the central lowland belt, stretching from central Ayrshire to Midlothian and to mid-Fife, with Dundee and Aberdeen as in some sense northern outposts. Here were to be found rich coal and iron ore deposits, good harbours, estuaries and canals, and plentiful capital and labour. In this region, therefore, and more particularly in its heart, north Lanarkshire, heavy industry took root, drawing to itself the displaced, discontented or ambitious Scottish peasants, as

[1] Many commentators have been deceived by the fineness of the finished product into speaking or thinking of the shawl as being of cotton or silk, instead of essentially a woollen article.

[2] The 'pine' was the symbol of an Eastern fertility-cult and is nowadays regarded in Britain, and still more in America, as constituting a 'Paisley pattern'.

well as skilled iron-workers from England and gangs of 'navvies'[1] from Ireland.

Everything favoured the rapid extension of the collieries – the presence of coal of good quality, the needs of industry, the demands of the town-dwellers, whose numbers and standards of living both rose steeply, and the new modes of transport (shortly to be considered). Inventors helped, too, with new or better pumping and winding engines, and, from 1842, with cages running in slides, to raise men or coal from the deeper levels. The output stood at 8¼ million tons, from 425 collieries, in 1857, whereas it had been 2½ millions in 1814; Lanarkshire, with 15,580 out of Scotland's 32,971 coal-miners in 1851, contributed nearly half the total. And all these figures were rising year by year, to reach, for example, 12,700,000 tons from 490 collieries in 1864.

For pig iron production the basic invention was that of James B. Neilson, whose hot-blast process (1828) used but two tons of coal (instead of the seven of the cold blast) to produce a ton of pig iron. An immediate expansion of the industry took place in Old Monkland parish, where plants were set up at Gartsherrie (1828), Dundyvan (1833), Calderbank (1835) and Summerlee (1836), while further south Coltness works began in 1837, and the celebrated 'Dixon's Blazes', which were to illumine Glasgow's night sky for a century to come, were first lit in Govan in 1839. The Scottish output increased phenomenally, especially after 1835:–

Pig Iron Output
(in thousands of tons)

1825	30
1835	75
1845	476
1857	918

To achieve this last figure, some 2½ million tons of iron ore were extracted. From 1839, too, a substantial number of small forges were set up for making malleable iron by the puddling process,[2] and by 1853 the production of wrought iron in Scotland amounted to 136,000 tons.

Many engineering works meanwhile came into operation, manufacturing spindles and looms for the textile factories, steam engines

[1] So called because they were originally engaged as unskilled labourers to dig the courses of the 'navigations' or canals.

[2] See *supra*, p. 133, n. 1. The concentration of malleable iron works in the Coatbridge area of Old Monkland is again remarkable.

and boilers, iron rolling mills, mining machinery, locomotives, marine engines, bridges and cranes, spades, shovels and nails. By mid-century, also, the iron-built and propeller-driven steamship was an established success, and shipbuilding was on the threshold of a big advance, though its output in 1851 stood at the modest level of 136 ships of 30,100 tons.

Improvements in transport both fostered and benefited from industrial activity. The turnpike roads, amounting by 1858 to 6,233 miles, administered by 243 trusts, and the seven canals gave good service, but for the carriage of goods, and to some extent for passenger transport as well, it was the steamship and the railway that mattered. The growth of Scottish shipping, aided by the deepening of the Clyde, which, with fifteen feet at low water, was by 1830 an ocean seaway, was very steady:–

	Number of Vessels		*Total*
	Sail	*Steam*	*Tonnage*
1820	2,851		273,411
1828	3,143		300,836
1840	3,479		429,204
1850	3,432	169	522,222
1860	3,172	314	623,791

Thus, while the expansion in numbers during these forty years was about 22 per cent, the increase in average size was from 96 to nearly 179 tons; but it is noteworthy that sailing ships still outnumbered steamships by ten to one in 1860.

This was, indeed, the heyday of the famous tea clippers of Aberdeen, including such great names in the annals of seafaring as the *Cairngorm*, *Black Prince* and *Thermopylae*: the Deeside yards were busy with their construction from 1839 to 1869. It is ironical that such vessels, with their sharp prow, their narrow beam and their towering spread of canvas all conducing to high speed, should have been devised just when sail was destined to yield to steam for marine transport. The clipper represents the summit of achievement in the world of sail, and, like the Paisley shawl in the factory age, or the stage-coach in the railway era, can be regarded as a protest, gallant if doomed to final failure, on behalf of fine craftmanship against the mastery of the machine.

The conquest of the Atlantic by steam owed much to the line that was formed in 1839 by Samuel Cunard, the Nova Scotian, in conjunction with George Burns, the Scots shipowner, Robert Napier, the Scots engineer, and others; its first four ships, the *Britannia*, *Acadia*, *Caledonia* and *Columbia*, were all built on the Clyde (1840). Scottish enterprise was also to the fore in the founding of the White Star (1825), the Clan (1845), the Anchor (1852) and the Donaldson (1858) lines.

The immediate forerunner of the Scottish railways was the line linking Kilmarnock and Troon, which, from 1810, was conveying coal, timber and grain by horse-drawn carriages.[1] It was, however, the ample coal supplies of Old Monkland parish that attracted the early planners and gave the railway its true start. Here, from the spot that was to become Coatbridge, the lines fanned out – the Monkland-Kirkintilloch to the north (1826),[2] the Ballochney to the east (1828), the Garnkirk-Glasgow to the west (1831), and the Coltness-Wishaw to the south (1833). The carriage of coal to centres of industry or population inspired these early routes, as it did the Edinburgh-Dalkeith line (1831). The remaining pioneer lines were the Dundee-Newtyle (1832), the Dundee-Arbroath (1838), and the Slamannan (which, in 1840, continued the Ballochney route to the Union canal).

A new phase began in 1840 with inter-urban services, inaugurated by the Glasgow, Paisley and Ayr line, and this was followed in 1841 by the Glasgow, Paisley and Greenock, and in 1842 by the most important of the early projects, the Edinburgh and Glasgow railway, running 46 miles between Haymarket and Queen Street stations. From 1845 to 1847 the 'railway mania' was at its height: it was a time when quite sound schemes were jumbled in the public mind with the madcap notions of foolish or shady promoters. In 1846, however, the North British company linked Edinburgh with Berwick, while, on the other side of the country, the Caledonian company joined Glasgow with Carlisle by way of the Clyde-Annan route (1848), and the Glasgow and South-Western railway provided an alternative approach through Kilmarnock, the Nith valley and Dumfries (1850). The forging of these links between Scotland and England was a tremendous boon for industry and agriculture. Meanwhile, to the north, the Edinburgh-Perth-Dundee railway was opened (1847), its route crossing the two firths by ferries, and the Scottish Central, Scottish Midland and other companies provided a line that reached Aberdeen in 1850. Between 1852 and 1863, when the Perth-Inverness link was completed by the

[1] Steam-power was tried in 1816 but not adopted until 1847.

[2] Kirkintilloch was chosen as terminus because it was a 'port' on the Forth-Clyde canal.

Highland railway, that company and the Great North of Scotland railway opened up the north-east.

The early railways sprang from independent local projects, but from 1848, with the formation of the Monkland railways, amalgamations were the order of the day, so that by 1864 five major and some seven minor companies remained:–

		Mileage	
Company	*Double track*	*Single track*	*Total*
North British	228	252	480
Caledonian	206	153	359
Glasgow and South-Western	169	81	250
Highland	7	226	233
Great North of Scotland	5	221	226
Edinburgh and Glasgow	115	31	146
Scottish North-Eastern	115	28	143
Scottish Central	70	43	113
Monkland	13	59	72
Others	–	83	83
	928	1,177	2,105

Economic expansion naturally stimulated new investment and banking activity. The year 1825 was marked, not only by the foundation of the National Bank and the Aberdeen Town and County Bank, but also by an English panic brought on by over-speculation. The government's proposal to forbid the issue of notes by the Scottish banks, which had weathered the storm, as well as by those of England, caused a *furore*; Sir Walter Scott, his patriotism and sense of justice outraged, voiced the national indignation in the fiery *Letters of Malachi Malagrowther*, and the unhappy suggestion was withdrawn. The 1830s saw the establishment of many new banks, including the Union in 1830 (as a fusion of earlier Glasgow banks), the Western in 1832, the North of Scotland in 1836, the Clydesdale in 1838 and the City of Glasgow in 1839, but an Act of 1845[1] prohibited the formation of any further banks of issue, and thus 'froze' the total at a maximum of nineteen.

Thereafter any change could only be reduction, by way of either fusion or failure. Amalgamations brought the survivors down to sixteen by 1857, and in that year a financial crisis shook one of them, the City of Glasgow, and destroyed another, the Western, for a loss of

[1] It followed the Bank Charter Act of the preceding year, which applied to England but not to Scotland.

nearly £3,000,000. Three of the remainder were absorbed between 1858 and 1864, at which date the existing banks may be listed thus:–

Bank	*Date of Founding*	*Branches*	*Note-Circulation (£000s)*
Union	1830	103	582
Commercial	1810	76	555
Royal	1727	74	535
Bank of Scotland	1695	60	493
British Linen	1746	52	490
National	1825	72	472
Clydesdale	1838	60	373
City of Glasgow	1839	94	364
North of Scotland	1836	34	218
Aberdeen Town & County	1825	31	145
Caledonian	1838	16	74
Central	1834	9	61

The American Civil War (1861-65) wrought a major change in the economy, for the cotton industry, tottering in the crisis of 1857, suffered deadly damage when the raw cotton supplies from the southern states were cut off. The west of Scotland, depending on fine muslins and other costly fabrics, was peculiarly vulnerable to adversity, for the tastes of the fashionable world are notoriously fickle, and the trade that was now lost was never recovered.[1] After the war investors preferred heavy industry, which became stronger with each passing year. Thus cotton in Scotland, having owed its rise in large part to an earlier American war (which had ruined the tobacco trade),[2] owed its collapse to another American war. The industry lingered on in a few large mills,[3] like Deanston (Perthshire), Catrine (Ayrshire), and several in Bridgeton (Glasgow), and also in such 'off-shoots' as the dyeing, bleaching and calico-printing of the Vale of Leven, thread manufacture in Paisley, carpet-weaving in Kilmarnock and Glasgow, and lace-making in the Irvine valley.

Linen underwent a milder form of dispersal and local specialisation. Dundee, completing the change to jute by 1890, forged close ties with Calcutta, which was first its source of raw material and next its competitor in manufacture. Dunfermline damask and Kirkcaldy linoleum were the leading 'off-shoots' from flax, while the Forfarshire mill-

[1] On the other hand, the cheaper cottons of Lancashire found a ready market in India. [2] See *supra*, chap. xii, especially p. 137.

[3] Some thousands of handloom weavers of cotton cloth were still making a precarious living.

towns, Arbroath, Forfar and Kirriemuir, clung to their traditional coarse linen fabrics. Some 300 woollen mills, scattered through the country from the Border towns to the far north, produced blankets and plaids, shawls and hosiery, yarn and knitting worsted, and, above all, the ever-popular tweeds.[1] The crafts of knitting and hand-loom weaving still flourished in remote parts like Shetland, Orkney and Harris.

Late Victorian times were emphatically the age of coal, iron and steel, which expanded even through the 'great depression' of 1873-94. Coal output, standing, as we saw, at 12,700,000 tons in 1864, was 25,482,000 in 1893, and it was still rising as the century closed. For pig iron a total of one million tons was reached and passed, with fewer but larger and more efficient blast furnaces: for example, Lanarkshire had fifty-nine furnaces in 1901 instead of the ninety of 1869, and seven out of the county's sixteen plants had been closed down altogether. The most remarkable development of the period was the displacement of wrought iron by steel for many industrial purposes. From 1856 the English inventions of the Bessemer converter and the Siemens-Martin open hearth furnace, rival processes for the production of steel,[2] made possible the large-scale commercial use of what had hitherto been a rather expensive metal. From 1871 new steel-works were being built, especially in the Motherwell-Wishaw area, and many wrought iron works were adapted for steel production, which rose from 241,000 tons in 1885 to 960,000 in 1900. With astonishing rapidity the iron ship gave way to the steel ship: whereas only 10·3 per cent of the tonnage launched on the Clyde in 1879 was of steel, the proportion in 1889 was 97·2 per cent.

By the close of the century the coal mines, pig iron furnaces, steel works, engineering shops and shipbuilding yards were so closely inter-dependent that an advance in one direction stimulated an all-round improvement. Scottish heavy industry was a strong component of British metallurgy, which led the world in the 1870s and 1880s. By the 1890s, however, Germany and the United States, making a late start almost 'from scratch', had become first-class industrial

[1] The name 'tweed' was itself a happy accident resulting from a Londoner's misreading of the trade term 'tweel', used to denote a cloth woven on the diagonal.

[2] Each of these processes converted pig iron into a mild steel by oxidising the impurities, such as carbon and silicon, in the iron; carbon passed off as carbon dioxide, other impurities in a slag. Broadly speaking, oxidation was effected in the Bessemer process by a blast of hot air *through* the molten pig iron, but in the Siemens-Martin by maintaining an oxidising atmosphere *above* the molten metal. The former was the more rapid but the less easily controlled process.

nations. By 1900 Britain had been passed by America in coal output, and by both America and Germany in steel production, while the competition in shipbuilding was also severe. Moreover, whereas the wrought iron puddling works and the iron foundries had relied on domestic coal or coke and on pig iron produced from local iron-stone deposits, steel-making demanded different ores, especially the haematite or phosphorus-free ores found in Spain, Sweden, even in England – but not in Scotland. Consequently, some three-fifths of the ores required by the steel-works had to be imported, so that some of the natural advantages which had promoted the rise of Scottish metallurgy had vanished by 1900.

The railway and the steamship filled a dual role in late Victorian times, for both of them were at once products of heavy industry and carriers for it.[1] The railway system was extended by double-tracking, by additional lines in the industrial lowlands, and by the opening of routes to outlying points, including Wick and Thurso (1874), Oban 1880), Fort William (1894), Kyle of Lochalsh (1897) and Mallaig, (1901). The biggest advance was the successful bridging of the Tay in 1887[2] and of the Forth (an outstanding engineering feat) in 1889 which greatly enhanced the speed and convenience of rail transport between the Edinburgh, Dundee and Aberdeen districts. By 1900 the 'big five' railway companies,[3] with over 3,500 miles of track, controlled practically the whole system.

It was mainly British ships, whether intended for coastwise or overseas trade, that were the products of Scottish shipbuilding: in 1893, for example, out of 200,140 tons constructed in the Scottish yards, only 24,440 tons were for foreign owners. The fluctuations in registered tonnage were as follows:–

	Sail		*Steam*		*Sail and Steam*	
Year	*Vessels*	*Tonnage*	*Vessels*	*Tonnage*	*Vessels*	*Tonnage*
1860	3,172	552,212	314	71,579	3,486	623,791
1870	2,715	727,942	582	209,142	3,297	937,084
1880	2,358	849,089	1,095	598,951	3,453	1,448,040
1890	1,560	809,048	1,616	1,099,332	3,176	1,908,380
1900	1,104	709,430	1,980	1,528,032	3,084	2,237,462
1914	494	153,323	3,441	2,675,720	3,935	2,829,043

[1] For short-distance passenger and goods transport, horse-drawn vehicles were indispensable: the motor-car was still experimental in the 1890s.

[2] An earlier bridge, of unsound construction, was blown down by a gale on 28 December 1879, with total loss of life on the train then in transit.

[3] These are the first five listed on page 240.

As these figures show, the long survival of sail alongside steam is as remarkable as is the steady increase in size, rather than in numbers, in both categories; from 179 tons in 1860, the average size of Scottish ship rose to 601 tons in 1890, and to 719 tons in 1914. The use of ever larger ships (calling for the regular improvement of docks, piers and port equipment) was necessitated by the growth of trade, which was truly astonishing throughout the period:–

Scottish Trade, 1824-1913

Year	*Value of Imports* (£000s)	*Value of Exports* (£000s)
1824	3,146	2,670
1850	8,957	5,130
1874	31,013	17,913
1900	38,691	32,167
1911	46,938	47,361

Over 90 per cent of the volume of commerce was latterly passing through the six principal ports, Glasgow, Leith, Dundee, Aberdeen, Greenock and Grangemouth.

As before, economic enterprise was fostered by banking progress. It is true that the record was marred by a major disaster in 1878, when, as a result of fraudulent misconduct on the part of its directors, the failure of the City of Glasgow Bank involved its thousands of clients in a ruinous loss of over £6,000,000. This highly distressing episode was, however, quite exceptional, for the other banks went from strength to strength. Already, in 1874, the Clydesdale Bank had set up three branches in Cumberland, though by an Anglo-Scottish accord further expansion into English territory was renounced, save that all Scottish banks got the right of maintaining London offices. In 1881, as a precaution against any repetition of the City of Glasgow catastrophe, they adopted 'limited liability'.[1] The Bank of Scotland absorbed the Central Bank in 1868 and the Caledonian in 1907, and in the latter year the North of Scotland combined with the Aberdeen Town and County, to reduce the total to eight, each of them a stable and substantial institution.

Amalgamation and consolidation were features of Victorian industry, as well as of railways and banking. The days had passed when

[1] The three older banks – the Bank of Scotland, Royal Bank and British Linen – were already 'limited' under the terms of the statute or charter of foundation; for the seven surviving nineteenth-century banks, hitherto 'unlimited', the utmost liability of the shareholders was now limited to the amount of the bank's nominal capital, equal to five times the paid-up capital.

the sons of Alexander Baird, by exploiting the rich mineral deposits of Gartsherrie, could launch a highly successful and individualistic coal and iron company, or when Robert Napier, essentially a marine engineer, could interest himself in coal-mines, blast-furnaces, shipbuilding and shipowning. In place of the lone venturesome capitalist had come, both in Scotland and in England, the vast, impersonal combine, with professional managers administering a ramified industrial empire, like the Fairfield Shipbuilding and Engineering Company (1885) or John Brown and Company (1899) in heavy industry; or the United Thread Manufacturing Company (1890) and the Calico Printers' Association (1899) in textiles; or, again, the United Alkali Company (1890) in chemicals and the Distillers' Company Limited (1877) in the liquor trade.

The main trends in the late nineteenth century are reflected in the census figures relating to occupations. Textiles, like agriculture,[1] suffered a drastic reduction – from 250,000 in 1851 to 175,000 in 1901. Within the group the ranking of the various branches was reversed, for at the later date jute was easily first, with over 39,000 employees,[2] wool and worsted second with nearly 25,000, linen next with under 24,000, and cotton fourth, with fewer than 15,000. By contrast, coal-mining accounted for over 100,000 workers, instead of the 33,000 of 1851; if we add the 23,000 engaged in iron and steel manufacture, the 35,000 in shipbuilding, 119,000 in engineering, and others in minor classes, we find heavy industry giving employment to nearly 322,000 persons, and constituting much the largest economic group in the nation.

Of the lesser industries, fishing, with 27,600 employees in 1901, had experienced a fair degree of prosperity. The white fisheries (mainly for cod, ling and haddock) had been conducted by line-fishermen from sailing boats, but in 1882 the steam-trawler began to operate from Aberdeen, the centre of the industry. The other, and larger, branch, the herring fishery, had known many good seasons intermixed with bad. The annual 'cure' of herrings had improved from 300,000 barrels in the early 1820s to half-a-million by mid-century, and to one million by the 1880s. Here, too, change came from 1898, when the steam-drifter made its appearance at Wick, one of the main herring ports (the others being Fraserburgh, Peterhead and Aberdeen). There-

[1] See *supra*, p. 232.

[2] More than 33,000 of these were in Dundee, including nearly 24,000 women workers.

after, while catches generally increased, the trend in both white and herring fisheries was towards larger boats, longer voyages to deeper waters, and the more commodious ports rather than the tiny, picturesque, but ill-equipped fishing villages.[1]

Naturally, the doubling of the population and the multiplication of the national wealth caused a great proliferation of secondary industries. Some of these had strong local roots: sugar-refining at Greenock, granite-cutting at Aberdeen, the shale-oil of West Lothian, the manufacture of sanitary appliances at Barrhead, and the annual whaling expeditions from Dundee and Aberdeen. Others were widely dispersed: paper-making, printing and publishing (though these were usually located in or near cities and large towns), brick-making (in brisk demand for railway tunnels and arches), pottery and glass, woodworking, the manufacture of furniture and clothing, boots and shoes, the baking of bread and biscuits, confectionery, brewing and distilling. Chemical and scientific advances put many a new product within the citizen's grasp: soap and food preservatives, the waterproofed coat-fabric to which Charles Macintosh gave his name (1823), india-rubber (being produced in Edinburgh from 1855), and the Dunlop pneumatic tyre, devised in 1887.

The years from 1896 to 1913, though they did see some recessions, were in general a time of booming trade, when exports – especially textiles, ships and machines – were doubled; from 1910 the prospects for heavy industry were at their brightest. Political rivalry with Germany led, from 1906, to a naval armaments race, and many of the *Dreadnoughts*, the new all-big-gun ships, were Clyde-built. At the same time, the leading maritime nations entered a feverish competition for the building of merchant ships, and particularly of the costly luxury liners designed for the lucrative Atlantic trade. On both counts the Clyde yards profited greatly, reaching in 1913 their all-time record output of 750,000 tons, equal to one-third of the United Kingdom total and exceeding that of all Germany. Shipbuilding was now Scotland's key industry, for busy yards meant orders spread in a steady stream through the coal mines, steel works, engineering shops and ancillary trades, so that prosperity in this one branch betokened general well-being. Thus, coal output also reached its peak in that

[1] A further tendency, arising from these changes, was towards the cessation of the traditional arrangement whereby the skipper and the crew shared the ownership and profits of their little boats. Now the trawl-owner emerged as a petty capitalist, and the members of the crew became wage-earning employees.

year, with $42\frac{1}{2}$ million tons. The barometer seemed to be 'set fair' for the Scottish economy.

Yet, beneath the surface all was far from well. In 1911 very large numbers were engaged in 'sheltered' and 'service' occupations that were, in the narrow sense at least, unproductive – fully 200,000 (or one in ten of all who were 'gainfully employed') in personal, and mainly domestic, service, over 140,000 in the food trades, as bakers, butchers, grocers and the like, some 125,000 on the railways, roads, harbours and ships, and other substantial numbers as shopkeepers and dressmakers, builders and contractors, teachers and clerks. Among the primary and producing occupations, farming accounted for only 200,000, fishing for 28,000, textiles for 164,500, whereas heavy industry, with no fewer than 433,500 (including over a quarter of the country's male workers), outstripped all these taken together.

There was something hectic and artificial about the ascendancy of heavy industry, which, as we have seen, had lost a portion of its former natural assets through its dependence on imported ores for steel-making. Again, the whole group had come to rely to an excessive degree upon foreign orders for the disposal of its products. Thus while the export of machinery struck the industrialists as a profitable and beneficial measure, they were finding that customers had an awkward habit of reappearing as competitors: the Dundee jute magnates had had the same experience following the despatch of mill machines to Calcutta, which was now a serious rival. Beyond the challenge of America and Germany in coal and steel, ships and engineering, lay yet another source of future weakness: coal was the broad base of the structure of heavy industry, but coal was yielding place as a fuel to oil, a commodity in which, apart from its limited shale deposits, Scotland was quite deficient. Though the true facts were hidden from most observers in 1913, the economy was over-expanded, insufficiently varied, and therefore peculiarly vulnerable to the chances and changes of trade currents, of world markets, and, above all, of war-time conditions, which became a grim reality in August 1914.

CHAPTER XXII

The Rise of the Social Services

IN SCOTLAND, no less than in any other country, the Industrial Revolution, considered purely as an economic process, represents a stirring triumph of human ingenuity and tenacity, involving such a mastery of the physical environment as enabled material wealth to be multiplied many times over. But man is always more than an 'economic animal', and it remains to assess both the impact upon social life of these vast changes, and the reaction of the social conscience to the challenge of the new conditions. For this purpose it is well to divide the period between 1821 and 1914 at the early 1860s, for those years mark a turning-point in the public attitude to health, hygiene, housing and other aspects of social welfare.[1]

The population of Scotland rose from 2,091,521 in 1821 to 3,062,294 in 1861, but the increase, amounting to 46·4 per cent, was unevenly spread among the counties. We have seen that rural depopulation had already shown itself in the census figures, and that some counties had passed their 'peak'[2]: three of these, Argyll, Inverness and Perth, had actually fewer inhabitants in 1861 than in 1821. At the other end of the scale, the ten counties that showed the greatest growth of population between the two dates accounted among them for 89·8 per cent of the whole Scottish increase, and the share of one of them, Lanark, was 39·9 per cent:–

County	*Population* In 1821 (000s)	In 1861 (000s)	*Increase* Numerical (000s)	Percentage
Lanark	244	631	387	158·4
Forfar	113	204	91	80·3
Edinburgh	192	274	82	43·1
Ayr	127	199	72	56·3
Aberdeen	155	222	67	42·9
Renfrew	112	177	65	58·4

[1] The leading modern authority on this field of study, Professor T. Ferguson, takes the year 1863 for the 'break' between his two volumes, *The Dawn of Scottish Social Welfare* (1948) and *Scottish Social Welfare, 1864-1914* (1958).

[2] Cf. *supra*, pp. 160, 232.

County	Population In 1821 (000s)	Population In 1861 (000s)	Increase Numerical (000s)	Increase Percentage
Fife	115	155	40	35·1
Stirling	65	92	27	40·6
Dumbarton	27	52	25	90·5
Linlithgow	23	39	16	70·4

The remaining twenty counties all recorded smaller increments, though it is noteworthy that one of them had a large percentage increase (61·7): this was Clackmannan, which geographically and economically belongs to the above group. Clearly, the rapid growth of the Scottish population arose almost wholly within the counties of the central lowland belt, as already defined,[1] and it followed upon the prosperity and expansion of heavy industry, of textiles[2] and of commerce.[3]

The augmentation of population was, in point of fact, even more concentrated than the county figures indicate, for only the towns – especially the industrial and commercial towns – had any big share in it. All the large towns became larger[4]:–

	Population (000s) In 1821	*Population* (000s) In 1861
Glasgow	147	395
Edinburgh	112	168
Dundee	31	91
Aberdeen	45	74
Paisley	26	47
Greenock	22	43
Leith	26	34

For rapidity of growth, however, some of the secondary towns, depending on coal, iron or textiles, were yet more remarkable[5]:–

[1] See *supra*, p. 236.

[2] Outside that belt, Roxburgh and Selkirk, containing the centres of the Border woollen industry, had substantial percentage increases of population – 32·3 and 57·4 respectively.

[3] The only other counties with an increase of more than one-third were Banff (35·6 per cent), Elgin (36·0) and Caithness (40·9); in each of these, a fairly stable agriculture was reinforced by valuable fisheries.

[4] In this table, in contrast to the earlier one (*supra*, p. 141), Edinburgh and Leith are entered separately, and the 1821 figure for Paisley refers to the town parish, without the Abbey parish. The 1861 figures are burghal.

[5] Some of these figures are mere estimates, for no enumeration of the smaller towns was made in 1821.

	Population (00s) In 1821	In 1861
Airdrie	49	129
Barrhead	20	60
Coatbridge	5	105
Galashiels	11	64
Hawick	37	82
Pollokshaws	38	76
Wishaw	10	61

Apart from the general drift from the country to the towns, two large migratory movements of the time demand attention. By the 1820s, as we have seen,[1] the seasonal flow of Highland harvesters was slackening off, but there was a steady infiltration of displaced crofters and discontented farm-hands into the Lowland towns. New settlers found their way by sea from the west Highlands or the Hebrides to Glasgow and Greenock, while thousands more made the short land-journey to the towns and villages just beyond the Highland line – Dundee, Longforgan, Perth, Crieff, Comrie, Callander, Dumbarton and Dunoon. Although many Highland immigrants tended to keep to themselves in their own little communities, their presence in the Lowland towns offered little or nothing in the way of a social or racial problem.

It was quite otherwise with the 'Irish invasion'. From the neighbouring island, vastly over-populated and perennially poverty-stricken, seasonal migration came some time before permanent emigration. During the Napoleonic wars, Irish labourers had come over in the late summer to work as shearers on the Lowland farms, competing with, and eventually eliminating, the Highlanders. The existence from 1818 of a steamship service induced ever larger numbers to make the crossing: by the 1820s between 6,000 and 8,000 were making the trip each year, and by the 1840s the annual exodus was about 40,000. In August 1849 the steamship *Londonderry* brought 1,700 persons on a single voyage, and the *Thistle* carried 1,900, though each of these vessels was under 300 tons. The adoption of the reaping machine from the 1850s caused a decline in the traffic; moreover, emigration to the United States was now at its height,[2] and was preferred by those who could afford the Transatlantic fare (about £4). On a diminished

[1] Cf. *supra*, p. 159.

[2] It is calculated to have amounted to about 1,300,000 persons during the year 1847-54.

scale, however, the migrants still came for hay-making, potato-lifting and turnip-gathering.

The outright settler was mostly drawn to other types of work – on the canals, harbours, roads and railways, or in the coal-mines and textile mills. Many thousands came in the 1820s, many more in the 1830s, and the census of 1841 showed 126,000 Irish-born inhabitants of Scotland, or nearly 5 per cent of the total. The partial potato failure of 1845 and the almost complete loss of the 1846 crop served as the sharpest of spurs, and the stream became a torrent. In June 1847, according to the *Glasgow Herald*, 'the streets of Glasgow are at present literally swarming with vagrants from the sister kingdom, and the misery which many of these poor creatures endure can scarcely be less than what they have fled'.[1] In 1849 the parish authorities were returning Irish paupers to Ireland at the rate of a thousand a month, but there was no guarantee that they would stay at home. It is reckoned that as many as 115,000 Irish persons became residents of Scotland in the decade 1841-51, and the census of 1851 showed the Irish-born as numbering over 207,000, or 7·2 per cent of the population. In each of the four western counties of Ayr, Dumbarton, Lanark and Renfrew, the Irish-born proportion was between 10 and 15 per cent, and in Glasgow it was 18 per cent – a figure which, with allowance for the babies born in Scotland to Irish parents, indicates a ratio of about 25 per cent for those of Irish birth or extraction. Of all British towns, Glasgow exercised the strongest 'pull' on the east-bound emigrant, but the numbers were also substantial in Paisley, Greenock, Kilmarnock, Airdrie, Coatbridge, Edinburgh and Dundee.

In the eyes of most Scotsmen, the Irish now in their midst, besides being strangers, had two grave faults. First, they were almost all miserably poor, so that, if they worked, they did not mind low wages for back-breaking toil,[2] while, if they did not work, they became charges on the poor's rates, generally in towns already burdened with severe pauperism. Secondly, they were mostly of the Roman Catholic faith,[3] and it did not help matters that a minority were Protestants from Ulster, since this fact served merely to reproduce in Scotland the religious feuds of their homeland. The 'Orange Walk', a parade held by Protestants on the anniversary of the battle of the Boyne (12 July),

[1] Quoted by Dr J. E. Handley, whose full account (in *The Irish in Scotland* and *The Irish in Modern Scotland*) has been much drawn upon for these paragraphs.

[2] They were sometimes used as strike-breakers, and were specially imported for the purpose, as in the coal and cotton disputes of 1837.

[3] They had their own churches from 1808 and their own schools from 1817.

was observed in Glasgow from 1821, and soon 'Orange-and-Green' faction fights caused bloodshed wherever the two breeds of Irishmen dwelt together. With little or nothing to lose, and inured to a potato-and-herring standard, most of the Irish in Scotland flocked to the congested industrial towns and lived in the utmost squalor and degradation, incurring the hearty dislike and hostility of the native Scots.

Town life in the factory age (which meant comfort and affluence for many) had its pleasant aspects. There were numerous gracious mansions in the New Town of Edinburgh and its northward extensions towards Dean bridge, and fashionable balls were organised by ladies of distinction in the Assembly Rooms on George street. Glasgow, too, possessed elegant and substantial houses, particularly around Blythswood square in the west end, and two miles beyond this stood the new Observatory and the Botanic Gardens, with a rich profusion of tropical plants. Dundee's merchants travelled by ferry steamer to and from their 'handsome marine villas' in the pretty township of Newport, on the south side of the firth of Tay, while the prosperous middle classes of Aberdeen had, in the College precinct of Old Aberdeen, as agreeable a residential quarter as was to be found in Scotland. The two chief cities had their permanent theatres, and the principal towns were visited from time to time by travelling companies. Other amenities included tea-gardens, popular concerts, circuses and menageries, and the sports of the period comprised golf, horse-races, prize-fights, quoits and cock-fighting (most of these being frowned on by many as frivolous or positively vicious). Glasgow's great July fair was the Mecca for conjurers, showmen, stall-holders and keepers of shooting-ranges. In the first half of the nineteenth century polite society put back the dinner-hour from five o'clock to six-thirty, but both the rising-bell at six o'clock, summoning the adults to the day's labour, and the eight o'clock curfew, warning all children of bed-time, were still sounded.

If life was normal and happy for plenty of town-dwellers, the prevalence and the magnitude of social evils are not to be denied. Over the working classes hung the baleful presence of poverty, dirt and overcrowding, and the deadly menace of unemployment, destitution and disease. Alike in the gaunt slum tenements of the cities and the sordid 'miners' rows' of the new communities, rooms were dark and damp, the air was fetid, and amenities were wholly lacking: the insanitary privy-midden was everywhere to be seen and smelt. The census returns of 1861 recorded 27 per cent of the population of Scotland as living in houses of one room (shared by varying numbers of persons up to fifteen), and 38 per cent in two-roomed houses, which meant that only one person in three came from a home with three rooms or more. In Glasgow and Edinburgh the city centre was one huge festering slum, and at their worst there was nothing to choose between the two. 'In the very centre of the city', said the chief constable of Glasgow in 1840, 'there is an accumulated mass of squalid wretchedness, which is probably unequalled in any other town in the British Dominions'; but in 1867 Edinburgh's Old Town had one close, with 59 rooms all served by 'a steep, dark stone stair, common to the whole', and occupied by 248 persons belonging to 56 families, although 'in this huge congress of dens there is no water, no water-closet, no sink'.

The mechanical and scientific wonders of the age did little to relieve the gloom of such places. Gas-lighting, it is true, had been available in Glasgow from 1818, in Edinburgh from 1820, in Aberdeen from 1824 and in Dundee from 1825, but only the well-to-do could afford the charges imposed by the private companies, and it was mostly used to illuminate the principal thoroughfares. Again, country habits lingered on, absurdly enough, in an urban setting: as late as 1863 there were, within the city-limits of Edinburgh, 171 byres, some of which, being located under dwelling-houses, 'proved a source of discomfort to the inhabitants above'.

From the appalling housing conditions, rather than from the factories themselves, sprang most of the social evils of the time – improvidence, malnutrition, vagrancy, delinquency, but above all intemperance and disease. By 1834 there was one spirit-dealer to every fourteen families in Glasgow, and cheap, raw whisky was the usual stand-by of the working class, whether taken as an antidote for bad weather, ill-health, exhausting work, grinding poverty, or domestic misery. Typhus fever was a constant and deadly visitor among the city poor from 1818, small-pox came back time and again to carry off the children of negligent parents,[1] and in 1832 occurred the first epidemic outbreak of Asiatic cholera,[2] which throve amid the filth of the industrial towns, producing 20,202 cases of sickness and 10,650 deaths. Scotland suffered heavily, too, in the ravages of cholera in 1848-49 and 1853-54, and there was a milder, but still frightening, return in 1866-67.

[1] Since it often reduced the number of hungry mouths to be filled, it was called, in the most cynical phrase of the age, 'the poor man's friend'.

[2] It had travelled from India, by way of Russia, Germany, France and England; and it went on to Canada.

Strenuous efforts were made by charitable and public-spirited persons to alleviate the sufferings of the poor. Habits of thrift were inculcated by savings banks and friendly societies, and the trade unions did what they could for the working man, though, from 1825 to 1867, they were treated by the law as little better than conspiracies to defraud the employers. During times of trade depression and lack of work, soup kitchens were set up, meal was distributed, and public schemes involving labour were adopted. From 1841 'ragged' schools in the cities were endeavouring to cope with the problem of the vagrant child.[1] A temperance society, thought to be the first in Britain, was founded in 1829 where it was most needed – in Glasgow – and this cause, like that of total abstinence, had many supporters; eventually, in 1853, Parliament introduced, through the Forbes-Mackenzie Act,[2] an overdue measure of state control of the liquor trade.

Devoted doctors did their best for the sick poor, but they had to contend with daunting difficulties: the few general hospitals could not admit the many fever patients during epidemics, competent nurses were almost unknown before the reforms of Florence Nightingale (1854-57), and doctors themselves were suspected of being 'body-snatchers' after the Burke-and-Hare scandal (1829).[3] Moreover, though willing to give free service to paupers, they knew not where to turn for the necessary medicines and dressings. It was the last straw for them to hear the periodic plagues characterised as God's punishment for men's sins, when it was clear to them that congestion and squalor were the prime causes of disease and death.[4]

Social welfare, so far as the state's efforts were concerned, was as yet in its infancy. Poor relief, it is true, improved from 1845,[5] for, whereas before the Act of that year only 230 parishes out of 894 had been assessed, by 1862 there were 759, while the number of poor-houses increased from 13 to 48. The poor's funds were, however, inadequate,

[1] Cf. *infra*, p. 268. [2] See *supra*, p. 203.

[3] William Burke and William Hare, Irish criminals of the lowest type, made a living by suffocating chosen victims and selling the bodies to Edinburgh anatomists for dissection; Burke was hanged, but Hare turned informer and escaped punishment.

[4] A proposal made in 1853 by the presbytery of Edinburgh, that a national fast should be observed throughout the country to prevent a recurrence of cholera, evoked from Lord Palmerston, then home secretary, a reply that is a little classic: the statesman expressed his preference for measures designed to free the poorer quarters of towns and cities 'from those causes and sources of contagion which, if allowed to remain, will infallibly breed pestilence and be fruitful in death, in spite of the prayers and fastings of a united but inactive nation'.

[5] For the terms of the Act of 1845, see *supra*, pp. 200-1.

the process of 'going on the parish' involved physical hardship as well as moral stigma, and it was only the grosser forms of destitution that were checked.[1] From 1833, again, the reformed burgh had useful powers of control, if it cared to exercise them, but compulsory legislation in health matters came only in the 1860s. Thus, polluted water was known to be a main factor in spreading infection, yet supplies were low in both quality and quantity. About 1830 Dundee's water was 'bright, sparkling and piquant to the taste', because it was in fact 'nothing but a very thorough purified sewage, to the properties of decomposition of which it owes its pleasant flavour'. Edinburgh was almost as ill-served, though Aberdeen and Greenock were rather better, but the real advance came only in 1859 with Glasgow's 'epic of municipalisation', when the Loch Katrine system, bringing water piped from a distant, pure and ample source, and constituting much the best scheme in Britain, was formally opened.

Loch Katrine was of good augury, for effective legislation and determined local action soon followed. Lindsay's Act of 1862[2] provided that new houses in burghs must have covered drains, that each house must have a water-closet (except where 'such works shall be impracticable'), and that the sheriff would inquire into the sanitary arrangements of any burgh with an unduly high death-rate, in order to promote remedial measures. In the same year, Glasgow acquired the right to 'ticket' its small houses, and so to give notice of the number of permitted occupants.[3] Medical officers of health were appointed in Edinburgh in 1862 and in Glasgow in 1863. Slum clearance began with the Glasgow City Improvement Trust in 1866, and, while the trust incurred criticism and had long spells of inaction, most of the older tenements were demolished to make way for newer houses in the course of the next forty years.[4] Edinburgh followed with its own trust in 1867 and Dundee in 1871, though the new building in these cities was left in private hands. The Public Health (Scotland) Act, 1867, was a landmark in social history: under its terms, town councils or parochial boards were empowered to remove nuisances, regulate offensive trades, provide proper water supplies and drainage, establish

[1] About mid-century outdoor relief ranged between £4 and £6 per annum for each pauper, while maintenance costs in poorhouses were just over 4s. a week in the early 1860s.

[2] *Supra*, p. 204.

[3] The sub-letting of space to lodgers was widely practised in the poorer and smaller houses.

[4] A second 'trust' was created in 1897.

hospitals, and generally take measures to prevent disease; above all, they might (and, if the Board of Supervision insisted, must) appoint medical officers and sanitary inspectors.

These principles were reaffirmed and expanded in such later statutes as the Housing of the Working Classes Act, 1890, the Burgh Police Act, 1892, the Public Health Act, 1897, and the Housing and Town Planning Act, 1909, but the duty of the local authorities to promote the health, welfare and comfort of the community was plainly laid down for the first time in the 1860s. The vital statistics suggest that action had been taken none too soon. The Scottish death-rate reached its peak in 1864, a bad year for typhus and other fevers, when it stood at 23·6 per thousand of population; the rate was highest in the principal towns, exceeding 30 per thousand in that year and again in 1869. A gradual improvement brought it down to 15·5 in 1914. The birth-rate also declined steadily, from a record height of 35·6 per thousand inhabitants in 1864 and again in 1876 to 26·1 in 1914. These concurrent downward trends made for a more stable and longer living population. The expectation of life at birth in 1861 was 40 years for males and 44 for females, and in 1911 the figures were 50 and 53 years. Yet, throughout the period, infant mortality – the rate of deaths in the first year in relation to each thousand live births – was distressingly high. Generally attributed to the scarcity and poor quality of milk, especially in cities and towns, infant mortality reached its maximum of 138 as late as 1897, and stood at 111 in 1914.

Between 1861 and 1911 the total population increased at each census, though not quite at the previous high rate: the figures for these two dates were 3,062,294 and 4,760,904. The rise (equal to 55·5 per cent in 50 years) would have been steeper had not the natural increase – the excess of births over deaths – been checked by emigration mainly to the United States, Canada and Australia; the net loss amounted to over 735,000 persons, or an average of 14,700 per annum. A small portion of the gross emigration was offset by the Irish immigration, which, while less than it had been before 1851, was still substantial. The great majority of the newcomers were Protestants from Ulster,[1] the movement was at its height between 1876 and 1884, and the influx was again considerable from 1899 to 1907. By 1911 the Irish-born in Scotland numbered 174,715, or 3·67 per cent of the total. More and more settlers were meanwhile arriving from England and Wales, and

[1] Thus, in 1876, out of 8,807 immigrants from all Ireland, 8,191 came from Ulster; in 1900 the figures were 1,968 and 1,646.

the census of 1911 showed 165,102 persons born in these countries (or 3·47 per cent).

Once again, the increase in numbers was unevenly distributed through the country. Fifteen of the thirty-three counties recorded reductions between 1861 and 1911, in six others the gain was slight, and the ten[1] counties already noted as fast-growing before 1861 now accounted among them for more than the total Scottish increase:–

	Population		*Increase*	
County	*In 1861* (000s)	*In 1911* (000s)	*Numerical* (000s)	*Percentage*
Lanark	631	1,447	816	129·1
Edinburgh	274	508	234	85·3
Renfrew	177	314	137	77·1
Fife	155	268	113	73·0
Aberdeen	222	312	90	40·9
Dumbarton	52	140	88	168·7
Forfar	204	281	77	37·7
Stirling	92	161	69	75·1
Ayr	199	268	69	34·9
Linlithgow	39	80	41	107·4

These ten counties contained in 1911 79·4 per cent of all the inhabitants of Scotland, while the eight counties forming the central lowland belt from Ayr to Fife held more than two-thirds of the population (66·9 per cent), although they covered only 13·2 per cent of the land-area of Scotland. (By contrast, the five predominantly Highland counties, forming one-half of the area,[2] had but 380,000 inhabitants in 1911, or 8 per cent of the total.)

The rapid growth of the principal towns, and the still more remarkable advances of those secondary towns which were the creations of the later phase of the Industrial Revolution, are again noteworthy features of the period:–

	Population (000s)	
	In 1861	*In 1911*
Glasgow	395	784
Edinburgh	168	320
Dundee	91	165
Aberdeen	74	164

[1] See *supra*, pp. 248-9. The two remaining counties, though small, had large percentage increases – Clackmannan (45·1) and Selkirk (135·4).

[2] Cf. *supra*, pp. 150, 160, 232.

	Population (000s)	
	In 1861	*In 1911*
Paisley	47	84
Leith	34	80
Greenock	43	75
. . .	. . .	. . .
Govan	8	90
Partick	8	67
Coatbridge	11	43
Motherwell	3	40
Clydebank	–	38

By the end of the nineteenth century 74·3 per cent of the population lived in 'urban areas' (defined for census purposes as built-up areas – whether burghs or not – with 1,000 or more inhabitants), so that municipal enterprise and welfare activities were of great interest to the majority of the nation. Long before 1900, in fact, the local authorities were administering a wide range of social services and public utilities. The cholera and typhus outbreaks had shown the importance of pure water supplies, and in 1869 public control displaced private companies in Edinburgh and Dundee, which had been among the 'black spots'. In the same year the supply of gas was taken over by the municipality in Glasgow, and this step, here as elsewhere, was the prelude to a steady lowering of the price to bring it within the ordinary citizen's reach. Local transport, in the form of horse-drawn tramcars, was provided by tramway companies, trading for profit, at Edinburgh (1871), Glasgow (1873), Aberdeen (1874), Dundee (1875) and other towns; in the 1890s these were municipalised and soon after they were generally electrified. From 1891 electricity itself became a civic service in Glasgow, though for some time it was used mainly to light stations and public buildings, and gas was preferred in the home. In addition, the town councils of the greater burghs maintained parks and museums, public baths and wash-houses, 'model lodging-houses' and room-and-kitchen dwellings for the use of the working classes.[1]

The medical history of the period turned upon a running fight, with the result for long in doubt, against infection, dirt and ignorance. The last visitation of cholera was in 1869, but typhus and typhoid fever, small-pox, scarlet fever and diphtheria still claimed many thousands of victims; tuberculosis, often concealed from fear or shame,

[1] Bo'ness (1902) and Hamilton (1904) were among the pioneers in the building of these small houses.

accounted for 17 per cent of all deaths in the 1860s and 11 per cent in 1911-15. Fever hospitals, at first small, temporary and ill-equipped, but gradually enlarged and improved, were founded from 1865 at Glasgow and later elsewhere, while the provision of dispensaries and sanatoria for consumptives started at Edinburgh in 1887. Between 1877[1] and 1897 the notification of infectious diseases became compulsory, and this requirement was extended to tuberculosis in the years 1912-14. By the close of the period the number of patients in hospital was six times greater than at its opening, and fully four times as many lunatics and mental defectives were being treated in the numerous asylums.

Poor relief was until 1894 the responsibility of the parochial boards, and thereafter of the parish councils, but the principle was unaltered, that a pauper claiming relief must prove disability as well as destitution. The rate of pauperism reached its peak (nearly forty-two in each thousand) in 1868 and then declined to about twenty-one in 1914. Better standards of health, hygiene and living conditions had something to do with this trend, but so, too, had the operation of the 'poor-house test': if an applicant were in genuine need, he would be prepared to face the rigours of the poor-house. Meanwhile, a broader concept of what should be done for the weaker members of the community slowly took shape, and a beginning was made with the state's 'social services'. Old age pensions (1908), national insurance against sickness, disablement and unemployment (1911), and the first draft, for trial in the Highlands and Islands, of a state medical service (1913), mark the inception of what was to become familiar, a generation later, as the 'welfare state'.

When all is said, however, the main hope of social betterment lay in improved housing. Slum clearance was a first step, but not necessarily a cure in itself, for the new houses built in replacement might well be 'the slums of the future': thus, 70 per cent of the houses built in Glasgow in the period 1866-74 were of one or two apartments, although these were notoriously the types that were apt to become squalid and congested[2] within a few years. Larger homes did come into use, but only in a slow and patchy manner. In 1911 8·7 per cent of the population (compared with 27 per cent in 1861) lived in one-roomed houses, but the proportion of those dwelling in houses of two

[1] Greenock was the pioneer town in this respect.

[2] In 1871 8·5 per cent of those living in 'single-ends' in Edinburgh kept lodgers, while for 'room-and-kitchen' houses the proportion was 19·9 per cent.

apartments had actually risen from 38 to 40·9 per cent. Thus, half of the nation still had, in 1911, inadequate accommodation (for such was broadly the case with almost all these small houses), and the figure was lamentably high in most of the industrial towns: Armadale, by this test, came off worst in Scotland (with 82·8 per cent of its inhabitants living in one- or two-roomed houses), but ten others stood between 70 and 77 per cent – Coatbridge, Wishaw, Clydebank, Kilsyth, Lochgelly, Govan, Galston, Barrhead, Airdrie and Motherwell. Glasgow's figure was 62·5 per cent, Dundee's 63, Paisley's 65, though Edinburgh (37·2) and Aberdeen (38·6) were distinctly better. Clearly the housing 'drive' had only just begun in 1914.

While the social problems of Victorian and Edwardian times were real and pressing, there were forces making for stability and contentment. Life could be particularly agreeable in those old county-towns which stood apart from the main currents of industry and offered their inhabitants pleasant residences, good shops and schools, perhaps theatres, museums and other amenities: such were Dumfries, Ayr, Stirling, Perth, Inverness and Elgin. Again, within a prosperous and expanding economy, the greater part of society enjoyed steady wages and steady prices. The case of the hand-loom weaver was the pathetic exception: the wages of other labourers in the period 1861-1914 ranged between 12s. and 22s. a week, and the men with special skills made up to 38s. or 40s. Prices, if anything, tended to drop under the full impact of free trade, so that, of the basic foodstuffs, the four-pound white loaf fell from 1s. in the early part of the century to 6d. or less, tea from 6s. or 8s. a pound to 2s. 6d., and sugar from 9d. to 3½d. In supplying the working classes with cheap groceries, and incidentally inducing them to save, the many local co-operative societies were highly successful from the 1860s on.

The use of leisure became more important with the reduction of the working day from 11 or 12 hours to 8½ or 8, and the gradual adoption, from the 1850s, of the Saturday half-holiday. The cultural life was fostered by concerts and plays, by museums, libraries and art galleries. The fashionable sports of the gentry included fishing, shooting and deer-stalking, while shinty and curling had larger followings, and several of the Highland 'gatherings' drew much support. The golf courses of St Andrews and North Berwick on the east coast, and Prestwick and Troon on the west, became internationally famous. While golf was native to Scotland, cricket and bowling were imported from England. From beyond the Tweed, also, came the two 'codes' of football, which took their modern shape in 1873 with the formation of the Scottish Rugby Union and of the Scottish Football Association. The pioneer clubs in 'soccer' came from the west – Queen's Park, Clydesdale, Vale of Leven, Renton and Third Lanark – and they and other teams disputed, from season 1873-74, the right to the Scottish Cup and, from 1890-91, the championship of the Scottish League. The tremendous vogue enjoyed by football had one curious impact on social life, for the feuds between Protestant and Romanist, which were peculiarly virulent among the Irish settlers, inspired intense partisanship for the Glasgow rivals, Rangers and Celtic, and, in a milder way, for the two chief Edinburgh clubs, Heart of Midlothian and Hibernians.

From about 1885 the 'safety' bicycle and the motor car, each with its clubs, races and rallies, were really sporting devices. They can be reckoned serious forms of transport only from about 1900, and more particularly from 1904, when the motor bus began to take the place of the horse-drawn bus as one of the principal public carriers. By 1914, though the railways and tramways were profitable and much-used enterprises, horse-drawn carriages, cabs and carts still held their own, for transport in town and country, against the growing competition of the internal combustion engine.

CHAPTER XXIII

Victorian Scotland: Mind and Spirit

BY THE close of the reign of Queen Victoria, the aims of the political reformers had been largely attained (the exclusion of women from the franchise constituting the challenging exception to the tale of democratic advance); Scotsmen were playing their part in the building and defence of an overseas Empire that was as much a source of pride to them as to Englishmen; the economy had been transformed and material wealth enormously increased, though ill-regulated change and the mal-distribution of prosperity had bequeathed grave social problems to the twentieth century. It remains to consider the record of this age of liberty and progress in matters of religion and education, literature and the arts.

The ecclesiastical life of Victorian Scotland was over-shadowed by the Disruption – its genesis, fulfilment, consequences and aftermath. An atmosphere of sectarian strife overhung the counsels of the ministers, and the unhappy memories of 'Forty-three' embittered relations within the Presbyterian fold. Much, and perhaps all, of this might have been avoided, for, had Church and State shown beforehand half the wisdom and restraint that were brought to bear after the event, the Disruption probably need not have occurred at all. The 'rump' General Assembly of 1843, immediately after the departure of the Free Church contingent, and now under unfettered Moderate control, took steps to nullify the Veto Act, it reversed the deposition of the Strathbogie ministers,[1] and it repealed the Chapel Act. For its part Parliament, convinced too late of the seriousness of the crisis in Scotland, passed the Benefices Act that same summer (1843), authorising any presbytery, on receiving valid objections from a congregation, to reject a presentee.[2] Next year the *Quoad Sacra* Act provided for the disjunction of a part of a civil parish and its erection as a separate ecclesiastical charge, if a majority of the heritors approved and adequate maintenance for the new church and minister were arranged from teinds or other sources of revenue.

[1] See *supra*, p. 185.

[2] Promoted by George Gordon, fourth earl of Aberdeen, who was foreign secretary under Peel (1841-46), this statute was commonly called 'Lord Aberdeen's Act'. He had, while in opposition to Melbourne's Whig administration (1835-41), tried in vain to get Parliament to adopt some such measure.

Such a conciliatory spirit was highly commendable, but the damage had been done. The Church had so far lost its national character that it was thought wise to strip it of its powers of local government. Poor relief, as we have seen, was secularised in 1845 and education in 1872,[1] while in 1853 university professors, except in the theological chairs, were released from the requirement to subscribe the Westminster Confession of Faith. Despite these concessions to the spirit of the age, the Church made steady progress, undeterred by the taunt that her pastors preferred their livings to their principles. She did change somewhat with the times, and more and more of her ministers came to be men with a gentler faith and broader sympathies, like Dr Norman Macleod, of the Barony church, Glasgow, who edited, from its inception in 1860, the widely-read and highly-esteemed monthly magazine, *Good Words*, or Dr Robert Lee, of Greyfriars, Edinburgh, who installed stained-glass windows in 1857 and a church organ in 1864. The Church of Scotland claimed to be stronger in 1869 than all the other Presbyterian churches taken together. So strong, indeed, did she feel that, abandoning the Moderates' former attachment to patronage, the General Assembly petitioned Parliament for its abolition. Gladstone refused to take this step, but Disraeli did in 1874, when the members and adherents of each congregation were empowered freely to choose their own minister.

It might have been thought, and it was thought within the establishment, that the disappearance of this ancient grievance would clear the way for the readmission of the Free Church congregations, but, for reasons presently to be considered, this was not to be. For the rest of the reign the Church of Scotland continued on its quiet way, enjoying the support of many of the more conservative-minded, exercising a strong influence on the universities and schools, but making little impact upon the dissenters. With over 1,400 parishes and ministers in 1901, it had not succeeded in drawing back into the fold a single group of those who had left it.

For the dissenters it was a time of growth and change, of reunion and further schism. From its start the Free Church differed from earlier secessions by asserting its national scope: schools as well as churches had given up the state connection in 1843, schoolmasters' stipends, like those of ministers, were sacrificed, but now all the services of religion and education[2] were promised and provided. It

[1] See *supra*, pp. 200-1, 206.

[2] For the Free Church schools, see *infra*, p. 268.

was headed by a General Assembly instead of a mere synod, and it had its own colleges for the training of its clergy, Chalmers being principal and professor of divinity of the Edinburgh college until his death in 1847. With fervent enthusiasm it tackled the task of building and organising, its 'sustentation fund' was soon able to guarantee a fixed stipend,[1] and the Census returns of 1851 credit it with 889 places of worship and 495,000 sittings.[2]

In May 1847 the two dissenting bodies that were next in size to the Free Church, namely the United Secession and Relief Churches, finding themselves in agreement on all essentials, came together to form the United Presbyterian Church. The 'U.P. Church' (the initials were in common use for two generations) was strong,[3] popular and vigorous, and its members had long been at one in denying any validity to the *idea*, as to the *practice*, of a state establishment of religion: they were purely and simply 'voluntary'.

The second half of the nineteenth century brought both triumphs and troubles for the Presbyterian sects. The Free Church, marked by purity of conduct and missionary zeal, proved attractive to the two surviving representatives of earlier schisms, each of which in turn united with it – the Synod of United Original Seceders[4] in 1852 and the Reformed Presbyterians[5] in 1876. In each case, however, a non-uniting remnant continued the name and being of the separate community.[6] Outside as inside the establishment there was some movement of thought. The most famous 'heresy trial' of the century was that of William Robertson Smith, a professor and a Hebrew scholar of note at the Free Church College, Aberdeen, who was deposed in 1881 for taking a too 'historical' view of the Old Testament, though it was in keeping with modern ideas of Biblical criticism. Again, the obligation to subscribe the Westminster Confession of Faith (hitherto absolute for all Presbyterian clergymen) was relaxed, with some allowance for liberty of conscience, by declaratory Acts passed by the United Presbyterians in 1879 and by the Free Church in 1892. The second of these measures caused a minor secession, for in 1893 a number

[1] By 1864 the minimum stipend was £138, compared with £158 6s. 8d. for the Church of Scotland.

[2] The numbers for the establishment were 1,183 and 767,000 respectively.

[3] The 1851 Census gave it 465 places of worship and 288,000 sittings.

[4] Dating in their then form from 1842: see *supra*, p. 185.

[5] Organised in 1743: see *supra*, pp. 45, 100.

[6] Small numbers were involved in these 'secessions from a secession' – some ten congregations in 1852 and 13 in 1876.

of ministers and congregations, principally in the Highlands and Islands, broke away from the Free Church in protest against any softening of the traditional standards of belief, to form the Free Presbyterian Church, the strictest and most orthodox of all sects.

The main interest of the period lies in the attitude of the Free Church to the principle of establishment, in which Chalmers, Candlish and their fellows firmly believed: their hostility was against the existing state connection, which infringed the rights of the church and robbed it of spiritual independence through the evil law of patronage. No 'voluntaries' by conviction, Free churchmen became of necessity 'voluntaries' in action – and highly successful 'voluntaries' – so that in time their theories were re-shaped to fit the new facts. The first generation of leaders passed away, and the younger men who came forward scorned the notion of returning to the establishment, even after the abolition of patronage, and turned instead to the United Presbyterians. The new head of the Free Church was the able and scholarly Dr Robert Rainy (1826-1906), who succeeded Candlish in 1874 as principal of New College, Edinburgh, and, by the vigour of his faith and personality, dominated the ecclesiastical life of the entire nation for thirty years. It was he who inspired and guided the negotiations for a new union,[1] and he saw his life's work crowned in 1900, when the United Free Church was formed by the amalgamation of the Free Church, with over 1,100 congregations, and the United Presbyterian Church, with more than 600; the new body claimed to be about equal in strength to the Church of Scotland. Once again, a minority[2] stood aloof from union, asserting that it alone was faithful to the principles of the Disruption and therefore entitled to the entire Free Church property – a claim that was to have an interesting outcome in the law courts.[3]

During the reign of Victoria the Episcopal Church, having already adopted the Thirty-nine Articles,[4] became even closer in spirit to the Church of England. Its clergymen were made eligible, in 1864, for benefices in the sister church beyond the Tweed. Again, Anglican settlers in Scotland naturally sought fellowship with the Episcopal Church and tended in turn to make it more 'English' in tone, while

[1] As early as 1872 he had declared for disestablishment of the Church, so that he was already a 'voluntary' in principle.

[2] The U.P. Church was unanimous for union; it was only the ultra-conservative elements in the Free Church, adhering to the abstract idea of a 'state church', that insisted on continuing as a separate body.

[3] See *infra*, p. 306. [4] See *supra*, pp. 186-7.

many sons of the nobility, gentry and merchant class were sent to English public schools, where they were usually exposed to powerful Anglican influences. Moreover, the Episcopalians' own school at Glenalmond, opened in 1847, was itself an Anglican and 'high church' institution. By 1901, accordingly, though it remained a 'church of the people' in the north-east, the Episcopal Church elsewhere came to be identified with upper-class and English minority groups. With some 46,000 communicants, it had then 170 regular charges and over 50 missions – numbers that indicate growth, but growth not quite up to the rate of increase of the population at large.

It was mostly among communities of English and Welsh workers and their families that the chapels of the Methodists and Baptists were set up. Representing the native tradition of 'independency', the Congregationalists flourished in a modest way, absorbing in 1896 a majority of the 'Morisonians' (or the Evangelical Union).[1]

As the Episcopal Church became more English in affinity, the Roman Catholic community became overwhelmingly Irish in membership. The tremendous increase in the number of Romanists (due almost solely to the presence of Irish immigrants and their descendants) is suggested in the following estimates of population[2]:–

	Roman Catholics (in thousands)	*Percentage of Scottish Total*
1827	70	3·0
1851	146	5·0
1878	333	9·2
1901	446	10·0

There were 117 places of worship in 1851; by 1878 252 priests served 129 missions or parishes; and by 1901 one in ten of the population was a Romanist.

This remarkable growth did not pass without notice or challenge. Anti-papal sentiment, as we have seen,[3] flared up in 1845 in protest against Peel's Act for recognising and endowing Maynooth college for the training of Irish priests, and again in 1850 against the proposed assumption of territorial titles by Romanist bishops in England, a scheme which was denounced, in Scotland as in England, as 'papal aggression', and which led the government in the following year to

[1] See *supra*, pp. 180-1, 186.

[2] These statistics are taken from James Darragh, 'The Catholic Population of Scotland', in *Innes Review*, VOL. IV (1953), p. 58.

[3] *Supra*, p. 202.

bring in a prohibitory Act. The spread of a more tolerant mood is suggested by the fact that in 1878, against only mild opposition, a Romanist hierarchy was quietly instituted in Scotland itself; instead of the three vicariates, the Church was reorganised in six bishoprics, loosely based on a selection of pre-Reformation dioceses – Aberdeen, St Andrews, Dunkeld, Argyll, Glasgow and Galloway. Two-thirds of the total membership were then concentrated in the bishopric of Glasgow.

The educational reforms of the period flowed in part from the religious changes, in part from the adoption of the principle of popular election. Step by step the schools were transferred from ecclesiastical control to a system that was at once secular and democratic, and the universities too became less authoritarian and more responsive to popular ideals.

Prior to 1833 Parliament had contented itself with settling the level of schoolmasters' stipends, leaving it to heritors, kirk sessions and presbyteries to manage the affairs of the parish schools, allowing town councils a free hand with the burgh schools, and abstaining from any notice of academies and other private institutions. In that year a new departure was made when Parliament endorsed a scheme of grants for the erection of schools in Great Britain; though England alone, with the greater need, benefited from this first subsidy, annual sums of £10,000 were provided from 1834 to assist the building and maintenance of additional parish schools in Scotland. From 1838 the so-called 'parliamentary schools' were authorised in *quoad sacra* parishes: the heritors were to supply the buildings, the government the salary.[1] In 1839 a committee of the Privy Council was set up to administer grants-in-aid, school inspection was begun, and grants became subject to the acceptance of inspection. Many schools bowed to this measure of central control, but for long many more retained complete independence.

A parliamentary report at this time gives us a fairly full picture of the educational field. There were in 1834 about 1,000 regular parish schools, together with some 400 schools linked in one way or another with the establishment – 'Society', 'Assembly' and 'Sessional' schools.[2] The 270 endowed and subscription schools formed a special and somewhat superior group, but in direct competition with the parish schools

[1] In the period 1839-64, 695 'parliamentary' schools were built, including 364 connected with the Church of Scotland, 305 with other Presbyterian churches, and 16 with the Episcopalians.

[2] For the origins of these categories, see *supra*, pp. 105, 164.

stood about 350 schools belonging to the Relief and Secession churches (to be combined in 1847 as the U.P. Church). Most numerous of all – in excess of 2,000 – were the 'adventure' schools, run for profit (or rather to yield a bare livelihood) and including many a 'dame school' – which might mean no more than the 'ben-the-house' of a cottage, where a few boys and girls were taught the rudiments by a 'decayed gentlewoman'.

Confusion and rivalry were intensified by the Disruption, when 360 teachers 'came out' to join the Free Church. The growth of this new group was rapid – to over 500 in a few years and to over 600 in the 1860s.[1] By 1867, too, there were 74 Episcopalian and 61 Roman Catholic schools. The girls' schools of the S.S.P.C.K. had by this time mostly given up spinning and weaving in favour of sewing and knitting, reading and writing: in 1872 there were 76 of these sewing schools, besides 194 ordinary 'Society' schools. Another category was that of the 'ragged' or industrial school, started at Aberdeen in 1841 by Sheriff William Watson, and vigorously developed at Edinburgh from 1847 by the Rev. Thomas Guthrie of the Free Church, with the object of reclaiming the unkempt and illiterate 'street arabs'. The work of such institutions, numbering some twenty, was, from 1854, supplemented or superseded by that of the reformatory schools for the training of young delinquents.

The advanced schools at the opening of our period comprised over forty burgh or grammar schools, together with a smaller but increasing number of academies, and a marked trend of the times was for these two types, the old and the new, to merge in a single entity, which, under one name or the other, offered a wide range of subjects, classical and modern, literary and scientific. An older burgh school might be taken over by a well-endowed new foundation, as in the case of Madras College,[2] in St Andrews, opened in 1833 under the will of Dr Andrew Bell,[3] a pioneer of the monitorial method (under which the older pupils directed the studies of the younger). Again, the High School of Dundee was the result of the amalgamation in 1859 of a grammar school, an 'English' school and an academy. Glasgow Academy (1845), on the

[1] The Free Church schools were frequently located in the newer villages or other new centres of population, and thus benefited the entire community – one of the few happy consequences of the Disruption.

[2] The term 'college' was frequently applied in the nineteenth century to what were simply large schools, with several masters.

[3] It was also under his will (1831) that Cupar got what came to be called the Bell-Baxter school.

other hand, is an example of the quite separate school. By the 1860s there were over 80 'higher class' schools, as they were beginning to be called, varying from some that were both parochial and burghal to the three 'English-type' boarding schools – for Loretto (1829) had been joined by Merchiston Castle, in Edinburgh (1833), and by the Episcopalians' Trinity College, Glenalmond (1847).

Parliament at length intervened to tidy up the confusion and gradually to evolve a national system. By the Parochial and Burgh Schoolmasters Act, 1861, parish teachers were relieved from religious tests, and their supervision was transferred from the presbyteries to the universities. The maximum salary was fixed at £70 for men (or £80 if there were two of them to share the one stipend), and at £30 for women teachers. Between 1864 and 1868 a royal commission, known from its chairman as the Argyll commission,[1] surveyed and reported on no fewer than 4,450 schools, and it was partly as a result of its recommendations, partly as a companion measure to the mild English statute of 1870, that the Education (Scotland) Act was passed in 1872. All Presbyterian schools in burgh and parish were taken over by the state, their administration was entrusted to school boards, to be elected in each burgh or parish,[2] and schooling became compulsory for all to the age of thirteen; moreover, the 'higher class public schools' under the control of town councils were also placed under the boards. The allocation of parliamentary grants fell to a committee of the Privy Council, called the Scotch[3] Education Department. The private, Episcopalian and Roman Catholic schools were not affected by the Act.

Another change inspired in the main by the Argyll commission concerned the charity schools run for necessitous children by the endowed hospitals and trusts, but no longer required with the state undertaking responsibility for elementary education. In the 1870s and 1880s such schools were transformed into fee-paying day-schools, the rights of 'foundationers' under trusts being preserved by the grant of bursaries to poor day-scholars. In this way a number of famous schools (or 'colleges') came into being or were given a new form, including George Watson's, Daniel Stewart's, the Edinburgh Ladies and James Gillespie's, all in Edinburgh, Hutchesons' and Allan Glen's

[1] George, eighth duke of Argyll (1823-1900), was a leading Whig politician, who served in various offices under Aberdeen, Palmerston and Gladstone; his historical writings include *Scotland As It Was, and As It Is*.

[2] By 1901 there were 978 of them, a few unions of boards having been effected.

[3] The word 'Scotch' (customary in the nineteenth century) was expressly changed to 'Scottish' (in accordance with modern usage) in 1918.

in Glasgow, the Morgan in Dundee and Robert Gordon's[1] in Aberdeen; in one case the trustees, sensing the changed needs of the day, resolved not to found yet another hospital, but set up instead Scotland's fourth private boarding school, Fettes College in Edinburgh.

Of the other reforms of the reign the most important were the inception in 1888 of the 'leaving certificate' examination as a test of fitness for entrance to a university; the institution from 1892 of direct grants-in-aid for the furtherance of secondary education[2]; and the admission in 1899 of science as a subject for the leaving certificate. By 1901 the new national system, providing elementary education for all children, offering a variety of advanced curricula to the brighter pupils, and guaranteeing its teachers a reasonable competence,[3] was well established: the inferior old 'adventure' schools had disappeared, and most of the endowed schools had either closed or been transferred to the school boards.

Both teacher training and technical education made progress during the reign. From the establishment in 1836 of Glasgow's 'normal school',[4] the first of its kind in Britain, training colleges were set up in the cities, in association with the Church of Scotland, the Free Church, the Episcopalians and, finally, the Roman Catholics; it was mostly in the larger towns, too, that technical, agricultural and art colleges – often the product of the amalgamation of earlier and humbler schools – met the growing demand for their special branches of instruction.

For the universities, as for the schools, the mid- and late-Victorian periods were the great age of reforms. As we have seen,[5] certain grave defects in administration, finance and graduation called for remedies, but parliamentary action came only after a further and bitter law-suit at Edinburgh in 1845 and yet another, involving Glasgow, from 1854. The Universities (Scotland) Act, 1858, and the ordinances made by a royal commission under that statute, initiated the changes, and they were completed by a second measure (under the same title) in 1889. Each university became a self-governing corporation,[6] with

[1] This 'college' became in 1886 a combined secondary school and technical institution.

[2] For this purpose secondary education committees (representing equally the county council and the school boards) were set up in each of the thirty-three counties, while Edinburgh, Glasgow, Dundee, Aberdeen, Leith and Govan had each their own committees.

[3] Most male teachers were getting £100 a year or more, and women teachers £80-90. [4] Cf. *supra*, p. 166. [5] See *supra*, p. 168.

[6] The 1858 Act was above all a blessing to Edinburgh University, freeing it from the control of the town council, under which it had for long chafed.

its business affairs (appointments, finance and works) under the university court, and academic matters (teaching, examination and graduation) left to the senate. While the latter simply comprised all the professors, the former was given a 'balanced' constitution, representative of the university and municipal dignitaries, of the senate and of the graduates (who were now organised as a consultative body called the general council).

As one result of the reforms of 1858, faculties of arts, divinity, medicine and law[1] were established, with a basic bachelor's degree in each case except arts (where the M.A. displaced the B.A., which was abolished in 1861), and the doctorate reserved for advanced work or as an honorary award. A fifth faculty, that of science, was added in 1893, and Edinburgh got a sixth, music. Within this systematic framework new chairs were founded, for example, in English, history, pathology, geology and engineering. In 1860 Aberdeen's two colleges were conjoined in a single university, while in 1897 University College, Dundee, privately set up in 1881, was made a part of St Andrews.

From the 1870s the admission of women was being warmly advocated by some and stubbornly resisted by others. St Andrews offered one solution in 1876 by way of a special diploma of L.L.A. (lady literate in arts), based on external study and examination, while Queen Margaret College began in Glasgow in 1883 as an independent centre of higher learning. From 1892, however, the universities themselves were thrown open to women, and Queen Margaret College was incorporated in Glasgow, to endure as a constituent college until 1935.

The nature and life of the student body – strong in arts and medicine, much weaker numerically in other branches – did not greatly vary from one university to another; for all alike, cheap lodgings in town, regular attendance at lectures, and austere living were the order of the day. As spokesmen of their interests and promoters of their welfare, the students' representative councils came into existence from 1884, while from 1885 students' unions served as centres of their social life. By 1901 there were over 6,000 students in Scotland – upwards of 2,800 in Edinburgh, of 2,000 in Glasgow, of 800 in Aberdeen and of 400 in St Andrews. The need for more accommodation impelled Glasgow, in 1870, to abandon the graceful but cramped Old College in the High street, in favour of a larger site at Gilmorehill, in the west end, and led Edinburgh, from 1883, to adopt the opposite device of retaining its

[1] Exceptionally, St Andrews did not institute a full course in law until 1939.

'old' buildings as a centre, but scattering some of the newer departments on detached sites.

The Victorian universities, if they did not quite maintain the dominance that had been theirs during the 'Athenian age', had still some of the sparkle of intellectual brilliance. The greatest figure was Glasgow's scientific genius, William Thomson, Lord Kelvin (1824-1907), but not far behind him came, in the world of science, Aberdeen's eminent physicist, James Clerk Maxwell (1831-79), and one who was principal in succession at St Andrews and Edinburgh, and among the founders of the British Association, Sir David Brewster (1781-1868); or Kelvin's own contemporary at Glasgow, the originator of antiseptic surgery, Joseph, Lord Lister (1827-1912); or, again, those who kept alive Edinburgh's great name in medicine, like the well-loved Sir Robert Christison (1797-1882) and the pioneer of anaesthesia by chloroform, Sir James Young Simpson (1811-70); or, in letters, John Stuart Blackie (1809-95) and William Edmonstoune Aytoun (1813-65), each of whom, from his university chair, sent forth verse that had a great vogue in the middle years of the reign.

The churches and universities, whose development we have been considering, naturally made their specialised contributions to literature. In divinity the writings of John Tulloch,[1] Norman Macleod and William Robertson Smith had great influence. The 'Scottish Philosophy' reached its culmination in the works of Sir William Hamilton,[2] the erudite Edinburgh metaphysician, and found its chronicler in James McCosh, who left Scotland to assume the presidency of Princeton College, New Jersey, in 1868, exactly 100 years after John Witherspoon had taken the same road.[3] Literary criticism had its academic exponents in the Glasgow logician, John Veitch,[4] and the Edinburgh rhetorician,

[1] St Andrews, small and poor as it was, beset by internal troubles and threatened several times with extinction, was saved by a line of remarkable principals, of whom Tulloch (of St Mary's College, 1854-86) was one.

[2] He edited the writings of his two greatest predecessors, Thomas Reid and Dugald Stewart (see *supra*, pp. 167, 168, 169); his *Lectures on Metaphysics and Logic* were published posthumously from the notes taken by many of his students (1859-61).

[3] Cf. *supra*, p. 177. *The Scottish Philosophy . . . from Hutcheson to Hamilton* was published in 1874. These two great presidencies forged enduring links between Princeton and Scotland. Witherspoon and McCosh were both prominent in American public life, and in 1913 one of their successors in the headship of Princeton, Woodrow Wilson (of Scottish Presbyterian stock), became president of the United States.

[4] See his *History and Poetry of the Scottish Border* (1877) and *The Feeling for Nature in Scottish Poetry* (1887). (His chair was that of logic *and rhetoric*, so that its scope extended to grammar and letters.)

David Masson, whose *Life of John Milton* (1859-80) is a monumental work of research and interpretation.

The historical works of the reign have a wider and more lasting appeal. They too rested on a solid foundation of painstaking scholarship and antiquarian labours, which are exemplified in the texts of the Bannatyne and Maitland Clubs,[1] and, long after their dissolution, of the Scottish Text Society (1882) and the Scottish History Society (1886); in such official publications as *The Acts of the Parliaments of Scotland*, *The Exchequer Rolls* and *The Register of the Great Seal*; and in a number of private ventures, like the sumptuous 'family histories' compiled by Sir William Fraser. These are for the serious student, and yet half a dozen historians of the time left works which can be enjoyed by the general reader and the scholar alike, and are as valid for the twentieth as for the nineteenth century.

Patrick Fraser Tytler's *History of Scotland*, though completed in 1843,[2] retains its interest and readability, and Cosmo Innes's constitutional studies – *Scotland in the Middle Ages* (1860), *Sketches of Early Scotch History* (1861) and *Scotch Legal Antiquities* (1872) – are still fresh, clear and suggestive. The ecclesiastical histories of John Cunningham the Presbyterian (1859) and George Grub the Episcopalian (1861) are best read in conjunction, as mutual correctives. John Hill Burton's *History of Scotland*, finished in 1870,[3] if couched in full-blown prose, has many merits and is by no means discarded today. And William Forbes Skene's *Celtic Scotland* (1876-80), though open to detailed criticism,[4] remains a basic work for all matters concerning the Highlands.

On the fringes of history, Victorian Scotland yields autobiographical writings of enduring worth, beginning with those of Lord Cockburn, which have already been mentioned.[5] Hugh Miller, geologist, author of *The Old Red Sandstone* (1841), and evangelical journalist, wrote one of the classics of the age in *My Schools and Schoolmasters* (1854), and this was followed by the highly popular *Reminiscences of Scottish Life and Character* (1857), by Edward B. Ramsay, dean of Edinburgh.

[1] See *supra*, p. 170. Comparable to them, though of less importance, were the Abbotsford Club (Edinburgh, 1833-66) and the Spalding Club (Aberdeen, 1839-70).

[2] Originally in 9 volumes, but re-issued in many other editions down to 1877.

[3] But the second edition (8 vols., 1873) is the better.

[4] This comment, of course, applies in some measure to all these works; indeed, it would be a sad reflection on subsequent historical learning if it did not!

[5] See *supra*, p. 145. The *Memorials of his Time* (1856) and the *Journals* (1874) – the latter coming down to 1844 – were both published posthumously.

Two other clergymen drew on their own experiences to produce comparable works – Norman Macleod's *Reminiscences of a Highland Parish* (1867) and A. K. H. Boyd's *Twenty-five Years of St Andrews* (1892) and *Last Years of St Andrews* (1896). Beyond history, too, the 'Celtic twilight' drew John Francis Campbell into the realm of myth and fable for his *Popular Tales of the West Highlands* (1860-62).

It is when we turn to creative and imaginative literature that the record of Victorian Scotland, for all its wealth and knowledge, its interest in religion and culture, seems peculiarly barren. The contribution of the one great writer of his time, Thomas Carlyle, was made to English literature[1] and had very little connection with the land and the people that had shaped his character. The poetry of the middle years of the century bears the stamp of the third-rate – Aytoun's *Lays of the Scottish Cavaliers* (1848), Blackie's *Lays and Legends of Ancient Greece* (1857)[2] – or of the pompous and pretentious – Alexander Smith's misfire of an epic, *Life-Drama* (1853) – or again of the precious and esoteric – verse with a special appeal to literary lawyers, like James Maidment's *Court of Session Garland* (1839) and George Outram's *Legal and Other Lyrics* (*c.* 1850). Nor has posterity thought very highly of such fictional successes of the age as George Whyte-Melville's twenty-odd tales of military and sporting life, though more value attaches to the north-eastern dialect novels of George Macdonald – *David Elginbrod* (1862), *Alec Forbes* (1865) and *Robert Falconer* (1868) – and to William Alexander's *Johnny Gibb of Gushetneuk* (1871). And a minor but serious historian, James Grant, came as close as any to lasting fame with his historical novels, *The Romance of War* (1846), *The Adventures of an Aide-de-Camp* (1852) and *The Yellow Frigate* (1855).

The last two decades of the century saw an upsurge of interest in Scottish themes and dialects, in the oddities and mannerisms of village and church life. James M. Barrie (1860-1937) set the fashion with *Auld Licht Idylls* (1888), *A Window in Thrums* (1889) and *The Little Minister* (1891). The tone became forced, the episodes and characters contrived, in S. R. Crockett's *The Stickit Minister* (1893) and *The Raiders* (1894), and in *Beside the Bonny Brier Bush* (1894), by 'Ian Maclaren' (the Rev. John Watson). At its sentimental worst, this cult was labelled 'the Kailyard school', and it had its verse counterpart in *Horace in Homespun* (1886) and *Ochil Idylls* (1891), by 'Hugh Hali-

[1] He moved to London in 1834 and made his home there.

[2] For these two writers, cf. *supra*, p. 272.

burton' (James Logie Robertson). A similar straining after effect – in this case the mystery and glamour of the world of Celtic romance – marked the tales, essays and plays, in prose and verse, of 'Fiona Macleod' (William Sharp), but a truer note was struck in the early novels of Neil Munro (1864-1930), *The Lost Pibroch* (1896) and *John Splendid* (1898).

But for the work of its one man of genius, the literary annals of the Victorian age would have been meagre indeed, but the day was saved by Robert Louis Stevenson (1850-94), although ill-health drove him to exile and an early death. Despite his modest view of his own talents, his novels and tales – *Treasure Island* (1883), *The Strange Case of Dr Jekyll and Mr Hyde* (1886), *Kidnapped* (1886), *The Master of Ballantrae* (1889), *Catriona* (1893) and the unfinished *Weir of Hermiston* (1896)[1] – rank next after those of Scott. And the light verse of Stevenson – mere trifles, in his eyes – includes some sprightly Scottish pieces that are worthy of Burns himself; for example, the slim volume called *Underwoods* (1887) provides these lines from 'Embro Hie Kirk':–

The Lord Himsel' in former days
Waled out the proper tunes for praise [*chose*
An' named the proper kind' o' claes [*clothes*
  For folk to preach in:
Preceese and in the chief o' ways
  Important teachin'.

He ordered a' things late and air'; [*early*
He ordered folk to stand at prayer.
(Although I cannae just mind where
  He gave the warnin'.)
An' pit pomatum on their hair [*hair-oil*
  On Sabbath mornin'.

In the cultural pattern of Victorian life the periodical press was a large element. Until its abolition in 1855, the levying of a stamp-duty[2] made the newspaper business a precarious one, and casualties were numerous, especially among papers begun during the first Reform epoch and again at the time of the Chartist agitation.[3] Yet many took root, to cover the country with a network of local journals, from

[1] The same high quality informs the best of his short stories, like *A Lodging for the Night* and *The Sire de Malétroit's Door*.

[2] It then stood at 1d. for each large sheet (4 pages), but had been as high as 4d. (in 1815). The duty on paper itself was abolished by Gladstone in 1861.

[3] See *supra*, p. 199.

the *Shetland Times* (1872) and *Orcadian* (1854) to the *Dumfries and Galloway Standard* (1843), from the *Buchan Observer* (1863) to the *Oban Times* (1861).[1] The early newspapers were, and have mostly remained, weekly[2] or bi-weekly, but the year 1848 brought the start of the *North British Daily Mail*,[3] to be followed by the conversion into dailies of the *Scotsman* (1855), *Glasgow Herald* (1859) and others. A further landmark was the appearance in 1864 of the *Glasgow Evening Citizen*, for its lead was followed in the chief towns, and yet another came with the *Scots Pictorial* in 1897.[4]

Perhaps the most remarkable of early Victorian newspapers was Hugh Miller's fiery and eloquent *Witness*, but it did not long survive its creator's death and was wound up in 1864. As the reign wore on, the *Glasgow Herald* and *Scotsman* gradually established their primacy and emerged as chief moulders of national opinion, both in the Liberal interest down to 1886 and thereafter Unionist; they were widely read and highly respected for their news and comment. By the end of the century the great majority of the inhabitants had some contact with one or more of the country's 200 newspapers.[5]

Among reviews, meanwhile, the *Edinburgh*, *Blackwood's* and *Chambers's*[6] held their own, though challenged at times by two quarterlies with high literary standards, the *North British Review* (1844-71) and the *Scottish Review* (1882-1900), and again by the spirited and iconoclastic *Scots Observer* (1888-1900).[7]

The best of early and mid-Victorian art shows much technical ability along traditional lines – the sentimental Highland landscapes of Horatio McCulloch and John MacWhirter,[8] or the homely Galloway scenes of the brothers John and Thomas Faed, or again the historical pictures of Sir George Harvey, Sir William Orchardson and John Pettie. In Scotland, however, from about 1880 – as in France with the Impressionists – a violent reaction against 'academic' values and techniques inspired the younger artists to make bold experiments and

[1] All these titles survive to this day.

[2] Two weeklies, originating in Dundee, became something of national institutions through the printing of several local editions – the *Weekly News* (1855) and the *People's Journal* (1858).

[3] This was the forerunner of the *Daily Record and Mail.*

[4] It was absorbed in 1923 by the younger *Bulletin* (1915-60).

[5] Most daily morning papers then cost 1d., evening papers ½d.

[6] See *supra*, pp. 170-1.

[7] It eventually changed its name to the *National Observer* and moved to London.

[8] A modern critic, Mr Ian Finlay, compares these 'ben-and-glen' romantics to the 'Kailyard' novelists: *Art in Scotland* (1948), p. 118.

to apply light and colour in a new and lavish way. For a generation the 'Glasgow school' set the tone of Scottish painting and brought wide fame to its members, W. Y. Macgregor, William McTaggart, E. A. Hornel, Alexander Roche, E. A. Walton, George Henry and the English artist, Joseph Crawhall; associated in spirit with their output were the sculptures of Pittendrigh Macgillivray, while Sir James Guthrie, renowned later as a portraitist, felt their influence strongly in his early work.

In architecture the revulsion against the conventional standards was slower, and much of the building of the time was ornate and affected, imitative either of the Gothic or of the classical styles, with the former choice giving the less happy, though the more admired, results. The taste of the time, running to excessive decoration, is exemplified in the Scott monument and Fettes College in Edinburgh, in Marischal College at Aberdeen and Glasgow University at Gilmorehill, in the spuriously 'Baronial' castles of Balmoral and Glamis, while the Glasgow terraces and churches of Alexander ('Greek') Thomson are among the best works of the neo-classicists. The protest against utter dependence on past models and over-elaboration of detail came with the straightforward, 'functional' buildings of Charles Rennie Mackintosh, who, having designed the Glasgow School of Art (1894) and several private houses, was to go on to European fame as a pioneer of modern styles.

Thus Victorian culture had its moments in regard to the things of spirit and mind – in religion the heroic devotion of the Free Church to its concept of truth and justice, in education a system that was sound, disciplined and available to nearly all boys, in literature the fruits of scholarship and a flash of brilliance in the works of Stevenson, and in the arts a reaction against mere tradition and in favour of a fresh and natural approach.

CHAPTER XXIV

War and Peace

FROM THE outbreak of the first World War on 4 August 1914 until the Armistice agreement on 11 November 1918, the energies of the nation were directed, with an intensity of purpose never approached in any previous conflict, to the struggle for survival and victory. In the sufferings and triumphs of those years the Scots had their full share. It was a Scot, Sir Douglas (later Earl) Haig, who served for a great part of the war as commander-in-chief of the main British armies. The magnitude of Scotland's contribution to the military effort is shown by the tremendous expansion of her regiments of the line: three of these – the Cameronians, the Black Watch and the Highland Light Infantry – each raised twenty-seven battalions, while the famous 'First of Foot', the Royal Scots, had no fewer than thirty-five battalions. The battle honours awarded to these and the other Scottish units attest their endurance and gallantry in all the scattered theatres of war. Names like Mons, the Marne, the Aisne, Ypres, Loos, the Somme, Arras and Vimy ridge recall the western front, the miseries of trench warfare, and the appalling casualties suffered in attempts to break the enemy's line, while Gallipoli, Salonika, Palestine and Mesopotamia became memorable for equally staunch fortitude in distant lands. Again, the war at sea, and particularly the unrestricted submarine attacks of 1917-18, threatened our sea-power, the merchant marine, and the nation itself, and here too Scotland played its part. From first to last, active service of all kinds claimed some 74,000 Scotsmen killed, and more than twice as many wounded.[1] While military service – by voluntary recruiting until 1916, and thereafter by conscription – became the normal lot of the fit adult, for the rest of the population it was a grim time of privation and shortage, though fortunately not of real danger.

Patriotic feeling inspired all ranks of society, and it was in the nature of things that, in May 1915, the bitter animosity that had so recently divided the political parties over the Irish question[2] was laid aside, and Conservative and Labour leaders joined the Asquith ad-

[1] The total casualties among the armed forces of the Empire were 3,286,090, including 996,230 dead.

[2] See *supra*, p. 222.

ministration to form a coalition government. The party truce was observed for the duration of the war, but in December 1916 the premiership was assumed by Lloyd George, who proved to be a vigorous and fiery war minister. The supersession of Asquith by his younger rival made a breach among the Liberals, which, though mostly concealed during the war, was to be a lasting cause of weakness and to prepare the way for the ultimate downfall of the party; meanwhile, the 'drift to the right' was furthered by the general belief that the Tories were essentially the war party and the Liberals the peace party.

Yet there was some activity on the 'far left' as well. The mass-production of the munitions of war led to the adoption of irregular labour practices, including much overtime working, the suspension of normal trade union restrictions, and the 'dilution of labour' (whereby women were taken on for the lighter, semi-skilled tasks, to free the reduced number of skilled men for the more vital jobs). These innovations struck many men as invasions of their hard-won rights, and some of them insisted on having their own 'dilution committees' to oversee any revision of work schedules. The militant socialists now came forward, under the lead of shop stewards' committees, to oppose the old-fashioned trade unions, and to advocate a broad 'industrial' union, dedicated to the class struggle and its own version of 'democracy'. The movement produced a 'Clyde Workers' Committee', as a model for direct action, in all industrial areas, to achieve government by workers' delegates. Though driven underground, the agitation survived until about 1922, and it foretold, not only the general post-war trend to socialism, but also the particular brand of revolutionary fervour that was to create, in the 1920s, the legend of 'Red Clydeside'.

By the time the fighting ended a renewal of the mandate of Parliament was due, and indeed overdue, for that Parliament, after limiting its own life-span, and that of its successors, to a maximum of five years,[1] had itself remained in being, because of the war-time emergency, for eight years. The general election that followed was fought on a new franchise and with new electoral arrangements, which had been introduced, in place of those dating from 1884-85 and no longer meeting the needs of the population, by the Representation of the People Act. This statute, passed in February 1918 and forming, in effect, a fourth reform act, greatly enlarged the electorate by giving women the right to vote from the age of thirty (against twenty-one for men): male public opinion had been influenced towards this momentous step, not

[1] For the terms of the Parliament Act, 1911, see *supra*, pp. 221-2.

so much by the often disorderly agitation of the pre-war 'suffragettes', as by the big part played by women in the war effort, both as auxiliaries to the armed forces and as workers in industry. Speculation as to how 'the women's vote' would go was soon to cease, as experience showed women divided, like men, between 'the right' and 'the left', in accordance with their economic background, their social interests and their political preferences. The reform was to be quietly completed by the Equal Franchise Act, 1928, giving the vote to men and women from the age of twenty-one: adult suffrage was thus achieved in just under one hundred years from the passing of the first Reform Act in 1832.

The 1918 Act, based on the census figures of 1911, gave Scotland 74 members out of an increased total of 707 for the whole of the United Kingdom,[1] and redistributed the seats in an entirely new way. Of the thirty-three shires, Lanark, much the most populous, got seven M.P.s,[2] while Fife and Renfrew each formed[3] two divisions (East and West), Six single-member counties remained – Argyll, Banff, Dumbarton Dumfries, Forfar and Linlithgow – while six pairs of smaller shires made up six separate constituencies – Berwick and Haddington Caithness and Sutherland, Galloway (that is, Kirkcudbright and Wigtown), Moray and Nairn, Orkney and Shetland, Roxburgh and Selkirk. So far it was plain sailing, but a radical departure from past practice was made with the remaining shires. The new device was to conjoin a small shire with the contiguous portion of a neighbouring and larger shire for the return of one M.P., leaving the rest of the large shire to elect one or more members by itself. Thus the counties of Aberdeen and Kincardine formed three divisions – Eastern Aberdeen, Central Aberdeen, and Kincardine and Western Aberdeen – while Ayr and Bute yielded three others – Bute and Northern Ayr, Kilmarnock, and Southern Ayr. Thus, too, the Act created the two consti-

[1] Scotland's total (74) corresponded to her relative population, but Wales (36) was slightly and Ireland (105) greatly over-represented, so that England (492) was in turn under-represented. Population-quotas for each seat allocated were as follows:–

England,	69,071;
Scotland,	64,317;
Wales,	56,450;
Ireland,	41,733;
United Kingdom,	63,956.

[2] The Lanarkshire divisions were:– Bothwell, Coatbridge, Hamilton, Lanark, Motherwell, Northern and Rutherglen.

[3] That is – and the comment applies equally to other shires – without the burgh constituencies lying within them.

tuencies of Clackmannan and Eastern Stirling, and Western Stirling; two others in Peebles and Southern Midlothian, and Northern Midlothian; and yet two more in Kinross and Western Perth, and the Perth division. Exceptionally, Inverness and Ross and Cromarty were rearranged in three divisions – Inverness, Ross and Cromarty, and the Western Isles (the last belonging geographically to both counties). With much ingenuity, therefore, thirty-eight seats were allotted to the Scottish shires,[1] with a fair approach to the ideal of equal electoral districts, though generous allowance was made for the thinly-peopled 'outer fringes' to the north and west.

Of the burghs, Glasgow, greatly extended in 1912 by the 'annexation' of her suburbs, got fifteen M.P.s,[2] and Edinburgh got five.[3] Dundee remained a two-member constituency, Aberdeen formed two divisions, each returning one M.P., while Paisley, Greenock and Leith each got its own member. Most of the old districts of burghs were merged in the shires, but six new or partly new districts were devised – Ayr, Dumbarton, Dunfermline, Kirkcaldy, Montrose, and Stirling and Falkirk. There were thus thirty-three burgh members, though the distinction between shire and burgh constituencies was no longer a strong one: geographical convenience, rather than any sharp difference in kind, dictated the drawing of the boundaries. Scotland's quota of M.P.s was completed by the combining of the four universities as one constituency, in which the graduates were to elect three members by proportional representation, a form of franchise intended to protect the rights of minorities among the voters.

Just before it was dissolved, the war-time Parliament passed another measure of importance for Scotland, the Education (Scotland) Act, 1918. School boards in parishes and burghs were to be replaced by specially elected education authorities in each of thirty-three shires and of five large towns – Glasgow, Edinburgh, Dundee, Aberdeen and Leith.[4] To these authorities, very much larger, fewer and more remote than the old school boards, went responsibility for all 'public' schools, including the 'transferred' schools of the Episcopalians and Roman

[1] Not until 1948 did a 'mixed-county' constituency, of the kind thus set up in Scotland, appear in England – Rutland and Stamford (Stamford being part of Lincolnshire).

[2] The Glasgow divisions were:– Bridgeton, Camlachie, Cathcart, Central, Gorbals, Govan, Hillhead, Kelvingrove, Maryhill, Partick, Pollok, St Rollox, Shettleston, Springburn and Tradeston.

[3] Edinburgh's divisions were named Central, Eastern, Northern, Southern and Western.

[4] The burgh of Leith was to be 'annexed' by Edinburgh in 1920.

Catholics. The statute[1] marks a long step on the road to centralisation, to the fostering of the larger at the expense of the smaller authorities.

The general election of December 1918 was held too soon after the end of hostilities to be any true test of normal political sentiments. Claiming that an emergency still existed, Lloyd George made an emotional appeal for continued support, to enable his all-party administration to win the peace as it had won the war. As a result, the coalition, comprising almost all the Conservatives, most of the Liberals and a section of the Labour party, outnumbered its opponents by over three to one, and won 60 of the 74 Scottish seats, including no fewer than 32 under a 'Conservative' or 'Unionist' label; of the 14 opposition members in Scotland, 7 were Labour, the other 7 'Asquithian' or independent Liberals.

The years that followed were a time of frustration and disillusion: the League of Nations did not fulfil its promise, the war debts were a crippling burden, agriculture and industry languished, and unemployment rose steeply. The period includes important housing legislation, but little otherwise of political significance for Scotland. One minor reform was enacted in 1919, when the Local Government Board became the Scottish Board of Health, supervising poor law and housing, while the Scottish Secretary was given an assistant minister, the parliamentary under-secretary for health. With the establishment of the Irish Free State in December 1921, the House of Commons, losing its Irish members apart from 13 representatives from Northern Ireland, was reduced from 707 to 615 – a measure which, incidentally, smoothed the path to power for the Conservatives.

The break-up of the coalition brought a real party contest in November 1922. Bonar Law, a Canadian Scot, led the Conservatives to a clear victory, by some 87 seats, over all his opponents, who now included more Socialists than Liberals. In Scotland, however, the Conservatives won only 15 seats and took third place. The 28 Liberals were equally divided between the 'national' (Lloyd Georgite) and 'independent' (Asquithian) wings. Labour held 30 seats, 10 of them in Glasgow, and advanced to first place; Motherwell actually returned a Communist (who kept his seat for only one year). In December 1923 Stanley Baldwin, having succeeded Bonar Law as premier, sought, but failed to obtain, popular approval of a policy of protection in place of free trade. Scotland again gave the preference to Labour, with 35

[1] For further comments upon its terms, see *infra*, p. 310.

seats[1] against 23 for the Liberals and 16 for the Tories, and the result of the election at large was a stalemate, for 258 Conservatives, 192 Labour members and 159 Liberals were returned; with some misgivings, the third party supported the second, and Ramsay MacDonald took 'office without power' as Labour's first premier. The Liberals – including 'moderates' who favoured the Tories and 'radicals' who leaned to Labour – held the balance of power in a delicate situation. Their dilemma sustained neither their dignity nor their unity, and, inevitably, further massive defections, both to right and to left, weakened the party in Scotland as in England and Wales.

The withdrawal of the Liberals' wavering support before long drove MacDonald to the polls, and the general election of October 1924 cleared the air after a confused and unsatisfactory period of transition. The result showed that, in a remarkably short space of time, politics had assumed a new posture. The Conservatives, with 416 out of the 615 M.P.s, came back to power with a very wide margin. That Scotland still stood, as in Victorian times, to the 'left' of England is suggested by the fact that the Tory advantage north of the Tweed was as narrow as it could be: that party carried 38 Scottish seats, leaving the Socialists, now the main opposition, victorious in 27. The reduction of the Liberal quota to 9 (out of 41 for the entire United Kingdom) suggests the drastic 'squeeze-out' of the centre party: never had Scotland returned so few Liberals, although the future was to bring yet more dismal records.

Economic dislocation and labour unrest reached their climax in May 1926 with a general strike, called in support of the coal miners, then in the midst of a seven months' stoppage. One of the very rare attempts by manual workers to secure a political objective by direct industrial action, the strike was yet conducted with restraint on both sides: riotous behaviour and police intervention were infrequent. The general council of the Scottish Trades Union Congress guided the strikers, while food and fuel supplies were managed by the Scottish Emergency Organisation, under the lord advocate. Though basic industry was completely halted, volunteer labour brought out 'skeleton' newspapers and ran limited transport services. The leaders of the strike faced by widespread hostility, called it off on the ninth day (12 May).

[1] Scotland's strong support of Labour was rewarded by the Cabinet appointments: MacDonald, himself a Scot, had four others among his senior colleagues – Lord Haldane as lord chancellor, Arthur Henderson as home secretary, William Adamson as Scottish secretary, and John Wheatley as minister of health.

Under the Baldwin administration, the Scottish Secretary was advanced in dignity (and in salary) by the elevation of his post to a Secretaryship of State (1926). In the same year a new Court of Criminal Appeal, comprising three judges, was empowered to hear appeals from the High Court of Justiciary (that is, from single judges) or from the sheriff court. The Reorganisation of Offices Act, 1928, changed the Scottish Board of Health into a Department of Health, the Board of Agriculture into another Department, and the Prison Commissioners into a third; these three 'departments', unlike the semi-independent *ad hoc* 'boards' of the nineteenth century, were staffed by civil servants working directly under a minister responsible to Parliament. In that year, too, as we have seen, the Equal Franchise Act gave women, like men, the vote from twenty-one, and this raised the total of Scottish electors to over 3,000,000.

Among the last group of statutes passed during the Baldwin ministry (May 1929) was one sweeping measure, the Local Government (Scotland) Act. The parish councils, district boards of control and standing joint committees, all dating from Victorian times, were abolished, along with the lately instituted education authorities. All powers, nicely adjusted to the rank and importance of each authority, were now to go to the county councils, town councils and district councils; for this purpose, each burgh was classified as a 'county of a city' (Glasgow, Edinburgh, Dundee and Aberdeen), or a 'large burgh' (with approximately 20,000 or more inhabitants[1]), or a 'small burgh' (the remaining 171 burghs[2]). Education was reserved for the thirty-one county councils[3] and the four city corporations, in each case to be administered by a 'standing' committee of councillors and co-opted members. Police power was entrusted to the counties and cities, and to such of the large burghs as had 50,000 inhabitants or more,[4] or had a police force in being at the passing of the Act.[5] The other major services, like public health and public assistance (the old poor relief), went to the large burghs, leaving to the small burghs one very important branch (housing), besides such local functions as lighting, cleansing

[1] But Arbroath, just under that figure, was included. There were (and in 1960 still are) twenty large burghs in Scotland.

[2] The total was increased to 174 by the addition of Pitlochry (1947), Stevenston (1952) and Bearsden (1958).

[3] Of the thirty-three counties, Perth was united with Kinross, and Moray with Nairn, for all major branches of administration.

[4] Only Paisley, Greenock, and Motherwell and Wishaw had.

[5] Clydebank, Falkirk, Port Glasgow and Rutherglen had none; i.e. they were already merged in their shires for police purposes.

and drainage. Some of the work hitherto done by the parish councils passed to the district councils,[1] which were, however, hampered by a rating power limited to 1s. in the £. Finally, earlier Treasury 'grants-in-aid' were consolidated in a new *bloc* grant, adjusted to compensate the local authorities for the loss of revenue incurred through the 'de-rating' of farms, factories, mills and railways, and this was to be distributed among the councils according to their estimated needs. Ingeniously drawn up, the Act is open to the objection that its abolition of the small and intimate, if 'amateurish', parish councils, on top of the disappearance of the school boards in 1918, deprived the elector, and in particular the country-dweller, of any chance of familiarity with the persons placed in authority over him: central direction counted for more and more, local initiative for less and less.

Meanwhile, Scottish home rule had reasserted itself as a live issue. Bills had come before Parliament between 1919 and 1927, only to be shelved, and the Scots Liberals had adopted, from 1924, a federal plan, whereby Scotland, retaining her representatives at Westminster, would elect a Scottish legislature for internal affairs. Official indifference towards all such schemes bred more extreme views and (from 1927) demands for independence.[2] Concurrently, a number of writers became interested in a cultural revival, but the unrest was far from being merely academic: concern with Scotland's economic plight added to the political discontents. In 1928, therefore, the Scottish Nationalist party was founded by R. B. Cunninghame Graham, Mr R. E. Muirhead and Mr J. M. MacCormick. Stressing Scottish grievances in finance and legislation, it attracted some public sympathy and won much attention from the press.

The general election of May 1929 returned Labour, with 289 seats out of 615, as the largest party, though still without a clear majority. Once again, it did better in Scotland, with 38 of the 74 divisions: making a clean sweep of all the seats in Lanarkshire, Dunbartonshire and Stirlingshire, it held a solid band stretching from Southern Ayrshire to the Kirkcaldy burghs. The Conservatives, strong in the farming counties and the residential areas, even in their hour of defeat retained

[1] The district usually included a number of neighbouring parishes, and the county council could delegate to the district council functions in addition to its statutory duties.

[2] See in particular two little books published in that year: *Albyn*, in which C. M. Grieve argued that the English union was reducing Scotland to a mere province, and *Caledonia*, in which G. M. Thomson saw the Irish as the chief menace to national well-being and self-respect.

22 constituencies, and 14 Liberals were returned, mainly from the Highlands, the south-west and a few burghs (Greenock, Leith and Montrose). Ramsay MacDonald's second administration ran into trouble on both flanks: Liberal support was hesitant, and the militant socialists denounced his government's timidity. With the beginning of the 'great depression' in the summer of 1931, the threat of a 'flight from the pound', insolvency and mass unemployment led the three main parties to form a 'National' government under MacDonald as premier. Supported by nearly all the Conservatives, a majority of the Liberals and a small Labour group, the new ministry went to the country, with only a few independent Liberals and the rank and file of the Labour party in opposition.

The result of the general election (October 1931) was the greatest triumph in British political history. The National government won 553 seats, losing 52 to Labour and 6 to independent Liberals. On this occasion the Scottish figures differed little from the English[1]: 67 government supporters were elected, comprising 50 Conservatives, 16 National Liberals and one National Labour (at Kilmarnock). Labour retained only 7 seats – 5 in Glasgow, Hamilton and the Dumbarton burghs – and Liberal independency had almost disappeared, while the few Communist and Scottish Nationalist candidates also fared badly.[2] This one-sided contest inaugurated a long period of 'National' rule, in which the ministry, like the war-time coalition, became more and more Conservative in fact, despite its label and the original 'radicalism' of its leader. Its bold and novel measures for overcoming the economic crisis included the abandonment of free trade in favour of full protection (1932); the establishment of the Unemployment Assistance Board and the transfer to it of duties hitherto discharged locally (1934); and Exchequer grants to improve and rehabilitate certain 'depressed' or 'special' areas – among them central Scotland (1934). If prosperity was slow to appear, something like stability had been reached by 1935.

The political situation was meanwhile highly confused. The hapless Liberals had to choose between a protectionist government and its socialist critics. Sir John Simon with one group adhered to the administration, Sir Herbert Samuel with another joined the opposi-

[1] The government failed to carry Wales – but that has long been a normal experience for an administration of 'the right'.

[2] Earlier in 1931, however, standing as a Scottish Nationalist, Mr (later Sir) Compton Mackenzie had been elected rector of Glasgow University – a post with something of a Conservative tradition.

tion, and the ordinary citizen was bewildered by the absurd fission of the once-great party into 'National Liberals' and 'Liberal Nationals'. On the extreme left, the Independent Labour party, led by James Maxton, member for Bridgeton (Glasgow), rebuked with fine impartiality both their late colleagues of the Labour movement and their traditional foes, the Tories. That socialism, weak at Westminster, still had strong roots in the country was shown by the municipal elections: Labour captured control of Glasgow, Greenock and Dunfermline in 1933, of Motherwell and Wishaw, and of Port Glasgow, in 1934. The moderate home-rulers of a new 'Scottish party' (1932) joined the earlier Nationalists to form a broader Scottish National party in 1934; their contention that Scotland was over-taxed and under-paid by the joint Exchequer[1] was a good slogan to rouse discontented patriots.

The National government, now predominantly Conservative, fought the election of November 1935 under Baldwin as premier. Its margin of 247 seats (431-184), though much less than in 1931, was still exceptionally wide, but Scotland's traditional 'bias to the left' showed itself again in the return of a relatively stronger opposition. Out of 46 government M.P.s, 37 were Conservatives, 8 were National Liberals, and one was National Labour; on the other side were 20 Labour members,[2] 4 Glasgow adherents of the I.L.P., 3 Liberals (from Caithness and Sutherland, Dundee and Paisley) and one Communist (from West Fife). The Scottish Nationalists did not make much impression, polling under 30,000 votes in eight constituencies.

The Parliament thus elected was to remain in being for nearly ten years – a record for modern times – and to see the war clouds gather and burst. For the second time, 'the lights of Europe went out' one by one before the explosive force of military aggression – in the Italo-Abyssinian war, the Spanish civil war, the remilitarisation of the Rhineland, and the incorporation of Austria and Czechoslovakia in Hitler's Germany. From 1936 rearmament became the order of the day – incidentally assisting the country's economic recovery – and conscription was adopted early in 1939 by Neville Chamberlain, who had succeeded to the premiership in 1937. All doubts were settled by the German attack on Poland (1 September 1939), and the nation

[1] The figures of national revenue and expenditure show the opposite to have been true: Scotland was, and was bound to be, under-taxed and over-reimbursed. See *infra*, pp. 297-8.

[2] Including Mr Malcolm Macmillan, fresh from a new conquest in the Western Isles.

again, as it had done twenty-five years before, devoted all its ingenuity, its fortitude and its treasure to the winning of a world war.

The issue of peace or war dominated the political scene in the years 1935-39, and yet some of the legislation of the time has its place in the record of social and constitutional progress. Unemployment insurance, protecting the industrial worker against adversity, was extended in 1936 to the farm labourer, and contributory pension rights were opened up to 'black-coated' workers (with salaries below £400 a year) in 1938. As another step towards centralisation, the 'trunk' or 'through' roads were transferred from county councils to the Ministry of Transport in 1936. In Scottish affairs the government, though firmly opposed to home rule principles, hearkened to criticisms of 'remote control' and 'London bureaucracy' by beginning the transfer to Edinburgh, in 1935, of the Scottish Office and the Scottish Education Department. In 1939, too, a second Reorganisation of Offices Act completed the reforms begun in 1928. The Scottish Home Department, a new creation, concerned itself with police, fire services and other matters of local administration, and absorbed the older Fishery Board and Prisons Department. To the Department of Health were annexed the Registrar General's branch and the General Board of Control (for lunacy). These two departments, along with the Scottish Education Department and the Department of Agriculture, formed the four divisions of the Scottish Office, located in St Andrew's House, Edinburgh, and answerable to the Secretary of State. Finally, one aspect of Scots law was modernised in 1938, when five grounds, new or modified, were laid down for divorce,[1] a subject that had stood almost unaltered since the Reformation epoch.

The last four years of peace saw the government's inflated majority slightly reduced through by-election losses. In Scotland Labour won Greenock from the Liberal Nationals and Dunbartonshire from the Conservatives, both in 1936; these changes gave the opposition parties a total of 30 members, against 44 for the government. The municipal elections showed a similar trend. Labour retained Glasgow, held Dundee briefly (1936-37), and, having lost Greenock in 1936, regained it in 1938.

Scottish political life had been transformed during the inter-war period. The Liberal party was a shadow of its former self; many thousands had drifted away to right or to left, leaving groups of nominal

[1] These were desertion (for three years instead of four), adultery, cruelty, habitual drunkenness and insanity.

Liberals as junior and dependent allies of the Tories, and only a few 'pockets' of sturdy radicals, carrying on the fight under their own banners in the far north and in some of the burgh seats. Labour had supplanted them throughout the central industrial belt, with unbroken records from 1918, for example, in Gorbals, Govan and Hamilton. The Conservatives, however, displacing the Liberals as anti-socialist candidates, were firmly entrenched in such residential urban divisions as Hillhead, Pollok and Southern Edinburgh, and also in the better farming and 'resort' areas, like Bute and Northern Ayrshire, Moray and Nairn, or Perth. Already by 1939, therefore, some fifty of the Scottish seats, almost equally divided between Tories and Socialists, had developed new but fixed party loyalties of their own.

The second World War, beginning on 3 September 1939 and lasting longer than the first, produced nothing like the trench warfare and costly attacks of the earlier conflict, so that, though the nation was as fully committed to the total war effort, the casualties suffered by Britain were fortunately much lighter. Scotland supplied 446,000 men for the armed forces, besides 29,000 in the equally hazardous service of the merchant navy, and 69,000 women in the branches open to them; in the two former groups, some 34,000 men were killed, while 6,000 civilians lost their lives, mainly in air attacks. The bravery and endurance that had distinguished the Scottish fighting units in the past were again shown in France, the Low Countries and Germany, in Greece, North Africa and Italy, in Malaya, Burma and the Far East. Outstanding among the Scots in high places was Sir Charles (later Lord) Cunningham, commander-in-chief of the Mediterranean fleet during the critical years 1939-42, and the vanquisher of the Italian navy at the battle of Cape Matapan in March 1941. For long, however, the news seemed to be all bad, and some of the defeats and reverses came sharply home to Scotland: the submarine attack on Scapa Flow, in the Orkneys, which resulted in the sinking of the battleship *Royal Oak* (14 October 1939); the encirclement and capture, despite its heroic resistance, of the famous 51st (Highland) Division at St Valéry-en-Caux (12 June 1940); and the devastating 'blitz' on Clydebank and the lower Clyde (13-14 March 1941). When victory, from being a distant dream, became a reality on 8 May 1945 (against Germany) and on 15 August of the same year (against Japan), the nation emerged from the shadows of danger and austerity with sober relief and thankfulness.

Partisan politics were suspended for the duration of the conflict. Before the end of September 1939, the three principal parties had agreed not to contest by-elections and to allow the 'sitting' party to supply the candidate for a casual vacancy. All local government elections were dispensed with by an Act of October 1939. And, at the nation's 'darkest hour' (May 1940), when Neville Chamberlain gave way to the great war leader, Mr (later Sir) Winston Churchill, the nation rallied and the parties closed their ranks, so that the administration, including all the chief Labour and Liberal politicians, became 'National' in fact as in name.

The electoral truce was faithfully observed by the main parties, but opposition came from various unofficial and independent candidates, and only three of the fifteen war-time by-elections were uncontested. The support accorded to minority groups suggests some local dislike of the parties' pact. In 1940, for example, a Scottish Nationalist polled over half as many votes as the Conservative in Tory Argyll. In 1943, again, the electors of Northern Midlothian returned a Conservative with a majority of only 869 over a candidate belonging to 'Common Wealth', a short-lived, 'splinter' group of the left. In 1944 the socialist stronghold of Kirkcaldy recorded a Labour margin of no more than 1,647 over a Scottish Nationalist. Restiveness boiled over into effective revolt in April 1945, when two government seats were lost: Sir John (later Lord) Boyd Orr, as an independent, displaced a Liberal National in the Scottish Universities, and Dr Robert McIntyre won a unique victory for the Scottish Nationalists by defeating Labour at Motherwell.

Some of the war-time legislation had lasting significance. The government took over the main railways from 1 January 1942, and all mining royalties (the coal companies' payments to land-owners) from 1 July of the same year: each measure can be regarded as a prelude to the full nationalisation that was to follow the war. An Act of 1943 authorised the North of Scotland Hydro-Electric Board to produce and distribute current from Highland water-power, and also required the board to promote the economic and social betterment of the inhabitants of that area. An Act of 1944 raised the school-leaving age in England to fifteen, and provided for 'further education' beyond that age; a similar Scottish statute was passed in 1945, just before the dissolution of Parliament.[1] It was now recognised that Parliament, with its electorates based on the census of 1911, was badly in need of full reform, but this task, it was thought, must await the return of peace. As a temporary measure, the number of M.P.s was raised from

[1] This statute, before it could take effect, was to be superseded by another with similar aims but in ampler terms, Labour's Education (Scotland) Act, 1946.

615 to 640, the additional seats going to England and mostly to the Greater London area, where vast new concentrations of population had developed. (These provisional arrangements, as it turned out, applied only to the general election of 1945, for thorough reform came in 1948.)

Of all the war-time plans and hopes, the Beveridge report, published on 1 December 1942, had the deepest impact on public opinion. This document recommended a comprehensive, contributory, national health service, affording full medical, surgical and dental care for men, women and children, as well as unemployment insurance, national assistance, workmen's compensation and children's allowances. Social insurance on this ample scale, banishing for ever the spectres of want, poverty and suffering through sickness or disablement, was deemed essential for the nation's well-being. There is no doubt that the noble ideals of the report impressed the mass of the citizens as worthy aims for a modern democracy. Capturing the popular imagination, they served as a touchstone for political rectitude and sincerity, a blue-print for the welfare state that would make the war worth winning.

CHAPTER XXV

'Too Many Eggs in One Basket'

THE NATURE and capacities of the Scottish economy seemed to be well suited to serve the needs of the nation in the years 1914-18, and the result was something like boom conditions. Order-books were full, profits were high, employment was assured, and wages rose steadily after a long period of stability. As had been the case during the Napoleonic wars, agriculture was stimulated by the reduction of imports which followed the diversion of shipping and the heavy loss of tonnage through enemy attack. With the main foods rationed, it became patriotic as well as remunerative for the farmer to 'grow more food': early in 1917 he was encouraged by the government to plough up grass-lands, and was guaranteed minimum prices for wheat and oats, the chief food-crops. Difficulties arose from shortages of labour, of feeding-stuffs and of fertilisers, but the Scottish acreage under grain crops increased by 21 per cent between 1916 and 1918.

Again, the textile mills benefited from the army's large demands for uniforms, blankets, shirts and socks, but it was heavy industry, already deeply rooted in the west of Scotland, that positively prospered under war conditions. Coal output had reached its peak of 42½ million tons in 1913; though this total was never again achieved or even approached, the 30 million or more tons that were produced in each of the war years were eagerly taken up by industrial or domestic consumers. Labour was in short supply, for miners were welcomed by the army, which had need of their skill and strength in a war that was for long based on trenches; with 20,000 fewer men at the collieries in 1918 than in 1914, wages rose from 6s. 9d. or 7s. a shift to about 13s. during those four years. Iron, steel and engineering, easily adapted to the new situation, were responsible for the production of many millions of shells, besides guns, cartridges, bombs and other munitions of war. The shipyards had all the work that they could undertake. For a time first place was given to naval construction and the repair of damaged vessels, but the great destruction of merchant shipping, and the discouragement of neutral tonnage, caused a return in some of the yards to merchant shipbuilding. The Clyde output reached a yearly average of just under 500,000 tons, compared with the all-time record of 750,000 tons in 1913.

All this hectic activity, this 'made' work, was in the long run injurious to the Scottish economy. Military and naval orders deflected industry from such profitable branches as locomotives, bridge-building and chemicals. Moreover, sea-borne commerce was confined to immediate needs – foodstuffs, iron ores and military stores – and the exports even of a 'sheltered' port like Glasgow were cut nearly in half. Exports were vital for Scottish industry, but now the exigencies of war obliged our manufacturers to abandon their foreign markets, and virtually invited the overseas buyers of Scottish ships, machinery, coal and textiles to seek other suppliers. Finally, the diversion of manufacturing energies towards weapons of destruction, which had little or no place in peace-time industry, was so costly that it was financed only through borrowing on a large scale: the 1918 budget reached the huge total of over £4,000,000,000, and the expansion of the national debt was bound to impose a very heavy load on posterity. Thus the economy of Scotland, over-concentrated on heavy industry, was driven further out of balance; with its limited range of 'capital goods', it was forced to suspend the commercial contacts which alone could enable it to dispose of those goods. Even before 1914 it had put 'too many eggs in one basket', but now the eggs were so precariously poised as to make breakages inevitable.

The return of peace and the restoration of normal trading conditions – for it was then 'normal' that Britain should practise free trade in a 'protectionist' world – showed up the defects, one by one, that had been intensified by war-time experiences. The hasty removal of controls brought depression first to agriculture. The price of wheat plunged from over 70s. a quarter in the years 1918-20 to 50s. in 1921, and grain acreages dropped sharply. Prices steadied after 1922, but the weekly wages of ploughmen, having soared to 53s. 9d. in 1920, stood at 37s. or 38s. between 1923 and 1932.[1] From 1925 the government fostered the sugar-beet industry; this new branch prospered in England, but scarcely at all in Scotland. The year 1929 brought another slump and another fall in prices – to 34s. for wheat in 1930 and 24s. 8d. in 1931 (the lowest figure as yet for the century). The farmer now stood on the brink of despair. The numbers engaged in

[1] The figures include estimates of the worth of payments in kind. For these and some other statistics that follow, see A. K. Cairncross (ed.), *The Scottish Economy* (1954).

agriculture had diminished from 183,000 in 1921 to 177,000 in 1931, and it is clear that a steeper decline would have taken place had urban industry been more attractive to the dissatisfied farm labourer. As for tillage, the war-time gains had been wiped out, and the acreage under crops and rotation grass was 7·4 per cent less than in 1914. The spread of mechanisation over the same period is reflected in the reduction in the number of horses from 209,000 to 150,000; cattle had meanwhile increased from 1,215,000 to nearly 1,300,000, and sheep from 7,000,000 to 7,800,000. Cropping was becoming ever less profitable.

Industry had its fluctuations, but times were mostly hard. Coal output stood at 31½ million tons in 1920, when miners' wages were 17s. 8d. a shift, but the following year brought a three-month stoppage, with the workers in bitter mood over the failure to nationalise the collieries. From 1922 part of the former export trade in coal was recovered, and the output in 1923 (38½ million tons) was the highest of the inter-war period. Wages, however, continued to fall – to 10s. 10d. a shift in 1924, 9s. 3d. in 1928, and 8s. 9d. in 1932 – and it was a seven-month stoppage of work in coal that precipitated the general strike of 1926,[1] which in turn made matters much worse by forcing manufacturers to import foreign coal. Most serious of all blows was the threatened exhaustion of Lanarkshire's rich veins of 'hard splint' coal. The Lanarkshire area,[2] indeed, once the most productive, showed a steady decline in output:–

Year	*Millions of Tons*
1910	23·7
1920	16·9
1930	15·2
1940	13·0

As seams approached the point of being worked out, labour costs rose for diminishing returns. The general decrease in Scottish production was thus most noticeable and most disturbing in Lanarkshire.

Merchant vessels were urgently needed after the war to replace the sinkings, and shipbuilding enjoyed a minor boom in 1919 and 1920, when the Clyde output reached the high level of 650,000 tons a year. By 1921, however, the position was difficult for all the metal industries:

[1] See *supra*, p. 283.

[2] In terms of coal production, this area included neighbouring parts of West Lothian, Stirlingshire and Dunbartonshire.

the number of furnaces in blast (which had stood at eighty-five at the war-time peak) dropped to forty, and unemployment reached the alarming rate of one in five of all the insured workers. From the mid-1920s every branch of heavy industry suffered from uncertain coal supplies, labour unrest, unsaleable surplus stocks and severe foreign competition. With imports underselling domestic manufactures, idleness and poverty stalked the streets of places like Motherwell, Coatbridge, Falkirk and Clydebank. The closing years of the decade were lit by one ray of hope: the American passion for ocean travel caused a brisk demand for new ships, and the annual output of the Clyde averaged 567,000 tons in 1928-30. Decline then set in again, and worse was to follow. Textiles, too, suffered grievously, for the mills could not produce articles to compete in price with the linens of Italy and Czechoslovakia, or with Japanese cotton goods, or with the Indian jute that meant stagnant trade and unemployment for Dundee.

The industrial statistics in the census of 1931 show the drift of workers away from the basic and traditional occupations. The two groups of 'mining and quarrying' and 'the manufacture of metals and machines' are roughly equivalent to 'heavy industry'; they employed 549,000 persons in 1921, but only 427,000 in 1931 – a decrease of 22·2 per cent. The branches with the sharpest declines were as follows:–

	Persons employed	*(thousands)*	*Percentage*
	In 1921	*In 1931*	*Decrease*
Coal mining	163	133	18·7
Iron smelting, etc.	42	28	33·4
Iron founding, etc.	54	43	21·3
General engineering	91	65	28·4
Shipbuilding	124	78	37·1

Among textiles the hardest hit was cotton, with a fall from 25,000 to fewer than 20,000 (21·2 per cent), while the labour force in woollens went down from 22,400 to 20,400 (8·7 per cent).

It was most unfortunate that the newer and lighter industries, whose growth might have compensated for these losses, failed at this time to take firm root in Scotland. Scottish firms, like Argyll, Beardmore, Arrol Johnston and Halley, had been among the pioneers of the motor car, producing vehicles of quality and renown, but all of them were victims of the trade recession. By the early 1930s only one motor company, the Albion, remained in Scotland, for the industry had by then gravitated to the English Midlands.[1] Similarly, Scotland's share in the making of aircraft, of musical instruments and of wireless apparatus was very small. The group of 'electrical engineering and manufactures' employed 9,500 persons in 1921, and 10,400 in 1931: this increase of only 9·1 per cent, at a time of major developments in the use of electricity, was another indication of failure to seize the opportunities of the new age.

The American stock-market collapse of October 1929 had a disturbing effect throughout the world, and led eventually, in 1931, to the greatest depression of modern times. Every branch of the Scottish economy, already badly shaken, experienced a sharp down-turn of fortune. Wheat dropped again, from 24s. 8d. in 1931 to 20s. 6d. at the end of 1933. The acreage under oats amounted to 860,000 in 1933, compared with 1,240,000 in 1918. Coal output sagged to 31,700,000 tons in 1930, and to 29,000,000 in 1931, which was (apart from the great strike-years of 1921 and 1926) the lowest figure so far for the century. Steel imports exceeded exports in 1931, and at one point in that bleak year only one furnace was in blast. Equally disastrous was the plight of shipbuilding: the Clyde output was 153,000 tons in 1931, 67,000 in 1932, and 56,000 (out of 74,000 for all Scotland) in 1933. A gaunt symbol of distress was the hulk of the great new Cunarder lying at Clydebank, with work suspended at the end of 1931 for lack of finance. Over a quarter of the insured workers were unemployed in the years 1931-33, and late in 1933 the total reached 407,000, or more than 30 per cent; in a town like Coatbridge, dependent on the iron industry, fully half the workers were idle. As recently as 1928 some 63,000 had been engaged in the Clyde area in shipbuilding and marine engineering; five years later the number had fallen to 48,000, but even of this reduced total nearly 65 per cent (31,000) were unemployed.

The most drastic of the National government's remedies for creeping economic paralysis was the abandonment, after eighty-six years, of free trade: in pursuance of a policy agreed with the dominions at the Ottawa Imperial Conference of 1932, full protection was adopted. Between 1932 and 1937 a system of import-controls and subsidies guaranteed the farmer a fair price for his wheat, oats and barley, beef, mutton and bacon. Iron and steel became liable to high import-

[1] Among the assets of the Midland firms was much experience with the kind of light castings needed for car construction, whereas Scottish industry was used to heavy castings.

duties, textile and other manufactures to generally lower tariffs, but many foodstuffs and raw materials were still to be admitted duty-free.

Among other anti-depression measures of the time, milk marketing boards were set up in Scotland and England, to ensure the orderly disposal of milk supplies and dairy produce; and similar schemes were evolved for pigs, bacon and potatoes. Work was resumed in 1934 on Clydebank's great ship, which, as the *Queen Mary*, was to give outstanding service in peace and war for a quarter of a century. With the foundation of the Herring Industry Board in 1935, a struggling and obsolescent branch of the fisheries got the promise of Treasury assistance towards its revival and modernisation. Endeavours were made (again with the help of a government grant) to induce new industries to settle in the 'distressed', 'special', or 'development' areas (including central Scotland), where unemployment was most severe. This line of attack on the problem began to yield good results with the establishment of industrial estates on selected sites within the distressed areas, affording factories to let, and roads, power, water and drainage services. The first of these estates in Scotland was opened at Hillington, on the south-western confines of Glasgow, in 1937, and others followed in 1939 in north Lanarkshire – Carfin, Chapelhall and Larkhall – where the need for rehabilitation was acute. From these measures, and also from the rearmament orders that began in 1936, a slow but steady improvement resulted, and the heavy burden of unemployment was appreciably lightened.

The figures for the national income illustrate economic conditions during the depression. It is estimated that the annual income *per capita* of the Scottish population was £83 in 1925; by 1932 it had dropped to £67, but it recovered to £83 in 1936 and reached £97 in 1939. Another sidelight on this subject is provided by the official returns on national revenue and expenditure. Under the 'Goschen formula' of 1888,[1] the just contribution of Scotland to the United Kingdom revenue had been fixed at 11 per cent, that of England and Wales at 80 per cent, and that of Ireland at 9 per cent; ideally, each part should draw the same proportion of 'local expenditure', so that the 'imperial' expenses would be shared according to means. In fact, Ireland's revenue consistently fell short of its quota, and finally dropped below 5 per cent, while its 'local expenditure' remained high, but Scottish revenue and expenditure were remarkably stable from 1891 to 1922, seldom varying from 11 per cent by as much as one per cent.

[1] Cf. *supra*, p. 217.

Discontinued after the Irish treaty of 1921, the Treasury returns (applicable now only to Scotland and to England and Wales) were resumed for 1931-32 and 1934-35. In the first of these years Scottish revenue was £67½ million, against £726½ million for England and Wales, and, as Scotland's 'local expenditure' exceeded £42 million, her contribution, by way of 'imperial balance', was just over £25 million; the record for 1934-35 was essentially similar:–

National Revenue and Expenditure (percentages)

	1931-32		*1934-35*	
	Scotland	*England and Wales*	*Scotland*	*England and Wales*
Revenue	8·50	91·50	8·63	91·37
'Local Expenditure'	12·20	87·80	12·39	87·61
'Imperial Balances'	5·62	94·38	4·96	95·04

At this time, therefore, Scotland, with about 10·8 per cent of the total population, was clearly not 'paying her way', as she had done, often with something to spare, down to 1922. Economic adversity had diminished her capacity to pay income tax, customs and excise, while raising her claims for unemployment relief, public assistance and the social services generally. With nearly one-ninth of the population, she paid little more than one-twelfth of the common revenue, got back one-eighth of the 'local expenditure', and so was able to defray one-twentieth, more or less, of the common burdens of the United Kingdom. The depression had gravely impaired the national solvency.

Certain 'services' (as distinguished from 'industries') were further consolidated in the inter-war period. War-time working under government control had taught the railways the benefits of close integration, and, while the system was returned to private ownership after the end of the war, it was re-grouped in four large companies by the Railways Act, 1921. From 1 January 1923, therefore, the North British and Great North of Scotland railways were merged in the London and North-Eastern group, while the Caledonian, Glasgow and South-Western, and Highland railways formed part of the London, Midland and Scottish group. At about the same time, certain English banks bought up the share capital of some of the Scottish banks, without disturbing their management or administration; thus, the National Bank became an 'affiliate', as it was called, of Lloyds Bank and the British Linen of Barclay's (both in 1919), while the Midland Bank acquired the like control of the Clydesdale (1920) and the North of

Scotland (1923). By way of a minor move in the contrary direction, two small English concerns, Williams, Deacon's Bank and Glyn, Mills and Company, became 'associates' of the Royal Bank of Scotland. Amalgamation was the key-note, too, in such fields as road transport, gas supply, and above all electricity, in which a comprehensive 'national grid' scheme, begun in 1927 and completed in outline in 1933, proposed to raise Britain's annual *per capita* consumption from 110 to 500 units, and to lower the average unit charge from over 2d. to 1d.

By 1939 economic recovery was well on the way. It is true that, as late as December 1939, the unemployed in Scotland still numbered 177,000, or 10·6 per cent of the insured workers; before long, however, this position was rectified, and the 16,000 returned as idle in 1944 represent the truly unemployable. If in some respects the happenings of the years 1939-45 recall those of 1914-18 – the sinkings of merchant ships, the loss of the export trade, food rationing, shortages and the all-pervading austerity – in others the economy rode the storm more safely. Learning from the mistakes of the first war, the government used its resources more intelligently in the second. Moreover, Scottish industry had already undergone its critical ordeal in the early 1930s, and, tempered in the fire of that long agony, it was in better condition to face a major war than it had been in 1914.

Advance preparations for war included the authorisation of the ploughing-up of grass-lands (1938) and the enforcement of conscription (1939). Then, in 1940, farm labourers got a guaranteed weekly wage of 48s. but were forbidden to change their work; in fact, the legal minimum was soon exceeded, and by 1946 wages had risen to 92s. Hill-farming was subsidised from 1941 at a rate of 2s. 6d. for each ewe and £2 for each cow. The farmers themselves, through their agricultural executive committees,[1] undertook the duty of securing proper use of the land. As had happened before, both the acreage under crops and the average yield rose to meet war-time needs: the tillage area amounted in 1943 to 2,121,000 acres, instead of the 1,480,000 of 1939 – an increase of over 43 per cent.[2] In many parts tractors took the place of the vanishing horse,[3] just as the Women's Land

[1] Similar bodies had operated in the first war, but they were much more effective in the second.

[2] On the other hand, though the cattle herds were maintained and even increased (from 1,349,000 head in 1939 to 1,460,000 in 1945), livestock numbers generally fell off because of the scarcity of feed: sheep, just over eight million in 1939, were below seven million from 1941 onwards, and both pigs and poultry were sharply reduced

[3] The total number of horses stood at 142,000 in 1939, and 117,000 in 1945.

Army filled the gaps in the labour force, while keen amateurs raised vegetables on their 'allotments'. Perhaps the most remarkable achievement, in a time of acute transport difficulties, was the moving of 470,000 tons of seed-potatoes, by land and sea, from the Scottish to the English farms during the winter of 1943-44.

Coal output, falling short of 30 million tons in 1940, was reduced in the course of the war to about three-quarters of that figure; but, as in the earlier struggle, miners' wages rose – from an average of 12s. 7d. a shift in 1940 to 20s. 7d. in 1944. For machinery, ships, textiles, linoleum and other products, the official policy ('concentration of industry') left one firm in each group to use the available labour and materials for the war effort, while other firms (with safeguards for commercial 'good-will') were put, in effect, on a 'care-and-maintenance' basis. Exports were cut to about one-tenth of the pre-war total, and imports, limited to essential foodstuffs and war materials, amounted to less than half. The Clyde ports and anchorages, less vulnerable than most, had a big share of the sea-borne traffic that still moved. Some inflation was inevitable, but it was kept within bounds by strict controls. The annual income *per capita* for Scotland was £166 in 1945, that is, exactly double the figure for 1925 and for 1936; but, if allowance is made for the change in money-values, the real increase was about 50 per cent. On the whole, the economy emerged from the struggle in 1945 in tolerably good shape, and basically sounder than had been the case in 1918.

In the period of the two wars the increase of population was less marked than formerly, and one decade, indeed (1921-31), showed a positive decrease:–

Population of Scotland

Year	*Total*	*Intercensal Change* (%)
1911	4,760,904	(+6·5)
1921	4,882,497	+2·6
1931	4,842,980	−0·8
1939[1]	5,006,689	+3·4

Among the most noteworthy instances of urban increase at this time were these[2]:–

[1] The figures, here and later, for 1939 are taken from the Registrar-General's estimates. No census was held in 1941, nor indeed before 1951, and the war-time estimates are of little comparative value because of absences on military service, the evacuation of civilians, and the presence of large numbers of aliens in certain parts. Hence the importance of the 1939 figures: they have a real 'scarcity value'.

[2] In this and the following table, the 1921 census is disregarded, since, being

Urban Population (in thousands)

	1911	*1931*	*1939*
Glasgow	784	1,088	1,128
Edinburgh	320	439	472
Clydebank	37·5	47·0	48·1
Grangemouth	10·2	11·8	14·0
Prestwick	4·9	8·5	9·9

The two chief cities had grown mainly by outward expansion: in 1912 Glasgow had 'annexed' Govan, then the fifth largest burgh in Scotland, and Partick, the ninth, while in 1920 Edinburgh had absorbed Leith, the seventh in population. Of the others, Clydebank, in addition to its shipbuilding, had some important industries, such as the manufacture of sewing-machines; Grangemouth throve as an oil port and a centre for chemicals; and Prestwick, besides being a favoured seaside and golfing resort, had, from 1935, an air-port that was nearly fog-free and admirably sited for the Transatlantic air service.

The nineteenth-century tendency for the central industrial counties to gain inhabitants, while the northern and highland counties lost them, still operated in the twentieth century:–

Population of Counties (in thousands)

	1911	*1931*	*1939*
Ayr	268	285	297
Dunbarton[1]	140	148	157
Fife	268	276	285
Stirling	161	166	174
. . .	. . .	. . .	. . .
Banff	61	55	53
Ross and Cromarty	77	63	62
Sutherland	20	16	15
Zetland	28	21	20

Another continuing trend at this time was the decline in both the birth-rate and the death-rate. The birth-rate, having been 26·1 per thousand inhabitants in 1914, stood between 17 and 18 on the eve of

taken on 19 June, when holidays had begun, it distorted many of the local details, especially by inflating the totals for 'resort' areas, including whole counties, such as Bute.

[1] This form, since 1929 the official spelling for the county, has won gradual if grudging acceptance; the burgh, meanwhile, officially retains 'Dumbarton'. So, too, with whatever reluctance, 'Zetland' must nowadays be preferred to the more usual 'Shetland' as the formal name of the county.

the second World War, and was just under 16·9 in 1945. The general death-rate dropped from 15·5 in 1914 to 13·2 in 1945, but the figures for infant mortality (deaths in the first year to each thousand live births) showed a sharper improvement: in 1916, for the first time, the rate was below 100 (at 97·1), and thereafter, with some fluctuations, it came down to 68·5 in 1939. The population was, therefore, an ageing one: the expectation of life at birth was in 1911 fifty for males, fifty-three for females, but in 1931 the figures were fifty-six and sixty, and they were still rising. Though the higher proportion of the elderly in the population and the correspondingly fewer children made for stability, the excess of births over deaths, left to itself, would have yielded a substantial natural increase. This increase was, however, checked by emigration. During the first half of the twentieth century, the net annual loss by migration averaged 22,010; it was much higher in the 1920s (when it caused an actual reduction in the population) and it levelled off in the 1930s. The contemporary inward movement, if less marked, was still noticeable; from 1921 the English-born (then amounting to 3·9 per cent of all inhabitants) displaced the Irish-born (with 3·3 per cent) as the largest non-native element in the population.

It was in housing, for long the weak link in the chain of social progress, that the big change of the time occurred. In the first World War new housing was negligible and dilapidation continued, so that over-crowding and slum conditions worsened. A royal commission, reporting in 1918, roundly denounced housing conditions alike in the city tenements, the industrial towns, the mining villages and the crofting townships. Between 1920 and 1939, some 250,000 new houses were built, many of them by speculative builders in 'housing schemes', and, while most of these were for sale and so were far beyond the means of the neediest, they afforded indirect relief to the housing situation in general. The improvement may be seen in the reduction of the proportions of the inhabitants of Scotland and of its two worst-housed cities living in one-roomed and two-roomed houses (notoriously the seat of the slum problem):–

Percentages of Population living in Small Houses

	1911			*1931*		
	In One Room	*In Two Rooms*	*Total*	*In One Room*	*In Two Rooms*	*Total*
Scotland	8·7	40·9	49·6	7·1	36·9	44·0
Glasgow	13·8	48·7	62·5	11·0	44·4	55·4
Dundee	9·9	53·1	63·0	8·5	47·7	56·2

There was still a long way to go, but the trend was in the right direction, and the good work was maintained between 1931 and 1939, though the lack of a census in 1941 deprives us of further means of assessing the results within our period. Again, the Housing Act, 1935, gave a legal definition of 'overcrowding', by authorising a rate of two persons to one room, three to two rooms, five to three rooms,[1] and so forth; although this standard was never enforced, it was recommended for the observance of local authorities, landlords and tenants.

Increasing urbanisation, improved health, longer expectation of life, slightly better housing – these are among the precise 'social statistics' of the time. Certain other changes, of equal importance, cannot be exactly measured. In the first place, the two world wars re-shaped the life and outlook of two generations in succession. Shaken out of their accustomed ways, subjected to new experiences and exposed to unimagined dangers, the young men and women could never be the same again: tradition lost much of its force and gave way to excitement and change. Youth took readily to scientific innovations and technical advances: they welcomed mechanical transport, electrical appliances, labour-saving devices and 'mass entertainment'. The steam railway and the electric tramway had been among the marvels of the Victorian epoch, but from 1920 fast road transport supplemented and gradually displaced the older modes of travel. The motor bus, the private car and the bicycle gave all ranks of society a mobility unknown to their grandparents, bringing the amenities of the town within reach of the country-dweller, throwing open the delights of the countryside to the townsfolk, and making it possible for all to engage in either work or play at some distance from home. Shopping excursions and country rambles, tours and picnics, holidays at the seaside, in the mountains, or abroad, came to form part of the pattern of life.

A new world of culture and entertainment opened up to fill the leisure hours of the masses. Museums and libraries, art galleries and theatres, evening classes, lectures and concerts still played their part, but most of them lost ground to the newer forms of instruction and amusement. The cinema, launched before the first World War, spread rapidly from 1918, while wireless sets found favour from the early 1920s. It was inevitable that some activities with a 'Victorian' flavour – the musical 'at home', the whist drive, the prolonged, formal dinner – should fail to charm the restless inter-war generation. Though

[1] Babies under one year were not counted, and any child between one and ten was to be reckoned half a person.

some of the old favourites maintained their appeal – especially the numerous Burns clubs in towns and villages – few people were now prepared to turn out in the evening to support a literary or debating society, an antiquarian or local history club, a philosophical or naturalist group. Yet the countryfolk, perhaps less sophisticated or less spoiled than the town-dwellers, adopted at least two entirely new developments with such enthusiasm as to ensure their success. The first Women's Rural Institute was founded at Longniddry, in East Lothian, in 1917, and by the time of the second World War over a thousand of them were bringing colour, gaiety and self-culture into the lives of the country-women; the year 1923 saw the start of the Young Farmers' Clubs, which similarly enriched the experiences, social as well as professional, of their men-folk.

With the changed attitude to the use of leisure, and the wider social opportunities afforded to all classes, the populace became both more temperate and more law-abiding, as the figures for the chief categories of offences indicate:–

	1913	*1938*
Drunkenness	49,860	17,446
Breach of the peace (petty disturbances)	51,874	22,154
Traffic offences	7,950	48,150

While the decrease in the first two categories suggests the milder manners and better behaviour of the new generation, the steep rise under the third heading reflects the enormous increase in the numbers travelling by road: as one critic put it, 'the vacuum left by the shrinking army of drunks and disorderlies has been partly filled by careless drivers'.[1]

One result of the shortening of the working day was that sport and recreation claimed more of the time of men and women. Town councils and private clubs provided golf courses and bowling greens, tennis courts, putting greens and swimming ponds, while rugby, cricket, hockey and athletics were fostered by schools and universities. Football, however, remained first favourite, by a wide margin, among organised games. In all towns and most villages, junior and juvenile clubs, school and amateur teams ensured at least one afternoon's enjoyable exercise each week for all who had the interest and the aptitude, but it was at the top, among the country's senior clubs, that

[1] Quoted from John Mack, 'Crime', in *The Scottish Economy* (ed. A. K. Cairncross), p. 229.

the 'glamour' of the game was at its strongest. Most of the large burghs had their clubs, each famous enough to draw thousands of spectators every Saturday. A special occasion brought out huge crowds: in April 1937 Hampden park, in Glasgow, contained 149,547 onlookers (a British record) for the game between Scotland and England, while the Scottish Cup final that year, contested by Celtic and Aberdeen, brought 146,433 persons to the same field. Among lesser sports, shinty appealed chiefly to the west Highlanders, salmon and trout fishing, as ever, had its devotees, grouse-shooting, deer-stalking and hunting were necessarily confined to those with wealth and leisure, while curling, skating and ice-hockey tended to move to indoor rinks.

Of the less strenuous forms of relaxation, billiards, badminton, table tennis, chess and draughts all survived from an earlier age, and the newcomers included darts, carpet-bowls and bridge. Above all, the 1920s were 'the Jazz age', when the fox-trot and the tango, the dance hall and the cocktail bar, struck a note of hectic gaiety. Cigarette-smoking and gambling now displaced drunkenness as the targets of the social reformers, and a little later, in the 1930s, many sober citizens were alarmed over the tremendous popularity of the football 'pools'. There was, however, much to be said in favour of the young men and women who grew up in the shadow of the great wars. Fresher and more varied food, together with a high degree of immunity from the infectious diseases that had been so deadly in the past, and a good understanding of hygiene, gave them a superior physique, while, despite their foibles and their restlessness, they were, on the whole, as sensible, as humane and as temperate as any preceding generation.

CHAPTER XXVI

Twentieth-Century Culture

THE REIGN of Edward VII (1901-10), opening on the morrow of the most massive unification ever achieved among Presbyterians, was to close on a prospect of yet wider reunion. In the interim, a sharp lesson was given anent the relations between church and state, as they actually stood in the eyes of the law. The non-uniting minority of the Free Church,[1] strong only among Highlanders and Islesmen, and popularly dubbed 'the Wee Frees', confidently claimed the entire patrimony of the Free Church and entered upon a long and bitter dispute with their late brethren of the majority, who, in their view, had sinfully countenanced 'voluntary' opinions by combining with the U.P. Church, and had therefore forfeited any title to the church property. The 'Wee Free' plea was repelled by the Court of Session, but, on appeal, was – to the chagrin of the majority – upheld by the House of Lords in 1904. The U.F. Church was thus taught that, while it was free to repudiate the 'state connection' of religion and to advocate disestablishment, it remained, as a property-owning corporation, subject to law and the law-courts. In the long run, no harm was done, for the Lords' verdict, if defensible as a point of pure law, was in practice unworkable, so that the matter was compromised by an Act of Parliament of 1905, which equitably divided the disputed property between the U.F. and Free Churches.

Soon a new spirit of accommodation informed the attitudes of the Church of Scotland and the U.F. Church, each of which appointed a committee in 1909 to explore the path to reunion. By the start of the reign of George V (1910-36), the issue of disestablishment had been dismissed, and in 1912 it was agreed to prepare a complete plan of union for presentation to Parliament. The outbreak of war in 1914 interrupted the work, but it was resumed with the return of peace. The mutual solicitude of the negotiating parties, and in particular the readiness of the Church of Scotland to modify its tenets and to yield on details, showed the ardent desire for union.

On one point the U.F. Church was adamant: it required a guarantee of freedom from parliamentary interference on spiritual or ecclesiastical

[1] See *supra*, p. 265.

matters. Accordingly, in 1921, the General Assembly of the Church of Scotland passed declaratory articles affirming its adherence to Reformed principles, asserting its right to legislate (without reference to the civil authority) on doctrine, worship, government and discipline, recognising the mutual obligations of church and state, and avowing the duty of promoting church union. These articles were embodied in the Church of Scotland Act, passed by Parliament in 1921 with a fine regard (not always shown in the past) for Scotland's religious scruples. Again, the U.F. Church (whose ministers had been sustained chiefly by the free-will offerings of its members) looked askance at the financial mainstay of the establishment, the 'teinds': such a compulsory tax on land, enforced by the state for the behoof of the church, was, in its view, an unworthy and unspiritual device. To overcome this objection, the Kirk abandoned the system that had served it for 260 years, and Parliament graciously met its desires.[1] The result was the Church of Scotland (Property and Endowments) Act, 1925, which made elaborate arrangements for the redemption (outright or by instalments) of the teinds, and for the administration of all Church revenues by the General Trustees. With statutory assurance of both the spiritual and the financial independence of the established Church, the U.F. Church had no further reason to hesitate, and the union was consummated in October 1929.

This union, much the greatest in Scottish ecclesiastical history, went far towards healing the breaches of two centuries, for the U.F. Church was the heir of the majority groups of the secessions of 1733, 1761 and 1843. In numbers, the union brought in 759,625 communicants of the Church of Scotland, belonging to 1,457 parish kirks, and, on the other side, over 510,000[2] members of the U.F. Church (which had been organised in 1,441 congregations). The united Church, with 1,284,449 communicants and 2,869 charges, was stronger than it had been at any time since the middle of the eighteenth century: it could now claim the support of 41 per cent of the adult population.

Impressive as it was, the union was not quite complete. A small

[1] The tact and understanding shown by Parliament in its dealings with the Kirk were in striking contrast to its temper towards the Church of England over the 'deposited book' controversy of 1929. Sanction was then sought for a modified prayer-book, desired by most Anglicans but disliked by 'evangelical' or ultra-Protestant M.P.s (including many Scots and Welsh members). Parliament, by rejecting this particular Anglican 'reform', showed its readiness to dictate to the Church of England on a purely ecclesiastical issue.

[2] Of the 538,192 members, only a tiny minority – certainly under 5 per cent – stood aloof from the union.

group within the U.F. Church, cherishing the 'voluntary' principle, continued[1] the name and separate identity of the parent church. Its affinities lying rather with the Congregationalists than with any other Presbyterian body, this sect went its own way.

The united Church had its problems. At the level of higher education and pastoral training, little difficulty was encountered. The three U.F. Church colleges (in Edinburgh, Glasgow and Aberdeen) were amalgamated with the faculties of divinity at the universities, the life-interest of the incumbents of the redundant professorial chairs being safeguarded. Church finance offered more trouble. Ministers' stipends had not greatly advanced since the Disruption: they had been overtaken by teachers' salaries and far surpassed by the earnings in the sister-professions of medicine and law. In 1929 the minimum stood at £300 with a manse,[2] but it was agreed that the sum should be increased to £400. This target was not reached until 1947, by which time the change in money values had made it worth actually less, in spending power, than it had been in 1929.

The root of the difficulty was the superfluity of parochial charges. The reunited Church, as the heir of the three great rival communions of the nineteenth century, had been bequeathed a multitude of churches in towns and villages, many of them erected out of a spirit of emulation rather than in response to real spiritual needs. Competitive church-building had divided communities into antagonistic congregations, provided far too many places of worship, and incidentally cheapened the ministry. Common sense, and the need to conserve the limited man-power and money-power of the Church, now required the elimination of redundant charges. Yet, over-churched in one way, the nation was under-churched in another, for the new suburbs and housing schemes were generally deficient in churches (as they were, indeed, in schools and other centres of communal living). Hence the problem was twofold – to reduce the churches in the older settlements, and to increase them in the newer. Rising costs were the obstacle in the way of the second of these aims, while the first was often impeded by congregational loyalties, for church, manse and minister could not simply be liquidated to ensure a neater organisation. Nevertheless, local arrangements were made when the opportunity arose, especially in a casual vacancy following death or retirement. By 1945, 489 unions

[1] To avoid confusion, the word 'Continuing' was used for a few years in the title of this body: the United Free Church (Continuing).

[2] The figure had been the same in both uniting Churches.

of congregations had been effected, and 37 other congregations had been dissolved, while 56 new churches (or church-halls) had been erected, to give a new total of 2,430 active charges.

For the smaller churches the period 1901-45 was not an eventful one. The Free and Free Presbyterian Churches remained as Highland bulwarks of ultra-Protestant orthodoxy, denouncing such signs of decadence as the popular addiction to drink, gambling and Sabbath-breaking. In the Lowlands, dwindling numbers of Reformed Presbyterians and United Original Seceders were Covenanters of an antique breed. Only the youngest body of Presbyterian dissenters, the U.F. Church, seemed to be holding its own, but the combined followings of all five sects amounted to less than 1·5 per cent of the total population. Rather stronger numerically, and largely drawn from higher strata of society (including English settlers and Scots educated at English schools), the Episcopalians made one change, which brought them yet closer in spirit to the Anglicans: in 1929 they adopted a Book of Common Prayer, which, being based on the prayer-book of 1637, recalled the heyday of episcopacy in Scotland.[1] Meanwhile, the Methodists, the Baptists and also (native to Scotland as was their church) the Congregationalists were sustained by the increasing settlement of English families,[2] and the Roman Catholic Church depended for its massive support, not on its handful of traditional Scottish adherents, or on its converts, but on persons of Irish origin or descent: by 1931 it had 607,000 adherents of all ages, or exactly one-eighth of the population. Thus, the national stature of the Church of Scotland was enhanced by reason of both the narrow appeal of its domestic competitors, and the alien character of its greater rivals.

The educational reforms of the period began with an Act of 1901, which, from 1 January 1902, raised the school-leaving age to fourteen. The age was to be further raised to fifteen under the Education Act, 1918, but 'the appointed day' from which the change was to take place was never named. A fresh attempt to achieve this aim was made in 1936, the date being fixed as 1 September 1939, but, as by a cruel irony that turned out to be the very day of the German attack upon Poland, the change was again postponed. The Education (Scotland) Act, 1945, drawn up by the National government and passed by Parliament just before the dissolution, once more raised the age to fifteen; but that statute was itself superseded by the Labour government's own Act, and the change was in fact to come as one of the post-war reforms.

[1] See *supra*, p. 8. [2] Cf. *supra*, p. 302.

In England the county and county borough had displaced the parish in 1902 as the unit of school administration, but Scotland's parochial tradition was strong enough to survive for a while. In 1908, indeed, the responsibility of the Scottish school boards was enlarged: they were given additional powers to provide school meals, free books and stationery, travelling expenses, medical inspection and continuation classes (beyond the age of fourteen), while a complete, contributory system of superannuation was established for the behoof of teachers.[1] Yet, as time went on, more and more functions (especially in secondary education) passed to the counties rather than the parishes,[2] and the big reform came with the Act of 1918, which, as we have seen,[3] substituted 38 specially elected education authorities (in counties and larger towns) for the 967 school boards. Besides sanctioning the raising of the school-leaving age, the Act transferred to these authorities the Episcopalian and Roman Catholic schools, though appointments to them were to be subject to the approval of the denomination concerned. New or wider powers were also given in relation to nursery schools (for children between two and five), to county libraries (for adults as well as pupils) and to bursaries (for secondary schools, training colleges and universities).

There was regret over the passing of the school boards, which had given faithful service and been reasonably well liked; but the day of the 'big battalions' had come. It was ironical, however, that the newcomers had but a brief life, for the Local Government Act, 1929, transferred all powers in education to thirty-five committees, chosen by county or city councils,[4] with the council members outnumbering the co-opted members. The Scottish system was thus brought into line with that which had prevailed in England since 1902.

The sharp increase in living costs during the first World War necessitated the revision of teachers' salaries (hitherto dependent on school board decisions). After negotiations with the teachers and the authorities, new 'minimum national scales' were adopted in 1919 for men and women teachers of the various categories,[5] and these scales

[1] After some chopping and changing, it was decided in 1926 that teachers should pay 5 per cent of their salary towards their superannuation, and that a like sum should be contributed by the employing authority. (Each contribution was raised to 6 per cent in 1956.)

[2] For the training of teachers, the territorial unit from 1906 was the 'province', or region based on each university centre.

[3] *Supra*, pp. 281-2. [4] Cf. *supra*, p. 284.

[5] Since 1906 three kinds of teachers' certificates, corresponding to their professional qualifications, have been recognised: the general certificate (for primary

held good until the end of the second World War, except that a war bonus was paid to compensate for a further rise in costs after 1939. In 1945 'standard' (instead of 'minimum') scales were laid down, and it was recognised that periodic adjustments should be made after consultation with teachers and educational authorities.

For the universities, again, the period opened with a momentous change. In 1901 the Scoto-American millionaire, Andrew Carnegie (1835-1919), having started his grand plan of establishing 'Carnegie free libraries' in cities and towns, set up the Carnegie Trust for the Universities of Scotland, with an endowment of £2,000,000.[1] This fund helped to encourage research and advanced studies, to expand scientific learning, and to provide playing-fields and residences; above all, it assisted generously with the payment of students' fees. Supplementing the bursaries founded in earlier times, and in turn supplemented by county and town council awards, and by government allowances to ex-servicemen, the Carnegie grants ensured the preservation of the laudable old tradition of the 'open door' for the 'lad o' pairts' from a humble home.

Thus financially sustained, the student-body grew during the first half of the twentieth century. With Glasgow and Edinburgh competing for first place, and St Andrews and Aberdeen rivals at a lower level of numbers, the total rose slowly until the first World War, shot upwards after 1918 to reach a peak about 1930, then levelled off, to decline again in the second World War. The numbers of matriculated students in selected years were as follows:–

Numbers of University Students, 1901-45

Session	*St Andrews*	*Glasgow*	*Aberdeen*	*Edinburgh*	*Total*
1901-02	435	2,052	831	2,872	6,190
1913-14	508	2,916	1,069	3,283	7,776
1921-22	821	4,856	1,600	4,669	11,946
1930-31	930	5,531	1,314	4,437	12,212
1938-39	1,018	4,771	1,258	3,826	10,873
1944-45	1,014	3,562	988	3,294	8,858

There were still many students living in cheap and simple lodgings near the university, but the development of fast local transport (by

teaching and the first three years of secondary courses), the special certificate (for 'Honours' graduates taking special subjects up to university entrance), and the technical certificate, covering art, music, physical education and domestic science, as well as strictly 'technical' subjects.

[1] Similarly endowed, the Carnegie United Kingdom Trust (1916) was founded for 'charitable' purposes in general throughout the British Isles.

train, tram or bus) enabled a higher proportion than formerly to live at home, with the result that, at the worst, higher education might become merely a matter of attendance at lectures and examinations, instead of a whole-time experience in community living. This danger was a major challenge of the new age, baffling to most of the universities (in England as in Scotland), but met at St Andrews, already used to the residential ideal, by a bold policy, vigorously pursued under the principalship of Sir James Irvine (1921-52), whereby most of the women students and many of the men were accommodated in hostels and halls.

The expansion in staff fully kept pace with the increase in student members. In 1901, for example, Glasgow had 31 professors, 33 lecturers and 41 assistants, while in 1945 she had 54 professors, 4 readers, 202 lecturers and 75 assistants; and the record elsewhere was similar. Vast new developments took place in the range of subjects of study. The faculties of arts were widened, especially by the addition of modern languages and of sundry historical, economic and social studies. Specialised branches of medicine got new or fuller recognition – bacteriology, for example, and ophthalmology. But the greatest expansion – a positive burgeoning of new techniques and research projects – came in chemistry and physics, in other sciences, pure and applied, and in engineering: Glasgow, indeed, instituted a new faculty of engineering in 1923. With a multitude of new subjects demanding admission, the curricula for ordinary and honours degrees in arts and sciences were loosened and liberalised,[1] while from 1918 the degree of Ph.D. was available for award in any faculty, normally after three years of full-time research.

Unlike the nineteenth century, this period brought no royal commission to consider university affairs. Such intervention was now deemed unnecessary, since the university courts enjoyed, from 1889, the right (subject to inter-university and other consultations) to initiate legislation by ordinance. New machinery was, however, required to deal with the greatly extended system of government grants. In 1919, therefore, the University Grants Committee came into being, to give expert advice to the Treasury on the allocation of state monies and their distribution among the British universities.

[1] For arts the main change, involving a three-tier system (ordinary, higher and honours), with some opportunity for specialisation, was made in 1908, when also the teaching session was extended to twenty-five weeks by the addition of a short 'summer term'. For science the differentiation between the honours and ordinary B.Sc. degrees came in 1921.

The leaving certificate, awarded by the Scottish Education Department over an ever-widening range of subjects, was still the main avenue of approach from school to university, but from 1918 a conjoint body, the Scottish Universities Entrance Board, laid down minimum requirements and granted (or withheld) 'certificates of fitness', which normally constituted the student's claim for admission. With the populace at large, the universities developed contacts through the adult education courses[1] (of the lecture-and-discussion type) offered by their extra-mural departments: many courses were held in the university, and many of them were conducted by university teachers. At this time, too, centres of specialised higher education grew and flourished – technical colleges, training colleges for teachers, agricultural and commercial colleges, colleges of art and music, of domestic science and physical education.

Twentieth-century education in all its branches, while becoming more formal, more subject to regulation, with the passage of time, retained many pristine virtues – its democratic character, its availability to the poor but talented scholar, its insistence on a sound ground-work of general knowledge. If the better English schools, with their intensive studies in the sixth form, were now creeping ahead of even the best in Scotland,[2] if Oxford and Cambridge still tended to draw off the most brilliant and ambitious students, it remained true that, over the whole field of school and college, as an integral part of national culture, Scotland still held a real, though narrowing, lead.

In arts and letters the period 1901-45 had its achievements and its disappointments; most notable among the former were the many collective efforts of the time to stimulate cultural activities. Already in the old century, *An Comunn Gaidhealach* had been founded for the furthering of Gaelic language and literature, art and music (1891), and the annual *Mod* now became the centre and climax of keen but friendly rivalry in piping, singing and recitation. In a field of scholarship which had always been congenial to the nation, the Scottish History Society (celebrating its jubilee in 1936) continued to issue works of enduring worth, while the *Scottish Historical Review* had a quarter-

[1] The modern movement – which had its forerunner in the mechanics' institutes of the nineteenth century (see *supra*, p. 165) – owed its rise in 1911 largely to the vigour and drive of the Workers' Educational Association.

[2] Yet, to balance England's advantage as regards 'study in depth' and early specialisation, it should be remembered that Scotland offered (in the final years of school and also in the university courses) a broader sweep of education than that which was available at the corresponding stages in England.

century of fruitful labours (1903-28).[1] Musical and dramatic interests were promoted by the formation of the Glasgow Orpheus Choir (1905) and of the Scottish National Players (1921), while the popular response to the annual one-act play festival started by the Scottish Community Drama Association in 1927 showed that the amateur theatre had a strong appeal for all classes throughout the land. The year 1936 saw the establishment of the Saltire Society, with branches in the main towns devoted to the preservation of the distinctive Scottish tradition in literature and the arts.

The Georgian and Victorian epochs had been noteworthy for the prose works written by men of learning, and this scholarly cult was still prominent in Edwardian and neo-Georgian times. In particular, much interest attached to the writings of two leading politicians, for whom philosophy was a hobby and a relaxation – the first Earl Balfour and the first Viscount Haldane – and to the historical works of Peter Hume Brown, Andrew Lang[2] and Sir Robert Rait.

For Scottish fiction the new reign opened with a memorable book, *The House with the Green Shutters* (1901), in which George Douglas Brown (1869-1902) delivered a savage and biting counter-blast against the rose-coloured sentimentalities of the 'Kailyard school'.[3] In this grim study of tragic fate, Brown emphasised all that was sordid and unlovely in Scottish life and character, and showed the other side of the medal to that which had been presented in the works of Barrie, Crockett and 'Ian Maclaren'. A little later, Neil Munro, having achieved some fame with his early novels, struck a richly comic vein with his 'Para Handy' tales of a small Clyde coasting steamer (1904-6), but he returned to his former love, that of the Highland historical romance, with *The New Road* (1914).

The novels of Norman Douglas, John Buchan (Lord Tweedsmuir) and Sir Compton Mackenzie found their place in the realm of English letters, and the same is true of the short stories of R. B. Cunninghame Graham and Mrs Naomi Mitchison, and of the boisterous burlesques of Eric Linklater. Varied aspects of Scottish life were explored in A. J. Cronin's *Hatter's Castle* (1931), a novel reminiscent of *The House with the Green Shutters*, in George Blake's *The Shipbuilders*

[1] And, in the cognate field of Scots law and legal history, the Stair Society was instituted in 1934; its first publication, *An Introductory Survey of the Sources and Literature of Scots Law* (1936), was a work of exceptional value for scholars.

[2] The most gifted 'amateur' of his day, he was also noted for his light verse, folk-lore and fairy-tales.

[3] See *supra*, p. 274.

(1935), in Alexander McArthur's *No Mean City: a Story of the Glasgow Slums* (1935), and in Neil Gunn's graceful and natural tales of the northern Highlands. Outstanding among the attempts to recapture, in fictional form, the Scottish scene of the recent past was *A Scots Quair*, by Lewis Grassic Gibbon (J. Leslie Mitchell, 1901-35), comprising three separate novels, *Sunset Song*, *Cloud Howe* and *Grey Granite* (1932-34).[1] Gibbon made masterly use of the Scots vernacular to endow his descriptions of country, village and town, his vivid re-creations of east-coast characters, with an authentic tone and colour which, allied to his keen sense of the melody of words and phrases, raised his work to the level of an exquisite prose-poem.

At the turn of the century drama gained a recruit in the story-teller, J. M. Barrie, who went on to a wider fame with such plays as *Quality Street* (1901), *The Admirable Crichton* (1902), *Peter Pan* (a perennial favourite with the young since 1904), *What Every Woman Knows* (1908), *Dear Brutus* (1917) and *Mary Rose* (1920). Hard on his heels came James Bridie (Osborne Mavor, 1888-1951), whose dramatic ability shone forth brightly in *The Anatomist* and *Tobias and the Angel* (both in 1931), in *Jonah and the Whale* (1932), and above all in *A Sleeping Clergyman* (1933). In respect of musical composition, the period is best known for the *Songs of the Hebrides*, in which Marjorie Kennedy Fraser collected surviving Gaelic folk-songs – many of them otherwise doomed to perish – catching their spirit in lively (if freely altered) English versions.

Of the Scottish poets writing in English, John Davidson and Edwin Muir (also a distinguished essayist and translator) won critical rather than popular acclaim. The native Scots idiom was used with happy results in Charles Murray's *Hamewith* (1900), in Violet Jacob's *Songs of Angus* (1915 and later), in some of John Buchan's *Poems in Scots and English* (1917), and in the many ballads compiled or translated by Sir Alexander Gray from 1920. A form of 'plastic' Scots, blending archaic words with elements from the vernacular dialects, was devised from the 1920s for literary purposes, and the use of the new medium, now called 'Lallans', came to be considered the hall-mark of the 'Scottish Renaissance', a cultural revival parallel to the political and economic 'revolts' of the time.[2] Already Pittendrigh Macgillivray and

[1] If *Grey Granite*, unlike the earlier books, was marred by bitterness and intolerance, it should be remembered that it was the work of a sick man: the gifted author died in the following year – like Fergusson, Burns and Brown, cut off on the threshold of his prime.

[2] Cf. *supra*, p. 285.

Lewis Spence had been experimenting along these lines; a little later, William Soutar, William Jeffrey and others followed suit, but the most daring innovator in Lallans, the acknowledged leader of the group, was Hugh McDiarmid (C. M. Grieve, b. 1892), whose poems from the mid-1920s[1] marked the inception of a new vogue among native poets.

In art the impetus of the 'Glasgow school' persisted into the new century, but died away about 1914. In its place came a group of painters whose work bore a marked resemblance to that of the French impressionists, and who were styled 'the Scottish colourists' – Samuel J. Peploe, G. Leslie Hunter and F. C. B. Cadell. Another trio attained equal fame as masters of the art of etching – Sir D. Y. Cameron, Sir Muirhead Bone and James McBey. Again, if architectural distinction was sadly lacking in the public buildings, churches and 'council' houses of the time, Sir Robert Lorimer (1864-1929) received high praise for his adaptation to modern needs of historic Scottish modes, as in the Thistle chapel of St Giles, Edinburgh, in the restoration of the Scots Baronial castle of Dunderave, Argyll, and above all in the Scottish National War Memorial, within Edinburgh castle. In an allied field, Sir Patrick Geddes (1854-1932), professor of botany at University College, Dundee, from 1889 to 1914, followed a wayward academic custom by devoting himself, with vigour and success, to a subject other than his own 'profession', and so becoming a pioneer and expert in his 'side-line' of civics and town planning.[2] Thus, if there were hollows, there were also peaks of achievement in the arts, as in letters, in Edwardian and Georgian times.

[1] See especially his 'Sangschaw', 'A Drunk Man looks at the Thistle', and 'To Circumjack Cencrastus'; and his contributions (in conjunction with Lewis Grassic Gibbon) to *Scottish Scene* (1934).

[2] He was the father-in-law of Sir Frank Mears, who followed on in the line of eminent town-planners.

EPILOGUE

Post-War Scotland

THE WAR was over in Europe, but continuing against Japan,[1] when Labour withdrew from the war-time coalition to contest the general election, in July 1945, as a separate party. The Parliament had been in existence for almost ten years, and for nearly fourteen years the government had been consistently 'National' in name and predominantly Conservative in composition and policy; war-weariness now combined with a strong reaction against the party in power to produce a startling change in the posture of political affairs. In addition to the desire to give the 'outs' their chance against the 'ins', there was a general feeling that the time was ripe for bold social and economic experiments in nationalisation, full employment, town and country planning, and the whole apparatus of a 'welfare state' as outlined in the Beveridge report.[2] Moved in this way, the electors swung strongly to the left, giving Labour[3] 48·2 per cent of the votes cast, against 39·9 per cent to the 'Conservatives and their associates',[4] 9 per cent to the Liberals, and 2·9 per cent to all others. This verdict was sufficiently decisive to put Mr (later Lord) Attlee into power with an overwhelming majority: 393 of the 640 M.P.s belonged to his party, while Mr (later Sir) Winston Churchill's followers were reduced to 213, and the Liberals to 12.

The popular vote in Scotland differed little from that in the United Kingdom as a whole. Labour polled 49·6 per cent of the total, the Conservatives 41·8 per cent, Liberals 5·6 per cent, and others (Scottish Nationalists, Communists and sundry independents) 3 per cent. Here, then, the socialist advantage in votes was not much less marked than in England and Wales, but it brought a less abundant harvest of seats: out of the 74 in Scotland, 37 fell to official Labour candidates, the

[1] Cf. *supra*, p. 289. [2] See *supra*, p. 291.

[3] In both the United Kingdom and the Scottish percentages, the I.L.P. votes are included under Labour. The figures in each case refer to county and borough (or burgh) *contests*: i.e. they exclude the university votes (which are not strictly comparable and were, in any case, abolished in 1948) and also the few unopposed returns.

[4] This formula, henceforth in common use, embraced (besides Conservatives) such party 'labels' as 'National', 'National Liberal', 'Liberal National', and 'Liberal-Conservative'.

I.L.P. held three Glasgow divisions (Bridgeton, Camlachie and Shettleston), and the Communists retained West Fife. The Conservatives, with 32 seats, fared relatively better than their English colleagues. One independent member was returned (for the Scottish Universities), but the Liberals had not a single seat, though they came close to success in several constituencies: this seemed a pitiful end to the career of the party that had formerly been accustomed to carry most of the Scottish seats.

It was Labour's hour of triumph: there was no questioning its right to rule Britain in a changed and changing world – a world in which the old Empire gave birth to new nation-states in India, Pakistan, Ceylon and Burma (1947), but over which the threat of a fresh and devastating conflict loomed with the Communist conquest of the Chinese mainland and Russia's possession of the atom bomb (1949). At home, the first Attlee administration (1945-50) proceeded to enact a full socialist programme. Legislation of 1946 nationalised the Bank of England, the coal mines and the cable and wireless system, while electricity, the railways and a large sector of road transport were similarly treated by statutes of 1947. Nothing less than a social revolution was effected by the main legislation of the years 1946-48,[1] which put into operation the principal terms of the Beveridge report, with rather more emphasis on state control, and rather less on voluntary work, than its author had contemplated. A comprehensive national health service, including medical, surgical, maternity and dental care, full security against unemployment and disablement, national assistance and 'welfare' benefits for the needy, now came into force. Again, an Act of 1946 authorised the establishment of 'new towns' under their own development corporations, and another in 1947 ordered each local planning authority to prepare a detailed survey and a betterment scheme for approval by the central government. All gas undertakings were nationalised in 1948, and the Iron and Steel Act, 1949, proposed yet another instalment of state control, but the bitter controversy aroused by this measure induced the government to postpone its operative date to 1 January 1951, in order to permit an appeal to be made to the electorate.

Among the Labour enactments particularly concerning Scotland, the Education Act, 1946, raised the school-leaving age to fifteen (from 1 April 1947). Another statute of the same busy year (1946) authorised

[1] The statutes affecting Scotland were the National Insurance Act, 1946, the National Health Service (Scotland) Act, 1947, and the National Assistance Act, 1948.

amalgamations between neighbouring police forces, and in the course of the next ten years nine schemes of union were carried out, so that the forty-nine police forces were reduced to thirty-three. Thus, in the north-east, the county forces of Kincardine, Aberdeen, Banff, Moray and Nairn were combined, and, in the south-east, those of the three Lothians and of Peebles. In 1948, too, Parliament authorised the appointment of fifteen instead of thirteen judges of the Court of Session, thus restoring the rule which had stood from the sixteenth to the nineteenth century.

As there had been no overhaul of the parliamentary system since 1918 (when the population figures of 1911 had been used), reform was now overdue, and it was effected by the Representation of the People Act, 1948. Dual voting, by way of the university and business franchises, was abolished in favour of the maxim, 'one man, one vote', and all 625 seats in the new House became single-member constituencies.[1] Scotland retained 71 members (the old number, less the Universities' three members), and this figure meant a degree of deliberate over-representation,[2] in contrast to the under-representation that had obtained until 1885. Within Scotland 32 members were allocated to the burghs – 15 to Glasgow, 7 to Edinburgh, 2 each to Aberdeen and Dundee, one each to Paisley and Greenock, and one to each of four districts of burghs, those of Coatbridge and Airdrie, of Dunfermline, of Kirkcaldy, and of Stirling and Falkirk.[3] To the counties went 39 members, including 6 to Lanark, 2 each to Aberdeen, Dunbarton, Fife and Renfrew (the divisions being East and West in every case), and one each to Argyll, Banff, Dumfries and West Lothian. Seven pairs of counties were now to return one M.P. each: Berwick and East Lothian, Caithness and Sutherland, Galloway (that is, Kirkcudbright and Wigtown), Midlothian and Peebles, Moray and Nairn, Orkney and Shetland, Roxburgh and Selkirk. Finally, fourteen members were distributed among five pairs of disparate shires in a manner akin to that of the 1918 arrangement.[4] Thus Ayr and Bute got five members – one for the 'composite' division of Bute and North Ayrshire, and four others for purely Ayrshire divisions. One M.P

[1] Scotland's only two-member constituency, Dundee, gave way to two single-member divisions, East and West Dundee.

[2] While the average electorate for a Scottish constituency was just over 48,000 the figure was nearly 57,000 for England and over 55,000 for Great Britain.

[3] The Ayr, Dumbarton and Montrose districts were suppressed – that is, they were merged in county constituencies.

[4] See *supra*, pp. 280-1.

was to represent North Angus and Mearns, another Kinross and West Perth, a third Clackmannan and East Stirling, with the remainder of the larger county in each case having a separate member (South Angus, Perth and East Perthshire, West Stirling). The exceptional constituency of the Western Isles stood unaltered.

It was further provided in the Act that the annual municipal elections be held (like the triennial county elections) in May: this change, operative from 1949, marked a break from the practice of November polls which had prevailed since 1833. In 1949, also, it was arranged that periodic adjustments of the electoral divisions, to accord with population movements, should be recommended to Parliament by the four boundary commissions (for England, Scotland, Wales and Northern Ireland)[1]; this would obviate the need for a complete 'Reform Act' making wholesale changes once a generation. The Parliament Act of 1949 extended the principle of the similarly styled statute of 1911[2] by limiting the Lords' power of veto to one year instead of two: this enactment marked the utmost reach of Labour's constitutional reforms.

In 1948, meanwhile, the powers of the Scottish Standing Committee, which had played a useful but undistinguished part since 1907,[3] were greatly enhanced: by resolution of the House of Commons, Scottish bills could be referred to it for second reading debate as well as for the committee stage – that is, it could consider such legislation in principle and in detail. In addition, it was authorised to discuss the estimates relating to Scotland for six days in each session. The new arrangements gave Scotland something like 'a parliament within a parliament'.

In part this improvement stemmed from legislative convenience, but it was also in part a concession to 'nationalist' sentiment, which was much in evidence during the last years of the reign of George VI (1936-52). The success achieved at Motherwell in April 1945[4] was not repeated, but the favourable results of certain local plebiscites, as well as the approval of the General Assembly of the Church of Scotland from 1948, showed much popular support for the idea of a separate

[1] Previous boundary commissions had reported *ad hoc* on desirable schemes of redistribution of seats *before* each measure of parliamentary reform, and their recommendations had been embodied, for example, in the Acts of 1918 and 1948. Now, however, it was provided that *standing* boundary commissions should present reports, independently of any legislation, at intervals of not less than three or more than seven years. From 1954 the interval was lengthened to 10-15 years.

[2] Cf. *supra*, pp. 221-2. [3] See *supra*, p. 222. [4] See *supra*, p. 290.

Scottish parliament. In October 1949 the nationalists, often standing aloof from parliamentary contests, brought forth the Scottish Covenant, in which they undertook to work, in all loyalty, for a separate parliament; within two years they obtained over two million signatures (equal to well over half the registered voters). Yet the impact of this agitation on ordinary political life was slight. In the municipal elections, Labour won control of Dundee and Aberdeen in 1945, then lost these, as well as Glasgow, in the years 1947-50 (to regain them all from 1952-54). In parliamentary representation the chief changes of the time were the return to the Labour fold of the I.L.P. 'rebels' (1947) and one Conservative by-election gain, at Camlachie (Glasgow), largely as a result of Labour dissension (1948).

By 1950 the impetus of Labour's drive to power had mostly spent itself and the general election of February in that year, contested in part over the issue of nationalising iron and steel, was a bitter disappointment to the Attlee administration. With 315 seats out of 625, it had the slenderest of majorities over its opponents – 298 'Conservatives and their associates', and 9 Liberals.[1] One interesting feature of this election (and of all others during the 1950s) was the elimination of 'splinter' groups and candidates, such as Communists, I.L.P., Scottish Nationalists and independents. In Scotland, Labour was returned in 37 of the 71 constituencies, while Mr Churchill's supporters held 32, and the Liberals, faring better than in England, won 2 seats (Orkney and Shetland, and Roxburgh and Selkirk).[2]

Labour's tenure of office for a further period of eighteen months (1950-51) coincided with the Korean War, when the peace of the world seemed to be at the mercy of Communist aggression. In domestic affairs Labour's precarious majority proved nearly unworkable – it was described at the time as 'government by sneeze' – and, after the nationalisation of iron and steel had been forced through a sharply divided House, the raising of other controversial issues was impractical. Some Scottish nationalist extremists gained notoriety by removing the 'Stone of Destiny' from Westminster abbey on Christmas day, 1950, and transporting it to Scotland; it was returned in April 1951, and

[1] The Speaker and two Irish Nationalists completed the membership of the House.

[2] Over the whole United Kingdom, Labour polled 46·4 per cent of the votes cast in contested elections, while the Conservatives got 43·5 per cent, the Liberals 9·1 per cent, and all others 1 per cent. For Scotland the figures were 46·3 per cent for Labour, 45·2 per cent for Conservatives, 6·6 per cent for Liberals, and 1·9 per cent for the others.

the episode was soon dismissed from public memory as a foolish youthful prank.

Finding its position no longer tolerable, the Attlee administration was driven to make another appeal to the country, but the general election of October 1951, far from benefiting it, robbed it of the slight majority it possessed and ushered in a long period of Conservative rule. At this stage, it is true, the 'swing to the right' was little more than a gentle drift, involving the transfer of just over 20 seats, but it was enough to reduce the Labour forces to 295, and to increase their chief opponents to 321; the Liberal representation shrank to six. In Scotland the Conservatives won two seats from Labour (Berwick and East Lothian, and Rutherglen) and one from the Liberals (Roxburgh and Selkirk), with the consequence that, for the only time in our electoral history, the two major parties were at absolute parity, with 35 seats each: the Liberal member for Orkney and Shetland was 'odd man out'. The totals of votes cast showed that this was a fair enough result, only slightly favouring Labour: Conservatives polled 49·5 per cent of the Scottish votes, against 48 per cent for Labour,[1] with the balance of 2·5 per cent going to Liberals and others.

The administration that now took office under Mr Churchill (1951-55), besides denationalising the iron and steel industry and, in part, the road transport services, was noteworthy for several constitutional changes affecting Scotland. From November 1951 a minister of state occupied second place, after the secretary of state, in Scotland's governmental 'team'; and this new minister, normally being a peer, and therefore free from the exacting duties that tied the M.P. to London, could spend most of his time in Scotland. From February 1952 a third[2] under-secretary of state was added to give Scotland (already provided with its lord advocate and solicitor-general – the law officers of the Crown) something like a sub-cabinet.

A white paper of 1954 showed the impact of post-war conditions upon Scottish finance. The national revenue of Great Britain in 1952-53 amounted to £4,227 million, of which Scotland's contribution was £410 million, or 9·69 per cent, while her proportion of the population (in 1951) was 10·43 per cent. Scotland received £207 million, or 12·34 per cent of the total disbursed as 'local' expenditure, so that her

[1] The position was quite different in England and Wales, where the Conservatives got 277 seats with only 47·7 per cent of the poll, against 259 for Labour, with 49·5 per cent of the poll.

[2] The second under-secretaryship had been instituted in 1940.

balance, available for 'imperial' expenses, was £203 million, or 7·95 per cent of the total required. Thus, if Scotland, impeded by a heavier rate of unemployment than England, was still not 'paying her way', her situation was healthier than it had been in 1931-35.[1]

The first periodical report of the Boundary Commission for Scotland, submitted and approved towards the end of 1954, left Scotland with 71 seats out of an increased total of 630, made minor changes in the names and boundaries of some of the Glasgow divisions, and effected a few adjustments elsewhere. Its only major alteration was to take Peebles out of its pairing with Midlothian (now populous enough to warrant its own member) and to add it to Roxburgh and Selkirk, to form Britain's only three-county constituency.

In May 1955 the Conservative administration, now headed by Sir Anthony Eden in place of Sir Winston Churchill, repeated and extended the victory of 1951. A slight advantage in the votes polled throughout the United Kingdom[2] brought the government a net gain of over 20 seats and a working majority of 59 over all others: the new House included 344 Conservatives, 277 Labour members and 6 Liberals. Scotland gave the right wing parties 50·1 per cent of the total poll, against 46·7 per cent for Labour, but the only real change[3] in representation occurred in Central Ayrshire, where a Conservative displaced the Labour member, to increase the government supporters to 36, and to reduce Labour to 34.

Despite its strong position at home, the Eden administration ran into grave trouble in the autumn of 1956, when the Anglo-French attack on Egypt, coinciding in time with the brutal Russian suppression of the Hungarian revolt, seemed once more to bring the world to the brink of war. The danger was again averted, but the prime minister gave way to Mr Harold Macmillan.

In Scottish affairs, the years 1955-59 were fairly placid. In 1952 there had been vociferous objection from the more ardent nationalists to the numeral in the title of the new Queen, Elizabeth II, but little was heard of this after 1953. By 1958 both the major parties were officially opposed to the idea of a separate parliament for Scotland. The chief constitutional change of the time was effected by the Valuation and Rating (Scotland) Act, 1956, under which, from 1957, there

[1] See *supra*, pp. 297-8.

[2] The percentage figure was 49·7, against 46·3 for Labour (and 2·6 for the Liberals).

[3] Of the new constituencies, Midlothian fell to Labour, Roxburgh, Selkirk and Peebles to the Conservatives, while in Glasgow Craigton voted Conservative and Provan Labour. None of these results was a surprise.

was transferred to occupiers the liability for the rates which had been borne by owners under Scottish law and practice for 290 years.[1]

The election of October 1959 brought the Conservatives their third consecutive victory at the polls – an occurrence unique in modern political history. A net gain of 23 seats gave the government (with 365 supporters) an advantage of 107 over Labour (with 258); the Liberals, despite much effort and high hopes, remained unchanged at 6. The Conservatives had polled 49·4 per cent of the votes cast, Labour 43·6, and the Liberals 6 per cent. Only in two parts of the United Kingdom (where unemployment was higher than elsewhere) was there any 'swing' to Labour: one of these was Lancashire, the other was Scotland. The Conservatives had a solitary Scottish gain at Kelvingrove, Glasgow,[2] but four out of the five Labour gains in the entire country were made in Scottish constituencies – Craigton and Scotstoun (both in Glasgow), Central Ayrshire and Lanark. Thus Labour, against an adverse tide, increased its Scottish representation to 38, compared with 32[3] for the Conservatives and their associates; Orkney and Shetland was still in the Liberal fold. On this occasion, however, the luck of the ballot-box flattered Labour strength. Six of the 71 Scottish seats were won with majorities of less than one thousand – all six by Labour.[4] The Conservative share of the total Scottish poll was 47·9 per cent,[5] that of Labour 46·7 per cent.[6]

The close of the 1950s – marked in international affairs by the alternation of relaxed tension and renewed crisis – found the Conservatives more firmly in the saddle than ever. Of the five post-war general elections, Labour had unquestionably won the first two, in Scotland as in the United Kingdom, in votes cast as in members elected; in the next three, the Conservatives, while carrying England, were ahead of Labour in the Scottish popular vote, but had to be content with equality of representation in 1951 and with an actual deficit in

[1] Cf. *supra*, p. 18.

[2] This seat, Conservative in 1955, had been won by Labour at a by-election in March 1958.

[3] This figure includes Caithness and Sutherland, where Sir David Robertson, the former Conservative member, was now returned as an Independent, though with mainly Conservative support.

[4] Central Edinburgh, East Edinburgh, Glasgow (Craigton), Dundee West, Coatbridge and Airdrie, and Lanark.

[5] Even without Caithness and Sutherland, the figure would be 47·4 per cent.

[6] The Liberals got 4 per cent, the balance being divided between Communists, Scottish Nationalists (who ran second in Perth and East Perthshire, but did badly elsewhere) and various independents.

1959. In contrast to the position in England and Wales,[1] the verdict of the ballot-box in Scotland tended to be slightly distorted in favour of the Labour party: if there were any 'wasted' majorities, they were those of the 'safe' Tory seats in the counties. A composite picture of the five elections in the period 1945-59 would show Labour with an average holding of 37 Scottish seats, the Conservatives and their associates with 33, and the Liberals with one.

In and after 1945 the trend towards fixity of party loyalties, which was already strong before the second World War,[2] became more marked: the mainly residential, farming or 'resort' divisions inclined to vote Conservative, and the mainly industrial and 'working class' divisions to vote Labour. The political map of Scotland would indicate the northern mainland and the southern uplands as Conservative, the central lowland belt and the burghs (along with the Western Isles) as Labour, while the contest between them was doubtful only in or near the chief cities. No fewer than thirty-three of the seventy-one divisions had unbroken socialist records[3] during all five elections: these included seven Glasgow, three Edinburgh, two Dundee and one Aberdeen seats, and a broad band of county and burgh constituencies stretching from South Ayr to Kirkcaldy. The Conservatives and their allies consistently held twenty-six divisions, including four in Glasgow, three in Edinburgh, one in Aberdeen, and all the landward area north of the Argyll-Perth-East Fife line, as well as the extreme south-west. Hence, in only twelve constituencies was there a change of party allegiance at any of these five elections.[4] By this test, accordingly, a mere dozen seats in all Scotland could be termed 'marginal'.[5]

During the years 1945-59 the Scottish economy, though it had its black spots and its weak periods, was on the whole in a healthier state than it had been in the other 'post-war' period. Labour policy aimed at full employment, high wages and high taxation, even at the cost of

[1] The large 'wasted' majorities of the many 'safe' Labour seats in England and more especially in Wales meant that more votes were needed to elect each Labour member than for each Conservative. The reverse held good in Scotland.

[2] See *supra*, pp. 288-9.

[3] That is, if we include West Fife, Communist in 1945 but Labour regularly from 1950.

[4] These were Central Ayrshire, Berwick and East Lothian, Lanark, Rutherglen, Orkney and Shetland, West Renfrew, Roxburgh, Selkirk and Peebles, North Edinburgh, and four of the Glasgow divisions – Central, Craigton, Kelvingrove and Scotstoun. (In each case the latest name for the constituency is given.)

[5] Some of these twelve, it is true, seemed by 1959 to be moving out of the 'marginal' class towards a fixed political allegiance; but, to balance these, some other formerly 'safe' seats (both Labour and Conservative) appeared likely to become 'marginal'.

some inflation; war-time controls and rationing were retained, and certain essential services and industries were nationalised. From 1951 the Conservatives, while preserving the main features of the 'welfare state', halted the process of nationalisation, abolished many controls, tried to check inflation and to reduce taxation, and gave rein to 'free enterprise'. In fact, the area of agreement shared by the two parties was greater than the area of conflict, and between them they so directed affairs that the dreaded post-war depression (thought by some to be inevitable) did not come to pass.[1]

Agriculture benefited from the work of the Scottish Milk Marketing Board[2] and of the agricultural executive committees, made permanent in 1948 for the promotion of food production, good husbandry and estate management, and from the state subsidies in aid of hill grazings, marginal farming, the ploughing of grass-lands, drainage, bracken control, liming and fertilising. It is true that the acreages under the main crops, which had been much expanded during the war, showed some shrinkage:–

Land Use, 1945-59 (in thousands of acres)

	1945	*1952*	*1959*
Wheat	91	65	84
Barley	217	199	228
Oats	1,004	903	720
Potatoes	224	172	150
Turnips and Swedes	327	277	247
Total Crops and Fallow	2,011	1,743	1,546
Rotation Grass and Clover	1,332	1,479	2,813 (Rotation Grass and Clover and Permanent Grass combined)
Permanent Grass	1,082	1,169	
Total Crops and Grass	4,425	4,391	4,359

Thus the total tillage was diminished at this period by 465,000 acres, while the grass-lands increased by 399,000 acres, and the transfer from arable to pastoral farming is borne out by the livestock totals:–

Livestock, 1945-59 (thousands of head)

	1945	*1952*	*1959*
Cattle	1,460	1,576	1,892
Sheep	6,899	7,273	8,384
Pigs	171	446	428
Poultry	7,313	9,976	9,044
Horses	117	58	20

[1] True, one severe fuel crisis (January-March 1947) brought industry to a standstill and caused heavy unemployment, but this trouble passed and did not recur.

[2] See *supra*, p. 297.

The increase in cattle was marked and almost continuous, while the sheep total in 1959 was the highest ever recorded. The decrease in horses, on the other hand, suggests the extent to which farming was mechanised, for farmers were now buying or renting a wide range of tractor-drawn and other machines – ploughs, harrows and drills, broadcast sowers, cultivators and manure distributors, rollers and potato diggers, binders, mowers and combine harvesters. Not only was the horse disappearing from the scene: fewer hands were needed, and the numbers employed in agriculture[1] dropped from 117,000 in 1945 to 84,700 in 1959. More highly specialised than formerly, the farming of the 1950s was also more stable, productive and prosperous.

The traditional Scottish industries meanwhile had their troubles. Coal-mining was hampered by the many exhausted or uneconomic pits, especially in Lanarkshire, and, though good new seams existed in Fife, Lothian and Ayrshire, their exploitation was too slow a process to compensate as yet for the lost supplies. The annual output declined from over 23 million tons to under 20 million. In Scotland, as in Britain generally, pig iron and steel production rose steadily, to reach peaks of 1,059,000 and 2,626,500 tons respectively in 1957, though a slackening of demand thereafter brought a decline. Shipbuilding output was remarkably steady, fluctuating only between 440,000 and 570,000 tons a year. Apart from metal products (including ships, locomotives and machines), woollen textiles and whisky did well in the export trade, but the problem was still, as before the war, that of diversifying and modernising the Scottish economy. The paucity of the lighter, 'consumer' industries was reflected in the unemployment figures. Though not really high, the Scottish rate – ranging as a rule between 2 and 4·5 per cent – was usually twice as much as the British rate; and economic discontent, as we have seen, tended to fan the flames of political militancy and revolt.

Other difficulties afflicted rural Scotland and more especially the Highland region. Sheer physical geography had always made communications within, and out of, the northern parts of Scotland an awkward and perplexing problem: in the modern world, distance from the main centres of population, and slow or expensive transport, gravely hampered social and economic progress. To take one example only, the Aberdeen fish industry, in comparison with that of Hull or of Grimsby, suffered from high transport costs to southern markets.

[1] The figures exclude the 'self-employed', i.e. the farmer himself and his wife, and also any domestic servants.

Within the area itself branch railway lines, since here as elsewhere they did not pay, tended to be closed, first for passenger travel, and then for goods traffic as well; steamship services, particularly to the western and northern islands, were sharply curtailed. The extension of bus services and of goods transport by road could not compensate for all these losses, and the roads themselves, passing through thinly populated districts, were in urgent need of costly improvements (which were not forthcoming). It was this lack of proper communications, above all other ills, that handicapped economic ventures, old and new, to the north and west of the Highland line.

Post-war governments, both Labour and Conservative, strove in many ways to correct Scotland's economic imbalance. The Herring Industry Board (1935) and the White Fish Authority (1951) made grants to enable fishermen to acquire up-to-date vessels and equipment. A new Crofters' Commission (1956) helped to develop production from crofts and marginal land, while the Forestry Commission encouraged or undertook tree-planting, alongside local manufactures based on timber and its by-products. The North of Scotland Hydro-Electric Board provided both employment and power with such schemes as those of Loch Sloy, Dunbartonshire (inaugurated in 1950), Glen Affric, Inverness-shire (1952), Glen Shira, Argyll (1955), and Lawers, Perthshire (1956). And by 1959 some 70,000 new jobs had been created on the 21 industrial estates, including work on plastics and new fabrics, tractors and aero-engines, refrigerators, watches and business machines.

The 'service' industries began to adapt themselves to the new age. Railways, electricity and gas were nationalised, as we have seen, from 1947-48. The banks were reduced in number by amalgamation to five: the Clydesdale and North of Scotland combined in 1950, the Bank of Scotland took over the Union in 1954, and the National Commercial Bank (1958) was the outcome of yet another union; only the Royal Bank and the British Linen were unaffected by these changes. The trend in overseas trade continued to favour the larger ports, among which Grangemouth was now second only to Glasgow; the balance of Scottish imports and exports flowed mainly through Leith, Aberdeen, Dundee and Methil, in the east, and Ardrossan, Ayr and Greenock, in the west.[1] Transport improvements included the substitution, from

[1] For example, the total combined tonnages of imports and exports in 1951 were (in thousands of tons):– Glasgow, 5,779; Grangemouth, 3,263; Leith, 1,449; Aberdeen, 1,443; Ardrossan, 934; Ayr, 929; Methil, 929; Greenock, 580; Dundee, 548; Bo'ness, 209; Burntisland, 132; and Troon, 129.

1957, of diesel-powered for steam trains on certain routes, the scrapping of the once popular but now outmoded tramways,[1] and the opening, in 1959, of the Finnart oil terminal, on Loch Long, able to take the largest tankers afloat. By the close of the decade work was proceeding on the Forth road bridge and the Whiteinch tunnel under the Clyde at Glasgow, while plans were afoot for a Tay road bridge at Dundee and the electrification of the Glasgow suburban railways.

The newest types of industry came in with the Ferranti electronics laboratory in Edinburgh (1954), the nuclear power station at Chapelcross, Dumfriesshire, and the 'fast breeder' reactor at Dounreay, Caithness (both operative in 1959). At Hunterston, in Ayrshire, a vast nuclear power station was under construction, and – perhaps even better – Colvilles were building a steel strip mill near Motherwell: Scottish steel-making capacity had hitherto been directed mainly to plates and heavy rolled products, often intended for export, but the fabrication of sheets, it was confidently expected, would bring motor manufacturers to Scotland in the 1960s.

The need for better housing was meanwhile urgent. The output of new houses reached a peak of 39,548 in 1953, and by the close of 1959 nearly 380,000 had been built since the war. Moreover, to relieve urban congestion and to promote a healthier distribution of industry and population, three new towns were being constructed – East Kilbride (designated in 1947), Glenrothes (1948) and Cumbernauld (1955). Each of these, as well as many of the older burghs, agreed to take part of the 'overspill' from Glasgow, where a programme of slum clearance was under way, but whence, too, it was considered that a large proportion of the inhabitants must be 'decanted'.

The population trends of the time suggest an approach to stability: some typical changes are shown in the following table[2]:–

Population Changes, 1939-59 (in thousands)

		1939	*1951*	*1959*
	Scotland	5,007	5,096	5,192
Cities:	Glasgow	1,128	1,090	1,077
	Edinburgh	472	467	469
	Aberdeen	180	183	187

[1] After 1958 Glasgow alone retained its tramways, and these were in course of being abandoned – a process which was expected to be completed in 1963.

[2] The 1939 and 1959 figures are taken from the Registrar General's estimates for 30 June in each of these years, and those of 1951 from that year's Census Report.

		1939	1951	1959
Counties:	Lanark	510	525	555
	Midlothian	90	99	109
	Renfrew	323	325	337
	Argyll	62	63	56
	Berwick	26	25	23
	Orkney	22	21	19
Burghs:	Coatbridge	45	48	54
	Kilmarnock	40	42	46
	Perth	37	40	41

The industrial counties were still gaining, the agricultural ones losing, but rapid city growth was a thing of the past: the great development of public and private transport now made it possible for many to live in 'dormitory' suburbs and to travel to and from work. Glasgow, in particular, had passed its peak (in 1939) and reduced numbers were being recorded every year. Many burghs, on the other hand, continued to grow as their 'hinterland' lost – Wick and Thurso, for example, at the expense of Caithness, or Stranraer at the expense of Wigtownshire. Urban over-crowding and rural depopulation[1] still challenged the social planner.

The vital statistics of the time point to a fairly stable and healthy population. The birth-rate rose gently from about 17 per thousand, to reach or exceed 19 from 1957, while the death-rate remained at or near 12[2]; infant mortality dropped to 28 or 29 (to each thousand live births) by the late 1950s. Thus the expectation of life at birth was sixty-six years for males in 1958 and seventy-one for females. Population increase was, however, held in check by migration from Scotland, which often exceeded 20,000 per annum; England and Canada were favoured as the new homelands, and the departure of so many young and enterprising single men left the nation the poorer.

Other statistics serve to illustrate the improved housing standards. Whereas 44 per cent of the inhabitants of Scotland had been living in houses of one or two rooms in 1931,[3] the percentage in 1951 was 29·7; Glasgow's figure came down from 55·4 to 41·5,[4] Dundee's from 56·2

[1] In 1755 the five predominantly Highland counties had held 314,800 inhabitants, or nearly a quarter of the Scottish total (*supra*, p. 150); the estimate for 1959 was 337,600, that is, less than one-fifteenth of the whole.

[2] Among the medical triumphs of the period were the conquest of diphtheria and the very great reduction in the ravages of tuberculosis.

[3] Cf. *supra*, p. 302.

[4] The proportion varied widely between ill-housed and well-housed wards: it was as high as 85·9 per cent in Hutchesontown, and as low as 1·3 per cent in Craigton.

to 39·4. Again, the high wages of the 1950s[1] brought within reach of working class families amenities formerly undreamt of – private motor cars and holidays away from home, electrical refrigerators, washing machines, and (from 1952) television sets.

The school-leaving age was raised to fifteen from 1947,[2] and educational services were expanded until, in the country's 3,700 schools, ten times that number of teachers had charge of a school population of over 850,000. By January 1960 the average salary of the 'certificated' male teacher had been raised to £1,170, that of the female to £885.[3] At the universities, meanwhile, numbers rose to a post-war peak in 1948-49, and then levelled off somewhat:–

Numbers of University Students, 1944-58

Session	*St Andrews*	*Glasgow*	*Aberdeen*	*Edinburgh*	*Total*
1944-45	1,014	3,562	988	3,294	8,858
1948-49	2,195	7,555	2,228	6,806	18,784
1953-54	1,831	6,080	1,659	5,775	15,345
1957-58	2,391	6,695	1,984	6,586	17,656

University teachers increased to over 2,000 by 1957, including 224 professors. In response to the declared national need, expansion was most marked in science and technology, while, from the late 1940s, the colleges of dentistry, veterinary studies and agricultural science were all integrated into the university system.

The cause of church unity scored a minor triumph in 1956, when the United Original Secession returned to the Church of Scotland, and a major failure in 1959, when, after two years of anxious deliberation, a possible basis of union between the Churches of Scotland and England – involving 'bishops-in-presbytery' in Scotland and lay elders in England – was finally rejected. Meanwhile, the Kirk continued to put its own house in order. Between 1929 and 1958, 743 local unions of congregations and 63 'linkages' had been effected, while 49 congregations had been dissolved; in the period 1948-58, 120 new churches or hall-churches were completed. In 1958 the Church, with 1,315,630 communicants, had 2,280 charges. By 1959, too, the

[1] The United Kingdom average weekly wage stood in 1958 at £13 2s. 11d. for men, and £11 6s. 6d. for all workers.

[2] See *supra*, pp. 309, 318.

[3] The basic scales were £780-1,400 for first and second class honours graduates, £730-1,400 for third class honours graduates, and £710-1,180 for ordinary graduates. These scales applied to men teachers, but 'equal pay' was being introduced by stages and would be in full operation by 1961.

minimum stipend had been advanced to £725 (with a manse, and with £50 more in city and other exceptional charges). For the Roman Catholics, the chief event of the period was the institution, in 1948, of two new dioceses, Motherwell and Paisley, both of them in the archbishopric of Glasgow.

If, in a work like this, it is unwise to try to assess individual achievements in contemporary arts and letters, it is yet clear that post-war Scotland was rich in the fruits of that kind of collective endeavour which had accomplished much in earlier generations.[1] Sundry learned bodies, like the Scottish Text Society, the Scottish History Society and the Stair Society, continued their regular series of publications, and the *Scottish Historical Review*, suspended in 1928, was happily revived in 1947. The Saltire Society, besides issuing editions of Scottish poetry of both early and modern times, and making annual awards for buildings of architectural merit, founded in 1954 its own periodical, the *Saltire Review of Arts, Letters and Life*. The four Scottish universities undertook joint responsibility for two large-scale and authoritative works of reference, the *Dictionary of the Older Scottish Tongue* and the *Scottish National Dictionary*, and also for the existing folk museum at Kingussie. In 1948 Glasgow University established a full-time lectureship in Scottish Literature, and in 1952, under the auspices of Edinburgh University, a School of Scottish Studies started work in a group of related fields, such as folk-lore, folk music, place-names, archaeology and material cultures; in 1957 the School launched its own journal, *Scottish Studies*.

In cultural matters, however, there can be no question as to what was the outstanding development of the time: it was the inception, in 1947, of Edinburgh's International Festival of Music and Drama. Thereafter, year by year, the Festival drew large and appreciative gatherings from all parts, to see and hear orchestras, operatic groups, theatrical companies and individual *artistes* of world-wide renown; yet, even in this truly cosmopolitan assembly, a link was forged with Scotland's own literary past by the presentation of a modern version of Sir David Lindsay's *Pleasant Satyre of the Thrie Estaitis* (1948). In its austerely beautiful setting, the northern capital won fresh fame as a meeting-place for all citizens of the realm of arts and letters.

[1] See in particular *supra*, pp. 170, 273, 313-14.

Select Bibliography

A. Official Publications and Original Sources

Acts of the Parliaments of Scotland. Edited by Thomas Thomson and Cosmo Innes. Vols. IV-XII (1593-1707). H.M. Stationery Office, 1816-1875.

Annual Register, 1758. London, 1759 (and annually thereafter).

Baillie, Robert, *Letters and Journals* (1637-1662). Edited by David Laing. 3 vols. Bannatyne Club, 1841-1842.

Booke of the Universall Kirk of Scotland (Acts and Proceedings of the General Assemblies of the Kirk of Scotland). Edited by Thomas Thomson. Vol. III (1593-1618). Bannatyne and Maitland Clubs, 1845.

Brown, P. Hume, *Early Travellers in Scotland* [1295-1689]. Edinburgh, 1891.

——, *Scotland before 1700, from Contemporary Documents.* Edinburgh, 1893.

Burnet, Gilbert, *History of his Own Time.* Edited by O. Airy. 6 vols. London, 1823.

Calderwood, David, *History of the Kirk of Scotland.* Edited by Thomas Thomson and David Laing. Vols. VI-VIII (1600-1625). Wodrow Society, 1845-1849.

Carlyle, Alexander, *Autobiography* (1722-1805). Edited by John Hill Burton. Edinburgh, 1860. (Also new edition, 1910.)

Census of Great Britain, 1801: Abstracts of the Answers and Returns. H.M. Stationery Office, 1801-1802. (And decennially thereafter until 1841.)

Census of Great Britain: Comparative Account of the Population of Great Britain, 1801, 1811, 1821, 1831. H.M. Stationery Office, 1831.

Census of Great Britain, 1851: Tables of Population, Religious Worship and Education. H.M. Stationery Office, 1851-1854.

Census of Scotland, 1861: Report and Tables. H.M. Stationery Office, 1861-1864. (And decennially thereafter, except in 1941.)

Cockburn, Henry (Lord Cockburn), *Memorials of his Time* (1779-1830). Edinburgh, 1856. (Also new edition, 1910.)

——, *Journal* (1831-1854). 2 vols. Edinburgh, 1874.

Defoe, Daniel, *History of the Union of Great Britain.* Second edition. London, 1786.

Dickinson, William Croft, and Donaldson, Gordon, *A Source Book of Scottish History.* Vol. III (1567-1707). Edinburgh, 1954.

Fyfe, James G., *Scottish Diaries and Memoirs, 1550-1746.* Stirling, 1928.

——, *Scottish Diaries and Memoirs, 1746-1843.* Glasgow, 1942.

General Report of the Commissioners appointed to inquire into the State of Municipal Corporations in Scotland; and *Appendix, with Local Reports.* 3 vols. London, 1835-1836.

Keith, Robert, *An Historical Catalogue of the Scottish Bishops down to the Year 1688.* Edited by M. Russell. Edinburgh, 1824.

Mackenzie, Agnes Mure, *Scottish Pageant.* Vols. III-IV (1625-1800). Edinburgh, 1949-1950.

New Statistical Account of Scotland. Collected edition, 15 vols. Edinburgh, 1845.

Public General Statutes affecting Scotland. 3 vols. (1707-1847) and annual vols. from 1848 to 1947. H.M. Stationery Office, 1848-1948.

Public General Statutes passed in the 38th Year of the Reign of George III (1797-1798). London (the King's Printer), 1798. (And annually thereafter, to date.)

Register of the Privy Council of Scotland. First Series, Vols. VI-XIV (1599-1625). Second Series, 8 vols. (1625-1660). Third Series, 14 vols. (1661-1689). Edited by David Masson, P. Hume Brown, Henry M. Paton and Robert K. Hannay. H.M. Stationery Office, 1884-1933.

Registrum Magni Sigilli Regum Scotorum: Register of the Great Seal of Scotland. Vols. VI-XI (1593-1668). Edited by J. Maitland Thomson, J. H. Stevenson and W. K. Dickson. H.M. Stationery Office, 1890-1914.

Scottish Population Statistics. Edited by J. G. Kyd. Scottish History Society, 1952.

Sinclair, Sir John (editor), *The [Old] Statistical Account of Scotland.* 21 vols. Edinburgh, 1791-1799.

——, *Analysis of the Statistical Account of Scotland.* 2 vols. Edinburgh and London, 1825-1826.

Spottiswoode, John, *History of the Church of Scotland.* Edited by M. Russell and M. Napier. Vol. III (1596-1625). Bannatyne Club and Spottiswoode Society, 1850.

Statutes at Large. Vols. IV-XVIII (1699-1800). London (the Law Printer), 1769-1800.

Statutes of the United Kingdom of Great Britain and Ireland (1801-1869). 29 vols. London (the Law Printer), 1804-1869.

Terry, Charles Sanford, *The Forty-Five.* Cambridge, 1922.

——, *The Jacobites and the Union.* Cambridge, 1922.

Third Statistical Account of Scotland. By various Writers. Ayrshire; Fife; East Lothian; City of Aberdeen; City of Glasgow; Dunbarton; Aberdeenshire; Lanark; Argyll. Edinburgh and Glasgow, 1951-1960. In progress.

Wodrow, Robert, *Analecta, or Materials for a History of Remarkable Providences* (1701-1731). Edited by M. Leishman. 4 vols. Maitland Club, 1842-1843.

——, *History of the Sufferings of the Church of Scotland from the Restoration to the Revolution.* Edited by the Rev. Robert Burns. 4 vols. Glasgow, 1828-1836.

[*Note:* The official and semi-official documentation of modern times is complex, detailed and extremely voluminous, and no attempt has been made here to include more than a tiny fraction of these vital 'original sources'. Thus, the reports and minutes of evidence of a very large number of royal commissions and parliamentary committees of inquiry throw much light on such subjects as public health, sanitary conditions, poor law, housing of the working classes, and crofting in the Highlands. For all such parliamentary papers, apart from the official index volumes, reference may be made to P. S. King (publishers), *Catalogue of Parliamentary Papers*, 1801-1900 (London, N.D.), and to P. Ford and G. Ford, *Select List of British Parliamentary Papers, 1833-1899* (Oxford, 1953). Moreover, many of the more important of these papers are listed in the 'References' appended to the works of Professors Ferguson and Saunders, mentioned *infra*, under F. Similarly for the County Surveys issued by the Board of Agriculture during the years 1793-1816 (usually under the title *General View of the Agriculture*) the student may consult a handy list on pp. 445-7 of J. A. Symon, *Scottish Farming*, likewise noted *infra.*]

B. General Histories and Works of Reference

Black, George F., *The Surnames of Scotland*. New York, 1946.
Brown, P. Hume, *History of Scotland*. Library edition. Vols. II and III (1542-1910). Cambridge, 1911.
Burton, John Hill, *History of Scotland*. Second edition. Vols. V-VIII (1568-1748). Edinburgh, 1873.
Coupland, Sir Reginald, *Welsh and Scottish Nationalism*. Glasgow, 1954.
Craigie, Sir William (editor), *A Dictionary of the Older Scottish Tongue from the Twelfth Century to the End of the Seventeenth*. Chicago and Oxford, 1931- . In progress.
Grant, William (editor), *The Scottish National Dictionary . . . containing all the Scottish Words known to be in use or to have been in use since c. 1700*. Edinburgh, 1931- . In progress.
Jamieson, John, *An Etymological Dictionary of the Scottish Language*. New edition. 5 vols. Paisley, 1879-1887.
Lang, Andrew, *History of Scotland*. Vols. II-IV (1546-1746). Edinburgh, 1902-1907.
Livingstone, M., *Guide to the Public Records of Scotland deposited in H.M. General Register House, Edinburgh*. H.M. Stationery Office, 1905.
Mathieson, W. Law, *Politics and Religion: A Study of Scottish History from the Reformation to the Revolution*. 2 vols. Glasgow, 1902.
——, *Scotland and the Union, 1695-1747*. Glasgow, 1905.
——, *The Awakening of Scotland, 1747-1797*. Glasgow, 1910.
——, *Church and Reform in Scotland, 1797-1843*. Glasgow, 1916.
Meikle, Henry W. (editor), *Scotland: A Description of Scotland and Scottish Life*. Edinburgh, 1947.
Notestein, Wallace, *The Scot in History*. London, 1946.
Paul, Sir James Balfour (editor), *The Scots Peerage*. 9 vols. Edinburgh, 1904-1914.
Rait, Sir Robert, and Pryde, George S., *Scotland*. Second edition. London, 1954.
Scott, Hew, *Fasti Ecclesiae Scoticanae*. Revised edition. 8 vols. Edinburgh, 1915-1950.
Scottish Historical Review, Vols. I-XXV. Glasgow, 1903-1928. Vols. XXVI- . Edinburgh, 1947- . In progress.
Terry, Charles Sanford, *History of Scotland* [to 1843]. Cambridge, 1920.
Thomson, J. Maitland, *The Public Records of Scotland*. Glasgow, 1922.

C. Studies of Special Periods

The Seventeenth Century

Buchan, John (Lord Tweedsmuir), *Montrose*. London, 1928.
Firth, C. H. (editor), *Scotland and the Commonwealth* [1651-1653]. Scottish History Society, 1895.
——, *Scotland and the Protectorate* [1654-1659]. Scottish History Society, 1899.

Hewison, J. King, *The Covenanters, a History of the Church of Scotland from the Reformation to the Revolution.* Revised edition. 2 vols. Glasgow, 1913.
Lang, Andrew, *Sir George Mackenzie: His Life and Times* (1636-1691). London, 1909.
Mathew, David, *Scotland under Charles I.* London, 1955.
Robertson, A., *The Life of Sir Robert Moray*, 1608-1673. London, 1922.
Terry, Charles Sanford, *Life and Campaigns of Alexander Leslie.* London, 1899.
—— (editor), *The Cromwellian Union.* Scottish History Society, 1902.
——, *John Graham of Claverhouse, Viscount of Dundee.* London, 1905.
Willcock, John, *The Great Marquess: Life and Times of Archibald, 8th Earl of Argyll (1607-1661).* Edinburgh, 1903.
——, *A Scots Earl in Covenanting Times, being Life and Times of Archibald, 9th Earl of Argyll (1629-1685).* Edinburgh, 1907.
Willson, David Harris, *James VI and I.* London, 1956.

The Union and the Jacobites

Brown, Peter Hume, and Others, *The Union of 1707: a Survey of Events by Various Writers.* Glasgow, 1907.
——, *The Legislative Union of England and Scotland.* Oxford, 1914.
—— (editor), *Letters of the Earl of Seafield and Others* [1702-1707]. Scottish History Society, 1915.
Correspondence of George Baillie of Jerviswood, 1702-1708. [Edited by the Earl of Minto]. Bannatyne Club, 1842.
Dicey, A. V., and Rait, R. S., *Thoughts on the Union between England and Scotland.* London, 1920.
Fergusson, Sir James, *Argyll in the Forty-Five.* London, 1951.
Gray, John M. (editor), *Memoirs of Sir John Clerk of Penicuik* [1676-1755]. Scottish History Society, 1892.
Insh, George Pratt, *The Scottish Jacobite Movement.* Edinburgh, 1952.
Lockhart, George, of Carnwath, *The Lockhart Papers, containing Memoirs and Commentaries upon the Affairs of Scotland, 1702-1715.* 2 vols. London, 1817.
McCormick, Joseph (editor), *State Papers and Letters addressed to William Carstares.* Edinburgh, 1774.
Mackenzie, W. C., *Andrew Fletcher of Saltoun: His Life and Times* (1655-1716). Edinburgh, 1935.
Mackinnon, James, *The Union of England and Scotland.* London, 1896.
Menary, George, *The Life and Letters of Duncan Forbes of Culloden* (1685-1747). London, 1936.
Paton, Henry (editor), *The Lyon in Mourning, or a Collection of Speeches, Letters, Journals, etc., relative to the Affairs of Prince Charles Edward Stuart, by Bishop Forbes, 1746-1775.* 3 vols. Scottish History Society, 1895-1896.
Petrie, Sir Charles A., *The Jacobite Movement.* New and enlarged edition. London, 1959.
Pryde, George S. (editor), *The Treaty of Union of Scotland and England 1707.* Edinburgh, 1950.

Rose, Sir George Henry (editor), *A Selection from the Papers of the Earls of Marchmont* [1685-1750]. 3 vols. London, 1831.
Tayler, Alistair and Henrietta, *1715: The Story of the Rising.* Edinburgh, 1936.

Later Georgian Times

Craik, Sir Henry, *A Century of Scottish History: From the Days before the '45 to those within Living Memory.* 2 vols. Edinburgh, 1901.
Fergusson, James, *Letters of George Dempster to Sir Adam Fergusson, 1756-1813.* London, 1934.
Furber, Holden, *Henry Dundas, First Viscount Melville.* Oxford, 1931.
Matheson, Cyril, *The Life of Henry Dundas, First Viscount Melville.* London, 1933.
Meikle, Henry W., *Scotland and the French Revolution.* Glasgow, 1912.

Modern Times (since 1830)

Crewe, Marquess of, *Lord Rosebery* (1847-1929). 2 vols. London, 1931.
MacEwen, Sir Alexander, *The Thistle and the Rose.* Edinburgh, 1932.
Mackie, J. B., *The Life and Work of Duncan McLaren* (1800-1886). 2 vols. Edinburgh, 1888.
Turner, Arthur C., *Scottish Home Rule.* Oxford, 1951.
Wright, Leslie C., *Chartism in Scotland.* London, 1953.

D. Legal and Constitutional Studies

Barron, D. G. (editor), *Court-Book of the Barony of Urie, 1604-1747.* Scottish History Society, 1891.
Brunton, George, and Haig, David, *Historical Account of the Senators of the College of Justice.* Edinburgh, 1832.
Bute, Marquess of, Stevenson, J. H., and Lonsdale, H. W., *The Arms of the Baronial and Police Burghs of Scotland.* Edinburgh, 1903.
Fergusson, Sir James, *The Sixteen Peers of Scotland.* Oxford, 1960.
Mackenzie, W. Mackay, *The Scottish Burghs.* Edinburgh, 1949.
Mackie, J. D., and Pryde, G. S., *The Estate of the Burgesses in the Scots Parliament and its relation to the Convention of Royal Burghs.* St Andrews, 1923.
McLarty, M. R. (editor), *Source Book and History of Administrative Law in Scotland.* Edinburgh, 1956.
Malcolm, Charles A. (editor), *The Minutes of the Justices of the Peace for Lanarkshire, 1707-1723.* Scottish History Society, 1931.
Omond, G. W. T., *The Lord Advocates of Scotland.* 2 vols. Edinburgh, 1883. Second series (1834-1880), London, 1914.
Pagan, Theodora, *The Convention of the Royal Burghs of Scotland.* Glasgow, 1926.
Paton, G. Campbell H. (editor), *An Introduction to Scottish Legal History.* By various authors. Stair Society, 1958.
Pryde, George S. (editor), *Ayr Burgh Accounts, 1534-1624.* Scottish History Society, 1937.
Rait, Robert S., *The Parliaments of Scotland.* Glasgow, 1924.
Terry, Charles Sanford, *The Scottish Parliament: Its Constitution and Procedure, 1603-1707.* Glasgow, 1905.

Terry, Charles Sanford (editor), *Sir Thomas Craig's De Unione Regnorum Britanniae Tractatus*. Scottish History Society, 1909.

E. Ecclesiastical History

Bellesheim, Alphons, *History of the Catholic Church in Scotland*. Translated by D. Oswald Hunter-Blair. Vols. III-IV (1560-1878). Edinburgh, 1889-1890.

Burleigh, J. H. S., *A Church History of Scotland*. Oxford, 1960.

Cunningham, John, *The Church History of Scotland*. Second edition. 2 vols. Edinburgh, 1882.

Donaldson, Gordon, *The Making of the Scottish Prayer Book of 1637*. Edinburgh, 1954.

——, *Scotland: Church and Nation Through Sixteen Centuries*. London, 1960.

Fleming, J. R., *History of the Church in Scotland, 1843-1929*. 2 vols. Edinburgh, 1927-1933.

Goldie, F., *Short History of the Episcopal Church in Scotland*. London, 1951.

Grub, George, *Ecclesiastical History of Scotland*. Vols. II-IV (1521-1857). Edinburgh, 1861.

Henderson, G. D., *Religious Life in Seventeenth Century Scotland*. Cambridge, 1937.

——, *The Claims of the Church of Scotland*. London, 1951.

Highet, John, *The Scottish Churches: a review of their state 400 years after the Reformation*. London, 1960.

Mechie, Stewart, *see* under 'Social and Economic Conditions', *infra*.

Raleigh, Sir Thomas, *Annals of the Church in Scotland*. Oxford, 1921.

F. Social and Economic Conditions

Bremner, David, *The Industries of Scotland*. Edinburgh, 1869.

Cairncross, A. K. (editor), *The Scottish Economy*. Cambridge, 1954.

Chambers, Robert, *Domestic Annals of Scotland from the Reformation to the Rebellion, 1745*. Third edition. 3 vols. Edinburgh, 1874.

Colville, James (editor), *Ochtertyre House Book of Accomps, 1737-1739*. Scottish History Society, 1907.

Comrie, John D., *History of Scottish Medicine*. Second edition. 2 vols. London, 1932.

Davidson, John, and Gray, Alexander, *see* under 'Scotland Overseas', *infra*.

Ferguson, Thomas, *The Dawn of Scottish Social Welfare*. Edinburgh, 1948.

——, *Scottish Social Welfare, 1864-1914*. Edinburgh, 1958.

Franklin, T. Bedford, *A History of Scottish Farming*. Edinburgh, 1952.

Graham, Henry Grey, *Social Life of Scotland in the Eighteenth Century*. 2 vols. Edinburgh, 1899. Also several later editions, including illustrated edition (single volume), Edinburgh, 1937.

Grant, Isabel F., *Economic History of Scotland*. London, 1934.

——, *Everyday Life on an Old Highland Farm, 1769-1782*. London, 1924.

Gray, Malcolm, *see* under 'The Highlands and Islands', *infra*.

Haldane, A. R. B., *The Drove Roads of Scotland*. Edinburgh, 1952.

Haldane, Elizabeth S., *The Scotland of Our Fathers*. London, 1933.

Hamilton, Henry, *History of the Homeland*. London, 1947.

——, *The Industrial Revolution in Scotland*. Oxford, 1932.

Hamilton, Henry (editor), *Selections from the Monymusk Papers, 1713-1755*. Scottish History Society, 1945.
——, *Life and Labour on an Aberdeenshire Estate, 1735-1750 (being Selections from the Monymusk Papers)*. Third Spalding Club, 1946.
Handley, James E., *The Irish in Scotland, 1798-1845*. Cork, 1943.
——, *The Irish in Modern Scotland*. Cork, 1947.
——, *Scottish Farming in the Eighteenth Century*. London, 1953.
Johnston, Thomas, *History of the Working Classes in Scotland*. Glasgow, 1920.
Keith, Theodora (Theodora Pagan), *Commercial Relations of England and Scotland, 1603-1707*. Cambridge, 1910.
Kerr, A. W., *History of Banking in Scotland*. Fourth edition, revised by F. H. Allan. London, 1926.
McArthur, Margaret M. (editor), *Survey of Lochtayside, 1769*. Scottish History Society, 1936.
Macdonald, D. F., *Scotland's Shifting Population, 1770-1850*. Glasgow, 1937.
Mackay, William (editor), *The Letter Book of Bailie John Steuart of Inverness, 1715-1752*. Scottish History Society, 1915.
Marwick, W. H., *Economic Developments in Victorian Scotland*. London, 1936.
Millar, A. H. (editor), *The Compt Buik of David Wedderburne, Merchant of Dundee, 1587-1630*. Scottish History Society, 1898.
Mechie, Stewart, *The Church and Scottish Social Development, 1780-1870*. Oxford, 1960.
Nock, O. S., *Scottish Railways*. Edinburgh, 1950.
Plant, Marjorie, *The Domestic Life of Scotland in the Eighteenth Century*. Edinburgh, 1952.
Saunders, Laurance J., *Scottish Democracy, 1815-1840: The Social and Intellectual Background*. Edinburgh, 1950.
Scott, W. R. (editor), *Minute Book of the Managers of the New Mills Cloth Manufactory, 1681-1690*. Scottish History Society, 1905.
Scott-Moncrieff, R. (editor), *The Household Book of Lady Grisell Baillie, 1692-1733*. Scottish History Society, 1911.
Symon, J. A., *Scottish Farming, Past and Present*. Edinburgh, 1959.
Warrack, John, *Domestic Life in Scotland, 1488-1688*. London, 1920.

G. The Highlands and Islands

Browne, James, *A History of the Highlands and of the Highland Clans*. 4 vols. Glasgow, 1838. (Also later editions.)
Collier, Adam, *The Crofting Problem*. Cambridge, 1953.
Cunningham, Audrey, *The Loyal Clans*. Cambridge, 1932.
Darling, F. Fraser, *Natural History in the Highlands and Islands*. Glasgow, 1948.
Day, J. P., *Public Administration in the Highlands and Islands of Scotland*. London, 1918.
Grant, Mrs Anne, of Laggan, *Letters from the Mountains* [1773-1803]. 3 vols. London, 1806. [Other editions.]
Grant, Isabel F., *see* under 'Social and Economic Conditions', *supra*.
Gray, Malcolm, *The Highland Economy, 1750-1850*. Edinburgh, 1957.
Innes, Sir Thomas, of Learney, *The Tartans of the Clans and Families of Scotland*. Revised edition. Edinburgh, 1950.

Keltie, John S., *History of the Scottish Highlands, Highland Clans and Highland Regiments.* 2 vols. Edinburgh, 1875. (Also later editions.)

Kermack, W. R., *The Scottish Highlands: A Short History (c. 300-1746).* Edinburgh, 1957.

Mackenzie, W. C., *The Highlands and Isles of Scotland: A Historical Survey.* Revised edition. Edinburgh, 1949.

Millar, A. H. (editor), *Selection of the Forfeited Estates Papers* [1752-1784]. Scottish History Society, 1909.

Report of H.M. Commissioners of Inquiry into the Conditions of the Crofters and Cottars in the Highlands and Islands of Scotland. 5 vols. H.M. Stationery Office, 1884.

Skene, William F., *The Highlanders of Scotland.* Edited by Alexander MacBain. Stirling, 1902.

H. Tours

Boswell, James, *The Journal of a Tour to the Hebrides* [in 1773]. London, 1785. [Other editions.]

Burt, Captain Edward, *Letters from a Gentleman in the North of Scotland.* 2 vols. London, 1754.

Cobbett, William, *Tour in Scotland and in the four Northern Counties of England, in the autumn of the year 1832.* London, 1833.

Cockburn, Lord, *Circuit Journeys* [1837-1854]. Edinburgh, 1889.

Defoe, Daniel, *A Tour through the whole Island of Great Britain.* Vol. III. London, 1727. [Other editions.]

Franck, R., *Northern Memoirs* [1658]. London, 1694. [Other editions.]

Johnson, Samuel, *A Journey to the Western Islands of Scotland* [in 1773]. London, 1775. [Other editions.]

Macky, J., *A Journey through Scotland . . . being the Third Volume, which compleats Great-Britain.* London, 1723.

Pennant, Thomas, *A Tour in Scotland,* 1769; and *A Tour in Scotland and Voyage to the Hebrides, 1772.* 3 vols. Fifth edition. London, 1790.

Pococke, Richard, *Tours in Scotland, 1747, 1750, 1760.* Edited by D. W. Kemp. Scottish History Society, 1887.

Victoria, Queen, *Leaves from the Journal of Our Life in the Highlands, 1848-1851.* London, 1867.

——, *More Leaves from the Journal of Our Life in the Highlands, 1862-1882.* London, 1884. [Other editions.]

Wordsworth, Dorothy, *Recollections of a Tour made in Scotland A.D. 1803.* Edited by J. C. Shairp. Edinburgh, 1874.

[*Note:* Sir Arthur Mitchell published a valuable 'List of Travellers and Tours, etc., relating to Scotland' in the *Proceedings of the Society of Antiquaries of Scotland,* vols. XXXV (1901), XXXIX (1905) and XLIV (1910). An interleaved copy is kept up to date in the National Library, Edinburgh.]

I. Education, Literature and the Arts

Cant, Ronald G., *The University of St. Andrews: A Short History.* Edinburgh, 1946.

Caw, J. L., *Scottish Painting Past and Present, 1620-1908.* Edinburgh, 1908.

Coutts, James, *History of the University of Glasgow.* Glasgow, 1909.

Cursiter, Stanley, *Scottish Art to the Close of the Nineteenth Century*. London, 1949.
Dickinson, William Croft, *Two Students at St. Andrews, 1711-1716*. Edinburgh, 1952.
Finlay, Ian, *Art in Scotland*. Oxford, 1948.
——, *Scottish Crafts*. London, 1948.
Grant, Sir Alexander. *The Story of the University of Edinburgh*. 2 vols. London, 1884.
Grant, James, *History of the Burgh Schools of Scotland*. Glasgow, 1876.
Hannah, Ian C., *Story of Scotland in Stone*. Edinburgh, 1934.
Henderson, T. F., *Scottish Vernacular Literature*. Edinburgh, 1910.
Kerr, John, *Scottish Education: School and University*. Cambridge, 1910.
Knox, H. M., *Two Hundred and Fifty Years of Scottish Education, 1696-1946*. Edinburgh, 1953.
Lang, Sir Peter R. Scott (editor), *Duncan Dewar: A Student of St. Andrews 100 Years Ago*. Glasgow, 1926.
MacGibbon, D., and Ross, T., *The Castellated and Domestic Architecture of Scotland, from the Twelfth to the Eighteenth Century*. 5 vols. Edinburgh, 1887-1892.
——, *The Ecclesiastical Architecture of Scotland, from the Earliest Christian Times to the Seventeenth Century*. 3 vols. Edinburgh, 1896-1897.
Mackenzie, Agnes Mure, *An Historical Survey of Scottish Literature to 1714*. London, 1933.
Mackie, J. D., *The University of Glasgow, 1451-1951*. Glasgow, 1954.
Millar, J. H., *A Literary History of Scotland*. London, 1903.
Morgan, Alexander, *Scottish University Studies*. Oxford, 1933.
Rait, Robert S., *The Universities of Aberdeen: A History*. Aberdeen, 1895.
Turner, A. Logan, *History of the University of Edinburgh, 1883-1933*. Edinburgh, 1933.
Wittig, Kurt, *The Scottish Tradition in Literature*. Edinburgh, 1958.

J. Scotland Overseas

Burton, John Hill, *The Scot Abroad*. 2 vols. Edinburgh, 1864. (Also later editions.)
Davidson, John, and Gray, Alexander, *The Scottish Staple at Veere*. London, 1909.
Gibb, Andrew Dewar, *Scottish Empire*. Glasgow, 1937.
Graham, Ian C. C., *Colonists from Scotland: Emigration to North America, 1707-1783*. Oxford, 1956.
Insh, George Pratt, *Scottish Colonial Schemes, 1620-1686*. Glasgow, 1922.
——, *The Company of Scotland trading to Africa and the Indies*. London, 1932.
Kirkwood, J. B., *The Regiments of Scotland*. Edinburgh, 1949.

K. Gazetteers and Topographical Works

Bartholomew, J. G. (editor), *Survey Atlas of Scotland*. Edinburgh, 1912.
Chalmers, George, *Caledonia, or an Account, Historical and Topographic, of North Britain*. 3 vols. London, 1810-1824. Also new edition, 8 vols. Paisley, 1887-1902.
Dawson, James Hooper, *Abridged Statistical History of Scotland*. Edinburgh, 1853. (Also later editions.)

Groome, F. H. (editor), *Ordnance Gazetteer of Scotland.* 6 vols. Edinburgh, 1882-1885. (Also later editions, in 1, 3 or 6 vols.)

Hartop, B. B., and Rodger, M. (editors), *Johnston's Gazetteer of Scotland.* Second edition. Edinburgh, 1958.

Mitchell, Sir Arthur (editor), *Macfarlane's Geographical Collections.* 3 vols. Scottish History Society, 1906-1908.

Watson, W. J., *History of the Celtic Place-Names of Scotland.* Edinburgh, 1926.

Wilson, John Marius (editor), *Imperial Gazetteer of Scotland.* 2 vols. London and Edinburgh, 1854. (Also later editions.)

L. Bibliographies

Black, George F., *List of Works in the New York Public Library relating to Scotland.* New York, 1916.

Ferguson, Joan P. S., *Scottish Family Histories held in Scottish Libraries.* Scottish Central Library, 1960.

——, *Scottish Newspapers held in Scottish Libraries.* Scottish Central Library, 1956.

Hancock, P. D., *A Bibliography of Works relating to Scotland, 1915-1950.* 2 vols. Edinburgh, 1960.

Introductory Survey of the Sources and Literature of Scots Law. By various contributors. Stair Society, 1936.

MacGregor, M. B., *The Sources and Literature of Scottish Church History.* Glasgow, 1934.

Mackie, J. D., *Scottish History.* Cambridge (for the National Book League), 1956.

Matheson, Cyril, *A Catalogue of the Publications of Scottish Historical and Kindred Clubs and Societies, 1908-1927.* Aberdeen, 1928. (*See* also Terry, *infra.*)

Meikle, Henry W., Beattie, W., and Wood, H. Harvey, *Scotland: A Select Bibliography.* Cambridge (for the National Book League), 1950.

Mitchell, Sir Arthur, and Cash, C. G., *A Contribution to the Bibliography of Scottish Topography.* 2 vols. Scottish History Society, 1917.

Stuart, Margaret, *Scottish Family History: A Guide to Works of Reference on the History and Genealogy of Scottish Families.* Edinburgh, 1930.

Terry, Charles Sanford, *A Catalogue of the Publications of Scottish Historical and Kindred Clubs and Societies, 1780-1908.* Glasgow, 1909. (*See* also Matheson, *supra.*)

——, *An Index to the Papers relating to Scotland described or calendared in the Historical MSS. Commission's Reports.* Glasgow, 1908.

Index